AF522339

PURCHASING AND MATERIALS MANAGEMENT

PURCHASING
AND
MATERIALS MANAGEMENT

Anand Kumar Sharma

ANMOL PUBLICATIONS PVT. LTD.
NEW DELHI - 110 002 (INDIA)

ANMOL PUBLICATIONS PVT. LTD.
H.O.: 4374/4B, Ansari Road, Darya Ganj,
New Delhi-110 002 (India)
Ph.: 23278000, 23261597
B.O.: No. 1015, Ist Main Road, BSK IIIrd Stage
IIIrd Phase, IIIrd Block,
Bangalore - 560 085 (India)
Visit us at: www.anmolpublications.com

Purchasing and Materials Management

First Published, 2006

ISBN 81-261-2821-6

PRINTED IN INDIA

Printed at Mehra Offset Press, Delhi

Contents

Preface

"Purchasing and Materials Management" as a paper is being taught at M.Com., M.B.A. and Other Management Courses at various universities and institutions. This book is designed as an introductory text to the above paper, encompassing vital information on all pertinent aspects. Thus the material presented here would be of interest as well as of great use to the students, teachers and professionals of Management Courses. This book will provide complete knowledge of objectives and policies of purchase management, material management, description of quality, make or buy decisions, purchasing research, legal aspects of purchasing, materials scheduling, purchasing capital equipment, material handling & warehousing, traffic and transportation, disposal of scrap and obsolete materials, material distribution control, storage of materials, etc. to the students.

The major topics dealt in this book are—Purchase Management; Material Management; Material Planning MRP & JIT; Description of Quality; Quality and Inspection; Capital Acquisition; Make or Buy Decisions; Purchasing Research; Price Determination and Negotiations; Legal Aspects of Purchasing; Materials Scheduling; Purchasing Capital Equipment; Material Logistics—Material Handling & Warehousing; Traffic and Transportation; Disposal of Scrap and Obsolete Materials; Inventory Control; Material Distribution Control; Storage of Materials; Management Information System: Materials etc.

It is hoped that all those will benefit from the contents of this book for whom it is meant. The author will feel amply rewarded, if motive is achieved.

Editor

1

Purchase Management

Any commercial transaction, however simple always involves a buyer and a seller. Thus purchasing is one of the basic functions in any economy. The buyer requires certain goods and materials to satisfy his wants on payment. He seeks a seller who can and is willing to supply him with what he needs. Together they negotiate a mutually satisfactory price and the deal is completed.

The winds of change are blowing in purchasing and supply. Continued upgrading of conformance quality standards, just-in-time approaches to material availability, long-term relationships with fewer suppliers and a win-win approach to negotiations instead of the more traditional adversarial or win-lose approach, are just some of the changes in the way procurement is managed. These changes are helping organizations to survive and succeed in a very competitive world.

Purchasing and supply is a necessary function in almost every organization, from the private household to the national government. This book is mainly about larger organizations which have purchasing and supply departments, but purchasing and supply is just as important in small organizations which do not employ full-time people to do the work, and it is hoped that the latter may also find this chapter useful.

Industrial Purchasing

Industrial purchasing is a highly refined, highly specialized version of this activity. Modern manufacturing firms spend, on the average, more than half their sales income on materials, goods, and services purchased from other companies. They assign this buying job to specialists who have the authority to select suppliers and commit company funds.

Purchasing's responsibilities have a direct effect on the company's financial and competitive position. The buyer, in addition to investing his company's money prudently, must satisfy the demands of the operating departments. Thus the "best" price that he constantly seks involves much more than selection of the lowest quotation.

In selecting a supplier and negotiating a price, the buyer must also be certain that what he is buying will *(1)* meet specifications and quality standards; *(2)* arrive in the plant on time to meet production schedules; and *(3)* be stocked in amounts sufficient to meet manufacturing requirements without causing excessive carrying expense. He (she) must see that the supplier gives prompt and adequate service.

Individual purchases can range from simple to highly complex. The buyer of an intricate electronic sub-assembly for a space rocket obviously faces greater problems than the buyer of No. 2 fuel oil. The electronic unit involves advanced engineering and exotic materials. Nothing like it may have ever been made before; neither the buyer nor the supplier has any real cost data to go on in negotiating a price, No. 2 fuel oil, on the other hand is a standard product, with basic specifications. The market Price can be found on the business page of the morning newspaper.

More complex purchases obviously require buying experts. It is in the relatively simple purchases, however, that justification for a specialized, centralized purchasing department can be found. An expert buyer of any commodity will do much more than check current prices. he (she) will study market trends in an attempt to anticipate price changes. He will analyze his supplier's shipping and his own company's storage methods for possible improvements that will reduce costs. He will, for example, study the long-range supply outlook and possibilities of substituting competitive fuels. In such studies, he will work closely with the plant engineer.

Smaller Business Transactions

Paul Bocuse, a world-famous French cook, employs about 50 people at his main restaurant; not enough to have a purchase department. But every day when he is in residence he shops personally at the Lyon market. According to him, a good cook is someone who knows how to buy produce. Franco Taruschio, who runs what is perhaps the best restaurant in Wales, also gets to the market in Abergavenny early to buy the best on offer.

As we read in the *Good Food Guide 1985*, 'nearly all the restaurants in this book take as much care over their ingredients as they do in the cooking. They have supported local producers, cajoled people back to the land, created new jobs by providing a market for small-scale operations that would otherwise be unable to compete with big factory farms.' This close attention to buying, and to developing new supply sources if existing sources do not meet requirements, are just the sort of policies adopted by large supply departments.

The Process Defined

Organizational purchasing is the process by which organizations define their needs for goods and services; identify and compare the supplies and suppliers available to them; negotiate with sources of supply or in some other way arrive at agreed terms of trading; make contracts and place orders; and finally receive, accept and pay for the goods and services required.

Purchasing is closely associated with other organizational functions, such as inventory management, stores operation, and transport. Production planning and control, in manufacturing organizations, and merchandizing, in distributive organizations, have to work closely with buying. Often some or all of these functions are combined with the purchasing function under a single head, the materials manager or supply manager.

Traditionally, purchasing objectives were defined as: to obtain the riiht quality of goods, in the right quantity, at the right time, from the right supplier, at the right price. These five 'rights' were often thought of in the context of a static environment, so that by a series of successive approximations it would eventually be possible to arrive at the final right answer for each one.

But in highly competitive world markets the environment is not static but dynamic, tending not towards equilibrium but always towards something new. Purchasing objectives continually need to be updated and revised. Arriving at the final right answer for some old product just as it is discontinued does nothing for the competitive position of an organization.

Proactive, rather than reactive; dynamic, rather than static, is the way in which the purchasing role is now conceived. Better quality, in more suitable quantities, just in time for requirements, from better suppliers, at prices which continue to improve, are the sort of aims set by the dynamic purchasing function today.

The broad scope of Purchasing's interest and authority makes inadequate the classic definition: "Purchasing is the activity responsible for getting the right material to the right place, at the right time, in the right quantity, at the right price."

Purchasing or more precisely, procurement can be called that function responsible for the phase of the materials cycle from the time an item is requisitioned until it is delivered to the user. This includes direct responsibility for selection of vendor, negotiation of price, and assurance of quality and delivery; it can also include direct or indirect responsibility for transportation, receiving, inspection and inventory control.

The Modern Concept

Most firms start off as very small organizations, growing in size as they become more successful. The small firm consists of the entrepreneur who runs it and who usually started it, plus a number of other people to whom work is assigned which the entrepreneur either does not wish to do himself (such as perhaps packaging and despatch), or cannot do himself because he does not know how (such as, perhaps, preparation of final accounts), or else betause there are not enough hours in the day to do everything. In such a small firm, major purchasing decision are usually made by the head of the organization and minor purchasing decisions together with the detailed purchasing work fall to those in charge of any departments that exist. When a purchasing officer is appointed, his job may at first be seen as to do the legwork and the paperwork associated with purchasing, rather than to take the basic purchasing decisions.

Eventually, if the firm continues to increase in size, proper, departments are set up for all major functions, and it is at this stage that management needs to delegate to purchasing the authority and responsibility to identify and evaluate purchasing problems, and to initiate, recommend and implement effective solutions.

John H. Hill, president of Air Reduction Company, Inc., speaking before the National Association of Purchasing Agents, put the development of Purchasing in these terms:

"Purchasing traditionally has been considered a service function a place where money was spent/ not made... Recent developments have shaken this point of view. Good purchasing is essential to good profits. The difference between good purchasing and poor purchasing can be the difference between outstanding results and mediocre performance. Modernized purchasing departments have shown that skillfull procurement can out 5 to 10% from the total cost of goods purchased."

"A saving of 5% to 10% in the cost of purchases (in a company where purchases absorb 50% to 60% of the sales) is equivalent to 2½% to'5% of the sales."

This concept of procurement stands today as it did when it was first enunciated some three decades ago, and serves to define the objectives of a modern well-run purchasing department with broad responsibility. These may be listed as follows: Low prices for purchased materials and services; high inventory turnover; low cost of acquisition and possession; continuity of supply; consistency of quality; low payroll costs; favourable relations with suppliers.

Other objectives of the department include: new materials and products; greater standardization and interchangeability; product improvement and simplification; good relations with other departments; long and short term economic forecasts; reduction of transportation costs; favourable reciprocal relations.

A Complex Process

Organizational purchasing can be a complex process. Many people may take part, at various levels in the management hierarchy and in several functional departments. It can be a lengthy process: major 'one-off' decisions may take years to finalize. Even routine repeat orders that are placed immediately without consultation may be placed in accordance with policies previously laid down after much consultation and experiment over lengthy period of time.

It is made more complex by its detailed involvement with other decision and control processes such as:

(1) stock control policies and procedures which determine/control and replenish the range of items stocked;

(2) the physical supply cycle which goods pass through as they are despatched, transported, received, stored and either issued or sold;

(3) production planning and control which determines and controls the quantities of parts and materials required to meet production commitments;

(4) merchandizing which goods will be offered for resale and at what price.

It is when some or all of these other processes are combined in one department or under one head that the term materials management is used. The term purchasing and supply also suggests a joint consideration of purchasing with stock control and stores management without necessarily implying that all those concerned with carrying out the relevant activities report to a single manager. Purchasing works for every department in the business, and may be particularly involved with:

(1) The specification and design of the end-product;

(2) The quality control policies and procedures which set standards, assess capability, and control performance;

(3) The finance function that pays bills and is also particularly concerned with capital expenditure, terms of credit, budgets, and stock investment.

Organization Structures

The way purchasing and other supply activities are organized into departments, how tasks and activities are allocated to supply personnel, and the extent to which authority is delegated to the department head to decide matters in the supply area on his own responsibility, are all subject to considerable variation in practice.

For instance Fig. 1 shows two alternative ways of grouping together people working on materials-related activities. In part A, the purchasing manager is responsible for stock control as well as purchasing; in part B, purchasing, stock control, and also transport, stores, production control come unlder the same manager, now known as the materials manager.

Such organizational questions are considered in more detail in Vol. 4, *Corporate Management,* of this treatise. But an important

(a) Before

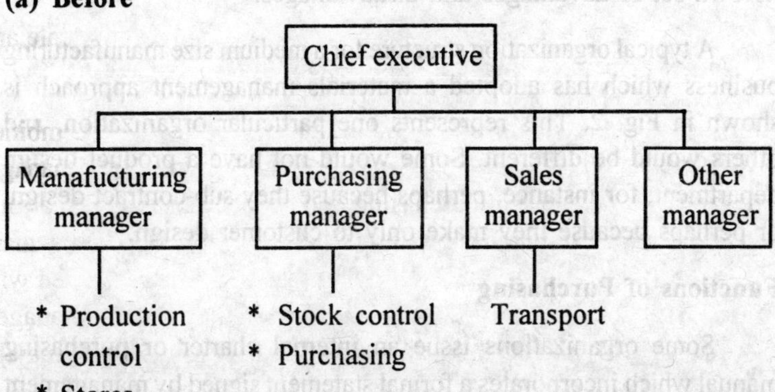

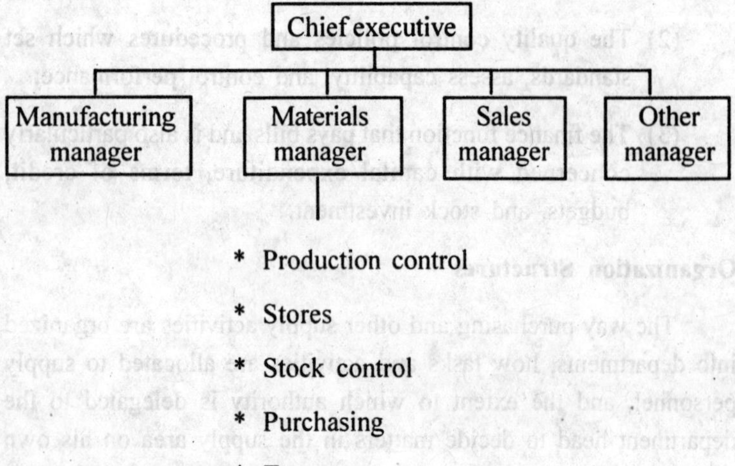

Fig. 1. The reorganization of materials management department.

point needs to be made in this chapter, which is that the management of materials contributes most effectively to general management and to the success of the organization if it is seen as a single process, from definition of requirements to delivery to customer.

It is not usually feasible to group all the activities involved into one department. Only the smallest firm can operate as a single department, and once more than one department has to be set up, alternative departmental groupings have to be considered, each with its own set of advantages and disadvantages.

A typical organization structure for a medium size manufacturing business which has adopted a materials management approach is shown in Fig. 2. This represents one particular organization, and others would be different. Some would not have a product design department, for instance, perhaps because they sub-contract design, or perhaps because they make only to customer design.

Functions of Purchasing

Some organizations issue an internal charter or purchasing manual which incorporates a formal statement signed by management

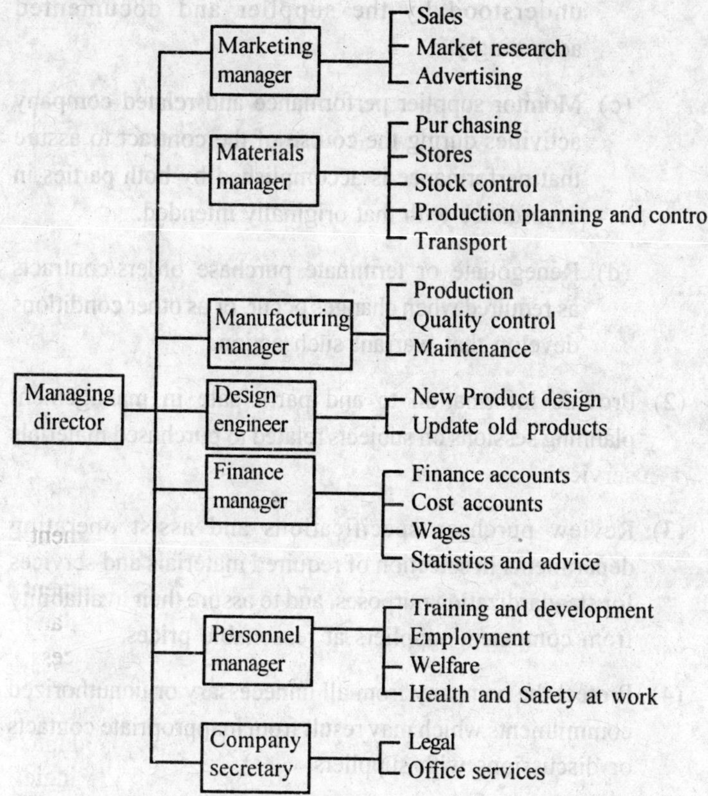

Fig. 2. A typical organization chart for a manufacturer.

of what services the purchasing department is expected to provide and what its responsibilities are. Croell (1977) suggests the following:

(1) Providc all materials and services that the company elects not to provide internally. In accomplishing this, purchasing must perform the following basic tasks.

(a) Select and develop as required, vendors capable of meeting company needs.

(b) Prepare and sign all purchase orders/contracts, so that the needs of the company and all pertinent terms and conditions related to the purchase are clearly understood by the supplier and documented accordingly.

(c) Monitor supplier performance and related company activities during the course of the contract to assure that performance is accomplished by both parties in accordance with that originally intended.

(d) Renegotiate or terminate purchase orders/contracts as required when changes occur, or as other conditions develop that warrant such action.

(2) Provide information to and participate in management planning sessions on subjects related to purchased materials services.

(3) Review purchase specifications and assist operating departments in selection of required materials and services for standardization purposes, and to assure their availability from competent suppliers at reasonable prices.

(4) Protect the company from all unnecessary or unauthorized commitments which may result from inappropriate contacts or discussions with suppliers.

(5) Dispose of all obsolete materials, equipment, or scrap that is no longer required for company operations.

Marketing and Purchasing

The buying department and the selling department are the two departments mainly concerned with external relations, with reaching out into the supply markets and the sales markets out side the firm. To what extent does it make sense to say that both are engaged in marketing? This question is partly semantic (what words mean and how they are used) and partly about what departments do and how their work is perceived.

Definitions and discussions of marketing have certainly been dominated by selling considerations in recent years, although not in earlier periods. Consumer product manufacturers in the West which were competing for discretionary spending by consumers took to the marketing concept in a big way. The marketing concept, so called, could be described as the realization that firms need to find out what their customers want and take steps to provide it if they are to prosper; rather than producing the goods they were interested in producing, they needed to provide the goods the consumer was interested in purchasing. The marketing concept was less prevalent in industrial marketing, where many firms remained firmly and indeed proudly product-oriented rather than customer-oriented.

Industrial marketing differs from consumer marketing in several ways. Firstly, it usually sells different products. It deals in heavy equipment, such as tractors and machine tools; light equipment, such as photocopiers and hand power tools; construction, for example, of factories, docks and housing estates. It sells raw materials, such as iron ore and coal; processed materials, such as steel bar, chemicals and plywood; components, such as ball bearings and electric motors and semi-conductors; consumable supplies, such as cleaning materials and cutting oils; and a variety of services, such as those of the forwarding agent, the contract painter, or machine maintenance.

Secondly, it usually sells to different customers. Consumer marketing aims at organizations, and these have different and often much more complex buying processes. Consequently, when products such as motor cars or typewriters are sold to both consumers and to organizations the marketing approach tends to be very different for the two.

As Webster and Wind (1972) point out,

> "industrial and institutional marketers have often been urged to base their strategies on careful appraisal of buying behaviour within key accounts and in principal market segments. When they search the available literature on buyer behaviour, however, they find virtually exclusive emphasis on consumers, not industrial buyers. Research

> findings and theoretical discussions about consumer behaviour often have little relevance for the industrial marketer."

Yet the total value of interfirm purchases of raw materials, components and semi-finished parts, finished parts, tools and supplies, is considerably greater than the total of sales to retail consumers. Rowe and Alexander (1968) quote an estimate to the effect that interfirm sales are worth about 2.5 times as much as sales to individual consumers—3.5 times as much if sales to the government are included. They conclude that:

> resource allocation, in effect the sorting or matching of needs to supplying ability,. is what marketing and selling is all about when looked at from the economist's viewpoint, and nowhere is this function more in need of being expertly carried out than in the area of interfirm transactions where industries are becoming interlocked in increasing interdependence.

This remains at least equally true if the words 'purchasing and supply' are substituted for the words 'marketing and selling'. It could indeed be said that the sorting or matching of needs to supplying ability is what purchasing is all about, and that in the area of interfirm transactions this often calls for marketing initiatives on the buying side.

This is sometimes described as 'marketing in reverse'. But one definition of 'to market', .in the most popular dictionary in the United Kingdom, is 'to buy or sell in market', and the very word 'market' derives from a Latin word which means 'to buy' (mercari). In earlier days the merchant venturers set forth through unknown seas and distant countries in search, not so much of customers although they had to have something to trade, but more of new suppliers of new products—spices, furs, carpets, turkeys, tomatoes, oranges—as well as of new sources of known materials such as gold, diamonds and tin. Sourcing, and buying generally was the venturesome and creative part of their marketing effort.

In the distributive industries, the selection and pricing of merchandise to sell is fundamental to marketing plans, and buying is therefore an important part of marketing for the retailer. In the manufacturing industries on the other hand, it is the selection and pricing of products to make which corresponds to this, and the procurement of parts and material to make them tends to be seen as part of the production process rather than part of the marketing process.

Even here, some buying activities call for creative and entrepreneurial skills, for commercial innovation and persuasion. It is widely feared that shortages of materials and certain products will be increasingly common as the twentieth century draws to a close. And Kotler (Kotler and Levy, 1973; Kotler and Balachandrian, 1975) for instance argues that in times of shortage the marketing problem shifts its location from selling to buying. The development of new suppliers is another example of purchasing firms marketing their buying requirements to the supply markets. And in the negotiation of major contracts (for the design and development of equipment at the frontier of the art) to meet customer requirements, the term marketing may well be equally appropriate to the proposals and arguments coming from each side (if indeed it is appropriate at all in this situation).

The increasing concentration of markets has been a noticeable feature of recent years and accounts for part of the difference between industrial marketing and consumer marketing. For example, if three detergent manufacturers sell to tens of millions of households, scientific studies can be made of the market and how it can be segmented, of marketing methods and how best to apply them. But if an industrial manufacturer sells to six major industrial customers plus a number of minor customers, the scope for science is less, and it is more a matter of art. The shotgun communications of mass media advertising are used in the first case; the sharpshooter methods of field salesmen and low budget advertising in specialist trade journals are used in the second case.

In many industries a small number of manufacturers produce most of the output; and in quite a high proportion of cases, a small number of customers take most of the output. Buying and selling are both affected by the situation; after all every purchase is someone's sale, purchasing and marketing are the two sides of one coin. Purchase cost analysis, negotiated prices based on mutually agreed figures for cost, larger and more expert departments both for buying and for selling, are typical features.

When two or three large firms supply equivalent or inter changeable products to the same market, at prices which each is reluctant to change because of the risk of retaliation by the others, two obvious ways to increase security as well as profits are: firstly by product differentiation, and secondly by cost reduction. Product differentiation makes the products seem less equivalent or, interchangeable to the customer. Cost reduction enables a manufacturer to increase profits without starting a price war.

Cost reduction initially concentrated on manufacturing costs, with much success in many firms. But as one managing director said:

> "we have over the years by dint of research, engineering development and good management, reduced operating costs to such an extent that now nearly 80% of total cost consists of purchased materials. Obviously it is important that buyers have an eye for more than the cheap price. Purchasing and supply have a major part to play in reducing cost and increasing profit."

Value Analysis and Pre-Production Purchase Analysis

Value Engineering as an organized effort to reduce costs on purchased parts and materials was originated in the purchasing department of the General Electric Company in the late forties. A parallel development was taking place in Ford Motor Company purchasing at the same time. Basically, it involved a study of every part and service to determine how much of its cost could be reduced without impairing its function. This included a search for alternate materials or manufacturing processes; elimination of unnecessary features; location of specialty suppliers who could make the part for less; substitution of standards for specials.

Purchasing's success with Value Analysis (the first major G.E. project resulted in savings of $300,000) led to extension of the technique to other departments. Value Analysis or Value Engineering is now a team effort involving Engineering, Production, and Purchasing in thousands of plants.

Purchasing has moved up its analytical efforts in many companies to the design stage of a product. At this point it is able to recommend, on the basis of its market experience; changes in design or materials to take advantage of new developments or new techniques available from suppliers. In one major television company, for example, an engineer from the purchasing department participates in design engineering discussions of new or improved products. Thus Purchasing gets involved in the designmanufacturing cycle long before prints are made and handed to it with requisitions.

Vendor Evaluation

With greater demands and greater responsibilities being placed on it. Purchasing has in turn taken a closer look at the most important link in the materials cycle, the supplier. Both new and established vendors are coming in for a more critical review of their plant and capabilities, financial condition, and performance. Regular physical inspection of suppliers facilities by teams from Purchasing, Engineering, and Production are not unusual.

Statistical measurement of vendor performance on price, delivery, and quality has become standard practice in hundreds of industrial purchasing departments. The techniques used vary from the relatively rough approach of asking buyers and using departments to rate suppliers on certain factors, to developing index numbers of performance from data taken from computers. In the latter case, weights are assigned to each category (*e.g.*, Price-40%; Quality-

30%; Delivery-30%). Index numbers are calculated for each factor, as well as for overall performance.

Inventory Control

Although stores are not always directly under the control of the purchasing department, Purchasing has an important stake in inventory control policy. How well inventory is controlled affects material shortages, the number of purchase orders that must be placed, possibilities of obtaining quantity discounts, expediting, and supplier relations—all Purchasing responsibilities.

Inventory control systems range from relatively simple to very elaborate, depending on the nature, variety, volume, and value of the items involved. A basic step in any systemis the segregation of items into three classes: high value, medium value, and low value. (Critical items, regardless of dollar value, Cure generally placed in the high value category).

Control procedures are then developed for each category, the stricter controls naturally being placed on the higher value items. This would include frequent review of future requirements, lead, time, quantity on hand, quantity on order, safety stock, etc.

The basic objective is to have the right part or material on hand when it is needed. But it is also important to keep average inventory at a minimum, so that carrying costs are kept down and money which could be used productively elsewhere is not tied up in inventory. On the other hand, frequent ordering boosts administrative costs. Purchasing agents therefore try to order in quantities in which ordering costs and inventory carrying costs are in balance, thereby giving them lowest over—all costs. This quantity-calculated through the use of standard formulates—is known as the Economic Ordering Quantity, or EOQ.

In the past few years, Purchasing has developed a number of techniques to shift some of the responsibility for carrying inventory on to the supplier. These include contract purchasing, blanket orders, "stockless purchasing" programmes, and commitment buying. Excluding minor variations, they all involve the same basic approach: to assure a given vendor a certain amount of business in a given period if he will maintain a stock of the item and release it as needed by the customer. This enables Purchasing to avoid piling up an inventory of the item, cut its ordering paperwork, and generally obtain a lower price on the basis of increased volume.

Reduction of Administrative Costs

Since the generation of paper is inherent in the purchasing function, close control of administrative costs is of continuing concern to the purchasing agent.

Purchasing has developed a number of procedures and methods designed to reduce clerical effort and costs and free personnel for more creative buying. These range from the universally used traveling requisition to punched card and punched tape systems to handle paperwork involved in repetitive purchasing.

Today Purchasing is also using integrated data processing systems to tie together purchasing, inventory, and production data. Computers are used to store purchase histories, price records, inventory figures, data on suppliers, engineering specifications, accounting records, and receving information. The machines are being used to write purchase orders, produce expediting documents, make vendor payments, figure cost data, and measure supplier performance.

As the administrative side of purchasing becomes more automated, its managerial and technical responsibilities will be broadened. Purchasing agents and buyers will have to have greater knowledge of manufacturing operations, materials and processes, and general economics. They will require greater skill in negotiating complex contracts with suppliers. They will have to possess a certain degree of skill in both financial and engineering analysis to evaluate vendors- or have that skill available to them in their own departments. All this in turn will increase the demand for purchasing executives who have a broad concept of the materials function, and the ability to manage every phase of it.

Purchasing Decision-Making

Retailers and wholesalers normally buy the merchandise they sell rather than manufacturing it themselves. This applies not only to small distributors, but also to the large chain stores which often not only select merchandise from what is available, but also draw up specifications themselves. While doing this they are talking to suppliers and finding firms which can supply goods to their specifications.

There are exceptions. Some retailers use backward integration into products or packaging to improve their competitive position, and some manufacturers aim to strengthen their competitive position by forward integration into distribution. Breweries, which are beer manufacturers, often own most of their retail outlets, and many filling stations are owned by the petrol manufacturers. Inhouse bakeries have become common in the superstores, an exception to the normal policy which is for shops to buy rather than make.

Manufacturers on the other hand normally make the products they sell, although a few products may be bought in to complete a range. They manufacture them from parts and material which are either produced internally or bought out, so that make-or-buy decisions have to be made at each stage in formulating manufacturing strategy. Outside processing may be used in addition to or instead of internal processing. Subcontracting also requires make-or-buy decisions.

Primary Objectives

The main goals of the purchasing department are:

1. To maintain a smooth flow of goods into the production process to assure continuous operation.
2. To obtain such goods at the lowest ultimate cost, thus contributing to the company's profit picture.
3. To maintain harmonious relationships with both internal and external personnel.

One specific objective is to obtain the correct quality goods best suited to perform the intended purpose. One does not have to buy a platinum valve when a copper valve will fulfill the required function.

Another aim is to obtain correct quantities of the goods needed to maintain continuous operation and at the same time keep the inventory at the lowest safe level. The purchasing agent must keep abreast of market conditions, such as price trends and availability outlook and the labor situation for potential shortages or late deliveries due to a possible strike.

Yet another important objectives is to obtain the goods at the lowest ultimate cost, always keeping in mind the quality, quantity, and service required. The purchase of ayear's supply because the reduced unit cost or reduced freight charges gibe the appearance of a low cost has to be contrasted with increased carrying costs, additional cash outlay, and the greater possibility for obsolescence, scrap, and shrinkage. The "low" price may suddenly be seen as higher than if the purchases were made in smaller quantities several times during the year.

A most important objective for the purchasing department is the establishment and maintenance of good communications with others within the organization, listening as well as dispensing information.

The same good rapport must exist with outside sources. The successful purchasing agent will readily admit that a large portion of his knowledge comes from capable suppliers. If he is receptive, this source of information is never ending and costs the purchasing agent only courtesy, honesty, and fair treatment in his dealing with the competitive suppliers. This information benefits the company when made available to interested inside departments.

To achieve these objectives the purchasing department must have the authority to carry out its responsibilities. This authority as well as the responsibility is found in the purchasing department manual, as is the policy and procedures for departmental operation.

The Purchasing Department Manual

The purchasing department manual announce the broad policies and the philosophy of top management and the narrower policy pertaining to the department, such as the authority, responsibilities, ethics, and interdepartmental and vendor relationships. The manual serves:

1. As a guide used in formulating the specific operating functions to be performed by department personnel.
2. As a guide for making decisions about unusual problems not included in the established procedures.
3. As a guide in making decisions about problems of a routine nature.
4. As the delegated authority upon which the director acts.
5. To tell everyone that the contents of the purchasing manual, as set forth, are with approval and support of top management.

As with all other functions of an enterprise, the manual must be flexible and additions or changes made as the situation demands. The manual influences the entire company's operation in regard to the purchasing function.

Good procedures need to be explicit and understandable, with the aim of achieving their objective in the shortest time by the simplest method. If the simple method does not accomplish the task for which it has been designed, it is useless. The procedure that proves adequate for one company may be inadequate for another. Procedures must be formulated in light of the conditions under which they will operate. Always review all procedures; the addition of another step may add a little cost but can save more in the long run and, thus be justified.

Purchasing Forms

All businesses have a variety of forms to aid them in their operation. The design of the basic forms used by the purchasing department must be clearly specified and illustrated in the purchasing manual. The design and copies of each form are determined by the distribution requirements of that form. Top management decides on who gets a copy of which form.

The purchasing department basic forms listed are not inclusive, and some may not be used in some companies.

Requisition Forms

There are two main types of requisition forms. The internal requisition or stores requisition is used by the departments to obtain materials carried in inventory. The external requisition is for the acquisition of goods from outside sources when such goods are not carried in stock. The traveling requisition is actually a reusable external requisition used by inventory control and by certain other departments when they are the only ones repeatedly using a particular item not carried in stores. The bill of materials is an external requisition form that lists all items needed for a particular product. It is usually issued by engineering.

Request for Quotation Form

This form is sent to a potential supplier when requesting price, terms, etc., about some item or service. The design of the form should reflect the information desired.

Quotation Tabulation Form

This form is used to list in a uniform manner all information submitted by the prospective supplier. The information is then tabulated by a clerk. This enables the purchasing agent to make an analysis of the quotations and arrive at a decision more rapidly.

Purchase Order Form

The purchase order form is the most important legal document used by the purchasing agent. When issued in reply to a quotation, the purchase order form acts as an acceptance of the supplier's offer. When issued to request goods or services, the purchase order form acts as an offer to the supplier, and, if accepted, constitutes a binding legal contract. A copy of the purchase order form is distributed to the appropriate departments.

Follow-up Form

This form is used by the buyer to record any and all information pertaining to the progress of the receipt of the order. Many companies use a copy of the purchase order form for such purpose. In some cases there may be a field expediting form when a visit to the supplier's plant is required to assure the quality of the goods.

Change Order Form

This form is an important contract vehicle and is used whenever any change is made and agreed to by both parties to the contract (buyer and seller). This form acknowledges in writing the agreed change. Telephone agreements must be followed with a written change order form.

Receiving Form

This is another copy of the purchase order form, usually without prices, to inform the receiving department of an incoming shipment as to its identify, quantity, and where it is to be delivered. There are usually two copies, one to be sent to finance and one for receiving's own files.

The Inspection Form

This may also be a copy of the purchase order form to be used by quality control to verify the quality of the goods received against the specifications.

Planning and Forecasting

Planning is the process of formulating a programme of action, and it must start with the setting of goals to be achieved. The process uses strategies and standards within the policy set up by top management. The allocation of funds is very important in this process to meet the objectives. There is now a trend to use "planning" and "budgeting" interchangeably.

Purchasing, with its commodity awareness, its access to and cataloging of the variety of indexes and national barometers, and its daily contacts with the supplier world, is in a natural position to aid in the budgeting forecasts of the departments within the organization. Planning is usually for one-year periods, with three-to five-year projection in mind. The long-range planning is particularly applicable for capital—facility or equipment—expenditures.

Forecasting is an important part of planning and is the starting point for establishing the quantities, time, and cost for each raw material and/or component needed to meet the production and sales forecasts for the period. Generally, the annual forecast is made about three months prior to the period's start and must be flexible to accommodate unforeseen changes in the economy.

The actual budgeting for purchased raw materials, component parts, etc., follows the forecasting process and is a planned approach for carrying out the purchasing function. Budgeting makes it possible to gain better control over expenditures for goods and services and to correlate these purchases to the actual requirements of the manufacturing functions of the company. This budgeting permits each department, and top management, to monitor its performance and actual usage against its forecast. Purchasing with its interdepartmental relationships contributes to the planning and forecasting for the entire organization. Such participation involves:

1. Assisting various segments of the organization in "building" their individual budgets by supplying costs for goods and services.

2. Assisting in monitoring the physical goods expenditure against their individual budgets.

3. Building and monitoring purchasing's own budget.

The materials manager must develop a plan for all activities pertaining to the handling of materials. To do this the materials manager must know what objectives are to be met, gather all relevant facts, develop alternate solution routes to take, analyze these, and make the final decision as to the best route to follow. After all, planning is nothing more than choosing a definite route to take from a range of alternates. Every plan, like every function, must be followed up to ascertain its effectiveness and its problems and should be flexible enough to meet any necessary change.

Network Scheduling Systems

The first step of any plan, like the first step of any problem, is the gathering of facts, which means doing some research. Purchasing planning and research can be aided by the use of the "Critical Path Method" (CPM) or by the "Programme Evaluation and Review Technique" (PERT). Both these systems are based on the same 'concepts, although differing in details, and can be designed to make planning more effective.

The CPM technique was developed by DuPont and Sperry Rand in 1955 through 1957 for plant maintenance of chemicals. Later it was used in scheduling construction efficiency. This technique resulted in reducing the maintenance time in DuPont's Louisville works from 125 to 78 hours. The PERT method was developed for the navy in 1958 to plan and control the Polaris ballistic missile project, which involved about 3,000 separate contracting organizations. The PERT technique developed is credited for reducing the estimated time of the project by two years.

These network planning systems are representations of the required activities and events that take place in a production schedule. Some of the terminology used includes the following terms.

1. The *network* is a visual display of planned sequence and inter-relationships of events and activities indicating the critical path schedule and the slack schedule in the activity sequence needed for the finished product.
2. The *events*, shown usually as circles, are meaningful, specific accomplishments that do not use times or resources.

3. The *activities* are the time-consuming elements of a programme that separate events and are usually shown by an arrow. These values represent the most likely performance times.

4. The *critical path* is the controlling chain of events through a network. Any slippage along this path will produce a slippage in the end event.

By means of PERT, the complete process flow can be quickly seen, relationships recognized, arid appropriate plans laid for both consecutive and parallel activities with regard to time.

The PERT method was developed through research into the uncertainty of activity time requirements. This probability distribution or activity time is based on three time estimates for each activity.

1. The *optimistic time* is the estimate of the shortest time an activity can be accomplished under the most favourable conditions.
2. The *pessimistic time* is an estimate of the longest time an activity can be accomplished under the most unfavourable conditions.

3. The *most realistic time* is an estimate of the most likely time for an activity to be accomplished. This would be the model value in a distribution of activity time.

As actual data on the progress of the activities comes in, it may be necessary to change the allocation of resources to deal with any critical situation and correct the production schedule. In any probabilistic model, there is always the possibility that a slack time or non-critical activity takes longer than estimated, or an activity on the critical path sequence takes less time than estimated. Then corrections must be made. Every plan should be flexible so that rapid feedback of information allows for reissuance of a correct and accurate production schedule.

The advantages of this technique are that it:

1. Provides means for careful planning of all activities and all variables involved.

2. Provides for constant feedback to assure that all activities are on schedule.

3. Provides an overview of the entire procedure, with a clearer understanding of the interrelationships of the activities.

4. Identifies potential problems early so that resources can be diverted to avoid cumulative delays.

5. Makes it possible to accurately predict completion time for the project.

The PERT schedule permits purchasing to know what raw materials and component parts are needed when for the various activities. This permits the buyer to make the most economical purchasing and transportation decisions. The buyer, with the knowledge of the latitude of delivery time, can select low-cost suppliers who offer longer lead times. This is one way that purchasing can reduce the total cost of materials.

The CPM method was originally developed for engineering maintenance operations where a great deal of experience existed and the activity was known. This produced a deterministic model for the CPM technique. It is also used in construction projects, and the network shows the sequence of the activities required for the project with estimated normal times for each activity. There is a critical path, as with the PERT method, together with branches (slack time) relating to the sequence.

The Computer in Planning and Forecasting

With the use of the computer as a tool for management, the system can be fed detailed plans involving such activities as setting manpower levels, determining production schedules, and stating inventory policy. This tactical planning should result in a series of logical, day-to-day operating systems. The system can be set up so that all conditions are monitored and measured against the standards from the plan (the estimates), and in case of deviations, the system world automatically notify the manager responsible. Adjustments would be made as required.

All enterprises have specific goals to achieve, and planning is tool for achieving them. That is, planning helps choose one method from a range of alternatives. The computer can aid by testing the alternatives and does not involve costly development of complicated mathematical models. The planner can ask a wide range of questions to be answered through simulation. The data are fed into the computer, and various situations are created that have different results. All these simulations permit top management to assess the probable result of a policy decision before it is put into effect.

With the PERT network system, the purchasing department has contact with the entire project and is in an excellent position to ensure the availability of the right quality and quantity at the right time. The technique for using computer technology is to control the many interrelated events of the project. The PERT system in the computer can quickly indicate when a crucial delivery is approaching or passed and alert the purchasing department to follow-up and/or expedite the delivery of the needed material.

With the speed of the computer, direct search concepts can be used in the solution to planning problems and accurately find the lowest combination of costs for any given project. The essential in planning problems is to look ahead to see what impact projected demand changes would have on the present decisions that may be made. If the short-term demand for the first quarter is projected to increase, followed by a decline in demand, what is to be done to keep overall costs down? Top management, to keep costs at a minimum, may absorb the increase in demand by drawing from inventory or by use of overtime rather temporarily increase the work force. Costs over the entire planning period would be minimized.

The budgeting function is an important factor in the overall financial posture and cash-flow control. The departments seek to obtain approval from top management for future expenditures for their individual objectives and look to the purchasing department in ascertaining an estimate of those costs. The success of today's manufacturing company is proportional to its ability to rapidly gather, transmit, and interpret all information detailing all activities of the company. The communication capability of the computer is needed to deal with the increased complexity of doing business. The data are fed into the computer and displayed at departmental terminals to monitor and control all operating activities. This computer communication capability had proven a great help to management in operating more effectively.

Organizations communicate and function on the basis of information. It is the prime medium by which different groups and departments react, function, and proact. Data is the lowest denominator of information. It is the measure, notation, observation, or other item that records something. Information is data put into a useful context for decision-making or action.

Data and information are dealt with in three basic ways in purchasing. First is forms, which are the basic data documents of purchasing. Forms are used for a variety of purposes in the operation and control activities of the department. Second is reports, which are summary documents indicating the need for possible corrective action or for compilation of routine activity statistics. Third is management information systems, which are any information, treatment, and reporting process designed for specific objectives.

Forms constitute the basic information needs of a purchasing operation. They serve a variety of purposes, some of which are: to report or inform, request, record, instruct, follow-up, authorize, cancel, order, apply, acknowledge, estimate, route, schedule, and claim. Many forms are used in purchasing. It is good practice to conduct audits upon forms with an eye toward simplifying, eliminating, or removing problems that arise with them. Some functional considerations about forms are: *(1)* they should follow the flow and sequence of the work involved, and *(2)* they should be designed with the information needed in mind and how to achieve the desired action by the target persons to whom it is sent, the method of identifying the form, and the copies and distribution of each one. Reports needed and used in purchasing revolve around the monitoring of order progress, the triggering of action at needed points in time, and the capturing of buyer performance and activity. Some common reporting systems are discussed as follows.

Order status is often reported in detail for each order as well as in summary form. Open orders are those that are currently outstanding with the goods expected to arrive sometime in the future. The open order status detail acts as a "tickler" device to prompt follow-up communication with vendors to assure the goods will be received at an expected time.

The vendor deliver rating is valuable for the future selection of vendors. The data captured for this report system includes vendor name, plant, product, quantities ordered, prices paid versus expected, quality order cycle times, order-to -receipt time performance, and any knowledge relating to other plants of the firm buying from each vendor. This is key system for noting the quality of each vendor. It is useful in the vendor selection decision.

Purchases for Stock

In order to replenish stock as it is used up, or (a much better way to think of the process) in order to provide for expected future demands after allowing for stock on hand, stock control will originate purchases by issuing requisitions. These may be general purpose requisitions as described earlier, but much use is also made of travelling requisitions and buy-lists or schedule requisitions.

Travelling requisitions are documents which travel from the originating department to purchasing in order to initiate a purchase, and then after transaction details have been recorded on them travel back to the originating department where they are filed for future reference and for use again the next time the item is required. They have nothing to do with travelling expenses or with requests to visit an overseas supplier. Alternative names for travelling requisitions are permanent order cards and perpetual requisitions.

Buy-lists (also known as blanket or schedule requisitions) are used when a large number of items need to be ordered at one time. This happens with some stock control systems and also with some production planning systems. No special form is used for these schedules of requirements. Often they are retained in the computer system as planned orders and not printed out as hard copy until action needs to be taken by purchasing.

In smaller organizations, the same person may be responsible for deciding what is to be ordered for stock as well as for actually ordering it—such as the buyer/first sales in a department store, the manager of a small retailer, the purchaser / stock controller in a small manufacturing firm.

Purchases for Production

Parts and material required to make products to meet manufacturing schedules are normally supplied from stock, in the case of both common use and inexpensive items. For expensive or bulky items, and those used in large quantities, material requirements are planned week by week, or even day by day, and deliveries are timed so as to meet needs with little or no stock.

Material requirements for manufacturing schedules are notified to purchasing in the same way as stock requirements, by general purpose requisitions, travelling requisitions, or buy-lists, which may be retained in the computer system until they need to be actioned.

In some small organizations the purchasing and stock control department is given a master production schedule showing what end-products are due out week by week, plus parts lists for the end-products. They calculate materials requirements, adjust for stock, and place orders accordingly. This is now usually done on a computer, using MRP soft ware.

Enquiry Procedures

General buyers' guides give you a long list rather than a short list of potential suppliers. This can be cut down by sending to the firms listed a preliminary enquiry giving brief details of the requirement, and asking firms, if they are able and willing to supply the requirement, to give some details about capability, performance record, financial status and other matters useful in drawing up a short list. These preliminary enquiries are usually called requests for information (RFI). In connection with construction contracts they are often called pre-qualification questionnaires, since the aim is to 'prequalify' or make a preliminary selection of potential suppliers who appear qualified to undertake the work.

Existing commitments or future plans may make it difficult for a supplier to bid for the requirement, in which case the supplier should say so. The purchaser should be pleased by this responsible attitude and keep the firm on the list of potential suppliers.

Having prepared a short list of possible suppliers, the next step is to send out formal enquiries or requests for quotation (RFQ), or tender forms. If a preprinted form is used it should not look like the order form and should not need to have such messages as 'This is not an older!' printed across in in large letters. It should either 'be a specially designed form such as the one shown in Fig. 3. or else should be a version of the normal letterhead with such words as 'Your quotation is invited not later than...for the supply and delivery of the goods specified below, subject to the terms and conditions printed on the back of this form', preprinted

REQUEST FOR QUOTATION

ALEXANDER CONTRACTS PLC.

122 Beker Street lo on WCI 3RG

TELEX 32148& 32273

TELEPHONE 01-222666

Please quote' this Reference in any correspondence or Telephone Call

----------		

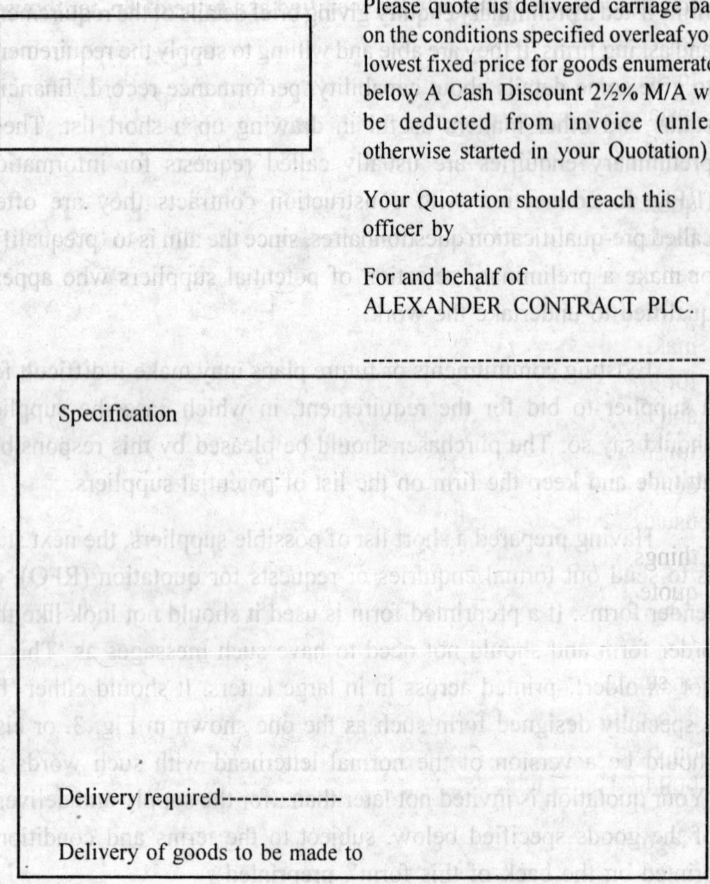
Please quote us delivered carriage paid on the conditions specified overleaf your lowest fixed price for goods enumerated below A Cash Discount 2½% M/A will be deducted from invoice (unless otherwise started in your Quotation)

Your Quotation should reach this officer by

For and behalf of
ALEXANDER CONTRACT PLC.

Specification

Delivery required------------------

Delivery of goods to be made to

Fig. 3. Request for quotation.

to save typing. With the increasing use of word processors pre-printed forms of this kind are used less than before.

One dictionary definition of 'quotation' is: 'amount stated as current price of stocks or commodities'. So a supplier could in principle reply to a request for quotation by saying 'we are currently selling this article at £p per thousand and delivery is usually about four weeks from receipt of order'. This is indeed a quotation but it is not an offer to sell so much as a statement of fact. Or a supplier could reply, as many do, by saying 'in reply to your enquiry we offer to supply you with the articles specified at a price of £p per thousand for delivery four weeks from receipt of your order.' This is an offer to sell, which can be converted into a contract by acceptance, for instance by sending an order.

Or a supplier could reply in similar words on a preprinted quotation form, with a set of terms and conditions printed on the back which are not the same as the buyer's. This is also an offer to sell, but if the buyer accepts it using a purchase order form with different terms printed on it he is not in law accepting the offer but making a counter-offer. They are regarded as relatively unimportant for a transaction which is one of a series between a regular supplier and a regular customer. They are important for an isolated transaction, for instance to build a new factory, where buyer and seller may never deal with each other again. For constructional work of this kind it is usual to use standard forms of contract which cover most of the things which could go wrong, and it is also usual for suppliers to quote for the work on tender forms.

A tender has been defined as 'a written offer to execute work or supply goods at a fixed price', and this offer is usually made on a form supplied by the purchaser, or the engineer or architect acting on behalf of the purchaser. This enquiry procedure is normal for building and civil engineering contracts.

Negotiation

The four main price negotiation situations are:

(1) An established supplier wants to increase price.

(2) The buyer wants an established supplier to reduce price.

(3) A potential supplier wants to get the business and oust the established supplier.

(4) There is no regular supplier and this is a new purchase.

Negotiations about price changes usually turn on costs. Suppliers in a position to dictate price do not need to negotiate. Suppliers who do negotiate need to make out a reasonable case.

Buyers negotiate many other matters apart from price: terms and conditions of contract, tooling, transport, quality control arrangements, delivery and stockholding arrangements, in fact any aspect of the agreement which is not standard.

Negotiation should not be difficult between reasonable persons who want to reach a mutually satisfactory agreement quickly, upon a matter they understand. Lengthy and arduous negotiations occur mainly when one or more of the parties are not being reasonable, and when large numbers of people are affected by the result.

A common mistake is not preparing thoroughly enough. Inadequate preparation is sometimes attributed to lack of time, but everyone has all the time there is; no-one's day has more th 24 hours in it. Faulty allocation of time might be nearer the mark.

Another mistake is trying to score a great victory. Win-Win' negotiations do not lead to the defeat of one side and the victory of the other, since buyer and supplier are not at war with each other. The aim in this kind of negotiation must be a mutually satisfactory solution. Trying to win every point is the result of not thinking the situation through. Most commercial negotiations occur between buyers and sellers who intend to continue trading with each other; whose objectives cannot rationally include leaving the other party stone cold dead in the market; who cannot therefore be said to have succeeded in achieving their objectives unless the other party is also reasonably satisfied with the outcome.

Preparation for Negotiations

Objectives, and tactics, are the two areas where advance planning and preparation can pay off.

In considering objectives, the major issues and the minor issues should be spelled out. The other parties' needs should be considered: what are they really after? How can we satisfy some of their needs? What do we stand to lose or gain, and what do they stand to lose or gain, if settlement is not reached? What are the relevant facts and figures? Often these have to be collected and collated in consultation with colleagues in other departments—in finance, engineering, production or sales. Long-term objectives such as the future supply pattern should not be left out of account when planning a short-term negotiation such as the price to be paid or the supplier to be chosen for a particular contract.

In fixing objectives for a negotiation, some margin for manoeuvre should be left. We might for instance aim at a settlement price of Rs. 10000, while hoping to settle for £8000 and being willing to agree at most to Rs. 12000. These are precise figures but do not send the negotiator into battle with his hands tied.

In considering the tactical plan, we have to consider relative bargaining strength. How much the seller needs the business, how sure he is of getting it, and how much time there is to reach agreement; how much the buyer needs the seller's product, what alternatives are open to him, how much time he has to develop alternatives, how much business he has to give the supplier, and what cost and price data he has; these are particularly relevant. TIme and location of meeting have to be settled. The home player has a small advantage. It is hardly enough to justify booking a hotel room to make sure of a neutral meeting ground.

In fixing the tactical plan, what questions to ask, and how to word them; what approaches the other side may come up with, and how to counter. them; and the order in which issues will be tackled, are the main things to plan.

Conduct of Negotiations

The reasonable negotiator begins on a positive friendly note, perhaps by referring to a past history of mutually satisfactory transactions. He shows clearly that he intends if at all possible to come to a mutually satisfactory settlement of the points at issue as soon as he can. He deals systematically in succession with the various points. He concludes by recapping what has been agreed, and he confirms this in writing the following day. He does not attempt to put one over on the other side by smuggling into the confirmation matters that were not mentioned in the recap. His plain and evident intention is to reach agreement on terms which satisfy both sides. Provided that the other party is also reasonable, it is one the whole a pleasure to do business with him. It cannot, however, be denied that unreasonable negotiators sometimes enjoy an underserved success.

Some practical advice is as follows:

(1) DO give plenty of thought to the other party's probably objectives, tactics, and attitude.

(2) DON'T waste time scoring debating points, proving your opponent wrong, or otherwise showing off.

(3) DON'T let emotional reactions such as rage or pride cloud your thinking.

(4) DON'T do all the talking; ask questions, listen to the answers.

(5) DON'T keep your eyes on the papers. Watch your opponent's body language: his eyes, physical attitudes, and facial expressions. Most people signal their feelings and attitudes quite clearly, even while saying verbally something rather different.

(6) Be ready to modify your approach.

(7) If you seem to reach an impasse on one point and your do not seem to be getting anywhere, switch to another point; say 'Let's leave that one for the moment. How about ?' When the less controversial point has been settled, the sticky one may look less sticky. Or else suggest a break for coffee, conference, referring back.

(8) Have a list of points at issue and work through it systematically, ticking off points as they are dealt with and recapping periodically.

(9) If you gain an important concession, think of something you can concede in turn. If on the other hand you have had to yield on some major point, use this as a lever to gain some *quid pro quo*.

(10) The alternatives are not win or lose, as Gerry Nierenberg has pointed out: 'The creative negotiator is where there are no wars, no strikes, no lockouts. The old cliches of the playing field, I win, you lose, survival of the fittest, winner take all, don't apply to commercial negotiations in an advanced cultural system.

❐

2

Material Management

HISTORICAL BACKGROUND

The managing of materials in industry in this country has been a real problem ever since the end of the Second World War. We came through the days of shortage and deprivation immediately following the end of hostilities, and, through the years that followed, heavy demand for materials and supplies created, in some areas like the chemical industry and others, a situation where rationing became necessary in order to keep industry ticking over. This was followed by continuous spasms of stop-go for our economic fortunes, which again put a great strain on the availability of materials; all this at a time when the impact of the Japanese, German and French had not been much in evidence in the world market-place.

Over a long period these circumstances created an atmosphere where what was important was getting supplies in any possible way in order to keep things moving, and a turning away from any possibility of real materials control.

Up to the early sixties the stock controlling of materials was very much a 'seat of the pants' decision and it was not until this time that the first breakthrough came, in the form of algebraic formulae from the United States. By their application to the conditions prevailing within an organization, it was possible to determine what was considered to be an economic order quantity. From this innovation things moved quickly and soon the computer specialists were getting busy to provide us with more useful data which, given time, would help those responsible for materials control to make more accurate assessments of requirements.

By now, the market-place was becoming a larger place in which to shop and money was fast becoming the dearest item to buy. Because of our seeming inability to obtain a good share of the increasing export market at this time, mainly due to our inability to meet the delivery dates required by our potential overseas customers, plus a creeping apathy being shown in industry, a study was made of the causes of this new situation. The results showed that the lack of availability of materials on time and their control after receipt by our manufacturers was the main cause of the problem and, in order to overcome this for the future, a new concept of total materials management was evolved and presented to industry.

Because of the self-interest of individuals and the traditional reluctance to change, this new concept did not take off right away. By the end of 1967, however, many forward-thinking companies had considered its application and were prepared to give it a chance. By now out share of exports had shown little improvement because, although our export figures were showing a gradual monthly increase, measured by the decline—now already begun—in the value.of the rupee, the seemingly improved position of exports was not there in real terms.

Over the years between 1967 and 1973, still more companies entered upon a system of materials management and the overwhelming consensus of opinion by now was that 'it worked'; those who had proved this wished that they had introduced it much earlier. It still continues to grow in popularity and today it is forging ahead fast in manufacturing industry.

We do not need to labour on the tribulations which befell us through inflation in the three years following 1973, when many companies went to the wall and others had to be propped up financially. It was bad enough to have to cope with the malignancy of inflation, which hit us with a ferocity never before experienced in this century. We had always had to cope with inflation as a legacy of the past years, but never in this dimension. That in itself presented a man-sized problem to cope with but, as if this was not enough, we had, running in parallel, a world, recession. These two forms of cancer during four years of struggle acted as a great block against obtaining the true benefits of materials management at a time when its acceptance was widespread and the benefits assured. Buyers could no longer place long-term contracts and the economic position was forcing companies to manufacture only against known demand, which caused deliveries of materials to run out, the inevitable inflation of stock holdings, and the consequent tying down of badly needed cash; and taxation did nothing to help the overall position.

It would not be unreasonable, therefore, to say that modern materials management has, until now in the eighties, had a very chequered career, through economic and other storms, and that it is perhaps only now possible for us seriously to study its effect on the future of British manufacturing industry, with a view to making a real endeavour to ensure that it is going to work.

Whether there is an upward swing in worldwide trade in the near future or not, sheer economics and outside competition are going to force us to make radical changes in order to reduce our material costs to a minimum and keep our selling prices competitive. If we fail to do this, our overseas market can only shrink, with all the disastrous effects that would have upon our future economic outlook.

If the upswing in world trade were to get into top gear rather quickly, and there is nothing to suggest that this could not happen, we think that our manufacturing industry would find itself, once again, at a great disadvantage in trying to grasp, with any speed, the opportunities that this upswing could provide. This is simply because we have not taken advantage of the time that the worldwide depression has given us to equip ourselves for this situation.

The modern concept of materials management is now widely acclaimed in forward-thinking, productive industry in this country, but if we are to become really effective against giant competitors for our share of world trade then companies, large, medium and small, who have not yet begun to consider this new concept and who would like to see their productivity increased, their costs reduced and be in a position to deliver on time, will have to give urgent and serious consideration to its immediate introduction.

Computers, like minimum stock levels, will do nothing to prevent us running out of stocks of materials and components. No matter how much paper we have floating around our organization, or how many bodies we employ to push it about, the plain, simple truth remains: if we do not have the materials and compqnents available in sufficient quantity in the stores at the time they are needed, then all else becomes totally irrelevant. The inquests do not help, rolling heads bring about nothing, and the Money and the time lost cannot be recovered.

Senior management should have taken steps to avoid the necessity for the inquests and the rolling heads, which even in themselves cost money for their execution! Modem materials management creates involvement on a scale not hitherto conceived, and this involvement embraces board management as well as middle management. It gives encouragement to the shop-floor personnel to know that, when they start a job, the materials will flow without interruption until the job is completed; thereby putting the challenge to finish on time on the operator, who it has been proved, can meet this challenge and be reasonably satisfied with his reward.

Some Results of a Survey in UK

The concept was originated as a result of a survey carried out by eminent industrialists to discover the root cause of the poor reputation of UK manufacturers in respect of late deliveries to customers at home and overseas. In the export market we were failing to maintain a growth rate of any significance, and overseas complaints of customers were increasing.

At the time there had been an upsurge in the quality of the goods being manufactured, thanks to the efforts of the Institute of Quality Assurance. We were also benefiting, as exporters, from favourable rates of exchange in many parts of the world. Oil revenues have since changed this particular advantage.

We had no lack of manufacturing skills or capacity (albeit the capacity being used was nothing like as modern as some of our competitors). What then was wrong? Why was our export growth losing ground?

This was the reason for the review. The results led to the conclusion that delivery was the major factor. Our inability to deliver on time. Our inability to create confidence in buyers, both at home and overseas, that our delivery promises would be met. That as the cause of markets being lost to manufacturers in both the home and the overseas markets.

Buyers in the United Kingdom were asked: 'Why buy in Germany when we can produce it in the UK?'

The answer was the same in most cases: 'We cannot obtain delivery on time.'

Overseas buyers were asked the same question and their reply was even more ironic: 'We like your goods, we would like to buy from you, but you cannot ship on time.'

The next logical step was to ask, if the problem is bad delivery, what is the cause of our failure to deliver on time?

The review revealed that this was down to an overall lack of control of materials, which is the major ingredient in producing finished goods on time. There were discovered such things as materials arriving late, interrupted production lines due to selfcreated emergencies, a lack of control of materials in the production area, and so on.

It would take too long to catalogue the many examples of disastrous circumstances which the survey revealed; suffice it to say that it called for very drastic action to try to improve the position and create a healthier atmosphere in world markets, where increasingly our competitiveness was being challenged more vigorously.

As a result of the investigation a 'blueprint for industry' was evolved, whereby materials would, or could, be tightly controlled right from the time a customer's order was received, through all its stages until it became a finished product being dispatched to a satisfied customer on time.

This blueprint was an integrated system which welded together the five facets of management directly concerned with material control into a team whose task was, in broad terms, to achieve the following objectives:

1. Reduce the cost of materials.
2. Bring the inventory in line with demand and thereby reduce the investment.
3. Increase productivity to a maximum.
4. Make certain that finished products were ready to satisfy customer's orders at the time they were promised for delivery.
5. Reduce wastage and reduce obsolescence to a minimum.
6. Enhance the company 'image' at all times.

This blueprint was entitled Materials Management, and the five facets of management that make up the materials management team are:

1. Stores management.
2. Stock control management.
3. Purchasing and contracts management.
4. Production planning and control.
5. Materials control management.

As time passes, and as many more companies, no matter what their size, become more fully acquainted with the great benefits to be derived from the concept of total materials management, so we shall here less and less of the purchasing department per se and the stores department per se, and so on, but a great deal more about materials management.

This is a totally integrated team of functional heads, who should all be qualified experts in their respective fields, and who, will be coordinated either by a materials manager with direct access to the board room, or, alternatively, a materials director who is already a member of the board.

The strong integration, which will always be so necessary among the members of the materials management team if it is to operate successfully, has at long last broken down the compartmentalization which for far too long has existed between the various functions.

At the time this blueprint for industry was evolved, the production planning and control manager was invariably under the control of the works manager or works superintendent, and similarly the materials control manager was to be found in the same position. Now they have been welded into a strong and effective materials management team.

Organisation of Modern Materials Management

The tree structure of the new concept is shown in Fig. 1. The post of director operators, who heads this team, does not necessarily involve a new appointment to the board; it could be an existing director having a knowledge of this area of activity being given the responsibility of coordinating the efforts of the five-man team of specialist managers. He would hold regular meetings, possibly at

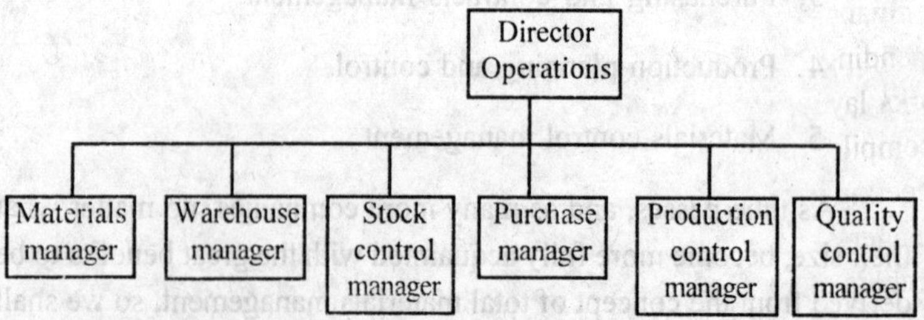

Fig. 1. Flow of the materials management decision making.

weekly intervals, with the five managers collectively, who would report progress against forecasts and detail any likely problems which could lead to production not being maintained strictly on time. He must, if necessary, be ready to use his influence, position and experience to smooth out these problems promptly, both inside and outside the boardroom. 'This involvement by the board of directors is imperative to the success of the whole organization, and the board must be willing to shoulder its responsibilities in this respect. In doing so, they will hold together a team of experts rather than a number of individuals preoccupied with empire-building and self interest, who are blind to the main objective of manufacturing what is needed at the lowest cost and delivering it on time. By achieving that objective we shall begin to retrieve, once more, our industrial self-respect and show our customers that we intend to keep to our delivery promises, no matter what.

Each of the five managers is of equal status and each will be well trained in his field of operation, as well as being fully involved in the overall objectives of the organization. Each must be essentially a team man, who knows the vital importance in integration. He must practise this in all things and strive always to promote it, thereby dispelling the antiquated ideology of compart mentalization, which has existed for too long.

The *materials manager* is responsible for producing a complete masters chedule of materials requirements to cover the whole of the production plan (or sales forecast) for the whole twelve months of the financial year, or as far ahead within the year as can be forccast depending on the type of business. This he compiles either from works layout sheets with or without the aid of the computer, but it is compiled in totality; in detail and including every requirement. After a meeting between the production control manager, the stock control manager, the purchasing manager, and the production manager and members of his team, the production programme is planned and the right decisions taken as to how much of the totality of materials requirements are to be made, in-plant and how much will be bought outside. These are decisions of paramount importance and involve all three materials managers, especially the purchasing manager, whose advice on make or buy will be respected and accepted. When these decisions are taken, the master schedule of materials requirements is then studied by the. materials control manager and broken down into schedules, one for the made-in items, the other for the bought-out items.

The schedule for the made-in items is passed to the production control manager who will be responsible for planning, in detail, the whole production required to complete this schedule week by week, apportioning to each week the amount of production necessary to complete the plan on time.

The *production control manager* has the unenviable task of making certain that his made-in parts are coming off the production lines on time to ensure complete synchronization with the boughtout parts, so that at the right point on the production line both made-in and bought-out parts synchronize perfectly and go forward to become a finished product on time to be sent to the finished products store for dispatch on time. Failure to achieve this synchronization on the part of the production control manager and the purchasing manager can only result in the cash flow of the organization being badly affected by having made-in parts accumulating in stock, waiting for bought-out parts, or vice versa. Either way, money is unnecessarily tied up and customers are alienated by late deliveries.

The *stock control manager* receives both schedules and must measure what free stock will be available to meet the needs of the schedules, what is outstanding on commitment and what quantity is still required to meet both schedules to cover both the bought-out requirements and the materials required to make the made-in parts. He then passes the requests for all the materials and parts requirements to the purchasing manager, defining in detail how much and at what rate he wants it to be delivered so that only the right amount of stock is available at all times, thus avoiding overstocking or stockout.

The *stock control manager* is constantly watching for obsolete, redundant and slow-moving stocks to keep these to the minimum, listing them and having them dealt with by the stock review committee and disposed of promptly, realizing that he can only show a return on the money invested in stocks if the stocks are kept on the move all the time. He plays an important role in standardization and rationalization, knowing that the greater the degree of each that can be achieved, the greater will be the power of the purchasing manager to go into the market-place and buy 'right'.

The *purchasing manager* has the responsibility of purchasing everything requested by the stock control manager at the .right price and applying all the purchasing techniques' required to achieve this. He must portray the correct image of the organization to all those with whom he deals, making sure that at all times he is protecting the organization and the board against litigation and malpractice, and constantly demonstrating his integrity. He must see his function as a profit centre rather than a cost centre, by using sound purchasing judgements and constantly employing source protection and cost reduction exercises so as to safeguard the supply line of the organization in all circumstances.

The purchasing manager, the stock control manager and the stores manager have not only to deal meticulously with all the items of made-in and bought-out parts and see that they are made available in the right quantity at the right time, but they must also provide and control in exactly the same manner all those many consumable items which help to oil the wheels of production. These items are just as important as the production materials; with them, much can be done to smooth industrial relations, but without them the production lines can be brought to a halt just as quickly as by not having the materials for the actual manufacturing of products.

The *Stores Manager*—last, but by no means least in importance-has the responsibility for physical control of all stores and ware-houses as well as accountability at the end of the financial year. He has a major role to play in integrating with the production control manager to ensure that his requests are promptly met, to extract items physically from stock, correctly lay them up and transfer to work-in-progress ready to be loaded onto the production lines as required. He has to report promptly the stockout situation to the production control manager and the stock control manager. His function has to operate smoothly and efficiently so that it is always complementing good stock control. He will, among other activities, raise lists of obsolete, redundant and surplus materials for action, provide information to form the basis of consideration for rationalization and standardization, and have a very keen eye on all incoming materials and parts to ensure the organizatibn is getting value for money.

There is a five line of difference between the Stock Control Manager and Material Manager. The stock control manager is responsible for having all stocks available in the stores, both in the quantities and at the time required, up to the point where they are withdrawn by the production control manager who takes over and steers these materials through all their operations in the production processes, keeping the production manager fully aware of progress and anything that can happen operationally to stop the finished products rolling off the production lines on time and as planned. In very forward-thinking organizations the materials control manager has been given an added role or responsibility: to be the link-man between the members of the materials management team and the research and development department and the drawing offices. Any materials required for design changes, modifications or new products will be advised to the material control manager by R and D and DO personnel before drawings and designs are finalised so that he can check with the materiats managemertt team that such materials can be made available for the foreseeable life of the modification or new product; that they can be abtained somewhere in the market-place far this period as standard produced materials and will not have to be specially made thereby increasing their purchase price approximately twelve times); and, most important, when is the right time to introduce them. The right time is when the stock of old materials can be run down to zero; the new take-over at that point. Good planning and cooperation can achieve this.

The benefits of this coordination lie in large-scale reductions in stocks of absolete, redundant and surplus materials which are unnecessary and often crippling in their effects. It can be seen that this concept of materials management means that this highly skilled, closely knit team of specialists will in future be controlling materials from the time of the raw material requisition right through all the stages of processing and storage until the finished product is ready for dispatch to the customer. Expediting, which will be all important, will move from the purchasing manager to. the stock contral manager, who is nearer to. the scene of operatians and can therefore take action earlier. Priority actian can be better decided by the stock contral manager, and analysis has shown that only some 20 per cent of all we purchase annually really needs the application of specialist expediting. This moving of the expediting will simply ensure that the instructions of the purchasing manager, in relation to delivery only, have been carried out by the supplier on time. Success in achieving this will still further reduce stackholdings, and help the cash flow situation.

Many small organizations will be unable to. support a five-man team of specialists but the concept can still be applied. It simply means, for example, that stores and stock control, or perhaps stores, stock control, and purchasing, will be under one functionol head. Whatever the grouping of functianal heads they must abviously be efficient, well-trained, competent managers, fully comprehending their role and able to provide a high standard of integrated effort.

Finally, it is up to the board to see that diversification is not allowed to interrupt the concept for the sake of appeasing someone's ego.. As an example, the stores manager is the manager of the stores and, whether these store-houses cantain tools, oils and greases, finished products, raw materials, piece parts, packaging, flammable materials, stationery, maintenance spares, or anything else, they shauld all be under his control. In future the stores manager will have to be sufficiently experienced to be capable of laying out and managing any kind of storehouse, no matter what it contains, and be able to demonstrate this ability to the board. It is pointless nominating a stores manager but having the tool stores and maintenance stores under engineering, and finished products stores under marketing. This is wrong and should be eliminated; only by having total control can one have effective control.

This chapter has been anly an introduction to the concept. Later chapters will give more details, but those who are now working to. the concept acknowledge its benefits and know what it has done to. smooth out problems and eliminate bottlenecks, enhance productivity, reduce costs, and give a higher service level with a lower investment in stockholdings by ensuring that stocks are 'right', in line with the productian plan. One wonders whether the concept would help you to improve things?

Materials Management: A Conceptual Analysis

Materials management is an indispensable core activity of all types of organisations. All organisations are continuously involved in procurement, storage, and stock replenishment of different types of materials. In some of the industries the cost of materials input ranges between 45% to 85% of the product cost. Thus, the slightest efficiency in the materials management releases substantial gains to the organisation in terms of cost and capital requirement. Due to such strategic role materials management has assumed greater importance in the modern management. In fact, along with other areas of management like production, marketing, finance and personnel, materials management has been recognized as fifty key area of the management of the organisations.

In India and Iran materials account for around 66% and in the U.S.A., Japan, U.K., Italy and Mexico 59%, 56%, 61 %,62% and 64% respectively of the total cost of product. The study conducted by the RBI on company finances relating to 1650 selected medium and large scale public limited companies reveals that the investment in inventories constitutes 37.2% of total assets, 59% of current assets and 90% of total working capital requirements.

In India, materials cost is about 66%, labour cost 15% and overhead about 19% of the total cost. It has been observed that in

India, in both private and public sector materials cost as percentage to total cost is quite high as compared to advanced countries. It has been estimated that about 90% of working capital in most of the Indian industries remains locked-up in inventories as against 36% in industrial advanced nations. These facts make out a strong case to study materials management with the objective to improve operating efficiency and reduce working capital lock-up.

Materials management covers efficient management of materials —planning and programming, purchasing, inventory control, receiving, warehousing and store-keeping, materials handling and disposal of scraps and surpluses. The Dictionary of American Production and Inventory Control Society defines the materials management as under:

"Materials management is a term to describe the grouping of management functions related to the complete cycle of materials flow, from the purchase and internal control of production materials to the planning and control of work-in progress, to the warehousing, shipping and distribution of finished products. It differs from the materials control in that the latter term traditionally is limited to the internal control of production materials."

The materials management would embrace all activities concerned with materials except those directly concerned with designing or manufacturing the product or maintaining the facilities, equipment and tooling. It would embrace the activities performed by major departments such as purchasing, inventory control, receiving and inspection, stores, traffic and physical distribution.

Materials management views materials flow as a system. Thus, it includes:

(i) anticipating material requirements scientifically;

(ii) sourcing, obtaining and inspecting materials;

(iii) introducing materials into the organisation;

(iv) storing and handling materials, and disposal of scraps and unserviceable items;

(v) monitoring the status of materials;

(vi) replenishment of stocks; and

(vii) strengthening materials information system.

Symbolically materials management concept may be presented as:

$$MM = P_1 + P_2 + C + I$$

P_1 = Purchasing

P_2 = Procurement

C = Inventory Control including Stores Function

I = Materials Information System

MM = Materials Management

The modern approach is to have an integrated materials department headed by a materials manager with the purchase manager under him. The other functions included in the integrated materials set-up would be stores, inventory control, planning, cost reduction, transportation, value engineering, etc.

Objectives of Materials Management

The successful operation of any organisation depends, to a large extent, on the availability of goods and services of the right quality in the right quantity at the right time, from the right source, at the right price. These basic requirements can be suitably amplified and modified by the needs and objectives of the individual organisations. The materials management objectives may be studied' under two major segments:

(i) Primary, and (ii) Secondary.

The primary objectives include scientific purchasing, storage, inventory control, quality standards, operating efficiency, etc. The secondary objectives cover such functions as locating new suppliers, vendor rating, vendor development, purchase research, value analysis, value engineering, variety reduction, standardisation, human resource development, etc.

Some authorities on materials management have given its objectives as under:

(i) Provide an uninterrupted flow of material supplies, and services required to operate the organisation.

(ii) Keep inventory investment and loss at a minimum.

(iii) Maintain adequate quality standards.

(iv) Purchase required items and services at lowest ultimate price.

(v) Maintain the organisation's competitive position.

(vi) Find or develop competent vendors.

(vii) Standardize, where possible, the items bought.

(viii) Achieve harmonious, productive working relationships with other departments within the organisation.

(ix) Accomplish the purchasing objective at the lowest possible level of administrative costs.

Purchase Planning

Materials planning is the most neglected area in the purchasing activity in developing countries. Over-ordering and under-ordering materials are consequences of lack of planning in materials management field. Over-ordering is marked by over-investment and unproductive use of costly working capital. Under-ordering is characterized by equipment and material shortages that cause unnecessary delays and costly interruptions in executing the commitments. Ill-planned purchasing at macro and micro levels have a powerful inflationary potential. Thus, purchase planning is the most important function that distinguishes the buyer as a purchase manager.

Purchase planning may be defined as the scientific way of determining the materials requirements within economic investment policies, undertaking purchasing research activities, and determining stress areas' to reduce lead time, etc. There are four broad purchase planning techniques that exert far-reaching influence on the effectiveness of materials management. They are *(i)* budgeting, *(ii)* demand forecasting, *(iii)* purchasing research, and *(iv)* network analysis.

Budgeting has long been recognized as a useful tool in managerial planning and control. A company budget is a device which balances the planned allocation of expenses with forecasted income during a specified period of time. Budgeting enables executives to draw out the future course of action through mutually acceptable decisions and to control it through performance dynamics. From materials management point of view materials / purchase and operating budgets are important. Demand forecasting is the technique of evaluation of available information to predict future trends. The accuracy of forecasting depends on the data used and its analysis. In the present discussion, focus of attention is the forecasts for inventory planning and control as a guidance to purchasing.

Forecasting may be judgmental or analytical. The first involves human judgment and intuition, therefore, is 'subjective' and the second is mathematical-statistical and therefore, is 'scientific'. The scientific technique is based on analysis of data and a quantitative expression of their interrelationship. However, scientific fact and human psychology and interconnected. Therefore, a synthesis between the two may produce better results. But till now two kinds are viewed differently, one with scepticism and the other with some kind of reliability as the. only available analytical-scientific technique to estimate possible trend of future demand.

R. G. Brown in his book 'Statistical Forecasting for Inventory Control' has distinguished between 'forecasting' and 'prediction'. He has used the term 'forecast' to mean the projection of the past into the future, which literally means 'to throw ahead', to continue what has been happening, reserving the term 'prediction' for management's anticipation of changes and of new factors affecting demand. He has further elaborated this in his book, 'Smoothing, Forecasting and Prediction of Discrete Time-Series' as "our everyday life presents countless situations where one must somehow estimate what will happen in future, as a basis of reaching a decision or taking action. In some instances, the estimate is reached subjectively; in others, an objective computation is advisable. Predictions are sometimes used as an input to forecasting, and forecasts are sometimes a basis for predictions".

The purchasing research wing is charged with the responsibility of obtaining, organising and interpreting data which facilitate purchasing and hence improve total purchasing performance. A formal purchasing research programme serves as a purchasing planning instrument. The general objective of such a programme is to undertake indepth investigations which improve purchasing and on the whole increase materials management's contribution to organisation's goals. Mr. Albert Kreig, manager of purchasing research for the American Cyanamid Company, classifies the purchasing research staff functions into three primary jobs and one special project area:

(i) Procurement Planning

(ii) Research on Purchased Materials

(iii) Research on Purchasing System

(iv) Special Projects.

In addition to the above other activities that can be covered under purchasing research are vendor rating, vendor development, vendor-vendee relationship, standardisation and specifications, design planning, materials requirement planning (MRP), etc. MRP consists of a set of logically related procedures and policies designed to translate total requirement of materials into time-phased net requirements and the planned coverage of such requirements for each component of inventory item needed to implement the schedule. It is both an inventory control and scheduling technique.

Critical path scheduling is another basic technique that can be used for planning and controlling complex projects composed of a large number of interrelated and interdependent activities. There are no less than fifteen specific techniques derived from the basic critical path scheduling concept. The best known of these are PERT (Programme Evaluation & Review Technique) and CPM (Critical Path Method). CPM was originally developed in 1955 by the Du Pont and Remington Rand Companies for use in coping with complex plant maintenance problems. PERT emerged in 1958 through the joint efforts of the United States Navy, the Booz Allen and Hamilton Consulting firm, and the Lockheed Missile and Space Division in connection with the Polaris weapons programme.

Inventory Control

Inventory may be defined as a detailed list of all those movable items which await fabrication or shipment. The items which await further fabrication in the manufacturing process may be raw-materials and consumable stores. The items awaiting shipment to consuming centres may be the finished products. Hence, inventory may be stated as the detailed descriptive list of stores and stocks. Inventory consists of:

(i) Raw-materials

(ii) Components

(iii) Work-in-progress

(iv) Finished products.

Inventory control system aims to answer two fundamental questions; one—when to order and two—what quantity to order? It may be defined as a set of policies and procedures by which an organisation determines what materials it should hold in stock and the quantities of each that it should carry without entailing costs involved in overstocking, understocking or out-of-stocking. Maintaining minimum inventory investment, needs little or no explanation to the materials manager of today, who has been under extreme pressure to keep inventories under control.

Inventory is maintained basically to ensure operational smoothness. It is the materials management's responsibility to ensure that this operational smoothness is carried out at the minimum cost commensurate with efficiency. This is done through inventory control. The increasing size of manufacturing units and consequently number and variety of items in stock are mainly responsible for the development of modern inventory control techniques. Inventory carrying costs are today as high as 25%10, *i.e.*, if a company has Rs.10 lakhs worth of inventories it spends Rs. 2.51akhs to carry them in its stores. The wide variety and complexity of the requirements of modern industry also necessitates conscious inventory management. The larger the range of inventory, the greater the number of problems in inventory, investment, procurement, handling, accounting, shortages and stock-outs, deterioration and obsolescence.

In the industrial economy of today, there is a greater pressure for maintaining liquidity than in the trading economy of the past. It has, therefore, a greater reason to be alert about the working capital turnover. The best way to secure a rapid turnover of working capital is to control inventories. It is, therefore, apparent that an integrated approach for inventory control is essential. Without control the inventories have a tendency to grow beyond economic limits, tie-up funds and increase the cost of maintence or the carrying cost. At the same time non-availability of inventory involves the cost of stock-outs, reordering costs and additional transit costs. A rigorous inventory control ensures the purchasing and storing costs at the lowest possible without affecting production and operational efficiency or operational preparedness.

The costs that are affected by each specific decision must be determined when deciding how much inventory to carry. The following classes of costs are involved in inventory decisions:

(a) Ordering costs

(b) Inventory carrying costs

(c) Out-of-stock costs

(d) Capacity associated costs.

Details of the above variables will be discussed in the subsequent chapter.

Classification of Inventories

Effectiveness of inventory control stands on systematic inventory classification. Organisations often apply selective control over the inventories to keep them within limits without jeopardising the operational efficiency. As its name implies, selective control means that there are variations in the method of inventory control from item to item and this differentiation is on selective basis. Inventories can be divided into eight different types. However, synthesis of two or more classifications is normally adopted by the organisations to exercise rigorous inventory control. The classification is as under:

Classification	Criteria
1. ABC-Always Better Control.	Annual value of consumption of the items concerned.
2. VED-Vital, Essential and Desirable.	Criticality of the component or material with respect to production.
3. FNS-Fast Moving, Normal Moving and Slow Moving.	Issue frequency from stores.
4. SDE-Scarce, Difficult to obtain and easily available.	Purchasing problems with respect to availability.
5. HML-High Price, Medium Price and Low Price.	Unit price of materials.
6. GOLF-Government controlled, ordinarily available, Local and Foreign	Source from which the material is obtained.
7. SOS-Seasonal and off-seasonal.	Seasonality.
8. XYZ	Inventory value of stored items.

Inventory Control Models/Methods

In most of the realistic inventory situations certainty does not exist. Both usage and acquisition lead time usually fluctuate and cannot be completely predicted. Demand or usage of items can be greater or lesser than anticipated due to external and internal factors. Also, the acquisition lead time can vary from favourable to unfavourable due to the supplier or transhipment problems.

The basic approach under all inventory control methods is to fix limits or levels which, when reached, would indicate that the stock needs replenishment. The quantity of inventory required or purchased in any organisation is determined by the following variables:

(i) Safety Margin

(ii) Reorder Point

(iii) Buffer Stock

(iv) Lead Time

(v) Standard Order Quantity

(vi) Maximum Level

(vii) Economic Order Quantity (EOQ).

The following inventory control systems have been developed to cope up with the situations where the demand or the lead time or both fluctuate:

(i) Perpetual Inventory Control Method.

(ii) Periodic or Imprest Inventory Control Method.

(iii) Optional Replenishment Method.

Probabilistic Inventory Model can be used to determine stock level under a situation where demand is a random variable, following either a discrete or a continuous probability distribution. This model is out of the scope of present research work. Hence, it has not been discussed. However, perpetual inventory control, periodic inventory control and optional replenishment inventory control methods will be discussed in the chapter on inventory control.

Stores Management

Stores management is an indispensable part of the overall function of materials management. An organisation can have various types of stores like raw-materials, components, semifinished and finished products. The task of storekeeping relates to safe custody and preservation of the materials stocked, their receipts, issue and accounting. The objective is to efficiently and economically provide the right material at the right time and in the condition in which it is required. The stores function of materials management is mainly concerned with accepting, storing, handling and issuing of materials and also with processing the necessary documents to record transactions. In general, the stores department is designed to achieve the following functions:

(i) To make a balanced flow of raw-materials and components efficiently and economically to meet operational requirements.

(ii) To receive and issue all materials including the finished goods.

(iii) To store and handle materials efficiently.

(iv) To carry out stock-taking.

(v) To accept and store scrap and other discarded materials as they arise.

The main scope of stores department is as under:

(i) Storage of materials.

(ii) Handling of materials.

(iii) Classification and codification of materials.

(iv) Physical verification.

(v) Provide instant information about the materials status to the top management for strengthening materials information system.

(vi) Stores accounting and materials valuation.

(vii) Management of surplus, scrap and unserviceable items.

Details of the above variables will be discussed in the chapter on stores management.

Power Scenario in India

For a developing country like India, electricity is the most commonly used form of energy. Indeed it is the fulcrum on which rests the future pace of growth and development. As the tempo of development increases, the demand for electricity also increases.

Since independence, India has multiplied electricity generation capacity over 55 times. India's generating capacity has increased from a meagre 1362 MW in 1947 to about 76,718 MW in 1993-94. Electricity generation which was only about 4.1 billion KWh in 1947 has risen to a level of around 323 billion KWh in 1993-94. The total transmission lines of all categories at the end of 1993-94 were of the order of 4 million ckt. kms. as compared to 29,271 ckt. kms. in 1950. The number of villages which have been electrified are over half a million as compared to only 3061 in 1950. Despite these impressive achievements, most regions in the country face severe power shortages. The per capita electricity consumption in the country, in spite of a rise to a level of 270 Kwh from 15.6 Kwh in 1950, is one of the lowest in the world. We are far behind the level of consumption in developed countries which ranges from 8000 Kwh to 25000 Kwh per annum.

In its quest for increasing availability of electricity, the country has adopted a blend of thermal, hydel and nuclear sources. Of late, emphasis is also being laid on non-conventional energy sources—solar, wind and tidal. The need for all round development is putting a heavy burden on India's limited sources. Mobilisation of resources for achieving self-sufficiency in the electricity sector assumes high priority.

Hitherto, development of the electricity sector has been primarily the responsibility of the Goverrunent, with a relatively small contribution from private enterprises. However, it has been now realised that the resources needed to set up enough capacity to make a dent in the power deficit are too enormous to be mobilised by the public sector alone. For the 8th Plan (1992-97), the Central Electricity Authority (CEA) had estimated a need based capacity addition of 48,000 MW, which was scaled down to 30,538 MW taking into account the availability of resources. At present we have energy shortage of about 8% and peak shortage of 19%. Even with the planned capacity addition of over 30,000 MW, the shortages in the terminal year continue to be at the same level as at present. As a matter of fact, the situation is likely to be worse than at present as slippages in the planned capacity addition may occur. In this background, the Government has resolved to mobilise additional resources to help bridge the gap in supply by encouraging greater investment by private enterprises in the power sector.

GOALS OF MATERIALS MANAGEMENT

We will next examine in detail some typical objectives of materials management. Each, in some way, contributes to the achievement of some overall company objective. If the contribution is made directly by the materials function, we call it a "primary" objective. If it is indirect, and results from the materials department's assistance to another department in achieving its objectives, we call it a "secondary" objective.

Primary Materials Objectives

Almost every materials department has at least nine primary objectives. These are low prices, high inventory turnover, low cost of acquisition and possession, continuity of supply, consistency of quality, low payroll costs, favourable relations with suppliers, development of personnel, and good records.

(1) Low Prices. Obtaining the lowest possible price for purchased materials is the most obvious materials objective and certainly one of the most important. If the materials department reduces the prices of the items it buys, operating costs are reduced and profits are enhanced. This objective is important for all purchases of materials and services, including transportation.

(2) High Inventory Turnover. When inventories are low in relation to sales (inventory turnover = sales ÷ average inventories), less capital is tied up in inventories. This in turn increases the efficiency with which the company's capital is utilized, so that return on investment is higher. Also, storage and carrying costs of inventories are lower when turnover is high.

(3) Low-cost Acquisition and Possession. If materials are handled and stored efficiently, their real cost is lower. Acquisition and possession costs are low when the receiving and stores departments operate efficiently. They also are reduced when shipments are received in relatively large quantities (thereby reducing the unit cost of handling), but they are increased if average inventories are boosted with the large shipments.

(4) Consistency of Quality. The materials department is responsible for the quality only of the materials and services furnished by outside suppliers. The manufacturing department is responsible for quality control of manufacturing processes. When materials purchased are homogeneous and in a primitive state (*e.g.*, sand and gravel), quality is rarely a big problem for materials personnel. But wher. the product is in a highly advanced stage of manufacture and specifications are a tremendous challenge for suppliers to meet consistently (*e.g.*, components of interplan etary rockets), quality may become the single most important objective of materials management.

(5) Continuity of Supply. When there are disruptions in the continuity of supply, excess costs are inevitable. Production costs go up, excess expediting and transportation costs are likely, and so on. Continuity of supply is particularly important for highly automated processes, where costs are rigid and must be incurred even when production stops because of lack of material.

(6) Low Payroll Costs. The objective of low payroll costs is common to every department in the company. The lower the payroll, the higher the profits—all other factors being equal. But because no department can do its job without a payroll, the objective of low payroll must be viewed in proper perspective. It pays to spend $1.00 on additional payroll if earnings can thereby be boosted $1.01 through achieving other objectives.

(7) Development of Personnel. Every department in the company should be Interested in developing the skills of its personnel. And each department head should devote special effort to locating in junior posts men and women who have the leadership potential the company needs for continued success and growth. They should try to develop these highpotential men and women as the company's future executives; the company's future profits will depend on the talents of its managers.

(8) Favourable Supplier Relations. Manufacturing companies rely on outside suppliers to a far greater degree than is generally recognized. This makes favourable relations with suppliers extremely important. A company's standing in the business community is to a considerable degree determined by the manner in which it deals with its suppliers. A company with a good reputation in supplier relations is more likely to attract customers than one with a bad name.

Suppliers also can make a direct contribution to a company's success. Their product development and research efforts can be of tremendous assistance to their customers. Although such efforts naturally help the supplier too, it is important to remember that suppliers are human beings who respond to fair treatment. If a company has good relations with its suppliers, it will be far more successful in its efforts to stimulate superior performance from supplier personnel—extra service, cooperation in cost-reduction projects, a willingness to share new processes and ideas, and so on.

(9) Good Records. Good records are considered a primary objective of materials management, although paper work is a means to an end, not an end in itself. They contribute to the role of the materials department in the company's survival and profits only indirectly. They are necessary and. useful; they help materials personnel do a better job. While this can also be said of office equipment, the maintenance of the materials department's stock of typewriters, adding machines, and the like would hardly be considered a primary objective. Good records, however, are considered a primary objective in the purchasing and traffi phases of materials management for the same reason that they are a primary objective in the accounting department.

Secondary Objectives

The secondary' objectives of materials management are not nearly so limited in scope and variety as the primary objectives. Since, they represent the materials department's contribution to the achievement of the primary objective of some other department, they can vary widely from industry to industry.

There are literally hundreds of possible secondary objectives in materials management. Among the more common ones are reciprocity, new materials and products, economic make-or-buy decisions, promotion of standardization, product improvement, good interdepartmental relations, accurate economic forecasts, and alertness to possible acquisitions.

(1) Favourable Reciprocal Relations. When a company deliberately buys from its own customers as much as possible, it is practicing reciprocity. Sound reciprocity involves a balancing of the advantages and disadvantages of using one's buying power as an instrument for getting sales. Similarly, suppliers will use their own buying power as a sales tool.

In the consumer-goods industries, reciprocity is rarely a problem; sales are spread among many users. In producer-goods industries, however, reciprocity is a way of business life, particularly among industries where there is little product differentiation and prices are uniform. The materials department in such industries often coordinates its purchases with the sales department to make certain that company customers get favoured treatment.

(2) Product Improvement. This is perhaps the single most important objective of the engineering department. Materials personnel can assist, however. Their economic knowledge can supplement the technical skills of the engineers on programmes to boost profits through product change. The engineering of practically any product is basically a compromise between design and economic objectives. Materials personnel can help engineers achieve their design objectives more economically by suggesting materials or components that will do a better or equivalent job at lower cost.

(3) Economic Make or Buy. Make-or-buy decisions are often sparked by materials personnel since they are the group most intimately concerned with the selection of supply sources. By no means are they solely responsible for these decisions, however. As pointed out in the previous chapter, make-or-buy decisions should be a committee effort, representing the points of view of all departments in the company. The materials department, in its regular reviews of cost and availability of materials, often will spot the need for new make-or-buy decisions and should refer them to the committee for action.

(4) New Materials and Products. Engineering and manufacturing man agers are always interested in new products and materials that will help them operate more efficiently and thereby achieve one of their primary objectives. The materials department can help, because its personnel deal regularly with the suppliers responsible for the new developments. When they learn of anything of interest, they can call it to the attention of the interested parties in manufacturing, engineering, or other departments.

(5) Standardization. The fewer the items that need be controlled, the simpler and more efficient the materials management process. Thus it is to the interest of materials personnel to promote standardization and simplification of specifications. The engineering groups are primarily responsible for standards and specifications, but materials personnel can make a substantial contribution. They can periodically review stock to weed out nonstandard items; they can promote the incorporation of standard components into product designs to reduce cost; and they can promote standardization with suppliers.

(6) Inter-departmental Harmony. The materials department deals daily with every other activity in the business. It not only can contribute to the success of every other department, but its own success depends On how successful it is in gaining the cooperation of personnel in other departments. In practice, most materials managers are fully aware of the importance of good interdepartmental relations. To prevent disputes, they are careful to define departmental responsibilities clearly (this will be discussed later in this chapter) and also try to familiarize others with materials objectives, policies, and organization.

(7) Acquisitions. Most company managements are interested in growing, not only by internal expansion but also by acquiring other businesses. It is no easy job to identify a possible candidate for acquisition and then to make the necessary overtures for eventual merger. The materials manager can often play an important role in acquisitions, since he normally has, through dealing with his many suppliers, more contacts with the outside business world than other executives in the company.

(8) Forecasts. To manage materials well, some conception of the future outlook for prices, costs, and general business activity is necessary. In large companies, professional economists make forecasts that are used for both sales and purchase planning. Materials personnel translate these general forecasts into specific forecasts for purchased materials. They may also provide the conomists with data for forecasts because, more than any other group itt the company, they are intimately familiar with the market and general business conditions through their daily contacts with suppliers.

Achieving Objectives

The primary and secondary objectives of materials management discussed above would be applicable to most manufacturing companies. However, these objectives vary in relative importance from industry to industry and even among companies within an industry. One company may devote considerable effort to one objective while another may concentrate most of its efforts on a different one. Four examples which can illustrate this point are given below.

(1) Holding Down Prices. In the tanning and woolen textile industries, the raw material is always available at a price. But price fluctuations can be violent. Wool and hides (and other commodities, like crude rubber, zinc, and copper) have been known to double or triple in price within six months or decline by a proportionate amount.

For users of the materials, the key objective is to pay minimum prices for them. It overshadows all others in importance. A shrewd materials manager can save 10—or even 100-times as much by intelligent timing of purchases as he can hope to save through achievement of other materials objectives.

(2) Assuring Reliability. In the aerospace industry, consistency of quality (*i.e.*, reliability) is all-important. Almost any minor component can cause a $1,000,000 missile to malfunction. The odds favour failure. Because of the very complexity of the product, even a 99.9 percent quality standard may be inadequate. With this standard one part in 1,000 will be unsatisfactory. Since each missile contains morel than 1,000 parts, it is then likely that each would contain a compment that will fail.

(3) Regulating Inventory. In companies making a wide range of complicated products (instruments, machine tools, a similar items), the key problem usually is inventory turnover. Not only must the company have thousands of items available for product, but often it stocks tens of thousands of repair parts for customer service. If demand is erratic, there is always the danger that inventories will become unbalanced. The materials manager strives to prevent srockouts without tying up too much of the company's capital in inventory.

(4) Cutting Operating Costs. If purchase prices are stable and inventory fluctuations are minimal, then the most important contribution the materials manager can make is to do his job at minimum cost. His focus will be almost entirely on how to maintain the same level of basic performance at lower operating cost. In hospital materials management, for example, this may be the single most important economic objective.

POLICIES AND PROCEDURES

After the materials manager determines the relative importance of his objectives, he devises a programme to achieve them. In directing the programme, the materials manager wants to manage by exception if possible. That is, he wants to delegate the achievement of the programme completely to his subordinates. If everything goes according to plan, the materials manager does not interfere. But if something goes wrong because of a basic defect in the plan, the materials manager wants to learn of it. He may have to re-evaluate the objectives and devise a new plan or take other remedial steps.

Written policies and procedures permit management by exception. They guide routine performance. With them, management decisions are needed only when an exceptional problem arises.

Definitions. Policies are broad, overall guides to performance. Procedures are the specific administrative actions needed to carry out policies. Policies define in general terms the basic jobs of each department and its relation to other departments; they are derived from the general goals and objectives of the department itself and the company as a whole. Procedures are derived from policies. They describe routine operations in great detail.

Examples. One big aircraft and auto parts manufacturing company includes low prices and favourable vendor relations among its materials objectives. To achieve these objectives, it has a written policy that "negotiations with vendors regarding price, terms, quality, etc. should be initiated, conducted, and concluded by the purchasing department."

This policy might be carried out with a number of procedures, such as a buying procedure whereby no purchase commitment is valid unless it is approved by a member of the purchasing department, or a procedure that prohibits anyone in departments other than purchasing from interviewing supplier salesmen without written approval of the purchasing agent.

A company with a policy of stimulating maximum competition among suppliers (in order to achieve an objective of low prices) might have a procedure calling for a minimum of three bids on each purchase.

Advantages of Materials Departments' Manuals

Progressive materials departments codify literally hundreds of policies and procedures in manuals that may include several hundred pages. They invest in hundreds of hours of high-priced specialists' time for preparing the manual. Moreover, such manuals are no good unless they are kept up to date, so frequent revisions are necessary.

After all this work, what usually happens? Nine policy and procedure manuals out of ten may not be referred to for months or even years. They just gather dust on supervisors' bookcases. Very few persons in a well-managed company ever have much need to refer to a manual. Each knows his job, and if he has any questions he simply asks his supervisor. New employees don't have much use for manuals, either. They normally learn their jobs by observing their fellow workers and through verbal instructions from their supervisors.

Yet the best-managed companies have manuals for materials policies and procedures. They have them because manuals promote good interdepartmental relations (a secondary materials objective), make supervision easier, encourage standard practices, improve procedures, and aid in training.

Clarify Inter-departmental Relations. Even the best organization structure represents, to some extent, a rather artificial division of work. Departmental responsibilities overlap. Each department must work with the others if the overall job is to be done. Written policies and procedures define interdepartmental relationships. Thus they prevent many unnecessary jurisdictional disputes and also can prevent duplication of effort.

Written materials policies are particularly important because the materials department must work with other departments on problems where it is sometimes hard to determine jurisdiction. For example, although the materials department is responsible for selecting suppliers, using departments certainly have a right to receive the materials they need and to solicit suppliers for advice. Without written policies, jurisdictional disputes are almost inevitable when two departments are independently working with the same vendor on the same problem.

Make Supervision Easier. With written policies and procedures, a supervisor need not develop original solutions to routine problems. Nor need he even explain routine procedures to his subordinates (although he may wish to do so to make certain they understand them). The answers are in the manual. In most cases, the manual need not be referred to because employees already know what is in it. But were there no manual as a basic record, employees would gradually forget certain details of little-used procedures, and the load on supervisors would be correspondingly greater.

Develop Standard Practices. Without written policies and procedures, each supervisor would devise his own procedures to fit his superior's not-always-consistent instructions. As a result, eventually the same job would be performed in many different ways. Operations would be less efficient, communication slower, and supervision poorer. With Written policies and procedures (called "standard practices," because that is what they are designed to promote), supervisors still deviate from routine when necessary, but they have basic guides to make them aware that they are deviating. These in themselves tend to prevent unnecessary changes in routine.

Improve Procedures. When a manual is prepared, procedures are subjected to closer scrutiny than they may have received before. Improvements are almost inevitable. Unnecessary paper work can be eliminated, and tighter controls can be instituted if necessary. Periodic review and revision of the manual can prevent sloppy practices from creeping back into the system.

Aid in Training. Although new employees are often lazy readers and prefer to get their training by watching and talking with fellow employees, the manual is helpful for reference. It is also useful to employees in other departments.

The job of preparing or revising a manual can be a training vehicle in itself. There is no better way to give a new high-potential employee a good grasp of the overall workings of the department and to permit him to apply his imagination and resourcefulness to improvements in procedures.

Preparing the Manual

The materials department probably has more need for a policy and procedures manual than any other department in the company, mainly because of its contact with outside suppliers. Almost everyone in every department likes to buy and feels particularly competent to buy the items he uses. Controllers like to buy their own accounting machines, maintenance superintendents prefer to select brands of cleaning compounds, and product engineers feel they should select suppliers of parts and materials. This results in difficulties, which make preparation of a materials manual an especially long and tedious job. Since most of the important policies and procedures affect other departments, the person writing the manual must submit a draft of the proposed policy to each affected department head for approval. In many cases, hours are spent discussing precisely how a given policy should be worded so that each department's prerogatives are protected.

The usual procedure in preparing a manual is to determine what is being done and then to describe each operation in writing. After existing procedures are analyzed critically, the materials manager and his staff try to put down in writing what they would like to have done, as regards both policies and procedures. Existing procedures are then modified to fit these goals and drafts are submitted to all interested department heads for approval. The whole process always takes a few months and occasionally more than a year.

The effort is worthwhile, however, written objectives, policies, and procedures provide the framework within which the materials organization does its job. But they are useless, of course, if the materials department does not also have the organization it needs to achieve the objectives.

❒

3

Material Planning MRP & JIT

In contrast to the classical inventory control approach to the planning and control of materials, the technique, known as material requirements planning (MRT), looks at a future requirement for the finished product in terms of a master production schedule and uses this and other information to generate the requirements for all the sub-assemblies, components and raw materials which go to make up the finished product.

This technique has, in essence, been used under different names for many years, particularly for the purchase of special materials in the jobbing industries, that is, the time-phasing of material ordering. However, the advent of low cost computing has brought the term material requirements planning to the fore in the planning and control of the manufacture of multicomponent assemblies. In fact, MRP forms the central module of the majority of commercially available production control software packages.

As has been mentioned, MRP is concerned with the manufacture of multi-component assemblies and relies on the fact that the demands for all sub-assemblies, components and raw materials are dependent upon the demand for the finished product itself. They are said to have 'dependent demands'.

There are also some items which have 'independent demands' that is the demand for them does not depend on the demand for any other item. Notably, the finished product itself usually has an independent demand in that it depends solely on the customer purchasing the product. Components and sub-assemblies may also have independent demands in the form of spare parts sales requirements.

It is interesting to note that in a recent survey, 92% of engineering companies produced assembled products, that is to say. they had to deal with a proportion of dependent demand items.

Independent demand items may be satisfactorily controlled using the classical inventory control approach, for example, the reorder level policy. However, for dependent demand items, MRP offers considerable advantages in ensuring that all the parts for the assembly of the product are available at the right time. It also reduces overall stockholding costs whilst improving the service that the stock is providing.

This example shows that a saving in stock holding costs is one of the objectives of an MRP system.

In order to carry out its calculations, the MRP package requires three tppes of information to be supplied, namely:

(i) The master production schedule for the finished product;

(ii) The bill of material which contains details of which raw materials, components and sub-assemblies go to make up the finished products; and

(iii) Information concerning the status of all materials held in inventory.

Having performed its calculations, the package then produces reports, the majority of which are concerned with what and when to manufacture or order.

This system is shown in general outline in figure 1.

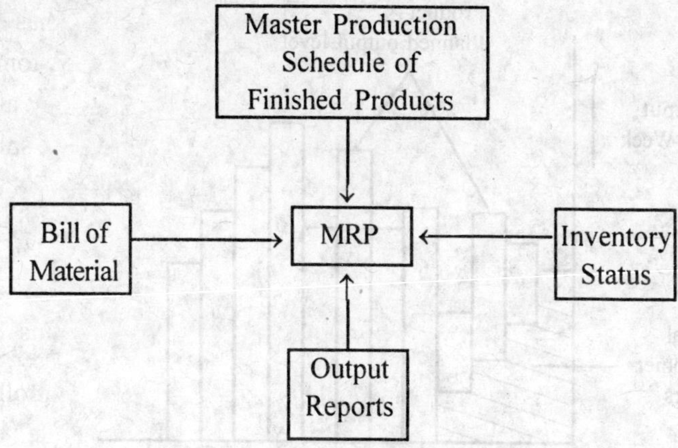

Fig.1. General MRP System Outline

1. Elements of the MRP System

The total MRP System (figure 1.) consists of several elements: the inputs, the package itself which carries out the calculations and the output reports. Each element may vary in its exact description, depending on the company and product in any particular case, but it is important to understand the purpose of the element and the various choices which are available.

2. The Master Prorluction Schedule

The master production schedule is a management commitment to produce certain volumes of finished products in particular time periods in the future and should not be confused with the term 'sales forccast'.

A master schedule is created for each finished product using known customer orders, sales forecasts and a knowledge of the manufacturing capacity. It is likely that the schedule will contain a major proportion of firm customer orders in the most immediate time periods and mostly forecasts in the later periods of the planning horizon (see figure 2).

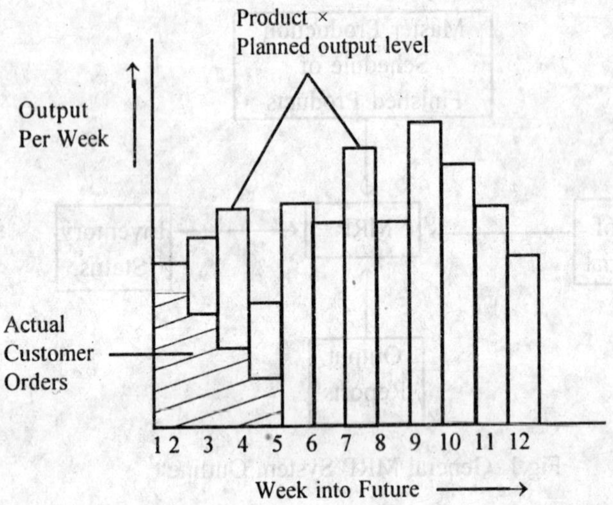

Fig. 2. Master Schedule for Product X

The length of the planning horizon is determined calculating the longest cumulative lead time for the finished product and adding a period of time to give the purchasing department visibility over future requirements, so that they are able to take advantage of bulk purchasing discounts. The longest cumulative lead time is the sum of all the lead times along the longest route from placing an order for a raw material to completing the finished product (see figure 3).

Today   Future

Assemble Product	Manufacture Parts	Purchase Material	Time to Permit Economic Purchasing

Cumulative Product Lead Time

Lenght of Planning Horizon

Fig. 3.Master Schedule Planning Horizon

For many companies in practice this will entail using planning horizons of between a year and eighteen months. Since the further ahead a forecast is made, the less accurate it is likely to be, it would be unrealistic to expect that no changes would be allowed to the master schedule, particularly in its later stages. There are however, increasing difficulties in making changes to the schedule the closer that the beginning or 'front end' of the schedule is approached.

One method of controlling the changes to the master production schedule is to split the planning horizon into time zones, each of which has different constraints on the type of change which can be made (see figure 4).

Essentially, that period of the schedule which represents finished products which are currently being a sembled should only be changed in emergency situations, since parts and sub-assemblies will have already been manufactured to the original schedule.

In that part of the planning horizon which represents parts currently being manufactured, it may be possible to alter the sequence of the finished products already scheduled, bear in mind material and capacity availabilities.

	Today			Future
Changes Allowed	Emergency only	Alter Sequence of Products Already Schedule	Alter Volume of Pro-ducts	Any Changes Allowed
	Assemble Product	Manufacture Parts	Purchase Material	Time to Permit Economic Purchasing

Fig 4. Changes Allowed to the Master Schedule

In the period which represents orders for materials that have been placed on suppliers, it may be feasible to alter the quantities of finished products on the master schedule if it is possible to make the consequent alterations of material quantities on the open orders with suppliers.

In the last section of the planning horizon. or 'back-end' of the schedule, which represents forward information for the purchasing department, it should be possible to make alterations to both the sequence and volume of finished products scheduled, presuming of course, that checks have first been made with the purchasing department regarding any major bulk material purchases which may have been made on the basis of the original information.

Apart from the sales of finished products, a company might also be concerned with the supply of spares in the form of components or sub-assemblies. As described previously, these items have independent demands. However, these independent demands can be incorporated imto a MRP system by adding them to the generated dependent demands for the items in the relevant time periods.

As with the master producticn schedule, the independent spare parts demands could be made up of firm customer orders and sales forecasts as in figure 5.

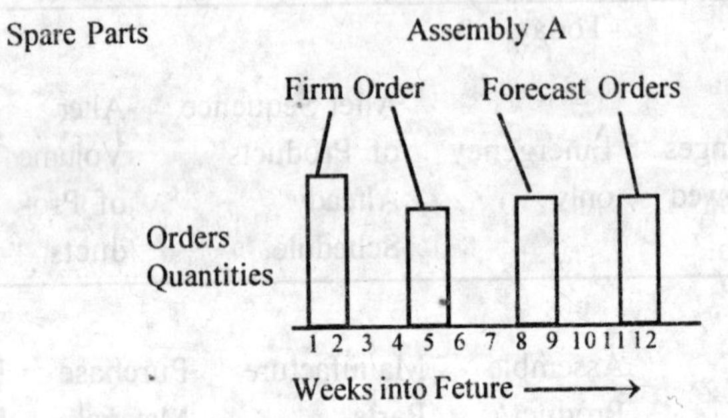

Fig. 5. Spares Demand for Assembly A

The time periods used in the master schedule will be a result of the degree of control required in the overall production planning and control system and for most companies it is accepted that time periods in excess of one week do not give sufficient control for the setting of priorities for manufactured components and their subsequent progressing.

Some companies have tackled the problem of the choice of time period or time 'bucker' by adopting variable lenth periods, as in figure 6 which give the possibility of greater control of the final assembly operations and less detailed control for the bulk purchasing of materials.

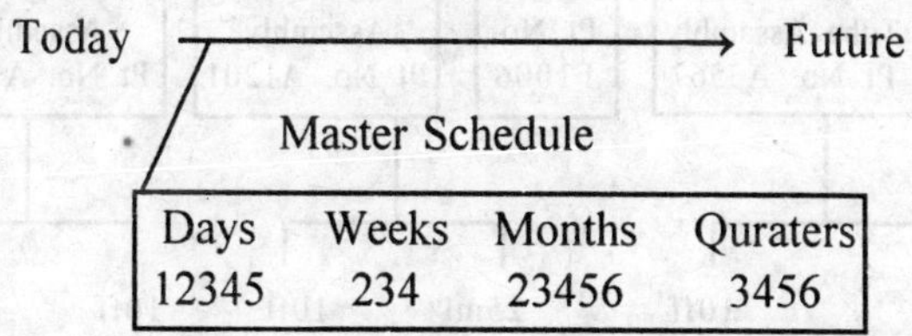

Fig. 6. Master Schedule with Variable Length Time Periods

The master production schedule should be, above all, a realistic picture of what can be achieved, based on past experience.

It will serve no useful purpose to use 'standard' rates of output or optimistic product on targets as the basis for the master production schedule since what will result are excessive inventories, an increasing backlog of unfulfilled requirements and difficult in setting the correct priorities on jobs.

3. The Bill of Material

The bill of material (BOM) is a file or set of files which basically contain the *'recipe'* for each finished product. The *'recipe'* in a manufactured goods environment consists of information regarding which materials, components and sub-assemblies go together to make up each finished product, held on what is often known as a Product Structure file; and all the standard information about each item, such a part number, description, unit of measure, lead time for manufacturing or procurement etc., held on what is often known as a Part Master file.

For each finished product a bill of material is originally created from the design and production engineering information. This information will initially be in the form of drawings and assembly charts 7 which together with information on the relevant lead times form the basis of the inputs to the BOM.

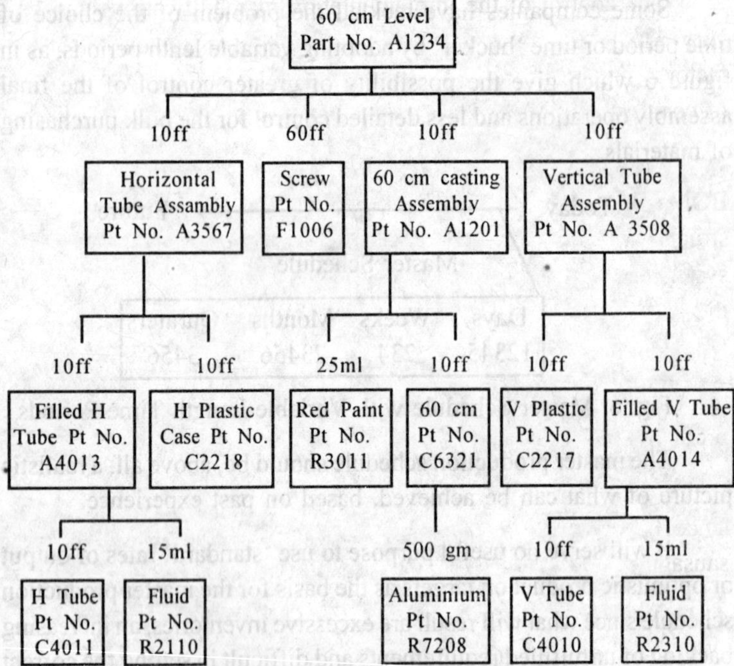

Fig 7. Assembly Chart (simplified) for Part No. A1234—a 60 cm. Spirit Level

Whilst most MRP systems can cope with part numbers allocated at random, whether they are numeric or alphanumeric, it is absolutely necessary for all parts or material within the organisation, in whatever form, to be given a unique part number. It may be, therefore, that bulk raw materials and sub-assemblies have to be allocated their own part numbers for the first time, if an MRP system is to be implemented.

It may appear obvious that the information on the BOM needs to be accurate, since inaccuracies can lead to incorrect items or incorrect quantities of items being ordered. However, the problem of file accuracy is complicated by the fact that in many operating environments there are continual changes to the BOM in the form of product modifications. These modifications may originate from many sources, for example: safety legislation, production process changes, improvements for marketing purposes, value analysis exercises, etc.

The control of the implementation of modifications can be a very time-consuming task for some companies, especially since factors such as the depletion of un-modified stocks and the timing of combined modifications have also to be considered.

One other piece of information that has to be recorded on the BOM is the assembly level at which the item occurs in the product structure. There is an almost universally accepted level numbering system which allocates level 0 to the finished product and increases the level number as the raw material stage is approached.

The number of levels of assembly breakdown is determined by the complexity of the product and can be as high as twelve for products as complex as aircraft engines.

The key characteristic of a bill of material should be its accuracy, since 'one can never produce mince pies on time using the recipe for sausage rolls!'

4. Inventory Status File

The inventory status file keeps a record of all transactions and balances of all stock throughout the organisation. The transactions are mainly receipts and issues, starting with the 'On Order' condition and eventually finishing with the issue of the completed product out of the factory. Other transations may record occurrences such as inspection rejects or stock adjustments as a result of physical stock checks.

Many organisations use the concept of the 'stock condition' to describe the stage which the material has reached, for example: 500 kgs of aluminium part no. R 7208 has been inspected and is in the raw material store ready for issue into Work in Progress. An example of a possible stock condition route is shown in figure 8.

If a greater degree of control is required, the work in progress stock condition may itself be split into a number of separate stock conditions, so that a batch of items may be monitored from one operation to the next (see figure 9).

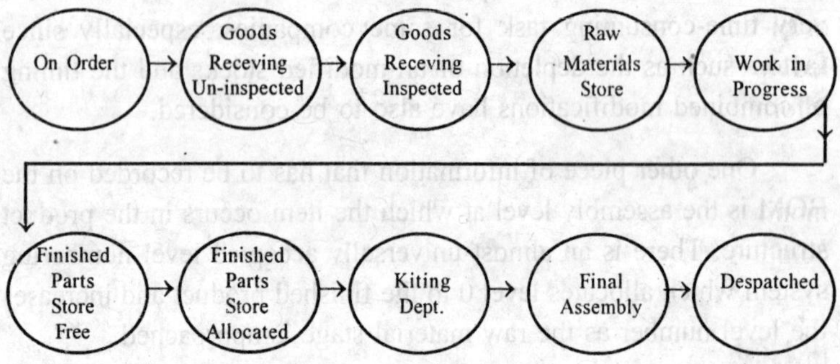

Fig. 8. Stock Condition Route for Aluminium Part No. R7208

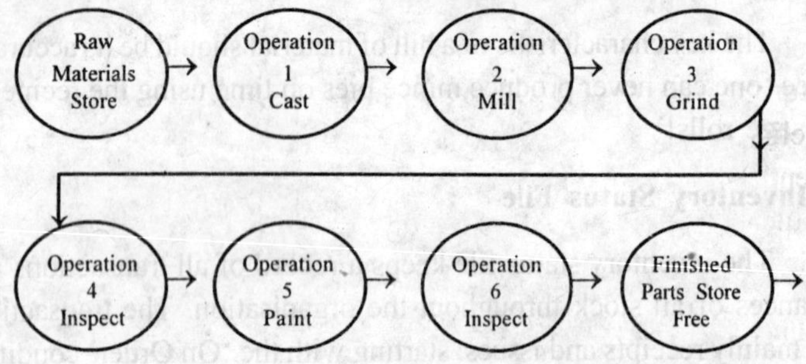

Fig. 9. Work in Progress Stock Conditions

It should be noted that as material progress from one stock condition to the next, its part number may also change. For example, when 6 screws (Part No. F1006) become part of the spirit level final assembly (Part No. A1234), the balance of Part No. F1006 (screws) in the 'kitting' condition is reduced by 6 and the balance of Part No. Al234 (assembly) in the 'final assembly' condition is increased by 1.

The actual method that is used to input the inventory transactions to the inventory status file may vary consderably. At one extreme, the information may be input on a batch processing basis using punched cards that have been punched from handwritten information.

In the early days of MRP, this method of updating with weekly or bi-weekly processing runs was most common, Unfortunately this led to considerable problems because of the untimeliness of the information.

At the other extreme, it is now possible to have automatic monitoring devices of work centres which feed numbers of items completed directly into the computer file.

Most MRP users are currently using either direct 'on-line' inventory updating perhaps using pre-punched cards through computer terminals on the shop-floor, or similarly using prepunched cards on a nightly batch processing basis.

As with the bill of material, one of the key features of the inventory status file should be its accurary. The other important feature is the timeliness of the information. Since this accuracy and timeliness will be critical to the running of the MRP system it is essential that those who will be involved with supplying this information should be thoroughly trained and made aware of the importance of their task.

5. The MRP Package

The MRP package carries out calculations on a level by level basis which convert the master schedule of finished products into suggested orders for all the sub-assemblies, components and raw matcrials. These calculations or 'requirements generation runs' are likely to be carried out on the computer every one or two weeks so that the situation is kept constantly up-todate.

At each level of assembly breakdown, the package undertakes three steps in its calculations before continuing to the next lower level. These steps are as follows:

(i) It generates gross requirements for the item by 'exploding' the 'planned start' quantities of the next higher level assembly, by reference to the bill of material structure file. *e.g.*,

A 'planned start' of 200 spirit levels (Pt. No. A1234 in week 15 would be exploded to give gross requirements of 1200 screws (Pt. No. F1006) in week 15.

(ii) The gross requirements are amended by the amount of inventory of that item that is expected to be available in each week *i.e.*, on hand plus scheduled receipts. This information is obtained from the inventory status file and the amended requirements are called the net requirements.

e.g.,

In week 15 a total of 800 screws are expected to be available, so the gross requirement of 1200 is amended to give a net requirement of 400 screws in week 15.

(iii) The net requirements are then offset by the relevant lead time for the item to give planned starts for initiating the manufacture or purchase of the item.

e.g.,

If the lead time for the screws (Pt. No. F1006) is 4 weeks, the net requirements of 400 screws in week 15 are offset as follows:

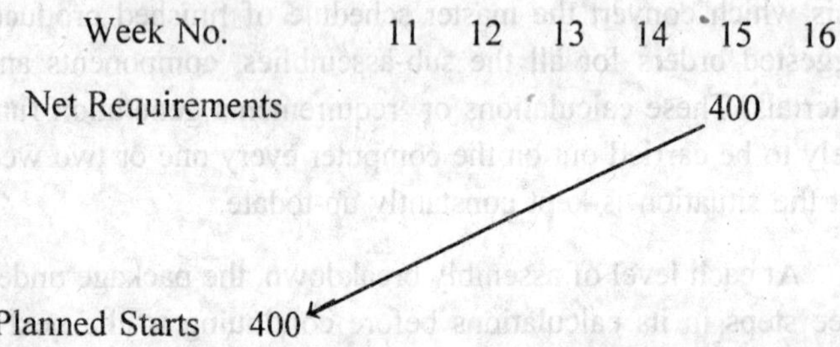

Week No.	11	12	13	14	15	16
Net Requirements					400	
Planned Starts	400					

To summarise, in its simplest form, the MRP package would calculate the requirement of screws for each period of the planning horizon as in figure 10.

The calculation ahead assumes that the only use of the screw (Part No. F1006) is in the assembly of the 60cm spirit level. If this were not the case and if its usage were common to other products assembled by the organisation, for example 40cm and 80cm spirit levels, then the gross requirements for the screw would have been the aggregated requirements generated from the planned starts of all the assemblies using that screw.

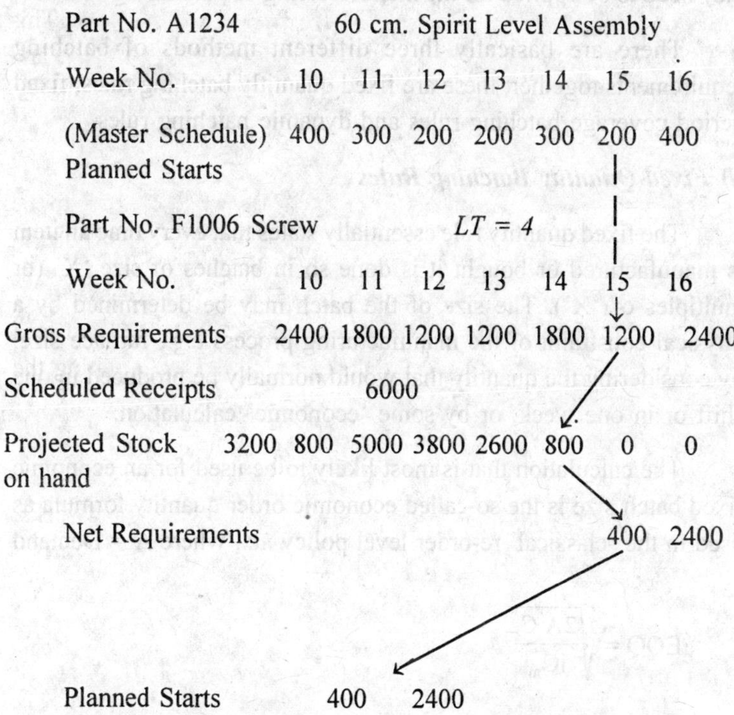

Part No. A1234 60 cm. Spirit Level Assembly

Week No.	10	11	12	13	14	15	16
(Master Schedule) Planned Starts	400	300	200	200	300	200	400

Part No. F1006 Screw *LT* = 4

Week No.		10	11	12	13	14	15	16
Gross Requirements		2400	1800	1200	1200	1800	1200	2400
Scheduled Receipts			6000					
Projected Stock on hand	3200	800	5000	3800	2600	800	0	0
Net Requirements							400	2400
Planned Starts			400	2400				

Fig. 10 MRP Calculation Example

6. Batch Sizing in MRP Systems

The simplified approach to the calculation of requirements has, so far, assumed that the net requirements would be translated directly into planned starts, resulting in manufacturing component schedules and purchasing schedules which do not take any account of the cost of machine set-ups or the cost of ordering. In other words, marking the requirements as they occur on a week by week basis, otherwise known as the lot-for lot policy, will certainly reduce overall stockholding costs, but will increase costs incurred through excessive set-up and ordering costs for small batches.

To take account of the total costs of managing the materials, that is holding costs and ordering or set-up costs, batch sizing rules may need to be applied for the manufacturing or purchasing of items.

There are basically three different methods of batching requirements together; these are fixed quantitly batching rules, fixed period coverage batching rules and dynamic hatching rules.

(i) Fixed Quantity Batching Rules

The fixed quantity rule essentially states that every time an item is manufactured or bought it is done so in batches of size 'X' (or multiples of 'X'). The size of the batch may be determined by a physical constraint of the manufacturing process *e.g.*, furnace size, by considering the quantity that would normally be produced in one shift or in one week, or by some 'economic' calculation.

The calculation that is most likely to be used for an economic fixed batch size is the so-called economic order quantity formula as used in the 'classical' re-order level policy *i.e.*, where A = Demand

$$EOQ = \sqrt{\frac{2A\,C.}{iC_m}}$$

per time period: C. = Set-up (or Ordering) Cost; and iC_m = Cost of holdlng one item for one period; (i being the holding interest rate and C_m the value of the item).

However, it should be noted that in an MRP system, the assumptions upon which the EOQ calculation is based are not valid, that is; a re-order level policy is not in operation and there is not continuous demand and a gradual depletion of stock of the item. Consequently, although the EOQ may be a guide to the 'best' batch size, it cannot be guaranteed that the implementation will result in minimising total inventory operating costs.

An example of the operation of a fixed quantity batching rule using the EOQ calculation is shown in figure 11.

Part No. C6321 60cm Casting LT = l Batch Rule = Fixed Quantity Batch Size=700

Week No.	20	21	22	23	24	25	26	27	28	29
Net Requirements	0	350	100	0	400	0	200	50	100	300
Batched Requirements	—	700	—	—	700	—	—	—	—	700
Planned Starts	700	—	—	700	—	—	—	—	700	—

Fig. 11. Example of a Fixed Quantity Batching Rule

Note: If A, (average demand) = 150 per week

$C_{s,}$ (set-up cost) = £500

$Ci_{m,}$(holding cost = £0.3.0 per item per week

$$\text{Then EOQ} = \sqrt{\frac{2\times150\times500}{0.3}} = 707$$

∴ Use Batch Size = 700

(ii) Fixed Period Coverage Batching Rules

Fixed period coverage rules calculate a batch size by batching together the net requirements for the next 'y' periods ahead. The coverage period may be chosen to fit in with a cycle scheduling approach to stop loading where, for example, machined components may be manufactured on a three weekly repeated cycle with one third of components starting in week 1, one third in week 2 and so on. If the choice is not determined. by this constraint, an 'economic' coverage period may be calculated by relating the economic order quantity calculation to an equivalent number of tjme periods' coverage.

An example of the operation of a fixed period coverage rule is shown in Fig. 12.

Part No. C6321	*60cm Casting LT = 1*								*Batch Rule = Fixed Period*	
									Period = 5	
Week No.	20	21	22	23	24	25	26	27	28	29
Net Requirements	0	350	100	0	400	0	200	50	100	300
Batched Requirements	—	850	—	—	—	—	650+	—	—	—
Planned Starts	850	—	—	—	—	650+	—	—	—	—

Fig. 12. Example of a Fixed Period Coverage Batching Rule

Note: Using the same information as in Fig. 3.14 the Fixed Period would be calculated as follows:

$$\frac{\text{EOQ}}{\text{A}} \text{ (average weekly demand)} = \frac{700}{150}$$

$$= 5 \text{ weeks.}$$

(iii) Dynamic Batching Rules

With dynamic batching rules, the computer uses an algorithm which attempts to arrive at a batching schedule which minimises inventory operating costs. One example of a dynamic rules is the least total cost or part period algorithm.This algorithm consists of computing the cumulatIve holding costs and stopping at the batch size just short of the point where cumulative holding costs exceed the set-up cost. It makes the cost comparison by first calculating the ratio of the set up cost (C_3) to the holding cost (IC_m) known as the part period value (PPV) *i.e.*, how many parts may be held for how many periods whose holding cost will equate to the set up cost. For example, using the data in Fig. 11, the PPV would be 500/.3=1667 part periods.

The Part Period Algorithm would calculate the batches as follows:

PPV=1667

Week No.	*Net Reqts.*	*Cumulative Batch Size*	*Inventory Held*	*Number of Periods*	*Cumulative Part Periods*
21	350	350	0	0	0
22	100	450	100	1	100
23	0	450	0	2	100
24	400	850	400	3	1300
25	0	850	0	4	1300
26	200	1050	200	5	2300(>1667)

∴ 1st Batch of 850 required in week 21

(Contd.)

26	200	200	0	0	0
27	50	250	50	1	50
28	100	350	100	2	250
29	300	650	300	3	1150

Second batch of at least 650 required in week 26 (on the next MRP run the net requirement of Week 30 may be included in the batch).

In this particular example the part period algorithm has produced identical planned starts to those shown in Fig. 12. although, of course, this will not always be the case.

Each type of batching rule has its own advantages and disadvantages. The fixed quantity rule is easily understood and may fit in well with manufacturing process constraints or suppliers' standard order sizes. However, it suffers from the drawbacks of generating orders at irregular intervals and compared to the other methods of batching, it generates higher stock levels.

Since the fixed period coverage rule is directly related to the future periods' requirements, it is more economical in terms of the overall stock levels generated and, as mentioned previously, it may fit in well with the balancing of the workload on the shopfloor. However, it may result in sizes of batches which fluctuate considerably especially if there are periods with zero net requirements.

Theoretically the dynamic batching rules, especially the part period algorithm, are superior to the other two methods of batch sizing in the reduction of costs. However, they suffer the disadvantages of not being understood as easily and of generating differing batch sizes at uncertain time intervals which, in turn, may lead to difficulties in shop loading.

In general, it should be noted that any batching that takes place at high levels in the assembly structure will affect the requirements for all the constituent items at the lower levels *i.e.*, requirements will be similarly bunched together and required earlier. Therefore, unless set-up or ordering costs are significantly high, it may be advantageous to generate planned starts on a lot-for-lot basis rather than batching, since this will certainly lead to lower holding costs and will keep the relative priorities on manufactured items realistic.

8. Setting Safety Stocks in MRP Systems

Safety stocks are held in any manufacturing system to cater for uncertainty. In an MRP system the major cause of uncertainty, that of the future usage of the item, has been mainly eliminated since items should be produced to meet a plan—the master schedule. Therefore, overall, safety stocks in an MRP system should be significantly lower than in a system using classical inventory control policies.

However, safety stocks are still needed because of uncertainties in supply both in terms of the variation of actual lead times and the variation of quantites supplied caused by inspection rejects and material shortages. There will also be changes of demand caused by short-term (emergency) changes to the master schedule and unexpected demands for items such as spares.

The statistical techniques of establishing safety stocks used in classical inventory control systems are mainly inappropriate to the material requirements planning environment. Alternative methods have therefore been developed for application to MRP which fall into three main categories which are fixed quantity safety stocks, safety times, and percentage increases in requirements.

(i) Fixed Quantity Safety Stocks

Fixed quantity safety stocks are introduced by triggering a net requirement whenever the projected stock on hand reaches a safety stock level rather than zero. Fig. 13 shows examples of MRP calculations with and without a fixed quantity safety stock.

Part No. C2218 H. Plastic Case *LT=1 Safety Quantity=0*

Week No.		13	14	15	16	17	18
Gross Requirements		200	300	200	400	300	500
Scheduled Receipts		—	—	—	—	—	—
Projected Stock on hand	600	400	100	0	0	0	0
Net Requirements		—	—	100	400	300	500
Planned Starts		—	100	400	300	500	—

(a) Without Safety Stock

Part No. C2218 H. Plastic Case *LT=1 Safety Quantity=150*

Week No.		13	14	15	16	17	18
Gross Requirements		200	300	200	400	300	500
Scheduled Receipts		—	—	—	—	—	—
Projected Stock on hand	600	400	150	150	150	150	150
Net Requirements		—	50	200	400	300	500
Planned Starts		50	200	400	300	500	—

Fig. 13. The Effect of a Fixed Quantity Safety Stock

(b) With Safety Stock

The calculation of the size of the fixed quantity stock should be related to the cause of the unexpected usage during the lead time. For example, if the unplanned demand is primarily as a rèsult of unforecasted spares demand for the item, than an historical analysis of this variation may lead towards the setting of a satisfactory safety stock level.

However, since in most cases variations in usage and supply could be the result of many factors and since there are not any 'scientific' methods of setting safety stocks in MRP systems, 'rule of thumb' approximations have been applied. For example, it may be satisfactory to initially set the safety stock level at one week's average requirement or one week's 'maximum' requirement. However, it is essential that the usage of the safety stock is monitored and the level then adjusted accor dingly *i.e.*, too frequent use of the safety stock would suggest the need for a higher safety level whereas infrequent use would suggest a lower one.

(ii) Safety Times

The safety time approach for setting safety margins in essentially 'planning to make items available earlier than they are required'. The intorduction of safety time is straight forward in that the net requirements are offset by the lead time and the safety time to produce planned starts. Fig. 14. shows examples of MRP calculations with and without a safety time.

Part No. C2218 H. Plastic Case *LT=1 Safety Time=0*

Week No.		13	14	15	16	17	18
Gross Requirements		200	300	200	400	300	500
Scheduled Receipts		—	—	—	—	—	—
Projected Stock on hand	600	400	100	0	0	0	0
Net Requirements		—	—	100	400	300	500
Planned Starts		—	100	400	300	500	—

(a) Without Safety Time

Part No. C2218 H. Plastic Case *LT=1 Safety Time = 1*

Week No.		13	14	15	16	17	18
Gross Requirements		200	300	200	400	300	500
Scheduled Receipts		—	—	—	—	—	—
Projected Stock on hand	600	400	200	400	300	500	0
Net Requirements		—	—	100	400	300	500
Planned Starts		100	400	300	500	—	—

(b) With Safety Time

Fig. 14. The Effect of Safety Time

The choice of the length of the safety time could, perhaps, be related to the variability of the manufacturing or procurement lead time of the item being considered. However, since other factors' may influence the use of the safety stock generated by the use of safety time, an arbitrary setting of the safety time and subsequent adjustment based on the monitoring of the usage of the safety stock is satisfactory.

(iii) Percentage Increases in Requirements

The setting of safety margins by the percentage increases in requirements method is particularly suitable for dealing with the variations in supply caused by scrap or process yield losses and are often implemented as 'scrap factors' or 'shrinkage factors'. This type of safety margin is introduced by increasing the net requirements by a factor to produce planned starts. An example is shown in Fig.15.

Part No. C2218 H. Plastic Case *LT=1 Scrap Factor = 0.05*

Week No.	13	14	15	16	17	18
Gross Requirements	200	300	200	400	300	500
Scheduled Receipts	—	—	—	—	—	—

Projected Stock on hand	600	400	100	0	0	0	0
Net Requirements		—	—	100	400	300	500
Planned Starts		—	105	420	315	525	—

(b) With Safety Time

Fig. 15. The Effect of a Scrap Factor

The size of the percentage increase in requirement should be directly related to the actual scrap or process yield loss for which it is supposed to be compensating. If this margin is to be used as a buffer against other variations then, again, an arbitrary setting may be made and subsequently modified based on the feed back of the actual use of the safety stock generated.

Safety stocks of finished products to provide a pre-determined customer service level should be set in the traditional fashion by analysing the operation of the sales forecast and translating the resulting requirements into a master schedule for the finished products.

9. Output Reports of MRP Systems

The principal outputs are the executive intructions to make or buy items in the form of requirements reports. Other, more specific reports may be produced such as 'projected on-hand summaries' 'projected shortages', 'expedite lists', 'cancellations' and 'supplier call-off schedules'.

Enquiries may also be made from the various input files, for example, from the bill of material, 'indented parts lists' and 'where used reports' could be obtained and from the inventory status file, 'stock status reports' and 'inventory analyses' could be generated.

In most, companies the reports and their formats are specified to fit in with the particular organisational requirements.

10. The Implementation of MRP Systems

The problems that are likely to be encountered in the implementation of an MRP system may fall into many categories but their solutions will be dealt with briefly under two main headings, *i.e.*, analysis of the system task and user involvement and training.

(i) Analysis of the System Task

Before an MRP system its implemented or even proposed, a detailed feasibility study should be undertaken to determine:

(a) How 'standard' are the finished products?

(b) What would be the size and complexity of the bill of material?

(c) What would be the volume of modifications to the bill of material?

(d) How accurate is the current product structure information?

(e) How accurate are current inventory records?

(f) To what level of detailed control would stock condition records need to be taken?

(g) What length of ylanning horizon would be necessary?

(h) How easily can finished product demand be forecasted over this planning horizon?

(i) What would be the level of changes to the master schedule?

It the questions above are investigated and answered satisfactorily at the feasibility study stage, then the implementation and eventual running of the system may encounter far fewer problems. Also, before implementation, user involvement and through user training are essential.

(ii) User Involvement and Training

The training should include an appreciation of the theory of MRP and more specific instructions for those who are likely to be involved in making particular decisions, for xample, covering topics such as:

(a) The effect of changes to the master schedule

(b) The effect of batching

(c) The effect of safety stocks

(d) The importance of BOM accuracy

(e) The importance of stock recording accuracy etc.

Before implementation, it is also essential that the top management of the organisation clearly defines the responsibilities for the creation and maintenance of the data on the various computer files; it is seldom satisfactory to make this the responsibility of the data processing manager!

Conclusion

The benefits that can result from the use of a material requirements planning system can be considerable, some companies with successful implementations quoting:

(i) Commonly 30 per sent reduction in component inventories

(ii) Better delivery performance and fewer stockouts

(iii) Up to 5 per cent increases in productivity

(iv) Up to 25 per cent less indirect employees engaged in stores, transport etc.

Apart from these sorts of benefits, MRP may also from the major input to other production planning and control sub-systems in the organisation, for example.

(i) Shop loading (scheduling), where MRP already supplies the vital information of item quantities and require dates;

(ii) Capacity planning, where, with the addition of a routeing file (or bill of operations), detailed loads on departments and work centre can be produced for each period of the planning horizon.

In order to obtain the benefits offered by the use of MRP some organisations may have to change their business methods quite considerably. For instance, instead of accepting orders and quoting delivery dates based, to a large extent, on guesswork and then progressing these orders through the manufacturing departments by the use of 'shortage lists' and 'priority lists' the company may now have to attempt to forecast sales much further into the future, commit themselves to master schedules, commence production based on these schedules and than allocate customer orders, as they arrive to the available unallocated products on the master schedule.

MRP has been used successfully in many different companies since the 1960s in the USA and since the early 1970s in the UK. It has applications in the manufacture of a wide variety of products ranging from aircraft engines to automobiles, from typewriters to machine tools, from batteries to generators and from lawnmowers to pharmaceuticals.

❐

4
Description of Quality

Materials management is a critical part of the planning and operating cycle activities of a firm. The following subactivities in the overall planning process require specific purchasing and materials management input.

* **Long-range Plan.** Purchasing and management resources, processes, and capacities (actual and desired).
* **Corporate Plan.** Sources as well as material availability, quality, and cost (now and future).
* **Operating Plan.** General timing requirements of goods for production market plan.
* **Production.** Provide goods and services when required.
* **Materials Management and Distribution Plans.** Plan for above production needs, anticipate and advise if possible disruptions foreseen, coordinate with firm's own and vendors' distribution activities, and maintain contact with vendors.

Purchasing and materials management provide periodic planning and continuous operating input to the four activities listed. In more and more firms, the task of production scheduling is being shifted to either materials management, distribution, or both. This shifting is made in recognition of the fact that purchasing materials management-distribution timing and quantity economies are greater than those typically accruing to production alone.

Kodak, for example, has integrated the function of production scheduling within distribution so that purchasing, inventory, and warehousing costs can be balanced with production and marketing timing and quantity considerations.

Materials management has stewardship responsibilities over inbound inventories. Inventories, in turn, have a major impact upon the overall financial performance of a firm. The double digit cost of capital experience at the beginning of the 1980s and the memory of products shortages and profit problems in the 1970s has led top management to direct attention to these areas. Inventories represent cash that could be used elsewhere by top management. In fact, excessive inventories have been the reason for some firms' failing.

In any case, it is imperative for the purchasing and materials manager to understand the overall role of the inventories he/she is responsible for within the firm. More and more firms are integrating inbound inventory investment, placement, and positioning into the entire strategic decision process. The income statement shows the results of sales and expenses for the year. It presents the total purchases and usually inbound freight costs for the year. Expenses for holding inventories, such as warehousing, handling, etc., are often found in "operating expenses."

The top management of many firms attempts to report low inventory dollar values at year end so that reported profits are low for taxation purposes. This practice assists in cash retention in the firm. During the 1970s many firms switched to LIFO inventory valuation in order to achieve this end. This is also the reason for year-end inventory liquidation efforts, including sales, promotions, and the write-off or write-down of excess, older or damaged goods and obsolete parts. Thus, what might be a good purchase timing decision during the year may run counter to the wishes of top management and the company treasurer near year end.

On the surface, the income statement shows inventories as a'major overall profitability component of the firm. In the JJC Corp., every $1 of sales results in a $.40 margin to cover operating expenses and taxes. These figures are of value when comparing year-to-year trends or looking at similar products sold by competitors. The balance sheet is a statement of corporate position on a given day. It shows the inventory holding of the firm at the end of the year. In this example twelve and one-half percent of all assets are represented by inventories, which are clearly assets that could otherwise be converted to less risky and more liquid receivables or cash.

The income statement and balance sheet together can be used to show other elements of inventory in the organization, including:

(1) **Return on Sales.** One measure of the firm often sought by analysis is profit in relation to sales. This ratio is net income after taxes divided by total sales.

(2) **Return on Equity.** Return on equity is profit divided by common stock and retained earnings. This figure is $60,000/$925,000 or 6.5 per cent for JJC Corp. It is a measure of how well the owners' investment in the firm is performing for them. Obviously, profit, as it is calculated by using purchases and inventories, is a factor in this measure.

(3) **Return on Assets.** A measure of how well the assets of a firm are being utilized is indicated by the return on assets. This figure is determined by dividing net profit by total assets.

(4) **Working Capital.** Working capital is the residual when all short-term liabilities are subtracted from short-term assets. Within this context, short term is usually about thirty days. In the ICC Corp. example, this is cash plus receivables plus inventories less accounts payables, or $500,00 less $75,000" or $425,000. This is a healthy position.

(5) **Acid Test.** The acid test is current assets without inventories less current liabilities. The argument for this measure is that inventories might not be easily liquidated within the short term. in the ICC Corp. this is $200,000 + $50,000 or $175,000. Within this measure, financial personnel and

top managers would prefer the firm's resources in cash rather than inventories. Many firms look healthy from a working capital standpoint but cannot pay bills from an acid test position.

(6) **Days Inventory on Hand.** Days inventory on hand is a rough measure of how many days of sales can be covered by the inventory on hand.

(7) **Inventory Turnover.** Inventory turnover is determined by dividing sales for the period by the average inventory. In the ICC Corp., this is $1,000,000/250,000 or 4.00 times. This figure is an efficiency measure of asset turnover. Again, industry comparisons are necessary.

The measures described here are keenly watched by top management and financial personnel. Generally speaking, a reduced level of inventory or inventory values is sought for favourable result in these measures. Each factor must be weighed by purchasing and materials manager in day-to-day operations and overall planning. Several of these factors are pertinent for analysis as we enter the mid-1980s.

First, it is still apparent that inventories are not the responsibility of one operating person. Inventories are generally fragmented between purchasing, materials management (when these are separate), production, and distribution. Thus, total inventory control is often spread among, many departments. This situation can cause unforeseen shortages or an unmanaged increase of inventories.

Often, the inventory flow records of these departments do not correspond to each other. Until there is singular control over goods throughout the firm, there will tend to be problems in controlling this fluid asset. Purchase and selling terms can have a key direct financial impact upon the firm. Goods purchased FOB receiving plant will reduce the overall holding of inventories by the amount of days in transit, versus those purchased FOB vendor's plant and sold FOB selling destination. While this action might have a favourable impact upon the reporting of the inventory position, it might represent a loss of transportation savings opportunities, especially on the inbound side.

Clearly, this is a factor ripe for analysis in the 1980s as the importance of transportation increases for purchasing managers. The make-or-buy decision plays a major role in inventory decision. The "make" alternative usually requires a larger overall investment in goods unless equipment is already on-hand. This cost and its resulting impact on the financial measures of the firm must become part of the make-or-buy equation.

Vendor performance and lead-time experience come into play here as well. Shipments from a great distance or from unreliable sources require a safety stock or lead-time inventory holdings. Such actions impact detrimentally upon inventory measures. This is particularly a problem with imported goods, which often must be paid for at the exporting port. Consignment purchasing is a favourable alternative when inventory financial impacts are involved. Consignment purchasing makes goods available without having them "on the books" until actually used. Goods are physically available without lead time and payment for the subsequent sale might actually be received prior to payment to the vendor. Of course, the liability for payment for the total lot of goods must also be considered. The financial aspects of inventories as they affect the overall firm are important considerations for top management. Corporate policy dealing with inventories will no doubt play more of a hand in the future. The purchasing and materials manager must understand these concerns as they relate to day-to-day acquisition and supply management tasks.

The objectives of materials management embody those for purchasing including lowest final cost, optimum quality, assurance of supply, and lowest possible administrative costs to the firm. Brought down to an operating level, specific materials management objectives exist.

Inventories represent cash and other liquid assets that were converted into physical product form having less flexibility and greater risk than cash, marketable securities, or credit power (through increases in accounts payables or other short term debt.) Firms continually seek to reduce inventories because they are seen as one of the cheapest forms of financing available to the firm. That is, cash released from reduced inventories is less expensive to obtain than that available by borrowing.

Inventories are also the subject of reduction efforts because they are a critical variable in the firm's return on investment. Firms A and B have equal sales, but Firm A has a very efficient materials and distribution management system that keeps its inventories very low. Firm B, on the other hand, has a higher inventory level. This phenomenon will tend to produce some distinctive differences between the two firms that are both overtly and covertly noted in financial records. On the surface, however, both sales and the reported cost of goods sold of both firms are the same. The first difference between the Firm A and B is that the inventory turnover (inventory on hand divided into the cost of goods sold) is higher in A (5 times) than B (1.2 times).

Second, Firm A requires less warehouse space for inventory than Firm B. This is disguised in less fixed plant and facilities assets ($1,500 versus $1,575). Third, Firm A can finance its assets out of short-term cash flow while Firm B must often borrow funds in order to cover its inventory purchases and holdings. This situation will be reflected in higher interest expenses. Fourth, Firm A's profit is higher due to lower interest charges and operating expenses of a smaller warehouse and inventory system. Fifth, Firm A will experience less risk in inventory holding because there is al ays less inventory on hand that can become damaged or obsolete. And sixth, Firm A has a higher return on investment ration (profit divided by assets), 11.25 percent versus Firms B with 7.7 percent. This occurs from the double impact of higher profits in the numerator and lower assets in the denominator.

While this example was both hypothetical and simplified, the impacts shown are real inside the firm, and they illustrate the reason why minimized inventory investment is one of the major goals of top, middle, and lower management.

Table 1

Impact of Inventories Upon the Firm

Financial components	*Firm A*	*Firm B*
Balance Sheet		
Cash/securities	$350	$300
Inventories	100	400
Other assets	1550	1575
Total assets	2000	2275
Income statement:		
Revenues	$1200	$1200
Cost of goods sold	(500)	(500)
Operating expenses	(250)	(300)
Profit after tax & interest	225	175
Cost of goods sold:		
Begin inventory	$100	$400
Add purchases	500	500
Total goods available	600	900
Less: end inventory	(100)	(400)
cost of goods sold	$500	$500

The second major materials management goal is to maximize that availability of inventory for production, consumption, or resale. This goal appears to be at the opposite end of the spectrum from minimum inventory investment, but it is crucial to the task of materials management, which is: provide all goods to the firms that are economically feasible while minimizing the funds required for doing so. This goal demands that material inventory be tightly controlled.

Firms that fall short of maximum inventory availability will often experience production downtime penalties, stockouts, and an overall loss of production and marketing productivity.

Minimized Logistics System Costs

This objective requires economical systems for storage, handling, information, communications, and management. This factor is found within the cost of purchased goods, work-in-process inventories, and the various costs for logistics activities that are usually reported in the category of operating costs in the income statement.

The Strategic Role of Materials Management

Strategy and its importance for the firm were discussed. On a materials. management and production level, strategy encompasses some specific factors, including:

1. **Capacity.** This factor includes physical system capacity and timing potential for handling and processing goods. Some firms actively build capacity in anticipation of product or industry growth.
2. **Facilities.** Production assets, handling entities, and purchasing/materials management system plants, equipment, record, and communication systems all comprise this facet of strategy. Some firms have strategically placed themselves in the marketplace by utilizing their own freight brokerage operation rather than calling one when shipments are needed inbound. By keeping close links with the market in this manner, the firm can take advantage of spot opportunities when they arise.
3. **Vertical Integration.** This forms of strategic placement entails ownership or control of entities supplying the prodution and materials management system and generally

includes private trucking operations that can provide cost and/or service advantages. In the extreme form, vertical integration can be noted with chemical and fertilizer companies that also own pipelines and tank facilities, or the ownership of the Bessemer and Lake Erie Railroad by U.S. Steel Corporation.

4. **Production Technologies.** Production technologies include the processes, machinery, formulas, etc. that the firm to produce a distinctive product either physically or cost-wise. In the materials management realm, this can include the method employed to maintain tight inventories or the system of maintaining a standardized raw product with final production upon demand. One South American processor obtained an edge on competition by developing a long-term storage system for tomato paste. Previously, the firm would have to rush multistage operations from raw tomato to ketchup, soup, etc. A year's market mix would have to be projected at the beginning of the six-week peak tomato season in March. Forecasting errors would result in some stockouts and other products in excess by November and December. The firm developed a sanitary storage medium for all output from a single stage, making the raw tomato into a standard paste. Any specific tomato-based product could then be made from the paste. This production materials management advantage enabled the firm to reduce the need for future production assets while it cut production scheduling problems and increased subsequent marketplace customer service.

5. **Quality.** This strategic advantage is pervasive from sourcing to handling/storage/inspection all the way through production. Quality is an attribute that exists in materials, design, or manufacturing processes. Adherence to high quality output requires a commitment of the entire firm. In many firms, however, quality assurance is left to the operational level where short-term cost targets can eclipse attention to product quality.

6. **People Talent.** People talent is another important strategic advantage that a firm can possess. This advantage ranges from management persons having special talents to production workers particularly adept at detailed assembly, or working with colours or tastes. In materials management, this can include persons who are able to very efficiently schedule production, negotiate, or conduct low-cost value analyses upon components and processes.

7. **Alternative Recognition.** This strategic advantage is more of a state of mind or an open process in a firm. It is the recognition that physical product handling poses trade-off ranges and decisions in plant and equipment, production planning and control, labour and staffing, and organization and management. Rather than strive for "the one way" of organizing and operating a system, this strategic advantage requires a management perception to problems and opportunities, the possible need for changes and adaptations, and the ability to change or accept alternatives when desirable. Again, alternative recognition is a corporate frame of mind that encourages new input rather than becoming entrenched with fixed methods.

The growth of distribution and materials management has brought an increased awareness of alternative recognition to many firms. There are many combinations of transportation-warehousing alternatives available. Many firms may use just one form large lot distribution. That is, there is no "one way" of distributing.

Purchasing personnel are now finding alternative methods of transporting goods inbound from different vendors. One method might be appropriate one time and yet another mode, at a different cost, would be best the next time. The objectives of materials management are supportive of those of purchasing and the firm as a whole. The key in anyone firm is to integrate the individual departmental goals into the overall corporate and marketing goals. Further, the firm must continually check for possible conflicts in both the objectives and the operational practices used by each department in carrying their individual goals out.

Materials management has not always received the attention it is today. Though these activities were always a part of purchasing and manufacturing, materials management as a discipline is a relatively new phenomenon that has grown since the 1950s. Following is a brief discussion about past practices and the trends that have caused materials management to become widely recognized.

Traditional organizational structures often had purchasing and manufacturing at an arm's length from each other. Purchasing had the goal of minimum material cost, and production was often evaluated on minimum unit cost obtained through long production runs. Even when purchasing was within manufacturing common emphasis was to supply the production line in ways that optimized purchasing's own operating conveniences and unit costs. Production scheduling was generally contained within manufacturing, and inventories acted as a buffer or reserve so that the operating necessities and conveniences of production could be maintained. By the 1950s, several factors led to changes in the organizational approach. One factor was product proliferation.

The growth in marketing, market segmentation, and an emphasis upon competition caused a growth in the number of separate products most firms produced and sold. This growth complicated the purchasing, manufacturing, and production scheduling tasks. These tasks became particularly problematic when the practice of infrequent long production runs of each product caused delays and stockouts in the delivery of specific products to customers. In this situation, marketing became a department in conflict with production scheduling. Product proliferation also led to large increases in inventory held within the firm.

Vertical integration was another factor that often caused firms to tighten the purchasing-manufacturing processes into what we today refer to as materials management. To achieve vertical integration it is necessary to coordinate the activities of interconnected plants.

Production runs, transportation, and work-in-process inventories must be coordinated in order to prevent problems and to optimize any economies sought in such arrangements. Lead time problems are another factor contributing to the evaluation of materials management.

The need to maximize inventory availability in face of uncertain vendor delivery and/ or in-transit transportation service requires a close link between purchasing and production scheduling. This problem often grows when procuring internationally or from sources distant from plants. Deteriorated rail service in the Northeast states during the 1970s caused problems for many firms when in-transit time on the Penn Central Railroad both lengthened and become erratic on many lines.

The development of the logistics concept greatly shaped materials management. This concept is recognition that trade-off relationships exist between interfacing functions. Further, whenever trade-offs exist, there are opportunities for total cost and service savings for the entire firm. Thus, many firms recognized that a unit cost increase from a shortened production run might have increased purchase order costs, but the firm saved a greater amount inventory and warehousing. This is only one example of such coordination which suboptimizes each of the major functions for the good of both and the firm.

Many management science techniques, including the use of the computer in production scheduling evolved during this period. These techniques presented new opportunities for analysis and cost/ service improvements in the materials management area. The advent of materials requirements planning (MRP) is one such tool that has had a great impact. Product shortages in the mid-1970s forced firms to link marketing, production, and purchasing in a way that more closely coordinated what was marketed in the best possible production schedule with what component products were available. Some firms made major organizational and coordination changes during this time that resulted in more formalized management entities.

Finally, recognition of the high cost of inventories in the late 1970s and early 1980s has led most firms to seek ways of reducing inventories without penalizing major economies in purchasing, production, and marketing. Inventory investment minimization, while maximizing its availability, requires centralized interdepartmental coordination in materials management. Materials management literature cities many examples of how specific firms adopted the materials management concept. Each company was shaped by specific events, impacts, and the personalities of those involved. All or most examples point to one or more of the factors highlighted in this chapter.

Examinations of firms will also reveal that no two firms are exactly alike in organization, function, or reporting lines of materials management. Boeing, for example, has a much more refined system than does a food processing plant that receives its vegetable supply only once yearly. Each firm has specific products, vendor/supply configurations, manufacturing arrangements, time con-straints, personnel talents, and information systems that all come into play with exactly how a materials management system will evolve.

Literature in the 1980s contains much contrasting information on various approaches used in materials management. In particular, the various approaches are often labeled as the U.S., Japanese, U.S. "just in time," and European approaches. Each approach will be presented and contrasted here to provide insights into how firms can structurally and procedurally address purchasing and production objectives. The U.S. has enjoyed extensive production capacity, labour goals, resource availability, and mass markets. Automation and large productive processes were economical because of large markets.

The quest for minimum manufacturing unit costs in many firms has lead them to optimize production lot sizes. Optimum run lot sizes are a function of balanced set-up costs, variable unit costs, and the scheduled needs of various products produced on each production line. Transportation vehicle sizes also come into play here, too, as rail car, truck, and container capacities enter into the inbound and outbound lot size equation. In the U.S., these capacities are quite large as railroad and highway size and weight limitations are larger in comparison to many other nations of the world. Further, transportation economics generally favour larger vehicles and single handlings of many shipments at once resulting in the form of lower unit carrier prices.

Inventory is used to buffer transportation, production, distribution, and sales when flow rates, availability, or demands are at different rates from each other. Purchasing usually has many materials sources available throughout the country, which requires selection monitoring and expediting efforts. The situation is intensified with the great product variety that is created and expected in our economy. Consequently, U.S. firms have emphasized materials delivery systems.

Many industries, and the automobile industry in particular, have recently been highlighted for quality problems. Quality and its control often are elements that are generally defined by top management but left to lower management levels for follow through and administration. In an effort to reduce unit production costs, line managers often opt for less inspection and the use of less than target quality components in order to avoid scrap, waste, return costs, or production inconvenience. Thus, quality is often treated as a trade-off against purchasing and/or production unit cost.

Quality frequently suffers because worker task assignment is often defined in very specialized terms either through the nature of line automation, labour skill rules, job descriptions, or both. This phenomenon creates repetitive and often boring jobs. It can prevent the worker from relating to the overall output of the line and the products of the firm as a whole. Here, too, lax attitude of commitment to the firm, its systems, and the quality of its products can become endemic. Vendor supply lines, transportation systems, production scheduling, and quality control are approached differently in many Japanese firms.

Large Japanese firms will often procure from small vendors that are in close proximity to their plant. This action minimizes lead time problems and often takes place several times a day, and in some instances a vendor's truck and driver are always at the firm's in bound dock. The driver acts as a production inventory monitor, supplier, and legal party in the purchase of goods. This minimizes inbound inventory for the manufacturer to such an extent that it is nearly non-existent: Vendors are informed weeks and months' in advance of production schedules.

Work-in-process and production activities are often "pulled through" the system according to the firm's sales and delivery requirements. The "pulling" approach is often organized around a system of KANBAN tickets that travel with small lots of goods through various production stages and are posted where all workers can see them. Workers may then relate subsequent production needs with what they are currently producing. This approach often permits a smoother, less hectic production rate than when machinery and manufacturing are running at maximum pace.

Observers of Japanese factories note that their high productivity is not necessarily attained through faster work activity. The pull-through system helps pace multiple production stages so there is little or no work-in-process inventory. In fact, safety stocks are regarded as a form of organizational waste. Inventories are further minimized through simplification of production set-up and changeover processes. Product variety is less than that found in the U.S., and this factor reduces the production lot problem 'somewhat. But, of most importance, is the drive to reduce production changeover efforts to an absolute minimum. This process is analyzed and implemented as an on-going, all-employee effort. This factor, combined with the almost real-time vendor delivery requirement, reduces the need to optimize production unit costs with run sizes that payoff any high changeover costs.

❐

5

Quality and Inspection

The first step in any acquisition is to determine what is needed. This is followed by a decision on the quality of the material or item required and the control and measurement of this quality.

Definition of Need-function

The term "need" is still a nebulous one. Every item to be purchased must perform a function. It must perform certain tasks. If it does not perform the function intended, the purchase may be a totally useless one and a waste of time, money, and effort. Similarly, quantity and price needs exist which are discussed in later chapters.

The function need requires some clarification. We seldom bother to think of the basic function the item must perform. We tend to speak of "a box" instead of "something to package this in;" "a bolt" instead of "something that fastens." We think of a steak, instead of something to eat; a bed, instead of something to sleep in; and a house, instead of a place to live. Note, that even when we issue an engineering drawing for a part, we really just say to a supplier, "Make this." And presumably, in our wisdom we have already made the decision that if the supplier makes the part as specified, it will perform the intended function. Seldom in our purchases do we dwell on this basic function aspect.

Why make an issue of this? It seems so simple and basic as to be hardly worth mentioning. But, actually, this is the heart of a sound purchasing system. Here lie the clues for improving the profitability of purchasing operations. A few simple examples will illustrate what is meant. A casual bypassing, of the function need frequently results in improper specification. For example, a hose will be too short, a lining will shrink, a bolt shear, a motor burn out, a paint peel, a machine vibrate, a vessel burst, a part won't fit, an insurance policy won't cover, and a host of other troubles of this sort arise. Many of these troubles will result from under estimating the function required or from negligence, error, or oversight, because certain functional needs have been forgotten or overlooked. We all laugh when we hear the story about the fellow who built the speedboat in the basement but couldn't get it out of the door. Yet, every day many people make this kind of mistake, perhaps not as glaring, or obvious, but often just as painful.

The answer to this problem, one will say, is to buy quality. As long as you buy good quality material you can't go wrong. Quality is really part of our function need. If the item is not of sufficient quality to perform the task required of it, it does not fulfill our function. Moreover, quality can be a cloak for various inadequacies. Buying the best quality, high alloy ½" screws will not help if 5/8" screws were needed in the first place. Buying high alloy screws when plain carbon mild steel ones will do is also going to increase costs unnecessarily.

If we define our basic functional need as a self-tapping or sheet metal screw, instead of a need to fasten together two sheets of metal of certain physical and chemical characteristics, we miss the first basic step in purchasing. We also miss the opportunity to investigate such alternatives as bolts, rivets, and spot welds, to name just a few. Frequently, and perhaps understandably, the tendency is to forget about the basic function need and to purchase something that will do the job for better or worse. This may become a dangerous guessing game that can lead to much trouble and cost a lot of extra money.

It is proper to emphasize here that in almost all industrial organizations the final responsibility for specifications lies with engineering.

Suitability

There is no such thing as quality divorced from an intended use. "Suitability" is more accurate.

The relationship between technical quality, on the one hand, and cost, on the other, is subject to a good deal of misunderstanding. Some persons appear to believe there are just two classes of goods in the market: one class purchased on the basis of quality and another in which quality is no considerable factor and which is sold entirely on a price basis. Such a conception is not sound. In every transaction, questions of price and quality are interrelated. The purchases made solely on a quality basis and with absolutely no reference to the price involved are so few both in number and in value as to make them practically negligible. On the other hand, goods in the so-called price class must have certain attributes of value or they could not command any price at all. The most that can be said, therefore, is that in some cases high quality is not as important as in other cases, and in some cases low-price merchandise is just as satisfactory to the buyer as high-price merchandise.

Reliability

In an effort to describe quality by a number the engineering profession has developed the concept of reliability: the mathematical probability that a product will function for a stipulated period of time. Originally, calculations like this were used in complex military electronic systems, but their use has spread into almost all types of products. The design of components in harmony with this concept allows for pre-determination of service calls and of what type at the design stage of equipment and, hence, the need for training of repair personnel and the size of spare parts inventory prior to actual manufacture. Complex military equipment is notoriously expensive to maintain with annual maintenance costs ranging from 60 percent to 1,000 percent of initial purchase cost.

Complexity is the enemy of reliability because of the multiplicative effect of probabilities of failure of components.

Consider a piece of equipment in which all parts have a reliability of 99.99 percent. If there are 100 parts, the overall reliability is reckoned to be 99 percent; 1,000 parts, 90 percent; 3,000 parts,

75 percent; 10,000 parts, 36.8 percent. The telstar communication satellite has more than 10,000 electronic parts.

Such calculations are not entirely realistic, for they depend on two assumptions: first, that the failure of a single component causes failure of the whole system and, second, that failure of one component does not hasten or delay the failure of another. But designers often take pains to compensate for the partial or complete failure of some critical components, so that the whole equipment is not put out of action. In many instances the second assumption is nullified by the fact that the failure of one component changes the environment so greatly—*e.g.*, by overheating—that nearby parts are likely to be affected.

The only way to get an entirely accurate reliability figure for a system is to build a number of the systems and test them until they fail. Unfortunately, in practice, the engineer can seldom do enough testing to get a figure that he can trust. It may be economically out of the question to fire off dozens of missiles or burn out many large radar receivers just to make a reliability prediction.

So usually the engineer must depend on what he knows about the reliability of components and synthesize a mathematical model that he hopes will enable him to predict accurately the reliability of the whole system. Fortunately, it is generally possible to get precise reliability measurements of most components by testing hundreds or thousands at a time. Sprague Electric Company, for example, has accumulated more than 200 million part-hours of test data on a top-grade capacitor developed for Minuteman. Such exhaustive testing is essential for developing what statisticians call a "confidence level" the extent to which the reliability figure can be trusted. "Without high confidence levels, all calculations of system reliability are risky."

The distribution of failures is normally considered to be exponential, with failures occurring randomly. This facilitates calculations by making the reliabilities of the components additive. Testing is also more flexible because of the time-numbers trade-off. The same inference may be drawn from 20 parts tested for 50 hours as for 500 parts tested for 2 hours. Exceptions like the Weibull distribution (which accounts for the aging effect) and the bath tub curve (which recognizes the high probability of early failure, a period of steady state and a higher probability of failure near the end of the useful life) can also be handled, but they require more complex mathematical treatment.

From a procurement standpoint it is useful to recognize the varying reliabilities of components and products acquired. Penalties or premiums may be assessed for variation from design standard depending on the expected reliability impact.

Quality

"Quality" is a combination of characteristics, not merely one. The specific combination finally decided on is almost always a compromise, since the particular aspect of quality to be stressed in any individual case depends largely upon circumstances. In some instances the primary consideration is reliability; questions of immediate cost or facility of installation or the ease of making repairs are all secondary. In other instances the lifetime of the item of supply is not so important; efficiency in operation becomes more significant. Certain electrical supplies suggest themselves as illustrations. While a long life is desired, it is more important that the materials always function during such life as they may have than that they last indefinitely. Assuming dependability in operation and a reasonable degree of durability, the ease and simplicity of operation may become the determining factor. For instance, it is well known that the mechanism of the modern typewriter makes it dependable under all ordinary usages but that it is not essential for a typewriter to last indefinitely. Given these two factors more or less standardized among various types of machines, the determining factor is the ease with which the machine can be operated. What constitutes a satisfactory quality, therefore, depends largely on what a person is seeking in particular goods.

Perhaps an illustration will be helpful:

Paper towels come under the classification of bibulous papers, which are characterized by absorptiveness, loose formation, and softness. Blotting paper is a well-known example of a paper in this group. Towel and blotting papers are similar in their absorptive requirements, but the former must possess much greater strength than blotting papers. Unlike the latter they must be comparatively thin to have the required flexibility and yet must possess much greater strength than blotting paper so that they will not break under the severe conditions of usage. A good grade of paper toweling has two or three times the strength of blotting paper of the same fiber composition. In evaluating paper towels, therefore, the main consideration, in addition to absorptiveness and softness, is the strength.

Decision on "best buy"

The decision on what to buy involves more than balancing various technical considerations. The most desirable technical quality or suitability for a given use, once determined, is not necessarily the desirable quality to buy. The distinction is between "technical" quality, which is strictly and entirely a matter of dimension, design, chemical, or physical properties, and the like, and the more inclusive concept of "economic" quality. Economic quality assumes, of necessity, a certain minimum measure of suitability but considers cost and procurability as well.

If the cost is so high as to be prohibitive, one must get along with an item somewhat less suitable. Or if, at whatever cost or however procurable, the only available suppliers of the technically perfect item lack adequate productive capacity or financial and other assurance of continued business existence, then, too, one must give way to something else. Obviously, too, frequent reappraisals are necessary, although a worklable balance between technical and economic quality has been established. It copper rises from $0.70 a pound to $1.00 or more its relationship to aluminum may change.

The decision on what constitutes the best buy for any particular need is as much conditioned by procurement considerations as by technical quality. "Best quality" and "best buy" are one and the same. It should be clear that neither the engineer, the user or the production man, on the one hand, nor the purchasing officer, on the other, is qualified to reach a sound decision on the best buy unless they work closely together.

Importance of Service in Determining Quality

Surely, with many items the service the vendor performs in connection with these items is quite as important as any attribute of the product itself. Many goods bought require no service; standard basic raw materials passing into manufacture are usually in this class. Many machines are so simple in construction that any ordinary mechanic can make repairs. At the other extreme are machines so complicated and delicate in adjustment that the manufacturer believes he can warrant satisfactory performance of the machines only if his trained employees service them. One reason why the International Business Machines Corporation and the United Shoe Machinery Corporation originally had a policy of leasing many of their machines instead of selling them outright is that these companies wished to control the servicing of machines. The vendor feels that in his own interests he should supervise installation of the equipment, train the operators to be engaged on it, and perhaps provide occasional inspection afterward. Servicing may include expert repair, as in typewriters. To cover some types of service, vendors issue guarantees, covering periods of varying length. The value of such guarantees rests less upon the technical wording of the statement itself than upon the goodwill and reliability of the seller. Service, however, extends to considerations other than those of the type mentioned. Service by vendor may properly be said to include willingness to make satisfactory adjustments for misunderstandings or clerical errors.

Many vendors specifically include the cost of service in the selling price. Others absorb it themselves, charging no more than competitors and relying for the sale upon the superior service. One of the difficult tasks of a buyer is to get only as much of this service factor as is really needed without paying for the excessive service the vendor may be obliged to render to some other purchaser. In many instances, of course, the servicing department of a manufacturing concern is maintained as a separate organization.

Responsibility for Determining Quality

It is generally accepted that the final verdict on technical suitability for aparticular use should rest with the using department. Thus, questions on the quality of office supplies and equipment may be settled by the office manager; the quality of advertising material by the advertising department; maintenance supplies by the maintenance department; and operating supplies by the production department.

The ultimate responsibility for the quality of manufactured items should rest primarily with the engineering department charged with design and standards involving raw or semiprocessed materials and component parts. Basically, the immediate decision is an engineering-production decision. The person responsible for converting primary materials or semimanufactured articles into the finished product is the person who should have the authority to determine what is to be required. It is the purchasing agent's task to keep the cost of material down to the lowest point consistent with the standard quality required in the completed product. Purchasing's right to audit, question, and suggest must be recognized if this task is to be successful.

Purchasing fails to live up to its responsibility unless it insists that technical quality factors be considered and unless it passes on, to those immediately responsible for quality, suggestions of importance that may come as a result of its normal activities. The procurement officer is in a key position to present the latest information from the marketplace which may permit modifications in design, more flexibility in specifications, or changes in manufacturing methods which will reduce the cost of materials without detracting from their performance. Unless the engineer and the production executive are willing to consider the information presented by the procurement officer in attempting to determine the "best buy," the full benefits of effective operation of the procurement function are lost to the firm.

Purchase Analysis Section

A development further emphasizing the effort to equip the purchasing department to deal more adequately with these technical problems is creating a purchase analysis section within the department. The basic aim of purchase analysis is to determine what constitutes good value to assist in negotiations. In this respect there is nothing new about the idea. What is new is the increased emphasis placed on purchase analysis using a separate group of purchase analysts to coordinate this particular activity into an organized programme. They work constantly in close cooperation with the engineering and production units of their own company and with vendors to determine designs, processes, and materials resulting in optimal value. These analysts are part of the purchasing department and are trained materials men and experienced engineers. In such companies as the Ford Motor Company, General Electric Company, and others, they evaluate each product or component, piece by piece. They are concerned primarily with two questions: is its usefulness proportionate to its cost, and is a new or lower cost equivament material or process available?

It should be emphasized that final responsibility for applying purchase analysis rests with the buyer. What an analyst seeks to do is to combine information on products, manufacturing methods, costs, prices, and markets, furnishing skilled advisory service to the buyer, who in turrr coordinates the whole pricing operations and negotiates with vendors.

Description of Quality

In any company it is not sufficient for the using department merely to know what quality is desired; that quality must be capable of reasonably accurate description. In no other way can the using department be assured of getting exactly what it wants. Although the responsibility for defining the quality needed usually rests with the using department in the first instance, the purchasing department has, a very direct and immediate responsibility in checking the description given. The purchasing department should not, of course, be allowed to exercise its authority arbitrarily or to alter the description and change the quality or the character of the item being procured. It should, however, have the authority to insist that the description be sufficiently accurate and detailed to be perfectly clear to the supplier with whom the purchasing department must place the order. The purchasing officer has the direct responsibility of calling the attention of the using department to the added expense resulting when the description calls for an article not standard and likely to be more expensive for that reason.

The description of an item may take anyone of a variety of forms or, indeed, may be a combination of several different forms. For our discussion, therefore, "description" will mean anyone of the various methods by which a buyer undertakes to convey to a seller a clear, accurate picture of the required item. The term "specification" will be used in the narrower and commonly accepted sense of referring to one particular form of description.

The methods of description ordinarily used may be listed as follows and will be discussed in order:

1. By brand.
2. By specification:
   a. Description of physical or chemical characteristics;
   b. Material and method of manufacture;
   c. Performance.
3. By engineering drawing.
4. By miscellaneous methods, such as:
   a. Market grade;
   b. Sample.
5. By a combination of two or more of the above.

Description by Brand

There are two questions of major importance in connection with the use of branded items. One relates to the desirability of using this type of description and the other to the problem of selecting the particular brand. Both these questions call for some detailed consideration.

Description by brand or trade name indicates a reliance upon the integrity and the reputation of the supplier. It assumes that the supplier is anxious to preserve the goodwill attached to a trade name and is capable of doing so. Furthermore, when a given supply is purchased by brand and is satisfactory in the use for which it was intended, the purchaser has every right to expect that any additional purchases bearing the same brand name will correspond exactly to the quality first obtained. The brand name is put upon an article to identify its origin. The manufacturer uses a brand name so that any goodwill cultivated among satisfied customers may redound to his benefit and profit and not to that of the distributor or of some other person. To protect this goodwill, however, it is essential that consistent quality be provided. Failure to maintain a consistent quality results in loss of confidence in the article by the users and, consequently, in ill will rather than goodwill.

There are certain circumstances under which description by brand may be not only desirable but also necessary:

a. When, either because the manufacturing process is secret or because the item is covered by a patent, specifications cannot be laid down.

b. When specifications cannot be laid down with sufficient accuracy by the buyer because the vendor's manufacturing process calls for a high degree of that intangible labour quality sometimes called "workmanship" or "skill," which cannot be defined exactly.

c. When the quantity bought is so small as to make the setting of specifications by the buyer unduly costly.

d. When, because of the expense involved or for some similar reason, testing by the buyer is impractical.

e. When the item is a fabricated part so effectively advertised by the maker as to create a real preference or even insistence on the part of the purchaser of the article in which it is incorporated.

f. When operating men often develop very real, even if unfounded, prejudices in favour of certain branded items, a bias the purchasing officer may find almost impossible to overcome.

On the other hand, there are some definite objections to purchasing branded items, most of them turning on cost. Although the price may often be quite in line with the prices charged by other vendors for similarly branded items, the whole price level may be so high as to cause the buyer to seek unbranded substitutes or even, after analysis, to set its own specifications. There are a great many articles on the market which, in spite of all the advertising, have no brand discrimination at all. Thus, the purchaser may just as well prefer using trisodium phosphate at 14 cents per pound as a branded cleaning compound costing 20 to 24 cents per pound.

A further argument, frequently encountered, against using brands is that undue dependence on them tends to restrict the number of potential suppliers and deprives the buyer of the possible advantage of a lower price or even of improvements brought out by competitors through research and invention.

If a purchase is to be made on the basis of brand, how is one to select the particular brand to buy? The buyer is, of course, confronted by many questions, of which quality, although primary, is but one. Testing provides an answer.

Brand Testing. The original selection of a given brand may be based either upon specific test or a preliminary trial. Once selected, it may or may not be subjected to periodic comparative tests. The brand tests are, in most instances, brought to the attention of the buyer by salesmen, although the purchasing officer may initiate an inquiry.

When salesmen offer samples for brand testing, the general rule apparently followed by purchasing men is to accept samples only of brands that have some chance to be used, although if there is any question about possible use, purchasing officers are more likely to accept samples than to reject them, since they are always on the lookout for items that may prove superior to those in current use. For various reasons, however, care does have to be exercised. For one thing, the samples cost the seller something, and the buyer will not wish to raise false hopes on the part of the salesman. Sometimes, too, the buyer lacks adequate facilities for testing.

To meet these objections, some companies insist on paying for all samples accepted for testing, partly because they believe that a more representative sample is obtained when it is purchased through the ordinary trade channels and partly because the buyer is less likely to feel under any obligation to the seller. Some companies pay for the sample when the value is substantial; some follow the rule of allowing whoever initiates the test to pay for the item tested; some pay for it only when the outcome of the test is satisfactory. The general rule is for the seller to pay for the sample on the theory that, if he really wants the business and has confidence in his product, he will be willing to bear the expense.

Use and Laboratory Tests. The type of test given also varies, depending upon such factors as the attitude of the buyer toward the value of specific types of tests, the type of item in question, its comparative importance to the company, and the buyer's facilities for testing. At times a use test alone is considered sufficient, as with paint and type-writer ribbons. One advantage of a use test is that the item can be tested for the particular purpose for which it is intended and under the particular conditions in which it will be used. The risk that failure may be costly or interrupt performance or production is, however, present. At other times a laboratory test alone is thought adequate and may be conducted by a commercial testing laboratory.

Frequently, a preliminary laboratory test is given to determine whether or not a use test is worthwhile.

The actual procedure, in accordance with which samples are handled, need not be outlined here. It is important that full and complete records concerning each individual sample accepted should be made out and filed. These records should include not only the type of test but the conditions under which it was given, the results, and any representations made about it by the seller.

Description by Specification

Description of desired material on a basis of specifications constitutes one of the best known of all methods employed. Like many of the other methods, it is used at one time or another by probably the great majority of manufacturing companies and governmental agencies for at least some part of their requirements. A great deal of time and effort has been expended in making it possible for purchasing officers to buy on a specification basis. Closely related to these endeavours is the effort toward standardization of product specifications and reduction in the number of types, sizes, and so on, of the products accepted as standard.

These efforts have been expended in the belief that, regardless of the particular type of specification, there are advantages in buying on specifications. Among them may be mentioned the following:

1. Adequate specifications are evidence that thought and careful study have been given to the need for which the material is intended and to the particular characteristics of the material demanded to satisfy this need.

2. Specifications constitute a standard for measuring and checking materials as supplied, preventing delay and waste that would occur with improper materials.

3. They are of definite value to the large consumer wishing to purchase identical material from a number of different sources of supply, either because no one manufacturer possesses the productive capacity to meet all the buyer's requirements or because the buyer

considers it good policy. To ensure identity of materials secured, adequate speeifications are almost indispensable.

4. Purchase on a basis of specification tends toward ensuring more equitable competition. This is why governmental agencies place such a premium on specification writing. In securing bids from various suppliers, a buyer must be sure that the suppliers are quoting for exactly the same material or service.

5. When the buyer specifies performance, the seller will be responsible for performance.

While there are certain distinct advantages in buying on specification, using specifications does not constitute a panacea for all difficulties involving quality. The limitations involved in using specifications fall into seven classes:

1. There are many items for which it is practically impossible to draw adequate specifications.

2. Although a saving may sometimes be realized in the long run, the use of specifications adds to the immediate cost. If, therefore, the article desired is one not purchased in large quantities and does not need to conform particularly to any definite standards, it is frequently inadvisable to incur the additional expense of attempting to buy such materials on a specification basis. Some purchasing directors, when sending specifications for a special item, request the vendor to quote on the basis of the specifications and at the same time to indicate whether or not a standard article closely approaching the one specified is available and, if so, to quote a price on the standard article, indicating how it differs from the specifications submitted.

3. Compared with purchase by brand, the immediate cost is also increased by the necessity of testing to insure that the specifications have been met.

4. One of the difficulties arising from the use of specifications come from carelessness in drawing them when they are likely to give the purchaser a false sense of security.

5. At thc opposite extreme is setting up specifications so elaborate and so detailed as to defeat their own purpose. Unduly elaborate specifications sometimes result in discouraging possible suppliers from placing bids in response to inquiries.

6. Unless the specifications are of the performance type, the responsibility for the adaptability of the item to the use intended rests wholly on the buyer, provided only that the item conforms to the description submitted.

7. The minimum specifications set up by the buyer are likely to be the maximum furnished by the supplier.

If after weighing these advantages and disadvantages, the buyer decides to purchase, on a specification basis, four major choices are available: specification by physical or chemical characteristics, by material or method of manufacture, by standards, or by performance.

Sources of Specification Data

Speaking broadly, there are three major sources from which specifications may be derived: *(1)* individual standards set up by thc buyer; *(2)* standards established by certain private agencies—either other users, suppliers, or technical societies; and *(3)* governmental standards.

Individual standards require extensive consultation between users, engineering, purchasing, quality control, suppliers, marketing, and, possibly, ultimate consumers. This means the task is likely to be arduous and expensive.

A buyer needs to be quite sure not only that it is best to acquire a given item on the basis we are now considering but also that there is no standard specification available serving this purpose equally well. A common procedure is for the buying company to formulate its own specifications on the basis of the foundation laid down by the governmental or technical societies. To make doubly sure that no serious errors have been made, some companies mail out copies of all tentative specifications, even in cases where changes are mere revisions of old forms, to séveral outstanding manufacturers in the industry to get the advantage of their comments and suggestions before final adoption.

Standard Specifications

If an organization wishes to buy on a specification basis, yet hesitates to undertake to originate its own, it may resort to one of the so-called standard specifications. These have been developed as a result of a great deal of experience and study by both governmental and non-governmental agencies, and substantial effort has been expended in promoting them. They may be applied to raw or semimanufactured products, to component parts, or to the composition of material. The well-known SAE steels, for instance, are a series of alloy steels of specified composition and known properties, carefully defined, and identified by individual numbers. When they can be used, standard specifications have certain definite advantages. For one, they are widely known and commonly recognized. This makes them readily available to every buyer. Further more, this standard should have somewhat lower costs of manufacture. Finally, because they have grown out of the wide experience of produce is and users, they should be adaptable to the requirements of a great many purchasers.

On the other hand there are certain disadvantages limiting the value of standard specifications. One of the most commonly urged objections is that just because they are standard, some of them are of necessity so broad as to be unsuited to the requirements of particular users. In some instances, too, certain so-called standard specifications have not been, as yet, sufficiently well accepted to warrant such designation.

Standard specifications have been developed by a number of non-governmental engineering and technical groups. Among them may be mentioned the American Standards Association, the American Society for Testing Materials, the American Society of Mechanical Engineers, the American Institute of Electrical Engineers, the Society of Automotive Engineers, the American Institute of Mining and

Metallurgical Engineers, the Underwriters Laboratories, the National Safety Council the Canadian Engineering Standards Association, the American Institute of Scrap Iron and Steel, the National Electrical Manufacturers' Association, and many others.

While governmental agencies have cooperated closely with the above mentioned organizations, operations for compiling specifications have been conducted independently in developing standards for use in purchasing for. the various governmental departments and agencies. The National Bureau of Standards in the U.S. Department of Commerce compiles commercial standards. The General Services Administration coordinates standards and federal specifications for the non-military type of items used by two or more services. The Defense Department issues military (MIL) specifications for items involving all types of military equipment.

Standardization and Simplification

No consideration of specifications would be complete without some reference to the efforts to standardize and simplify them. Some comments need to be made on this movement from a procurement angle, although no extended discussion is possible here.

In many discussions of this subject, these two terms are used as meaning much the same thing. Strictly speaking, they refer to two different ideas. "Standardization" means agreement upon definite sizes, design, quality, and the like. It is essentially a technical and engineering concept. "Simplification" refers to a reduction in the number of sizes, designs, and so forth. It is a selective and commercial problem, an attempt to determine the most important sizes, for instance, of a product and to concentrate production on these wherever possible. Simplification may be applied to articles already standardized as to design or size, or it may be applied as a step preliminary to standardization.

There are several sales aspects to the simplification-standardization movement. To the extent that standardization occurs, the salesman is compelled to stress not diversity in production as much as better product or service at the same price or of the same product at a lower price. It is just at this same point that a problem is created. If the product the buyer is purchasing is itself a completed product consumed in its finished form, then some reasonable measure of diversity in suppliers' offerings may well be desirable to get as large a degree of suitability for his particular use as possible. As N.F. Harriman has so aptly said in his Standards and Standardization: "Standardization is a useful servant but a bad master." That variations in completed products may have embodied a substantial measure of standardized components is no draw-back to the buyer. Because it facilitates replacements, it becomes a positive advantage. The problem from a selling angle becomes one of how to secure all the advantages of technological improvement, of originality and advanced design, to have "something better" to sell, while at the same time securing the economies of production.

For the industrial product the answer to this dilemma is probably to be found in two different areas. The first is in the large measure of cooperation among the production, procurement, and sales divisions that we have stressed so continually.

A second part of the answer is to be found in stressing not standardization and simplification in the end product but the component parts. By so doing, the production economies are combined with individuality of end product. So, too, can be obtained the procurement advantages of low initial cost, lower required inventory, and diversity in selection of source.

Specification by Performance

Performance specification is a method employed to considerable extent, partly because it throws the responsibility for a satisfactory product back to the seller. Performance specification is results and use oriented, leaving the supplier with the decisions on how to make the most suitable product. This enables the supplier to take advantage of the latest technological developments and to substitute anything that exceeds the minimum performance required.

The satisfactory use of a performance specification, of course, is absolutely dependent upon securing the right kind of supplier.

There are also some buyers who may resort to such specifications as an alibi for not going to' the trouble of getting an exact method of description or of locating more satisfactory sources. Finally, particularly because of the difficulty of comparing quotations, the price paid may prove rather high.

Miscellaneous Methods of Description

Description by Market Grades. Purchase on the basis of market grades is confined to certain primary materials. Wheat and cotton' have already been referred to in this connection; lumber, butter, and other commodities will suggest themselves. Purchase by grade is for some purposes entirely satisfactory. Its value depends upon the accuracy with which grading is done and the ability to ascertain the grade of the material by inspection. Setting up a definite series of grades sufficiently numerous to cover all major and perhaps minor divisions and the common acceptance of these grades by the trade are, of course, essential. The grading, furthermore, must be done by those in whose ability and honesty the purchaser has confidence. It may be noted that even for wheat and cotton, however, grading may be entirely satisfactory to one class of buyer and not satisfactory to another class. The differences between the' upper and the lower limits of the recognized grades of wheat are such as to make possible delivery of wheat not at all suited to the user's requirements. It is for this reason that miners buy only by sample or after physical examination of the wheat. Another difficulty arises in cases in which cotton is bought on the cotton exchange contracts permitting delivery of various grades of cotton and adjustment of payment on a basis of the commercial differences in price between the grades delivered. Although this method may be satisfactory for a cotton merchant, it will not serve a cotton manufacturer.

Description by Sample. Still another method of description is by submission of a sample of the item desired. Almost all purchasing officers use this method from time to time but ordinarily—there are some exceptions—for a minor percentage of their purchases and then more or less because no other method is possible.

Good examples are: items requiring visual acceptance, *e.g.*, wood grain, colour, appearance, etc.

Combination of Methods of Description

A company frequently uses a combination of two or more of the methods of description already discussed. The exact combination found most satisfactory for an individual organization will depend, of course, upon the type of product made by the company and the importance of quality in its purchases. There is no one best method applicable to any single product, nor is there for any particular company a best method of procedure. The important thing for the individuals is to keep in mind that the objective of all description is to secure exactly the right quality, neither better nor worse, at the best price that can be secured.

Metric Conversion

North America is currently engaged in a major planning programme to convert to the metric system of measurement. Plans call for industry-wide changes in stages and a high degree of participation and consultation between companies and government. The International System of Units or "SI" ,in abbreviated form has the advantage of simplicity and universality. It is expected that the conversion will be largely accomplished over the next ten years. Since the conversion of industries and individual organizations is expected to follow voluntary lines, metric conversion committees of national associations are expected to play a major role. The National Association of Purchasing Management recommends that every corporation form a metric conversion committee to plan for orderly internal change. The materials manager and purchasing manager are obvious candidates to head such a committee.

CONTROL OF QUALITY—INSPECTION

Purpose of Inspection

Just as the purpose of adequate description is to convey to the vendor a clear idea of the item being purchased, so the purpose of inspection is to assure the buyer that the supplier has delivered an item which corresponds to the description furnished. Regardless of how reliable the purchaser may have found the seller to be in the past and regardless of the care with which a manufacturer may inspect his product before he ships it, mistakes and errors of various sorts do occur. No such body of past experience exists when new suppliers are being tried, and their products must be watched with particular care until they have proved themselves dependable. Unfortunately, too, production methods and skills, even of old suppliers, change from time to time; operators become careless; and occasionally seller may even try to reduce production costs to the point where quality suffers. Thus, for a variety of reasons, it is poor policy for a buyer to neglect inspection methods or procedures. There is no point to spending time and money upon the development of satisfactory specifications unless some adequate provision is made through inspection to see that the specifications are lived up to by vendors.

The type of inspection and the frequency and thoroughness with which it is conducted clearly vary with circumstances. In the last analysis, this problem resolves itself into a matter of comparative costs, the question at issue being, how much must the company spend in order to ensure proper compliance with its specifications?

What is Reasonable Inspection?

What is reasonable inspection? No formula will give the answer. The importance of inspection is in proportion to the importance of the quality. Even a small quantity of a material in which quality is highly important may call for very rigid inspection, and permissible variations from standard may be very small. Generally speaking, when quantities are small and considerable variations of quality are permissible, inspection is of less importance than when the contrary conditions prevail. Merchandise which is bought by brand may call for occasional inspection to ensure consistency of quality, but it is more than likely that a check on the results obtained by the using department would be satisfactory for this purpose. Products bought on the basis of grades must be checked as to their compliance with the grade specified. The same rule applies to purchases made on a basis of samples. Products which are bought on a specification basis are usually sufficiently important to require rather close checking.

While it is true that on items of major equipment and, in some cases, on fabricating parts, a very careful and detailed inspection is called for on every item delivered, inspection based on a test of samples taken from the shipment should, in the main, prove adequate. In all cases, of course, where the purchaser has any reason whatsoever to question the condition of an incoming shipment, inspection is necessary.

Specification of Inspection Method

In setting specifications, it is sometimes the practice to include the procedure for inspection and testing. This leaves the method of testing within the discretion of the buyer. Since methods may vary widely, they can be made unfair to the seller and be made grounds for rejection of merchandise almost at the whim of the purchaser. Specifying the inspection method is a protection to the buyer, since the vendor cannot refuse to accept rejected goods on the ground that he did not understand the type of inspection to which the goods would be subjected or that the inspection was unduly rigid. Instructions which indicate merely that a specified number of samples of a shipment are to be tested may have little vallie unless it is made clear how these samples are to be chosen. For instance, if all the samples are taken from the top of a certain solution, the results are likely to be very different from what they would be if the samples were taken from the bottom. Similarly, samples chosen from the beginning of a run from a die are likely to be different from the one-thousandth or one-millionth sample from the same die.

In such a situation, not only the method of selecting the sample but also the statistical limits (as distinct from the so-called engineering limits) to be imposed should be indicated. Indeed, it may be well for a company doing a large amount of buying of items that require statistical methods in sampling to work out in some detail a standardized statement of procedure, perhaps even with some discussion of the theory and practice involved. Such a statement placed in the hands of a supplier might avoid considerable misunderstanding.

Quality Control Department

Up to this point we have assumed that the responsibility of a quality control group is narrowly confined to the technical task of submitting incoming material to certain definite tests in order to answer the one question, does this item comply with the description as defined in the purchase order?—the answer always being a definite Yes or No. Granting that the primary objective of inspection is to answer this one question, does it follow that management has no right to expect more? If we are considering the function of inspection, more may very well be expected. If, on the other hand, we are considering the place of inspection in a particular company, then the answer will depend upon such factors as the organization of the company, its ability to maintain inspection facilities, and the character of the material used.

Actually, a number of duties other than straight testing of incoming material may be undertaken by the quality control group and very properly so. Thus, the quality control department should assist in setting specifications, if for no other reason than to pass upon the company's ability to test for compliance with them. Clearly, it is useless to call for characteristics the presence or absence of which cannot be determined. Again, the quality group can initiate material studies. It can be called upon to pass on samples left by salesmen. Frequently it must investigate claims and errors, both as to incoming items and as to out-going or finished products. It may pass upon material returned to stores to determine its suitability for reissue. Similarly it may be called upon to examine salvage material and to make a recommendation as to its disposition. It may also assist in assessing the quality assurance programmes in supplier's plants.

Location of the Quality Control Department

The location of the quality control department constitutes a relevant problem of administration. In most cases the work of inspection is performed by a separate department. The department's work may be divided into three parts: the inspection of incoming materials, the inspection of materials in process of manufacture, and the inspection of the finished product. The assignment of this work in such cases to a separate department is supported partly on the ground that if the inspectors of materials in process and of the finished product report to the executive in charge of production, there may be occasions when inspection standards are relaxed in order to cover up defects in production which, if discovered, would affect adversely the record of the production department. If the inspectors of incoming materials were under the administration of the purchasing director, there might, on some occasions, be a tendency to relax inspection standards in order to pass materials which the purchasing director had procured because of a substantial production in price but which did not meet the quality standards specified.

Since the production department is frequently expected to discover defects in materials during the manufacturing process, the contention is often held that it should also have responsibility for the inspection of material before it enters the manufacturing process. However, the inspection of incoming materials by a purchasing department is not parallel to this. The test being made is not of the purchasing department's own work but rather of that of the vendors. It is true that an undue number of rejections may reflect upon the buyer's selection of a source, but no one is more interested in eliminating unreliable vendors than the purchasing officer. The only exceptions to this statement are those cases in which collusion or dishonesty exists or the purchasing officer is buying on a price basis.

The really important things to keep in mind are:

1. Inspection involves not only purchased material and parts but also work in process and finished goods.

2. Inspection at any stage is a technical problem of where, when, how much, and how to inspect. Also, it frequently requires the use of more or less technical equipment.

3. The importance of quality varies from industry to industry and from company to company. This fact has direct bearing on the inspection problem.

4. Inspection should be remedial and preventive as well as negative. As has been pointed out, the constructive aspects of inspection are as important as that of testing.

5. Any organization for inspection involves intraplant administrative problems pertaining to personnel, cost control, and relations with various departments, such as stores and production units, records, and so forth.

6. The real purpose of all inspection is to get materials and parts of the sort needed. This cannot be attained in the long run without good vendor relations and a sound purchasing policy.

Occasionally, the inspection is conducted by the buyer (or under his auspices) in the plant of the vendor. A great proportion of the procurements by the armed services are so inspected. Inspection at the supplier's plant is undertaken for several reasons. The usual methods of inspection of the finished item may not be adequate. Latent defects not determinable may appear only after the purchaser has further processed the material or part. Again, the correction of defects, if attended to as soon as possible, avoids the additional costs of carrying the work on to completion, only to find the end result unacceptable. Furthermore, transportation charges incident to the return to the vendor of rejected material, especially on heavy material or that shipped long distances, can be avoided. On the other hand inspection at the plant has two definite disadvantages, even where otherwise apparently desirable. One is the heavy cost of securing, training, and supervising an inspection staff. The second is that the presence of inspectors in his plant may be strongly resented by the supplier.

A different kind of buyer inspection at the seller's premises takes place when selection, rather than production of a commodity, determines the quality and when price varies accordingly. Examples would include but are not limited to: veneer and saw logs, pulp wood, livestock, land, feed and mixed grains, used equipment, antiques, paintings, scrap, and professional contracts. Furthermore, on premise buyer inspection almost always applies in conventional auctions but almost never in the case of dutch auctions.

The Quality Capability Survey

The increased emphasis on reliability brought on by space age technology has created the requirement that suppliers be evaluated prior to the placing of an order and .that continuous subsequent monitoring take place. This "quality capability survey" has become especially wide-spread in the aero space and military industry with a reported use in excess of 80 percent of all cases. It is interesting that despite widespread use of this technique, recent research findings show the survey's results to be statistically questionable. This is unfortunate, because the ability to determine, a priori, whether one supplier has a better chance than another of meeting the desired quality standards is highly desirable. Since the principle is obviously attractive, the real question deals with our future ability to develop a better test instrument.

Commercial Testing Labs and Services

The type of inspection required by a company may, in fact, be so complicated or so expensive that it cannot be performed satisfactorily in the company's own organization. In such cases some companies employ the services of commercial testing laboratories, particularly in connection with new processes or materials or for aid in the setting of specifications. The use of these agencies by manufacturers for any other purpose is limited; most companies do not use them at all and others only under unusual circumstances.

It is possible that the services of commercial testing laboratories are not used by some companies as much as they should be. Many of these laboratories are very dependable. They employ capable staffs and own the most modern of photometric, X-ray, electrical, chemical, and physical testing equipment. Their charges are commonly not unreachable for manufacturers in a position to use them. Standard testing reports of commonly used items are available from several commercial testing laboratories. They are the commercial equivalent of consumer's reports and can be a valuable aid.

Inspection Methods

Although it is not the purpose of this text to cover the choice of inspection methods extensively, it is proper to mention them briefly here in the recognition that procurement costs and performance may be significantly affected by this decision. The same inspection methods may be used by either the manufacturer or the purchaser. Since almost all output results from a manufacturing or transformation process of some sort, process quality control will be the first item discussed. This will be followed by screening and sampling which deal with items already produced. All quality control can be divided further into observations of attributes and variables. Attributes usually observed are whether the product is acceptable or not. For example, for an automobile assembly line, is the paint acceptable or not? In a hotel, have the rooms been properly cleaned or not? This type of yes or no inspection is usually based on the binominal distribution. The generating function for this distribution is:

$$P(r) = \frac{n!}{r!(n-r)!} P^r (1-P)^{n-r}$$

Output Inspection—100 Percent Inspection and Sampling

There are basically two major types of quality checks on output. One is to inspect every item produced. The other is to sample.

100 Percent Inspection or Screening. It is traditionally held that 100 percent inspection, or screening, is the most desirable inspection method available. This is not true. Experience shows that 100 percent inspection seldom accomplishes a completely satisfactory job of separating the acceptable from the nonacceptable or measuring or even higher may have to be done to accomplish this objective. Depending on the severity of a mistake, an error of discarding a perfectly good part may be more acceptable than passing a faulty part. In some applications the use of such extreme testing may increase the cost of a part enormously. For example, a 5 part may well end up costing $3.00.

If the test is destructive, 100 percent testing is impractical. The cost of 100 percent testing is frequently high. The testing is seldom fully reliable, because of worker boredom or fatigue, or in adequate facilities or methods, and, therefore, it is not 'often used in high-volume situations.

Sampling. The alternative to inspection of every item produced is to sample. How a sample is taken will vary with the product and process. The purpose is always to attempt securing a sample that is representative of the total population being tested. Random sampling is one commonly used technique.

The method of taking a random sample will depend on the characteristics of the product to be inspected. If it is such that all products received in a shipment can be thoroughly mixed together, then the selection of a sample from any part of the total of the mixed products will represent a valid random sample. The careful inspection of the sample will indicate what may be expected of the entire lot. For example, if a shipment of 1,000 small castings of supposedly identical characteristics are thoroughly mixed together and a random sample of 50 castings is picked from the lot and inspected and 5 are found to be defective, it is probable that 10 percent of the shipment is defective.

If the product has characteristics which make it difficult or impractical to thoroughly mix together, consecutive numbers can be assigned to each product, and then, through the use of tables of random sampling numbers (of which there are several) or a standard computer programme, a sample drawn by number is chosen for detailed inspection,

The general rule which the statisticians believe should be observed when drawing a random sample is: adopt a method of selection that will give every unit of the product to be inspected an equal chance of being drawn.

Sequential Sampling

Sequential sampling may be used to reduce the number of items to be inspected in accept-reject decisions without loss of accuracy. It is based on the cumulative effect of information that every additional item in the sample adds as it is inspected. After each individual item's inspection 'three decisions are possible: to accept, to reject, or sample, another item. A. Wald was one of the pioneers of sequential sampling development, and he estimated that using his plan the average sample size could be reduced to one half, as compared to a single sampling plan.

In a simple version of sequential sampling, often used by the military, 10 percent of the lot is inspected, and the whole lot is accepted if the sample is acceptable. If the sample is not acceptable, an additional 10 percent may be inspected if the decision to reject cannot be made on the basis of the first sample.

Computer Programs

Many quality control computer programmes are available in both real time, using remote terminals, and batch processing. They have resolved the tedium of extensive calculations and provide a range of applications not considered practical before DP introduction. All computer manufacturers and many service companies maintain these programmes for use by customers. Standard programmes, for example, include the selection of sampling plan, calculate sample statistics and plot histograms, produce random selection of parts, plot OC curves, and determine confidence limits.

Responsibility for Adjustments and Returns

Prompt negotiations for adjustments and returns made necessary by rejections are a responsibility of the purchasing department, aided by the using, the inspection, or the legal departments.

The actual decision as to what can or should be done with material that does not meet specifications is both an engineering and a procurement question. It can, of course, be simply rejected and either returned to the supplier at his expense or held for his instructions as to its disposition. In either case it is incumbent upon the buyer to inform the supplier whether the shipment is to be replaced with acceptable material or to consider the contract canceled. Not infrequently, however, a material may be used for some other than the originally intended purpose or substituted for some other grade; At any rate, it is altogether probable that some private readjustment is called for. A third alternative sometimes open to buyers is to rework the material in their own plant, deducting from the purchase price the cost of the additional processing involved. Finally, particularly in the case of new types of equipment or new material to which the purchaser is not accustomed, the vendor may send a technical representative to the buyer's organization in the hope that complete satisfaction may be provided.

A final problem growing out of inspection is that of the allocation, as between buyer and seller, of costs incurred in connection with rejected material. The following statement indicates the nature of the problem and the various practices in dealing with it:

The costs incurred on rejected materials may be divided into three major classes:

1. Transportation costs.
2. Cost of testing.
3. Contingent expense (for-work done on defective material before discovery of defect, handling, loss of production because of delay in receiving proper material, etc.).

The practice of allocating these costs varies considerably with various purchasing departments. The practice is affected to some degree by the kind of material rejected, trade customs, the essential economies of the situation, and the buyer's cost accounting procedure.

In practically all cases reported, transportation costs both to and from the rejection point are charged back to the supplier.

Very few companies report inspection or testing costs as items to be charged back to the supplier. Such costs are ordinarily borne by the buyer and considered by him as a part of his purchasing or inspection costs.

In a great many cases contracts or trade customs provide definitely that the supplier will not be responsible for contingent expense, yet this is perhaps the greatest risk and the most costly item of all from the buyer's standpoint. Incoming materials which are not of proper quality may seriously interrupt production; their rejection may cause a shortage of supply which may result in delay or actual stoppage of production, extra handling, and other expense. Labour may be expended in good faith upon material later found to be unusable, and not only the material but the labour thus expended is a total loss to the buyer. It is, in general, however, not the practice of buyers to allocate such contingent costs to the vendor. There is, however, a considerable minority practice in this respect upon the part of buyers who insist upon agreements with their vendors under which the vendor does assume a fair share of the responsibility for such contingent costs. This, it is true, is largely limited to that particular type of contingent cost which has to do with labour expended upon the material before discovery of its defective character.

Zero Defects Programmes

Starting in the late 1950s, the U.S. Department of Defense encouraged many of its suppliers to install incentive programmes aimed at defect prevention. These "Zero Defects Programmes" had the objective to reduce to zero the rejection rates resulting from failure to meet quality standards. Benefits achieved from the successful operation of these programmes included:

a. "On-time" delivery of products and materials which meet all quality specifications.

b. Lower costs because of less wasted materials.

c. Lower costs of inspection.

These motivational programmes generally rely on moral suasion. PRIDE (Personal Responsibility in Daily Effort) and various other titles have been applied to these programmes. It is useful to recognize that zero defects is usually not a process design possibility or a quality control system target. Machines are designed to operate within certain ranges, and all sampling plans are based on a certain percentage of consumer's risk and a probability of non-acceptable product. It is through the special care taken by operators, inspectors and assemblers that better than design performance is obtained.

Purchasing managers have used the concept of "zero defects" in non-defense industries to encourage suppliers to provide defect-free materials and products.

Importance of Inspection Records

Complete and well-documented records of the results of the inspection of materials and products received from suppliers are an essential element of any formal method of evaluating suppliers. In companies where the nature of the products produced requires strict control of quality, it is of great importance to the proper performance of the procurement function to select suppliers who can deliver materials and products of the specified quality.

A supplier who submits the lowest bid but furnishes materials which fail in part to pass inspection for quality may actually be a high-cost supplier. Interruptions of production schedules caused by lack of material which meets quality standards can be very expensive. The time required of purchasing personnel to obtain replacement and other adjustments for materials which fail to pass quality inspection also adds to costs.

❒

6

Capital Acquisition

Investment capital, financial analysis, or capital budgeting are terms used interchangeably for the same basic concept. For simplicity sake, we will refer to it as investment analysis. It is process of evaluating the expenditure in a project or long-term asset to determine its financial worth over its life or the period of commitment by the firm. It consists of relating the initial investment expenditure, or investment, to the longer term benefits derived from the project. It is used in the decision process for new products, factory buildings, equipment, machinery, and distribution facilities. Investment analysis also includes the decision process related to the lease versus purchase decision.

Investment analysis is presented here for several reasons. One, it is an area that requires much long-term planning, the benefits of which are often years in coming. Purchasing is often called upon to provide cost and availability estimates for capital assets as well as materials that will need during project life. Two, capital assets are bought infrequently, and they often involve very large expenditures.

Capital assets are not like the repetitive goods purchases made in normal raw material process capital items often involve costs that are not specifically known at the time of purchase thus complicating this problem further. And, three, capital goods must be carefully analyzed with a total life cycle cost approach. That is, the least costly asset might be the most expensive to operate over its life. This entire area is heavily involved in engineering, market planning, and financial analysis. The different nature of investment analysis often causes some firms to make it a separate function in purchasing.

The Investment Analysis Process

The entire cycle of capital projects falls into roughly nine distinct stages.

(1) **Idea Generation.** This is the initial conception and planning stage by a person or group. This stage does not generally last long. The cost of actually analyzing the worth of a project idea is high, so little hard development work will take place beyond cursory idea generation.

(2) **Initial Screening.** If an idea appears promising, it usually will undergo some form of top management screening before progressing much further. The purpose of the screen is to turn down ideas top management does not wish to pursue before too much time or money is spent on them. Additionally, approval from a screening often will provide funding and work assignments necessary for full detailed analysis. Purchasing is often involved in these first two stages by being asked for purchase prices, freight costs, and lead times for items necessary in the project. This information is known to be subject to change, only close ballpark estimates are necessary at this point.

(3) **Technical/Financial Analysis.** After top management approval, very technical engineering and financial data gathering and analysis begins. The person or group within marketing, distribution or production wishing the new asset or project usually conducts the analysis. Information is gathered from all areas such as marketing, production, accounting, finance, engineering, and purchasing. Here, purchasing is again requested for information about available machinery on the market, only this time more detailed cost and lead-time data is sought. The specific features of each item are analyzed in detail. This stage typically ends with a tentative idea as to which model or approach to obtain the total initial capital cost necessary to acquire it, and the estimated annual net benefits of the project into future

years. Computations to project payback and rate of return are also made.

(4) **Proposal.** This is the formal request document onto which the above cost, benefit, and rate of return information etc. is paced. It is usually a summarized form that is supported by back-up information. The proposal is what is used to formally request capital funds from top management for the project.

(5) **Implementation.** The construction or acquition phase is one in which purchasing is heavily involved. The physical task of acquiring the capital goods and optimally timing their arrival is a purchasing responsibility. Close coordination must exist in this phase with the person group who is launching the project.

(6) **Accept/Reject Decision.** This is the step at which top management decides whether to go ahead with or turn down the project. Purchasing is generally represented at these meetings. The approval is often in the form of signatures from all or a majority of all on these boards or committees. This is the purchasing departments authorization to began acquiring the needed items.

(7) **Financing Decision.** After project approval is obtained, then the decision of financing the project is often made. Financing might entail outright cash purchase, borrowing, selling stock or bonds, or any one of many types of leases. Purchasing usually provides specific information on prices and leases here.

(8) **Post Audit.** Many firms conduct audits of project performance once they are on steam. These audits are designed to ascertain whether the project is living up to initial projections and whether refinements are necessary in its operation. Purchasing will be called upon to provide an historical summary of all costs expanded to acquire and set up the asset.

(9) **Replacement.** Eventually the asset will require replacement or phasing-out. The cycle begins all over again with purchasing being asked what an estimated replacement unit will cost as well as how much the old asset will generate in net realizable value.

Purchasing is involved in most stages throughout asset project life. The tasks are non-repetitive. They often not available, and often involve estimates, since hard information is often not available, and often concern vendors who only are used a few times in a decade. The skills, approaches, and disciplines here are different from those of raw material or repetitive component purchasing.

Private Firm Project Analysis

Private firm project analysis is divided into three areas. First, is the basic information needed for financial analysis. This is the initial acquisition cost and the annual net cash benefits. Second, the financial worth of the project is determined using basic product/project information in a series of financial tools. Such approaches are employed by private firms that are seeking financial return analyses. Third, the evaluate approaches used in not-for-profit and government settings is presented. These are often different than those use in private settings.

Basic Financial Information

Two key bits of information are required before the financial feasibility of a project can be determined. These are: *(1)* initial capital cost, and *(2)* annual net cash benefits.

The initial capital cost consists of all costs required up to the actual start of the machine, operation,' or product sale. The following listing shows the items that are typically included in computing the initial capital cost.

Purchase price	$ 95,000
Freight	5,000
Site preparation	10,000

Installation	25,000
Training	15,000
Construction Interest Costs	5.000
Sub.	$160,000
Less: Investment tax credit	(10,000).
Total	$150,000

First, and always, is machinery purchase price and inbound freight. In addition, the firm will spend money for preparing the site, installation, training of workers and managers, interest on the construction loan, and the engineering and analytical work that goes into designing the project. If an old machine is to be replaced, then its dismantling costs are to be added, less whatever scrap value will be obtained from its disposition. A final and often overlooked element in this analysis is the investment tax credit. This is a reduction in income taxes normally payable by the firms due to fixed asset acquisitions made.

The tax credit is ten percent of the purchase and freight on assets of shorter depreciable lives. His tax credit, $10,000 in the above example, is an amount of taxes that the firm will not have to pay because it acquired this asset. The asset's initial capital cost, then, is $150,000. Annual net benefits is the second bit information needed in this analysis. These are the net cash flow results in each year of asset life. It is determined as follows. This is a two-step process that first requires project net profit to be determined. This is done using the standard income statement information used in accounting. The second step requires adding the "net after taxes" to the amount originally deducted for "depreciation". The sum is the net amount of cash that will result from the project during the year. This is the annual net benefit.

If a project has no actual cash flow, then it can be still justified by determining what net savings in expenses the firm will gain by switching to the new machine. This is a common approach used when new replacement machinery is being considered in a factory. Savings-type projects are perhaps easier to justify than new product ones because the former do not require estimates for revenues. Cost savings are perceived as easier to measure than a revenue and cost bearing project.

Financial Worth of a Project

The initial capital cost and annual net benefits are the two key items needed in financial investment analysis. A third is the present value rate, but this will be presented later. The common analytical tools used by industry are *(1)* simple payback, *(2)* discounted payback, *(3)* net present value, and 4) internal rate of return. Simple payback states how long it will take the initial investment cost to be recouped by the net benefits of the project. This can computed as follows.

YEAR	ACTUAL CASH FLOW	CUMULATIVE FLOW
0	($150,000)	($150,000)
1	60,000	(90,000)
2	60,000	(30,000)
3	60,000	30,000
4	60,000	90,000
5	60,000	150,000
	$150,000	

The cumulative column shows that at the end of year 2 the project will still have a deficit of total cash flows, but it will be in a surplus by end of year 3. The exact payback point is two years plus a fraction of a year. The fraction is determined by using the deficit in Year 2 without the brackets as a numerator over the total inflow in year 3. This is 30,000/60,000 or 5. Thus, the simple payback is two and one half years or two years and six months.

Simple payback has the benefit of being easy to understand. It is a basic measure of risk. The answer in terms of time, the lesser the time is the better, the longer it is, the worse. If a project still has a cumulative deficit at the end of its life, then it will not return its entire initial cost to the company. Simple payback has a disadvantage, however. It does not account for inflation, decreases in purchasing power of money over time, or the opportunities a firm might have in investing its funds elsewhere. In the above example, each dollar of $60,000 returned in year 5 is assumed to have the same dollar for dollar purchasing power or value as those returned in Year 1. This, of course, is false in any inflationary period. The present value factor, PVF, is a convenient tool to account for the above time value of funds. Table 1 is a present value table for rates up to 40 percent and up to ten years.

Many firms do not use the benefits accruing in a project beyond Year 5 even though a project might still be in existence. The rationale here is that the project must break-even in five years or less for the project to be approved. This is consistent with the long-term planning horizon in many firms. Discounted payback uses the above payback concept while accounting for the time-value of funds. It is computed using the firm's investment cut-off rate as supplied by the finance department. This rate is used to ascertain specific present value factors for each year from the table. In the example project, twenty percent is the rate used.

Year	Cash flow	20% PVF	value stream	Present Value stream
0	$(150,000)	1.000	($150,000)	($150,000)
1	60000	.833	49,980	(100,020)
2.	60,000	0.694	41,640	(58,380)
3	60,000	0.579	34,740	(23,640)
4	60,000	0.482	28,920	(5,280
5	60,000	0.42	24,120	29,400
			29,400	

The present value factor for the initial capital investment is 1.000 since present dollars each having one dollar value, are being spent.

The discounted payback is 3 + 23, 640/28,920 or 3.82 years. In simple terms the project broke-even in two and one half years. But, when the firm's time-value of funds is considered, the return takes place in three years and ten months. Again, discounted payback is expressed in time, the shorter the better. It is a measure of project risk. Net present value is the next financial evaluation toll. It seeks the total surplus of cash return from the project over and above the firm's opportunity rate. In the sample project, the net present value is $29,400, which is the sum of the fourth column or the last figure in fifth column. It is interpreted as the total surplus dollars earned from the project considering the firm's time value of funds or opportunity rate that could have been earned elsewhere.

If the net present value is zero, then the project just breaks even on this measure. If it is negative, then the firm would do better to invest in another project that would at least earn the cut-off percent rate of earnings, in this case twenty percent. But, the sample project is promising with a large surplus. Internal rate of return is the last investment tool. It is a percent figure of return. This can be compared to interest costs other investment alternatives or the inflation rate. It is found by multiplying various percent present value factors by the actual yearly cash flows until one of the percent PVFs results in the cumulative column summering to zero. The resent value percent that accomplishes this is the internal rate of return. At twenty percent a positive $29,400 results. The following table shows the results of other present value factors, PVFs.

P.V.F.	Cumulative Present value Stream
20%	$29,400
22%	21,840
24%	14,700
26%	8,100
28%	1,860
29%	-1,026

The internal rate of return for this project is about twenty-nine percent. These tools are often considered together because each one has a strength that others do not possess.

Risks in a project are evaluated by discounted payback. Project scale, magnitude, and feeling of surplus purchasing power earned is provided by net present value. Project "return" is illustrated with internal rate of return. Purchasing is involved with investment analysis in several ways. One, purchasing must use these various approaches when it seeks investments for itself such as computers, private fleets, or communications system. Two, purchasing's effectiveness in acquiring the sought items in a project is important. This means obtaining the capital item at or below the cost used in the original justification.

Cost overruns will cause decreases in the net present value and rate of return as well as a lengthening of the payback periods. For example, if the above project was $10,000 more than planned, the rate of return drops to twenty-five percent. There, a delay in acquiring the assets impacts the firm detrimentally as well. A six-month delay in project operation causes all the benefits to slide six months farther into the future. This makes the rate of return for this project twenty-four percent. Cost overruns and delays by purchasing have a great impact upon the total life returns of projects.

Leasing Versus Purchasing

A financing decision follow the project acceptances step. Financing can be gained through outright purchase or through one of many buying arrangements. Leasing has become a popular form of acquisition financing. It has been made even more attractive with the advent of "safe harbor" basing provisions in U.S. tax laws that permit firms incurring losses to still take effective advantage of depreciation and investment tax credits. Purchasing is often called upon to make the buy-or-lease decision. It is like an apple-orange comparison because there are benefits and draw backs to each choice.

Purchasing has the advantage of total control over the asset through but its entire life. The purchase decision is often the least expensive, since a leasing firm's profits are not being paid. The asset belongs to the owner after its effective life is past. This is an advantage with land, buildings, and airplanes, which can outlay appreciate over time. Finally, purchasing often involves a single cash outlay with none thereafter and only annual depreciation benefits coming to the firm. Leasing, on the other hand, provides the advantage of low initial cash commitment. A lease payment is paid rather than an entire purchase amount.

The lease payment also can correspond to the earnings of the asset. That is, after the first lease payment, earnings from the asset can pay for the subsequent ones. A lease arrangement might provide for machine installation earlier than a purchase. The buying power of the leasing firm might be so great as to pass on this economy to the lessee. An accounting benefit can also be obtained through a lease in the form of not having either the asset nor the lease obligation on the company books. This serves to increase the return on assets ratio.

Leasing is a low-risk way of entering into new areas. If the firm decides that the experience does not warrant continuation, a lease often can be easily terminated. Finally, many lease arrangements include training, administrative services, as well as maintenance and repair services. The problem at hand in many settings is to weigh the benefits of a lease against the additional costs typically associated with them. For example, truck or copier leasing is often more expensive than outright purchase, but the lease often avoids training, record keeping, personnel hiring, and maintenance necessities. The following approach can be used to evaluate how much the lease costs over and above the purchase on a time value of funds basis so that a comparative benefit and cost decision can be made by the firm.

An approach to evaluate the lease versus purchases includes 1) determining the after tax cash flow costs of the lease, 2) calculating the after-tax cash flow costs associated with the purchase, 3) subtracting the purchase cash flow from the lease cash flow to determine the annual and total cost difference of the lease over and above the purchase. 4) determining the above, after-tax cost difference in percent terms, and 5) evaluating this percent in relation to the after-tax cost of borrowing the funds for a purchase option: The following example illustrates the analysis using the project from the capital tools.

An asset can be purchased for $100,000, or it can be leased for $30,000 per year for five years. The costs of installation, etc. would be the same with each choice, but maintenance and training would be provided by the lease. The company tax rate is 30%.

Step 1: Determine after-tax lease cost.

Year	Before Tax Cash Flow	+	Lease Tax Shield	=	After Tax Cash Flow
0	$ 30,000				$ 30,000
1	30,000		($ 9,000)		21,000
2	30,000		($ 9,000)		21,000
3	30,000		($ 9,000)		21,000
4	30,000		($ 9,000)		21,000
5			($ 9,000)		(9,000)
	$150,000		($45,000)		$105,000

Note that the lease payment is at the beginning of each year. Since the company is in the thirty percent tax bracket, each lease payment shields $9,000 of funds from being paid in taxes. Year 5 is beyond the life of the lease, but the tax effect of the lease, but the tax effect of the lease payment in Year 4 is included in it.

Step. 2: Determine the after- tax purchase cash flows. The asset costs $100,000 and will be depreciated over five years for $20,000 per year. At thirty percent taxes, the tax shield affect will be $6,000 per year for years 2 through 5.

Year	Before Tax Cash Flow +	Lease Tax Shield =	After Tax Cash Flow
0	$100,000		$ 100,000
1		($ 6,000)	(6,000)
2		($ 6,000)	(6,000)
3		($ 6,000)	(6,000)
4		($ 6,000)	(6,000)
5		($ 6,000)	(6,000)
	$ 100,000	$30,000	$ 70,000

Step 3: Subtract the after-tax purchase cash flow from the after-tax lease cash flow.

Year	After- Tax Lease Cash Flow	After- Tax Purchase -Cash Flow	L.Minus P. Difference
0	$30,000	$100,000	($70,000)
1	21,000	(6,000)	27,000
2	21,000	(6/000)	27/000
3	21,000	(6/000)	27/000
4	21,000	(6/000)	27/000
5	(9,000)	(6/000)	(3/000)
	$105/000	$70/000	$35/000

Step 4: Determine the time-value percent difference between the lease minus purchase cash flows.

This is done in much the same way as the internal rate return is computed. That is, by trial and error, various percent value factors are applies in order to find which one creates a present value stream that sums to or close to zero.

TRIAL 12%	L-P	12%	Present
0	(70/000)	1,000	(70/000)
1	27,000	3.038*	82/020
5	(3/000)	.567	(1701)
			$10/325

PVFs can be added and multiplied as one when the cash flows for several years are equal.

The sum is too high on the positive side:

Attempt second trial using 16%.

TRIAL 16% L-P 16% Present

Year Flow PVF Val ue Stream

0 (70/000) 1.000 (70/000)

1-4 27/000 2.798 (75/546)

5 (3/000) .476 (1,428)

4118 too high

Trial 16% L-P 19% Present

Year Flow PVF Value Stream

0 (70/000) 1.000 (70/000)

1-4 27/000 2.638 71/226

5 (3/000) .419 (1/257) (31)

Nineteen percent the cost of the base over and above the purchase in percent time-value terms.

Step 5. Compare the extra cost of lease to cost of borrowing. This last step requires subtracting the after-tax cost of borrowing funds for a purchase from the after-tax cost of the lease.

Company cost to borrow 14% before taxes	
At 30% tax rate, after tax	
cost to borrow is	9.8%
Cost of lease over purchase (from Step 4) 1	9%
Cost to borrow for purchase	9.8%
True cost of financing by lease over and above purchase	9.2%

Purchasing, finance and the managers seeking to obtain the asset can now evaluate the convenience of having maintenance and training included on the lease. The cost of this service feature is $35/000 or 9.2% over five years. In some instances, a lease actually can be less than the cost of a purchase. This can occur when leasing company buying power is great and/or its cost of capital and tax rates are different than the lease.

Of course, if the lease cannot take advantage of the investment tax credit or depreciation for tax shield purposes leasing can still bring these total cost reduction elements to bear positively for the lessee.

Project Investment Analysis in Public Agencies

The previous analyses are used in private, for profit-firms. The intent of these tools is to evaluate the financial return, or cash profit, to the firm. In government settings, these tools generally are not appropriate because profit is not the sought after reason for a project. Instead, minimum total life cost is a more appropriate approach. Life cycle costing is applicable when the original purchase price is high, the asset has a long life, operating costs are large, and/or energy use is high. The basic concept allows two or more capital good alternatives to be evaluated on the basis of total purchase costs over their entire lives.

The key information needed for this analysis includes: *(1)* initial cost, *(2)* length of life, *(3)* salvage value, *(4)* maintenance and repair costs, *(5)* operating costs, *(6)* taxes and related benefits from depreciation, if any, *(7)* a discount rate for selected present value factors, and 8) escalation rates for operating and maintenance costs. Taxes and depreciation are not used in this analysis in public agencies, but should be included if used in for-profit firms. An example of two alternative machines will show how this can be applied. On the surface, Machine A often would be the one sought by purchasing managers because it has the least total initial cost of $ 107,500 versus $125,000 for B.

However, Machine A has a higher energy cost that has an expected inflation rate of ten percent per year and a higher maintenance cost, which is expected to climb by eight percent per year. Life cycle costing analysis requires adding all costs per year after they have been adjusted for inflation. The total yearly costs are then discounted using a present value rate appropriate for the organization. Even government agencies should use a discount rate, since they must often borrow funds on commercial markets. The sample problem uses a twelve percent rate, which is not an unlikely local, state, or federal government cost of A is higher than B, thereby over shadowing the benefit of a lower purchase cost. Thus, in this case, the asset with the higher purchase price has lower operating and downtime costs. Over the lives of both assets, Machine B costs less than Machine A.

Life cycle cost analysis is built into the initial capital cost and annual net benefit analyses of the financial tools used in private firm settings. It is appropriate to use in public agency, and not-for-profit organisation settings. It recognizes that the least purchase or lowest initial capital cost alternative is not always the best to acquire. Instead, the entire total life performance is pertinent for economic capital asset decisions. Conclusion creation, management,. and termination decisions are a major strategic area of the firm. Purchasing is involved with marketing at every stage of produce life. Too often managers in each area view the other at arms length. The ties must be close for-the firm to benefit.

Capital asset acquisition is also a part of the strategic planning process of the firm. Capital assets are used out strategic planning goals in the form of producing products for the firm. Capital analysis throughout asset life is a form of product management. Capital assets either assist the firm in reaching strategic goals, or they can restrict it by only being able to produce something the market no longer demands. Therefore, product management must be closely coordinated with capital asset use. Capital asset decisions are similar in public organization settings, though the use of capital assets there are some what different. Life cycle costing in public agency decision making considers more than purchase price alone.

The manager works with the present and the future, both now and in the future. As business conditions change, as staff turns over, and as volume climbs, it is, the manager who must compensate and adapt. While some changes in climate must be addressed with changes to the inventory system, others cannot.

The manager's challenge is to identify problems, select the best solution, and see that the chosen solution is properly implemented and effective. The system designer, however, is not left entirely out of the management picture. In order for the manager to do his or her job well, the designer must plan a manageable system.

The system must measure its performance and the performance of the people and equipment that work under its control. And it must provide the data platform on which other management decisions can be built. This chapter discusses these and other management concerns.

The topic of organization can be approached from several angles. The division of responsibilities among managers and supervisors and the structuring of reporting relationships are important to success in any business. But before responsibilities can be divided and structured, they must be identified. A discussion of the things that must be organized, particularly those that relate directly to inventory systems, divides easily into two areas: preinstallation and post installation.

First, it is important that the inventory manager and staff recognize the magnitude of change involved in the installation of systems such as the ones described in this book. Some businesses move directly from an all-manual environment to a sophisticated on-line inventory system. In these cases, it is obvious that the degree of change is great.

Other businesses simply move up from off-line environment. The inventory managers of these businesses may be the ones most likely to underestimate the degree of change involved. When systems are off-line, whether computer driven or manual, the consequences of an error are often hidden from the person who made the error.

Someone else suffers the consequences but not immediately and the error may not be traceable back to the person who made it.

In an on-line system, consequences are more immediate and people will find that they are making more errors than they had realized. Being human, many employees will fail to understand that they are now being held to a different and more exacting standard. They will, instead, blame their problems on the system.

The solution, of course, is training. Employees, and especially supervisors, must know the new systems well. They must understand not only how to do their jobs but also how to recover, from virtually every possible error. And they need enough visibility into the overall scope of the system to understand the consequences of what they do and how they do it. It is very difficult to provide too much training or to provide it in too much detail.

Training cannot be limited to a presentation of the new system and a description of how employees are to use it. Training cannot even be limited to hands-on practice on the system.

Training sessions must also be designed to produce a change in attitude. Slogans such as "the customer comes first," and "quality is job number one," must be joined with "accuracy is critical," and "do it right the first time."

An appropriate balance between these responsibilities is the key. Customer service, quality, accuracy, and productivity can and must coexist. Bank tellers, in one often-repeated example, are the material handlers of the banking industry. They receive, store, count, pick, and disburse the bank's inventory of currency. It is hard to imagine a successful bank that would allow tellers to perform transactions without keeping accurate and current records.

In a similar way, the material handlers in warehouses and stockrooms must adopt the "bank teller" attitude. Work must proceed one task at a time and no task can be started until the previous one has been fully and properly completed.

It must be generally known that sloppy work is detectable and intolerable. Training should not be limited to supervisors and material handlers. The inventory manager and staff must also be trained. It is difficult to effectively manage the use of a sophisticated, on-line system without a fundamental understanding of computers and how they work. Even a little programming experience can have value. Management training should include not only the functional aspects of the system but also introductions to the hardware and operating system used.

The system's database manager should be reviewed and the database manager's query and reporting language should be covered in detail.

It may be a good idea to place a systems person on the inventory manager's staff, even in businesses where a corporate data processing staff has responsibility for operations and technical support. This person can assume responsibility for a number of tasks, not the least of which might be advising the inventory manager in the use of the tools at his or her disposal.

Before training is even considered, the inventory manager should assume responsibility, unofficially if necessary, for supervision of the design process. It is, after all, going to be the manager's system when complete.

The inventory manager need not chair the design committee or even take part in all of its meetings. The inventory manager should, however, assure that the design committee is properly composed and that the people on the committee are competent.

As design work progresses and the system takes shape, the inventory manager should be involved in reviews. He or she should take or make time to read and comment on all documents created by the committee. Ultimately, only the inventory manager can decide whether or not the design provides all of the needed function in a way that will be useful and productive.

Another major pre-implementation concern for the inventory manager is the transition from the existing to the new system. These transitions are critical and can be the most difficult part of an inventory system development project. And, since the regular business of serving customers cannot be halted during the transition, the work ends up on top of existing jobs. The inventory manager is the one who must make sure that resources are available and that the work will get done properly and on time.

Modern on-line inventory systems use a great deal of information that older systems do not require. The collection and verification of this information can be an immense task. The amount of work involved is often underestimated, resulting in budget overruns at best and complete system failure at worst. Data maintained by the new inventory system can be divided into "static" and "dynamic" categories. Static data is information that changes relatively slowly and, therefore, can be gathered, entered, and verified in advance.

Dynamic data, however, changes much more rapidly. If entered in advance of the start-up date, it will be obsolete before it is used. Static data may be available from an existing system. If so, a programme can be written to transfer it to the new system. If not, however, it must be manually collected by people, entered, and verified. Temporary and part-time employees can sometimes be hired for this purpose, but knowledgeable supervision is required. Information that often must be collected manually includes:

— Location numbers, dimensions, and capacities

— Item dimensions and weights

— Vehicle numbers, capacities, and types

— Employee numbers, passwords, and access levels.

The first two items on this list, location and item information, often involve hundreds or even thousands of hours of work, particularly if items must be measured and weighed, one at a time.. This process alone can be a major management challenge.

Plans must be made to gather and enter the dynamic data at the last moment. Dynamic data may be available from an existing system or it may be necessary to close the facility for the time required to do a full physical inventory. Dynamic data required includes:

— On-hand balances by item and location

— Existing unit load numbers by item and location

— Existing lot and serial numbers by item and location

— Open customer, shop, and outbound transfer orders

— Open purchase and inbound transfer orders

The wise inventory manager will recognize that training and data collection activities do not end with the installation. Personnel turnover and growth both result in new employees who must be given at least as much training as the old employees received prior to the installation. Products and processes also come and go. Each requires the collection and verification of new information. Training and data collection activities must be ongoing. In addition, the inventory manager will find that he or she has assumed a new responsibility for identifying system problems. These problems can be left over from the original installation, or they can be the result of business or personnel changes.

System problems should be classified into two groups: those that can be solved with procedural improvements and those that require system change. The Inventory Manager will most likely be the focal point for these problems and for the management of the actions required to resolve them.

The achievement of an efficient, productive organization can only occur when people are equally efficient and productive. The inventory manager, therefore, needs a measure of the productivity of the people who work in the inventory facility, both as individuals and in groups. When systems direct people, as do modern inventory systems, it is relatively simple for the system to keep track of the tasks it has assigned and the time spent on each.

A report based on the file of completed transactions can summarize these tasks by shift, supervisor, work group, and employee. With appropriate logon procedures and passwords, the resulting information can be both accurate and revealing. If engineered time standards exist and if the inventory system is able to record time spent on non-productive tasks, the amount of work done can be expressed on the report in standard hours, and utilization, productivity, and efficiency ratios can be calculated, On the other hand, if no engineered time standards exist or if non-productive time is not collected, the report can be expressed in transaction counts, with different kinds of work shown separately. For experienced supervisors, transaction counts are usually adequate to determine which employees are accomplishing the most.

The inventory system can also capture and report instances in which employees make certain kinds of errors. It is these productivity and error-rate measurements that motivate employees to work accurately as well as quickly. If an employee is inaccurate, assignment of the next task will be delayed by the need to evaluate the last one, The employee is therefore affected not only by the nuisance of having to correct the work done but also by the resulting impact on, productivity measurements.

Managing Pilferage

Inventory pilferage is a significant problem for some business, particularly those with small, marketable products and those with consumer-oriented products. While no inventory system can prevent an employee from walking out with something in a pocket or purse, most pilferage is based on impulse. The inventory system can help reduce the rate of pilferage by limiting both opportunity and temptation. Here are several ways this can be done:

1. A fenced and locked security area can be created and, for selected items, the inventory system can be instructed to select only storage locations in this area.

2. Or, almost as effective and much more flexible, items requiring secure storage can be limited to locations that are beyond a normal person's reach. Employees who do not regularly work on high-rise equipment will then rarely see or handle them.

3. The system can limit the people who handle vulnerable items to a select few. This further limits both opportunity and temptation.

4. Security items can be picked last, possibly only minutes before shipment. This limits the time these items spend in the shipping area and limits the opportunity for pilferage,

5. Security items can be picked to special, sealable containers. If the containers are sealed and marked by the picker as part of the picking process, the opportunity for pilferage is further reduced.

6. Conveyor systems can be used to handle security items rather than entrusting employees with them. Both opportunity and temptation are reduced because fewer people handle the material.

Sometimes pilferage costs are higher than necessary simply because management lacks a measure of the size of the problem.

The inventory system can, and in appropriate businesses should, prepare a report of net inventory adjustments. While this report will include losses for reasons other than pilferage, those that are known can be filtered out and the remainder used as an indication of pilferage.

Items that show the largest downward adjustments over a significant period of time are candidates for some form of protection. The total facility wide adjustment is a measure of the total pilferage rate.

Another significant concern of the inventory manager is the rate at which assets are utilized. In an inventory facility, the assets of greatest concern are personnel, space, and equipment. Personnel utilization is measured by the productivity report. Space utilization can be reported by the inventory system.

The report should be available with summaries by warehouse area and such location characteristics as environment, demand, device, function, size, and weight capacity.

In addition, it can be useful to know the utilization of locations dedicated to an item versus those that are allowed to float and by single-item versus multiple-item locations. With an on-line system, the utilization of equipment, operated by the system can also be measured. When radio terminals are in use, lift truck utilization can also be measured.

In some businesses it can be taken one step further: the replenishment of the entire warehouse. Based on a user-maintained order point and order quantity, the inventory system can create purchase and shop requisitions.

After approval, purchase requisitions can be forwarded to the purchasing system for vendor selection and order placement.

Manufacturing orders can likewise be sent to the production control system for scheduling. This process can be further supported by the accumulation of usage information and the periodic recalculation of order points and order quantities.

Normal practice would require human approval of the recalculated order points and order quantities prior to use. This method of replenishment assumes that past demand rates will confine into the future unchanged. Since all products experience changes in demand sooner or later, blind use will eventually result in either shortages or excess inventories. Other techniques do consider demand forecasts and, therefore, are superior. However, MRP and DRP are complex and can be hard to implement. So, intelligent use of a simple replenishment method may be better for some low-cost, easily available products in some companies.

The employee productivity database contains a record of every material movement made in the facility and, for each, the amount of time spent on it. In addition to employee productivity, this database can be used to report warehouse labour cost by function.

If budget information is made available to the inventory system, a budget versus actual comparison can be added to the report.

A variety of reports can be created from the inventory system's database to measure quality and customer service.

Inbound quality can be measured from the results of incoming inspections and from the frequency of rejections resulting from those inspections. Outbound quality can be measured from customer returns.

Both reports are likely to be approximations, but in businesses where no other information is available, they are much better than nothing. Those businesses that have sophisticated quality systems should rely on them rather than the inventory system's database.

Customer service can be measured in a variety of ways depending on the data available in the inventory system.

On the shipments can be reported by comparing requested or promised shipment dates with the actual dates. Another useful customer service report is the fill rate report. Fill rate reports generally cover the orders shipped in a single day and report the percentage of lines that were filled, as opposed to being back ordered. Variations on this report will consider not only whether a line was completely shipped but also whether part of an order line was shipped. Measurements can be made as a percentage of either units or dollars or both.

❑

7

Make or Buy Decisions

Theoretically, a company has a choice of three basic decisions in sourcing a new product. It can:

1. Purchase the product complete from a contract manufacturer.
2. Purchase some components and materials and manufacture and assemble the balance in its own plant.
3. Manufacture the product completely, starting with the extraction of basic raw materials.

In practice, almost no companies can seriously consider the third alternative. Even relatively simple products require an amazing diversity of materials in various stages of fabrication. The largest, most highly integrated companies rely on outside suppliers for at least some components and materials. And some companies choose the first alternative and obtain a new product completely from an outside supplier. They usually do this either because they are a merchandising or engineering organization with no manufacturing facilities or because the product is not suited to their facilities. Sears, Roebuck's purchases of its own brands of appliances are a good example of the former; a business-machine maker's purchase and resale to customers of special forms to use in its machines is an example of the latter.

The general rule, however, is that an organization will make some things and buy others. This applies even to service organizations. Large hospital; for example, often operate their own print shops and laundries but are purchasers of food, drugs, and numerous other items. Both Service organizations and manufacturers sometimes generate their own electric power. They may even carry on service or manufacturing activities having nothing to do with their basic business, either because they happen to have the raw material or because the activity simply was not being performed by anyone else.

For manufacturers, make-or-buy decisions must constantly be made no manufacturer makes all of his own raw materials, so it is largely a matter of deciding at which stage of fabrication a component should be purchased. The company may buy a component complete from an outside supplier, buy it semifinished. or buy the raw material.

Make-or-buy Criteria

Companies usually prefer to do their own fabricating. They buy only raw materials or semifinished parts in cases where the following is true of the finished component:

1. Can be made mare cheaply by the company than by outside sup-pliers, or might require the company to rely on a limited number of vendors for its supply.

2. Is vital to the company's product and requires extremely close quality control.

3. Is readily manufactured with the company's existing facilities and is similar to other items with which the company has had considerable manufacturing experience.

4. Requires extensive investment in facilities that are not already available at supplier plants.

5. Has a demand that is both relatively large and stable.

Companies will usually buy a finished component from an outside supplier when:

1. They do not already have facilities to make it, and there are more profitable opportunities for investing company capital.

2. Existing facilities can be used more economically to make other components.

3. The skills of company personnel are not readily adapted to the making of the component.
4. Patents or other legal barriers prevent the company from making the component.
5. Demand for the component is either temporary or seasonal.
6. The supplier can utilize economically specialized equipment to make the product by grouping orders from several customers, and demand is not so great that any individual customer could economically utilize this equipment.

Other Factors. Some companies, by tradition, prefer to make almost every component of their products. Others prefer to buy as much as possible from outside suppliers. In general, an aggressive company in industry that is expanding very rapidly with many technological changes (*e.g.*, electronics) will prefer to buy many of its components from outside suppliers. In such industries, the company has many opportunities to employ its capital profitably through horizontal diversification-expanding its line of finished products.

A company in a stable or declining industry, on the other hand, has fewer attractive opportunities to invest its capital in expanding sales of its end products. It will be attracted, almost by default, to integration-making a bigger share of its sales dollar in its own manufacturing plants-in order to boost profits.

For example, the major auto companies have steadily increased the percentage of product that they make in their own plants. In most cases, they have been tempted to make the items that yield high profits to suppliers. Both Ford Motor Company and Chrysler Corporation have built plants to manufacture automobile glass, but it is no coincidence that neither has shown any signs of building textile mills to make up-holstery cloth for cars. Efficient glass producers earn about a 20 percent return on their investment, while in the highly competitive textile industry even efficient producers consider themselves fortunate if they average a 10 percent return.

A company may be effectively prevented from making an item by its own labour relations policies. If it is extremely generous with wages and fringe benefits for its employees, there will be some industries where it simply is not competitive even if its methods are better than those of potential competitors. For this reason, if no other, a high-wage employer like IBM or Eastman Kodak could probably never earn even modest profits in the low-wage textile industry. And it is far cheaper or the highly unionized auto companies to buy certain items from nonunion suppliers than to attempt to make the same items themselves.

Cost Comparison. When a company decides to make an item that it as been buying, it always eliminates the supplier's sales expenses usually eliminates some freight costs. If its production costs are identical to those of the supplier, the company also gains the supplier's profit and usually at least part of the fixed overhead expenses incurred by the supplier.

Suppose a supplier had the following unit cost on a component:

Direct material	$.20	
Direct labour	.10	
Variable overhead	.12	
Direct cost		$.42
Fixed overhead	$.08	
Manufacturing cost		.50
Sales expense	$.02	
Administrative expense	.06	
Total cost		.53
Profit	.01	
Supplier's price		.59
Inbound freight	$.01	
Buyer's cost		$.60

If a company were to make this item rather than buy it, it could conceivably reduce its costs from 60 cents per unit to 42 cents. This might be true if the company has idle equipment that could be used to make the part and if its only additional overhead expenses would be covered by the 12 cents allowance for variable overhead in the unit cost estimate. Even if the company had to invest in additional facilities and incur normal fixed overhead, its cost would presumably be only 50 cents per unit if it could use the facilities as economically as the supplier.

Savings Sometimes Illusory. Companies often are confronted with opportunities to make rather than buy that yield theoretical savings comparable to these. In Some cases they try to take advantage of them, But they often continue to buy the item even though they may be capable of making it. In most cases it is not to their advantage to make the item for a number of reasons, including:

1. The company's direct costs may be substantially higher than the direct costs of the supplier. The supplier presumably is one of the most efficient producers of the item and has achieved his existing costs only after management and labour have acquired considerable experience and even if the buyer can produce as efficiently as the supplier, his saving will be reduced by start-up cost. No company can immediately produce a new item at peak efficiency; costs on initial production runs are always well above standard.

2. A company has less flexibility with "make" items. It can easily change suppliers if it wishes to redesign the item so that it makes us of different materials. This can be expensive if the company has invested in equipment to make the item. Similarly, the company can exploit changes in market conditions on "buy" items and take advantage a lower prices offered by suppliers eager for new business.

3. Savings in overhead often are illusory. Fixed overhead rarely rises immediately after a company starts using idle facilities to make a part it has previously purchased, but eventually it creeps up. When business expands to capacity operations, fixed overhead increases and business be absorbed by each component that is produced.

Similarly. if business slumps, fixed overhead is underabsorbed, and unit cost rises. For example, the eight-cent allowance for fixed overhead in the preceding cost breakdown is valid only for a given volume. If business dropped 50 percent, the allowance would have to be doubled, to 16 cents. If the part were purchased from an outside supplier, he also would have difficulty absorbing fixed overhead when volume declines. But he would not dare try to recoup the added unit costs by increasing prices. In fact, competition might become so intense during a slump that he would be forced to cut prices.

4, There may be better profit opportunities in other areas. Each "make" part requires some investment in facilities, inventories, and top-management time. Even though this investment is profitable, the company may be able to earn even bigger profits by using its resources to expand the business it knows best-its end-product line.

Buy Instead of Make. Often companies decide to buy items that they have been making. In some cases they even dispose of plant and equipment used to make the item. Such decisions are almost always economic if the supplier's price is lower than the company's direct cash cost of making the part. Sometimes they are worthwhile even if the company has been making substantial profits on the item, for it may be able to use its resources still more profitably on other items.

Similarly, when a company's facilities are temporarily taxed beyond capacity, it may decide to buy part of its needs from an outsider supplier. For example, a company with a captive foundry may temporarily buy part of its castings from outside suppliers when business is exceptionally good. Even if the prices of the purchased castings are higher than the company's own costs, the company may not wish to increase its investment. In fo ndry facilities when the need for them may be temporary. When business drops off, the company can return to making all its own castings and need no longer rely on an outside supplier.

Companies that follow this practice may incur the resentment of supliers who get orders from them when business is good and they need them least and then lose the orders when business is bad and they need them most. Suppliers may not cooperate when the company wants to subcontract again. In addition, their ill will may have an adverse effect on the company's sales. Either the supplier may also be a customer or he may "knock" the company and its products to his own supplier, and customers. Ethical materials managers never try to convince suppliers that business is permanent when they know it will move back into the shop as soon as capacity is available to handle it.

Split Items. A company may simultaneously make and buy certain materials and components. For example, Ford Motor Company makes part of the steel for its cars in its own steel mills and buys the balance from independent steel producers such as National Steel Corporation. When a company does this, it enjoys most of the advantages of making without losing the advantages of buying. Its profits from making the item can be calculated precisely because there is an exact market price from the outside supplier. The company is protected, at least partly, against strikes at the supplier's plant or other supply failures. It enjoys the benefits of both its own and the supplier's improvements in technology. In addition, when a company has its own facilities to make an item, a supplier may hesitate to increase prices because his costs of production can be precisely estimated and the captive plant stands ready to take a bigger share of the business if it becomes profitable to do so.

A company often can reduce its average costs by buying part of its requirements and making the balance. The captive facility then can operate near capacity almost regardless of business conditions. When business is good, the supplier may make 50 percent and the captive plant 50 percent. When business is bad, the captive plant's production remains steady despite the decline in demand, and its share may increase to 80 percent or 90 percent, while the outside supplier feels the brunt of the business decline. His share drops to 10 or 20 percent of the business, and his actual output drops by an even greater amount. Need less to say, suppliers are not happy when they are asked to bear more than their share of a business slump, and sometimes they demand a contract providing that the percentage split be fixed regardless of general business conditions.

Controlling Captive Items

When a company makes and buys the same item, it knows precisely how competitive its manufacturing operations are ideally, every company would like the cost of each of its operations to be as low as those of the most efficient outside producer. The materials manager can render his company a real service by devoting a substantial amount of effort to locating shop items whose costs are higher than those of leading suppliers.

Stimulate Improvement. When captive manufacturing operations are at subjected to outside competition with frequent make-or-buy decisions, they may become complacent and inefficient. Their methods may not be up to date; they may be lagging in productivity, and their costs may be much higher than those of efficient outside producers. When this happens, the company's overall competitive strength can dwindle.

Suppose, for example, that one company making finished electric refrigerators were to attempt to make all of its components from basic raw materials, while a competitor elected to manufacture parts only when it could do so at substantially lower cost than it could obtain from outside suppliers. If the captive manufacturing operations of the integrated company had costs that were higher than the market prices paid for parts by its competitor, then its total product costs would be correspondingly higher. Its profits would be less despite its greater investment in facilities that would be needed to make all components.

All well-managed companies try to keep their manufacturing facilities up to date. They also try to keep costs under control with budgets and the like. If the component itself is not sold directly to a customer but is incorporated into one of the company's products, however, it never faces the acid test of market competition. The materials manager can help manufacturing simulate such competition by periodically reviewing various items made in captive operations to make certain that their production costs do not exceed market prices.

Decentralize Buying. Big companies go even further. They have decentralized organization structures in which one division may sell all of its output to one or more of the company's other divisions. For example, Ford Motor Company's Engine & Foundry Division sells its auto engines to the Ford Division, which is responsible for assembling cars and trucks.

In such a decentralized structure, the buying division (which is the unit responsible for the end product) treats the manufacturing division is much as possible as an outside supplier in order to simulate conditions; a competitive market. In some cases it can do this rather directly. For example, if the supplying division makes a product that the using division is also buying from an outside supplier, the market price is known. Similarly, if the manufacturing division makes something for difficult there is a published market price (steel or crude oil) it is not difficult to set a realistic market price.

Simulate Competition. A problem arises when the captive operation makes a product that is unique and for which quotations are not readily available from outside suppliers. For example, the Fisher Body Division of General Motors makes body stampings that are shared by all GM cars. No outside supplier is equipped to make these bodies in the quatities required by General Motors, nor would it ever seriously consider buying any major part of its body stamping needs from an outside supplier, because of its enormous investment in Fisher Body's facilities. Under such circumstances, the best the materials manager can do is to simulate market conditions for the captive operation. He can vigorously negotiate with the captive plant to get it to price its output at a level he feels would be competitive if alternate suppliers were available. In negotiating, he uses all of the cost analysis techniques that will be discussed in succeeding chapters.

Some materials managers spend a great deal of time on intracompany purchases from manufacturing plants. Why do they go to the trouble? After all, if a buying division persuades a supply division of the same company to reduce its prices by $1, the two divisions are just trading dollars. The buying division's profits go up $1 because of the lower price; the supplying division's profits decline $1. The net effect on overall company profit is nil.

Realistic Profits. One reason big companies go to such trouble is that they feel their manufacturing divisions will be more efficient in the long run if they are subject to as much competitive pressure as the materials manager can exert. Another equally important reason is that a company can calculate realistic profits for an operation only if its output is priced at market levels. If a plant whose prices are competitive does not earn adequate profits, either its management is at fault or it is in the wrong business. With realistic profit figures, a company can measure its managers' performance and also can direct new investments into areas that yield maximum profits.

Suppose, for example, that a television manufacturer makes his own cabinets. Each televison set costs $135 to make, and the company sells them to distributors for $150. Therefore the company makes $15 profit on each TV set, or 10 percent on sales.

If the company's cost of making each cabinet is $13.50, how much profit is the company earning by making its own cabinets? An amateur accountant might say that since the company is earning a 10 percent profit on each set it must automatically be earning 10 percent on each major component. But the fact is that it would be impossible to say whether the company's cabinets operation is profitable or not, since the company sells 110 cabinets. Possibly the company is producing a cabin worth $30 for a cost of only $13.50. In that case, it should expand its cabinet line to supply outside companies and go out of the TV set business itself. Or, as is more likely, the cabinet that costs $13.50 may be available from a specialist producer for $14. In that case,. the cabinets, with a return of less than 4 percent on sales, are eating into the company's profit margin. If the company can dispose of its cabinet plant and invest the proceeds in a more profitable part of the business, a an boost its overall profit margin.

Opportunity Cost. The materials manager is the natural link between company's own manufacturing operations and competitive operations of outside suppliers. Ideally, he should be constantly prodding manufacturing to make item he is currently buying, if these items are potentially profitable. At the same time he should be working to take items out of manufacturing that do not belong there.

The materials manager's basic yardstick for make-or-buy analysis is the company's own opportunity cost of capital. This of course, represents the return that the company should be able to earn on new investments. For example, a company that consistently earns a 15 percent return on its net assets probably has an opportunity cost of capital of about 15 percent.

The higher the opportunity cost, the more limited the company's ability to make things instead of buying them. For example, a highly profitable company with an opportunity cost of 30 percent or more would find it profitable to buy almost every component of its end product. The reason, of course, is that it is impossible to earn this sort of return in most businesses, and the company's own suppliers would have to settle for lower returns. Conversely, a company in a declining industry with declining opportunity costs and huge cash flow might be a lot less fussy and settle for a lot less.

Leasing

Companies with very high opportunity costs of capital often prefer to lease many of their assets. For example, a company that earns 20 percent on its own capital might prefer to lease a fleet of cars for its salesmen rather than buy them. The leasing firm might be willing to settle for a 10 percent return on capital. Consequently, even if the company could buy, sell, and maintain cars as efficiently as the leasing firm, its opportunity cost of capital would be so much higher that it would perfer to delegate the job to the leasing firm.

Leasing has grown enormously in popularity in recent years. A survey showed that 71 percent of the manufacturers participating leased capital equipment. Respondents also mentioned the types of equipment they leased. Office machines were most popular, with 31 percent of the mentions. Also mentioned were transportation equipment (23 percent), materials-handling equipment (18 percent), machine tools (17 percent), and other machines and equipment (II percent).

Advantages. Companies that lease do so both to avoid the resposibility of ownership and to make capital available for other purposes. They prefer to lease certain highly specialized types of equipment because they need not worry about its maintenance or possible obsolescence, all they need do is operate the equipment, with none of the responsibilities of owning it. In adddition, a company gets some tax advantage by leasing. Rent can always be charged entirely as an operating expense and thus is completely deductible from taxable income. On the other hand, if a company owns equipment, it must capitalize its cost. Depreciation charges deductible as operating expense must be spaced over the life of the equipment.

In some cases the lessor may be willing to pay for the lessee's tax privileges. Capital-intensive industries like airlines frequently generate more investment tax credit and accelerated depreciation than they can profitably use in reducing their own tax liability. One solution is to sell new equipment to third-party lessors who can make better use of the investment tax credits. The airline then leases back the equipment and enjoys the advantage of a financing scheme that does not increase the amount of debt on its own balance sheet.

Except when there is an extraordinary tax break, the lessee must pay for these advantages. The rent he pays not only includes an adequate amount to cover probable maintenance, depreciation, taxes, and other expenses but also a healthy profit for the lessor. Typically, a lessor might allow for a 10 percent return on his investment in calculating his rent. The return would be higher yet on equipment on short-term lease that is subject to high obsolescence, and it would be lower on buildings with very long-term leases.

Why then do most insurance companies and banks prefer to lease electronic data processing equipment when they are eager to make an investment with a guaranteed return of 5 to 6 percent? Such institutions rarely want to own this equipment. Its maintenance is much too costly and too highly specialized for them. When equipment is leased, the supplier must fix it if it breaks down. In addition, EDP equipment is subject to rapid obsolescence. This need not worry the lessee; he does not have to get rid of the old equipment when new models are developed or his needs change.

Companies also lease solely to use capital for other purposes. In some cases, they may even sell and lease back assets to get what amounts to a loan that is not shown as a liability on the balance sheet. For example, a company might sell one of its buildings to an insurance company and then sign a long-term lease for its use. The building becomes the equivalent of collateral on a loan for the insurance company, cold the lease includes a rent sufficient to cover depreciation of the property over its life as well as a return on investment. Sale and lease-back is desirable when the company either cannot raise money more cheaply with a direct loan or does not wish to impair its credit standing by having a loan show on its balance sheet, or it can make a larger profit on the proceeds from the sale of the asset than the return it gives the lessee in rent.

In the past, companies could also reduce financing costs substantially through sale and leaseback from municipalities in which their facilities were located. In order to encourage the company to build its plant and provide employment, a city would become legal owner of the plant, financing it with tax-free municipal bonds issued on the strength of the company's long-term lease of the facilities. This permitted the company to get financing for perhaps 4 or 5 percent instead of the much higher interest rate that would be charged if the financing were carried out through conventional channels. This tax loophole is currently available only for pollution-control projects.

Decisions to make, buy, or lease affect both manufacturing and materials activities. They should not be made without the approval of both the manufacturing manager and the materials manager. Other departments also help shape make-or-buy decisions, which are among the most basic decisions in the management of a business. Once the decision is made to buy, however, the materials manager and his buyers become the dominant factors in selecting the supplier. The next three chapters discuss the buying process in detail.

❐

8

Purchasing Research

Purchasing research is defined by Fearon (1961) as: 'systematic investigation and fact-finding to improve purchasing performance.' A certain amount of systematic investigation is done as a normal part of the buying process. Before dealing with a new supplier, or selecting a contractor for a major project, or taking the final decision on costly capital expenditure or on the adoption of some novel material, a competent purchase department would be expected to undertake a 'course of critical investigation; endeavour to discover new or collate old facts'—which is a dictionary definition of research.

Emergency investigations are also undertaken to solve problems, such as a sudden shortage or an unacceptable price increase; or in response to other exceptional situations, such as a change in the law.

But there is a problem for purchasing management in organizing research which goes beyond what is a prerequisite of some complex new purchase decision, or a crisis response. Rapid developments in technology, changes in the structure of the economy and continual evolution in the complex environment in which purchase decisions are made have made this problem more urgent. How can purchasing management make available to the buyer information which will improve purchasing performance now? How can future purchasing performance be improved by looking ahead, studying trends, exploring options, when buyers are fully occupied with the problems of today? The development of new systems, techniques and methods is another area which is difficult to handle on a part-time basis.

Consequently, some larger purchase departments include alongside the buying staff, people who are employed full-time on 'systematic investigation and fact-finding to improve purchase performance.'

Full-time research workers of this kind go by a variety of names, including: purchase analyst, cost analyst, systems analyst value analyst, commodity specialist, cost estimator, supply market analyst, purchasing research, purchasing services.

They are often grouped together in a separate section known as: purchase planning and research, purchasing research, purchasing services. Such a section may provide other information services such as a catalogue library or the preparation of management reports or expenditure budgets.

The technical qualifications of such personnel vary considerably and will depend on the nature of their work. Their personal qualifications are just as important. In providing a useful and appreciated service to buyers and to purchasing management their technical qualifications should be adequate to ensure that the service is useful; but to make it appreciated they need social or interpersonal skills. If buyers get the impression that research personnel are going to interfere with the way they buy, criticize their buying decisions and generally act as backseat drivers instead of helping them, then the back-up service provided by the section is not going to be fully used.

Personnel in other departments may contribute to research in the purchasing department. For instance, quality control engineers often assist in supplier evaluation, marketing research personnel sometimes help with supply market investigation, and systems or O and M people may be called in on systems and methods. Outside consultants are also used.

In organizations not employing full-time purchasing research staff, two methods are used by purchasing management to ensure that purchasing research is not confined to *ad hoc* or emergency investigations. The first is an individual approach, and the second is a collective approach.

The individual approach is to agree with individual buyers special projects. By an agreed date they must each complete an investigation and put forward recommendations, for instance on revised conditions of contract, on acceptance of hospitality, or on new sources. These projects arise from or are related to the normal work of the people concerned but are additional to it. In management by objectives, staff development schemes, and graduate training programmes such special projects are common.

Collective approaches usually attempt to focus the attention of all the buyers on the problem at a time. One purchasing manager refers to this as the 'roving spotlight.' Each month he turns the spotlight onto a new problem area. Particular aspects may be assigned to individuals but the whole department is expected to concentrate on the general problem.

The best way to keep interest alive may be to have a number of different approaches operating simultaneously. One large organization had one group looking at supplier appraisal methods while another group worked on system development with the computer specialists and a third group discussed long-term prospects with the corporate planning staff. Meanwhile all buyers were encouraged to read trade and commercial publications, attend exhibitions, visit suppliers, and contribute to planning and policy formation. Graduate trainees spent at least six months in purchasing research, and often did work which was of noticeably high standard but was not seen by the buyers as a threat to their prerogatives or an attack on their status.

Having organized a purchase research effort, either full-time or part-time, topics for research are selected. A thought-provoking definition of research was provided by C.F. Kettering: 'an organised process of finding out what you arc going to do when you can't keep on doing what you're doing now.'

Purchases for Employees

How far should the purchase department extend itself in making purchases for the private use of employees? Some companies encourage this; some prohibit it; most restrict its use to senior executives. It is a matter which company policy must regulate.

The typical employee purchase takes longer, and therefore costs more to handle, then the typical regular purchase. It is outside the usual routine, an isolated transaction rather than one of a series. The buyer will probably make a special effort to oblige a colleague who asks for something to be got for him wholesale. The accounting will probably be more complicated than for regular purchases.

However, most companies provide a whole range of fringe benefits for staff. These include subsidized sports facilities, subsidized canteens, legal assistance, help with tax problems, loans for house purchase, group life assurance, cash wedding presents, retirement pensions. Why should not a company add discount purchasing to the range if it chooses? But the purchasing time and processing associated paperwork ought to be charged to personnel or welfare rather than purchasing overheads. And it may turn out that the cost of providing the service is more than it is worth. Making a small charge for each transaction usually simplifies the situation considerably.

Disposal of Scrap and Surplus

Every manufacturer, unwillingly but unavoidably, manufactures scrap. Getting this off the premises for what it will fetch is a chore usually undertaken by the purchase department. Scrap and by product can even in certain cases generate sufficient income to rank as an appreciable secondary source of revenue.

Apart from the scrap and byproduct which is inevitably produced by manufacturing processes, any buying operation that caters for changing requirements will gradually, through failure to foresee changes, or simply through buyers' blunders, accumulate a stock of goods surplus to requirements. Often the buyers are the best people to dispose of this stock, for the following reasons.

(1) Buyers know the sources from which the goods were acquired. Suppliers might be interested in buying back the goods, perhaps for recycling.

(2) Buyers know the prices they paid for goods and consequently have some notion of the resale value of what is being disposed of.

For instance, the sales department of a diesel engine manufacturer would not be likely to know the market value of a lot of scrap bronze bushes, while the buyer who bought the bar stock they were made from should have a very good idea of what the bushes were worth.

(3) Potential customers for scrap and redundant items are not the same as potential customers for the end-product; rather they are like other raw material customers. They are members of the markets in which the buyers operate, rather than the markets in which the sales department operates.

Regular bulk scrap, such as steel and iron turnings and borings in a metalworking plant, is usually sold on period contracts awarded quarterly or annually and providing for frequent collection. Non-recurring or unusually valuable scrap is sold to the highest bidder after asking a few dealers and merchants to inspect and quote. There are also specialist firms who are in business to buy and sell surplus industrial equipment such as bearings, fastenings, machinery and office equipment.

The realization that the earth's resources are finite has led to an increased interest in recycling and reclamation; scrap is the one raw material which is increasing in supply.

Control

Any system of control will:

(1) set standards of performance;

(2) measure deviations from standard;

(3) identify reasons for these deviations;

(4) take corrective action.

Budgetary control is a typical example of this. Other control devices such as savings reports and cost ratios are used in the management of purchasing and supply.

Planning and control are closely connected. Plans are sometimes made far ahead, as in corporate planning; although here as the saying goes, 'plans are nothing—planning is everything.'

Corporate Planning

Corporate planning is a systematic attempt to plan the future of a corporation as a whole. It is an attempt to foresee the threats and promises which the future holds in store, on various assumptions as to the form the future might take, and to devise strategies to ensure that the organization is advantageously placed whatever happens. The larger organizations have most need to look further ahead. Small organizations can adapt more quickly to change. It is also when the environment is changing rapidly that forward planning is needed; if the future is going to be much like the present, forward planning can still be useful but will carry a lower priority.

The Need for Control

The measurement and control of the effectiveness and efficiency of an organization—how far it succeeds in achieving its objectives and how economically it uses its resources to do this is of great interest to managers. It could be argued that the usefulness of purchasing to the organization it serves is to some extent a function of the authority vested in it and the confidence which management has in it. This is affected by the way its performance is controlled and measured, which partly depends on data that can only be supplied by the buying department.

It has been suggested that the job of the purchasing department could be summed up briefly as:

(1) to get the goods required; to ensure they appear on time, with as little fuss and inconvenience to those who require them as possible, and without spending too much time and money on getting them;

(2) and in getting the goods, to buy wisely and well.

Success or failure in achieving the first of these objectives is not too hard to assess, and a variety of measures are used. The second objective is very hard to assess, buy it should not be ignored. Good buyers make good buys. If their performance is assessed on the basis of what it costs to employ them, how much they spend, how many requisitions they process and how many orders they place, and what proportion of goods arrive on time and are accepted by inspection, without taking note of their ability to make good buys, then something important is left out of the picture of buyer performance. What is not covered is an important aspect of the competent buyer's contribution to the company's survival and prosperity in competitive conditions.

Savings Reports

Many organizations try to correct this by calling for savings reports. It has to be laid down what is, and what is not, a 'saving'. If three quotes come in, how much is saved by accepting the lowest? Nothing, of course, if we never intended to accept the highest. If the bottom drops out of the market, how much credit can the buyer claim for lower prices? If we are honest, none: we cannot take credit for the sun shining in summer.

Many people do not like savings reports, regarding them as easy to fake, likely to lead to price chiselling, and perhaps also as boastful. This came out in a cartoon: Jackson was hitting a huge gong marked 'Another Jackson Cost Reduction!', While one colleague told another: 'Jackson likes management recognition.'

Savings reports do not provide data useful in running the business. They are about past history. But they may help management to identify and encourage the specific contribution made by the buyer. They may also produce better performance. If you have to report on how well you have carried out an activity, you will probably try harder to do it well.

Often targets are set for cost reduction, and the savings report will then be related to targets set. Targets may be set by cost reduction committees including people from design, manufacturing, purchasing, accounting, etc.

Many manufacturers have a range of products each of which may start in a small way, building up later to big sales if it is successful, only to be superseded eventually. Purchase departments that buy parts and material for the whole portfolio of products could well be set savings targets of 2% of purchase expenditure every year. (Bear in mind that every year some products will sell in much larger quantities than in the year before, with obvious cost reduction opportunities.)

Some firms negotiate savings targets individually with each buyer, on the basis of past performance and what is thought likely to happen in particular markets. One large company set an average savings target between 1-1.5% and 1.5% of spend: each buyer was expected to aim for savings of that order.

Cost Ratios

Cost ratios are used in controlling the operating costs of supply departments. These costs include wages and salaries, stationery and supplies, phone bills, telex and fax, travel and entertainment, and so on. It is always useful to compare this year's costs with last year's costs. The purpose of cost ratios is to relate operating cost to the work done.

The two ratios in common use are:

(1) the average cost of placing an order; and

(2) the average cost of spending Rs. 100.

The average cost of placing an order is obtained by adding up the total cost of operating the buying department for a year and dividing this by the number of orders placed in a year. Thus if it costs Rs £500,000 to run the department for a year in which it place 50,000 orders, the average cost of placing an order Rs. 10.

The average cost of spending Rs. 100 is obtained in a similar way, by relating operating cost to expenditure. Thus if it costs £500,000 to run the department for a year in which it spent Rs. 50 million, the cost of spending 100 is Re. 1.

Both ratios have to be used with caution. Department operating costs will be low in departments that do not employ properly qualified buyers. But this does not mean that the buying is done efficiently. Most of it is done in other departments. So the figures for the buying department do not really tell us what our buying costs us in relation to expenditure. If we employ qualified buyers and pay them the rate for the job, buying department operating costs of course go up; but for the company as a whole, costs would well come down.

And in principle we could get a very favourable figure for the cost of spending Rs. 100, simply by paying twice as much as the normal price. That would have our cost ratio. On the other hand, we could adopt more efficient procedures for handling small orders, so that we do not place so many orders. Result? Our cost per order goes up; so does our cost per Rs. 100 spent.

These examples show that cost ratios can give you useful indications that something has changed. They do not tell you if things have changed for the better or for the worse; you have to check up on that separately.

Head-Count

The number of people employed in the department—the 'head-count' is also something to watch. It can be related to the total number of employees, but not very precisely. We cannot assume that if the labour force doubles, the number of people employed in purchasing should double too. Nor can we assume that if the amount of money we spend on purchases doubles, we should employ twice as many people to spend it.

In one firm 50% of the total sales revenue was spent by the 0.5% of employees in the purchasing department, but this cannot be used as a guideline. Economies of scale apply. One survey found that in small firms purchasing employees numbered over 1% of the labour force, and in large firms they were less than 0.5% of the labour force. But differences between industries were greater than differences between big firms and small firms. In military electronics, 6% of the workforce were in buying; in computer manufacturers, 5%; in cutlery, 0.2%.

Vendor Rating

Vendor Rating is an integral part of most Quality Control and Quality Assurance programmes, vendor-rating schemes have evolved over a ten to fifteen year period from strictly numerical indices to the current practice of using descriptive evaluation.

Broadened Applications

The rapid expansion of quality assurance requirements in many industries has broadened the applicant on of vendor rating concepts from high-technology industries to industry in general. This trend has been spurred by the current climate of consumer demands for protection, supported by the courts in terms of major damage payments and massive recall programmes.

The intent of vendor evaluation is to determine, usually by pre-contract survey, if the intended vendors have "in place" the basic quality control procedures which will enable them to deliver products within specifications in timely and cost-effective manner. Such an investigation is desirable because the vendor is probably in a completely different industrial stream from that of the vendee.

A history of previous contract performance is a useful base to start from, but is actually not essential in the evaluation process. In most industries the evaluation process has become a team action, with members from purchasing, engineering, and quality assurance of the vendor and vendee companies meeting to exchange pertinent information. (Specific team make-up varies with the industry involved). A typical evaluation would proceed as follows:

(1) Vendee evaluation team meets at its work location to plan the evaluation.

(2) Vendee's purchasing representative contacts potential vendors and arranges for visits.

(3) Visit sequence is confirmed and vendor and vendee teams make final preparation for actual visits. Relevant documents, drawings, specifications, etc., are exchanged for study.

(4) Vendee team arrives at vendor plant or work location and briefs vendor management on the scope of the survey.

(5) The survey takes place, with both teams participating.

(6) Vendee team reviews its findings with vendor management.

(7) Vendee team returns to its headquarters and prepares a final report for its management group, with copies to the surveyed vendor.

(8) Vendor ratings are confirmed in purchasing, engineering, and quality assurance records.

The above sequence applies equally well to a complete five or six person team or a two person work party.

Scope of Survey

The scope of the survey normally includes:

(1) Personnel: Review of the key personnel who will be involved in any transaction.

(2) Engineering: Review of design methods and product integrity control.

(3) Production: Materials and inventory control, machine set-up and loading, control of scrap, surplus, or obsolete materials.

(4) Finance: Account systems, financial ratings, etc.

(5) Labour: Degree of unionization, strike history, etc.

(6) Marketing: Business profile-military, aerospace involvement.

(7) Quality Control: Manufacturing inspection and control procedures, instrument calibration procedures, engineering change control.

Evaluation. Survey results are tabulated, and the observations form the subject matter for a vendee conference to explore all possible good and bad points of (usually) three potential suppliers. A decision is then made as to which supplier will be the most economical and.logical choice (perhaps with upgrading) to meet contract requirements.

The foregoing account highlight the significant difference between the numerical schemes and present practices. Vendee companies are now prepared to change process cycles to meet vendor capabilities, and are also prepared to assist vendors to restructure their production and quality assurance system to meet vendee needs.

Most vendee teams regard the survey and its subsequent follow-up as an educational process, and are encouraged by their management to cooperate with the vendor in improving his quality assurance programme until it is acceptable as conforming to recognized standards. Various incentives are built into most programmes which reduce inspection costs for both parties and foster mutual understanding of product problems.

General Appraisals

A good driver will be aware of what information is displayed on the instruments, but will also be conscious of the fact that a lot can go wrong with the car or the way it is driven which will not show up on the instruments. Managers of large departments, however little or much they require in the way of regular performance checks and ratios and trend charts, know that these indicators, useful as they may be, cannot tell the whole story.

Very occasionally it may be necessary to attempt a full qualitative appraisal of the whole structure and performance of a supply department. The only qualification for making such an appraisal is exceptionally good judgement based on thorough knowledge of supply work. Making the appraisal objectively that is, so that several assessors would arrive independently at the same verdict is not easy.

Some of the many facets of departmental work which would have to be considered are: the state of long-term supplier relationships; the extent and quality of interdepartmental cooperation; whether the department is adequately staffed with people of sufficient ability who are adequately trained in the details of their work; whether duties are sensibly allocated and clearly defined; whether forms are well designed, systems and work routines efficient and sound and go with a swing, that is, flow instead of by turns slipping and sticking; whether the department is achieving the results required, making a real contribution. to efficient operation of the company, and improving its performance over the years.

Budgetary Control

Under budgetary control a manager within an undertaking is given financial limits within which he plans the activities under his command in accordance with the policy of the undertaking. Results are accounted for in such a way that continuous comparison is possible between actual and forecast results. If remedial action is necessary it can be taken at an early stage. Alternatively the budget objectives can be reviewed.

A budget is a financial and/or quantitative statement of the policy to be pursued during a defined period of time for the purpose of attaining a given objective. A manpower budget may be expressed in hours of work or number of men; an output budget may be expressed in product quantities, yards, or weight. Most budgets are in money terms because this is the simplest common unit. Despite this a budget is basically a programme of work to do and resources required to do it, even though it may be convenient to express it in money terms.

The budget is really a master-plan for the allotment of scarce resources. There seem always to be more things worth doing than money and other resources permit. Those in authority must decide between the claims of more hospitals or more schools, better roads or bigger universities, guns or butter. Their decisions are incorporated in the budgets that authorize expendit by spending departments during the ensuring year.

Budget procedure in local authorities and in central government departments entails three successive stages. First, requirements for the period are estimated: how much money it wants to spend and what it wants to spend it on. Second, the appropriate body considers the budget proposal and either accepts or amends it. The Treasury, the Cabinet (and Parliament) are the appropriate body for central government; the Finance Committee and the Council are the appropriate body for local government. Third, the budget as approved becomes the department's authorization to spend, and it becomes possible to check that the department does work to its budget.

All three stages involve much detail and many decisions. For the first stage all the department's activities must be costed out in detail. New projects must be weighed carefully; they have to be approved in competition with similar requests from other departments; they will not be judged solely on whether they will increase the service offered by the department. After preparation, and often in the course of preparation, experts outside the department who are employed as the public's watchdogs will subject it to detailed scrutiny. The final scrutiny of expenditure and the initial work of preparing the budget have turned out to be valuable aids in managing a big department, quite apart from their original purpose of enabling those who pay the piper to have some say in calling the tune.

The Business Budget

But while government budgets normally begin with proposals to spend money, business budgets normally begin with proposals to earn money.

The plans of a trading organization are usually limited by demand—how much of its products it can sell and what the customer will pay for them and the sales estimate is therefore the foundation of the whole budget. Profitability is a simple criterion for assessing alternative proposals, and it could be wished that some similar criterion could be applied to government budgets. Profitability is less simple than it may seem; it is long-term survival and prosperity of the organization rather than the maximum short-terms profit which is the aim. Maximizing income and minimizing outgoings are quite inadequate as guiding rules. In fact for such things as research, employee welfare, publicity, management must allot resources by judgement in the same way as a government allots national resources to alternative claims.

The sales budget, then, is an estimate of what will be sold in the period, and of what it will cost to sell it in salesmen's time and expenses, in advertising and other sales promotion activities, and so on. Next comes the production budget, a detailed plan for producing the things shown in the sales budget, with costs of materials, labour and overheads. Cash budgets and capital budgets will also be prepared, and there will be a budgeted net profit.

Events during the year may not fall out exactly as forecast in the plan, but the merit of an exact plan is that the unexpected, the exceptional, the operation which is not going to plan, can be identified.

Fixed budgets are only applicable to operations whose input and output can be tightly controlled. They are suitable for many government applications but few business applications. Even fixed budgets need some procedure such as supplementary estimates by which they can be adjusted if the occasion arises. But trading budgets must be flexible rather than fixed. An airline for instance made their budgets flexible by basing them on a standard variable cost per flight. They are adjusted to changing market conditions by leaving standing charges and overheads at the same gross figure as shown originally, but adjusting variable costs to the number of flights flown. Manufacturers' budgets need similar provision for adjusting to actual sales if these differ from the estimate.

Supply Performance and Standard Costs

The materials budget is part of the production budget in a manufacturing firm. Often standard costs for materials are calculated for each product, and the monthly materials budget is worked out by multiplying the quantity of each product which is to be made in the month by the standard materials cost for that product. Each month actual expenditure is compared with the budget, and if there is a variance the purchase department may be called upon to explain it. It has been suggested that: 'Material price standards can be used to control purchasing and even influence the Purchase Department to introduce new materials so that standard prices can be obtained.' A material variance might appear in the budget statement like this:

Month: April

Product: Widgets	Budget	Actual	Variance
Material consumption:	Rs 52500	Rs. 51700	Rs. 800

This is small enough. But there are two components in a material variance; either the quantity used may differ from the quantity, budgeted, or the price paid may differ from the standard price. In this particular case we might find that the materials budget is based on a budgeted widget output of 1,00,000 with a standard usage of 0.2 kg (0.51b) of material per widget at a standard price of Rs. 1.05 per 0.5 kg. We might find that in April actual usage was 47000 1b of material at an actual cost of Rs. 51700. The material variance would then be made up of both a price variance and a usage variance.

The price variance is the difference between actual and standard price multiplied by actual usage. Since we have found that actual price multiplied by actual usage is Rs. 51700; and since actual usage of 47000 1b of standard price of Rs. 1.05 per lb comes to Rs. 49350; the material price variance must be the difference between these figures, that is Rs. 2350.

The usage variance is the difference between actual and budgeted usage at standard price. In this case, actual usage is 47000 Ib and budgeted is 50000 lb. The difference is 3000 Ib, and at the standard cost of Rs. 1.05 per Ib gives a usage vanance of Rs. 3150.

In summary, we now have:

	Rs.
material price variance	+ 2350
material usage variance	– 3150
net materials variance	– 800

These figures disclose a 5% price rise, which is large enough to be looked into. Its effect on material costs has been masked by a 6% drop in consumption of material, in itself a discrepancy big enough to call for investigation.

As a purchasing yardstick, the price variance is incomplete. But it does measure how the materials cost of the product compares with what at some time in the past it was expected to be; and this is a most important fact, since company planning, in particular of prices, is based on it.

The budget helps to focus purchasing effort where it will do most good. If steel bar contributes 40% of a product's factory cost, then a 10% price rise for steel adds 4% to product cost. Doing something about that matters far more than shaving another two-paise a ream off typing copy paper cost. Costs can often be reduced even though prices are inflexible. In the case of steel we could ask if the right quality is being bought; could a different specification meet requirements and reduce costs; are there too many specifications, so that variety reduction could bring visible savings? Are the right sizes used and stocked? Is bright bar bought when cheaper black bar would do as well; or black bar where bright would more than save its extra cost through reductions machining time? Can something be saved in price, terms, or carriage costs by switching from manufacturer to stockholder or vice versa? Since steel comes cheaper in large lots, are quantity discounts fully exploited? Can the buyer negotiate special terms of some kind? Can the product be modified to use less steel, or some other material be substituted?

By drawing the buyer's attention to price changes which affect product costs significantly, budget variances enable the major purchasing effort to be directed at the right targets. By showing management how material costs are varying from expectations, they provide a means of encouraging good buying performance. But they should be regarded as a means of encouraging good performance and not as a measure of the performance achieved. Other wise buyers will get more credit than they deserve when prices are falling, and less than they have earned when prices are rising. In the latter case the variance may well remain unfavourable even though alert buyers have succeeded in keeping price rises below those suffered by competitors. On the other hand unfavourable variances may well be a sharp spur to alert and effective buying.

Departmental operating budgets cover departmental expenses such as salaries and wages, travelling expenses, postage and stationery, telephones and telex, furniture and equipment, etc. They provide an accounting check on the cost of operating the department, not of course on the performance given by the department.

Management by Objectives

Management by objectives (MbO) has been a popular technique. In consultation and agreement with his manager, the buyer develops a plan of operation in which a number of specific tasks or objectives are defined and time-tabled.

MbO has also been applied to stock control. In one example, 'the conceptual weaknesses, system deficiencies and operational shortcomings of the system of stock management were analysed to a limited extent using consultant specialists in operations research and data processing, and then a strong multidiscipline project team was established to investigate requirements and to devise the next-generation system.'

The targets or specific objectives agreed between the person concerned and his manager should be related to his normal work buy should be something extra or something new or something which had been neglected in the past. Discussion with other departments will often be necessary since there are nearly always interface problems in supply improvement plans: for instance in changing specifications, materials, suppliers, procedures and paperwork, working capital requirements, etc.

These targets act as incentives and provide yardsticks against which performance can be measured objectively. Properly administered, MbO can provide the individual with an environment in which he can grow, achieve high job motivation, and monitor his own performance instead of being policed by cost ratios and supervisors.

Materials Departments as a Profit Centre

The purchasing department as such does not make profits. Nor does the sales department or the manufacturing department. It is the organization as a whole that makes profits. But some qualification of this is needed in large organizations.

For measurement and motivational purposes it may be desirable to attribute portions of the profits earned to those departments primarily responsible for earning them. A multinational organization would normally treat each of its national 'departments' or subsidiaries in this way. A multiproduct organization may be organized in product divisions treated in this way, as quasi-firms with their own profit figures.

It is not possible to treat a buying department in this way, but supply department and materials departments can be treated as quasi-wholesalers. The buying department often has considerable opportunities to reduce material costs. A net cost reduction constitutes a contribution to profits, other things being equal, but it is misleading simply to equate cost reduction with profit increase, Buying personnel who favour the 'profitmaking' view of their work often stress the positive and creative side of it seeking out new sources or new specifications, commercial innovation by new types of supply arrangement, etc. These factors can indeed lead to a more profitable operation. When the buying department is combined with storage, stock control and transport, to form a materials department or supply department, it becomes possible to treat is as a quasi-firm which can earn profits or make losses, like a captive wholesaler. The purpose of doing this is to motivate supply people to behave like profit-minded businessmen instead of cost-minded service personnel.

THE BUYING PROCESS

Buying Process is directly concerned with four basic materials management objectives: low prices, continuity of supply, consistency of quality, and favorable supplier relations. The preceding chapter dealt with the selection of potential suppliers, or, more specifically, with the evaluation of a company's ability to supply. This chapter will discuss the process of selecting among a number of qualified potential suppliers. Essential to this process are an understanding of quality and an ability to evaluate prices quoted by competing suppliers for goods that sometimes vary in quality.

Quality is Paramount

Of the four basic buying objectives, quality may well be the most important. If the buyer does not get the quality of material need he gets nothing of any worth. Price, delivery, and favourable supplier relations become unimportant.

Quality is also the least understood buying objective. The price, delivery, and service objectives are fairly obvious. The quality objective seems obvious—but it is not. For example, professional buyers are always interested in paying the lowest prices for material and getting the delivery and service they need, but they do not necessarily seek the highest possible quality. On the contrary, they usually are interested in geting the minimum quality necessary for the material to perform its function satisfactorily. For example, for most applications silver is a higher quality metal than copper. It is easier to draw and has superior electrical conductivity. Yet silver is almost never used to make electrical wire, despite the fact that it is the best metal for this purpose. The reason, of course, is price Silver is 40 to 50 times more expensive than copper, which does adequate job.

Quality and Price. Quality is usually linked with price. A $6,000 Cadillac automobile is of better quality than a $3,000 Chevrolet.

Which car is the better value depends on its function. If the car is to be used for company errands, the Chevrolet is undoubtedly the car to buy. It will serve the function somewhat better than the Cadillac because it is shorter; and easier to maneuver. It will last almost as long, be cheaper to operate and maintain, and costs half as much. But if the car is to be use to impress company customers, the, Cadillac will probably serve the function more than twice as well as the Chevrolet.

Note that quality is related to function. In one sense, the Chevrolet is actually a higher quality car than the Cadillac. Similarly, a $3 pair of blue jeans can be of higher quality than a $50 pair of fine woolen slacks, if they are to be used as work clothes.

Every salesman tries to convince his prospects that his products are superior in quality to those of competitors. In fact, if a buyer tells a salesman his price is too high, the standard rejoinder is that the quality is high, too. In such cases, the buyer and the salesman both may be right. Then it is up to the buyer to determine if the salesman's company is offering the quality he really needs.

Setting Quality Criteria. Quality determination is only partly the buyer's responsibility. Also vitally interested are the departments concerned with using and specifying the purchased material. Ideally, the users and specifiers should set objective quality standards for each purchased item. Then the buyer need not concern himself with quality so long as the supplier meets those standards. Unfortunately, for many items this cannot be done in practice. Often it is impossible or impractical to establish standards sufficiently detailed so that the buyer would be assured of satisfactory quality if the supplier met them. Sometimes, the users and specifiers do not really know what standards should be set. They want the "best available at a reasonable price." In some cases each supplier's product is different and performance is the user's only really dependable guide to quality.

Thus quality criteria vary from product to product. No company can use the same criteria to measure the quality of every item it buys. And, regardless of the criteria used, quality is always a problem.

Specifications can rarely be so precise that an unscrupulous supplier cannot find a way to beat them. "It's amazing," one contracting officer for the U.S. army once said, "how ingenious contractors are in spotting loopholes in specifications." One supplier almost succeeded in selling back to the Army canned sweet potatoes that had been sold as surplus because they were spoiled. Other contractors have been successful in beating Army specifications

What Makes Quality?

Ethical suppliers will not try to pass off obviously shoddy goods but they can and do ship substandard merchandise. The quality of any material can never be better than the process by which it is made but, unfortunately, it can always be a lot worse. The basic theory behind modern quality control practice is that every process tends to produce material with specifications that fall within a predictable range. If the process is "in control" specifications are within this range, and if it is "out of control they fall outside it.

Role of Engineering. Quality determination usually begins in the buyer's engineering department. The engineer specifies the range of qualities that is acceptable and will sometimes even directly specify the process by which the product should be made. For example, suppose a product has a half-inch hole in it that is needed for ventilation. Almost any old hole will do and the engineer does not care how it is made. So he might just mark "½" D" on the blueprint to indicate the half-inch diameter. By engineering convention, this would mean that the hole could be made with a standard half-inch drill or punch, and the supplier need not worry about it. If the engineer were cost-conscious, he might go one step further. He would actively discourage close tolerances on this hole by marking the hole "for ventilation only" on the blueprint so that everyone would know that it could be made with the cheapest process that was available and that tolerances were not important.

Holes that the engineers really care about are marked either with tolerances or with the specific process. For example, an engineer might mark a half-inch hole on the blueprint as ".500" ± .006" or he might mark it ".500" REAM." With the former, the engineer does not care what process is used as long as the holes can be held within the desired tolerances; in the latter, he is requesting a specific operation-reaming. In the first case, the supplier can probably hold the hole to plus or minus 0.006 inch (or between 0.494 and 0.506 inch) with a single drilling or punching operation. In the second case, the requirement that the hole be reamed makes two operations necessary, since reaming is a finished operation that must be preceded by drilling or punching.

If the engineer does not indicate tolerances for the reamed hole, engineering convention would indicate that they should fall within the normal range of reamed holes but that, apparently, the dimensions will be no problem as long as the hole is reamed. On the other hand, the engineer is really interested in the diameter of the reamed hole, he should indicate this with specific tolerances.

Mean and Dispersion. In no case can the engineer require that a hole be exactly one-half inch in diameter, or 0.500000000 inch. Every process, regardless of how good it is, produces a range of dimensions. The more precise the process, the narrower the dispersion. But the engineer must always be realistic; he should never specify tolerances that are tighter than the process is capable of producing when it is in control.

If the process is in control, the mean characteristic is about equal to specification, and the actual range falls within that specified by the engineer. For example, a half-inch drilling operation might be in control if the mean diameter of the holes drilled was 0.500 inch and the range fell between 0.494 and 0.506 inch.

Quality can be statistically controlled if it is assumed that the process yields a normal distribution about its mean. In the example above, it would be assumed that the control limits of 0.494/0.506 inch were three standard deviations about the mean diameter of 0.500 inch. With a normal distribution, 99.72 percent of all occurrences would therefore fall between these control limits.

If a supplier is on the ball, he will be able to hold any process within its "natural" limits of three standard deviations. In fact, the materials manager who says he buys quality is really insisting that the supplier adhere to two basic rules:

1. Make the product by the required process indicated (implicitly if not explicitly) in the buyer's specifications.
2. Hold the process within three standard deviations of its normal range of fluctuation so that acceptable characteristics are achieved 99.72 percent of the time.

Buyers' Specifications

Suppliers usually will make an item by the required process. The buyer is normally concerned almost entirely with whether or not the supplier is keeping the process in control. He measures the effectiveness of the supplier's process with specifications. The buyer's quality control programme is only as good as the specifications by which quality is measured. There are three basic types of specification commonly used to measure quality: technical, performance, and brand name.

Technical Specifications. Quality can sometimes be measured objectively and impartially with instruments and gauges. The specifications may either be industrywide standards or be determined by the buyer's engineers. Most raw materials are bought to some industry or professional specifications. For example, the Society of Automotive Engineers, the American Iron and Steel Institute, and other organizations have developed specifications for steel. If a buyer orders one-inch bar stock made of SAE 4320 steel, he can define quality standards with considerable precision by using recognized industry specifications. When the order is delivered, his inspectors can measure the diameter, concentricity, and finish of the bars to see if they conform to standards. The quality laboratory can make an analysis of the steel to see if it contains precisely the right alloys in the right amounts. It also can test the material to make certain that its hardness, yield strength, ductility, and so on all are within the specified tolerances.

Similarly, if a company buys parts, its blueprints can specify the type of material and also the exact dimensions and other characteristics that are desired. For example, if the part is to be machined from the one-inch bars described above, the blueprint would indicate each dimension with its permitted tolerance. One dimension might be 0.875 inch with a tolerance of plus or minus 0.020 inch. In some cases much closer tolerances might be needed, but the engineer should never specify a closer tolerance than is really needed if the extra quality contributes nothing to the usefulness of the product.

Performance Specifications. When a company buys a finished product designed by the supplier, it is not particularly interested in a laboratory analysis of the materials or the dimensions of the product's components, Its primary interest is the performance of the product itself. Companies measure quality of such vendor-designed items as machine tools and maintenance, repair, and operating (MRO) supplies with performance specifications.

Performance specifications are sometimes combined with technical specifications. For example, one company requires that the aluminum paint used by its maintenance department dry tack-free in two hours and hard in six hours. It also specifies that the paint must not crack when a test panel is "rapidly bent 180° over a 3/8-inch diameter mandrel." Hiding and hardness qualities also are specified. All these are performance specifications. The company determines whether or not they are being met by applying the paint to a test panel and then measuring drying time and other characteristics.

The procedure for determining conformance to technical specifications little different. Tests are made on the product itself, not on its is application. For example, one technical specification requires that the paint be 13.5 percent pigment and a minimum of 59 percent nonvolatiles. Conformance to it can be determined in a laboratory, by heating the paint to boil off volatiles and by other tests.

Approved Brands. In some cases neither performance nor technical specifications can be developed satisfactorily. In addition, neither type of specification can be developed without incurring some costs. For this reason, most smaller organizations are forced to buy almost every thing on a brand name basis, and even very large organizations do some buying by brand name. For example, it would be difficult even for very large users to develop worthwhile specifications for products such as pickup trucks, copying machines, and electric typewriters. Each manufacturer's brand would be a little different, even though it might be designed to provide almost identical performance at the same prices charged for competing brands. Each manufacturer naturally would claim that his product was the best value. The only objective way the user could evaluate this claim would be to test several brands over a period of years to see if they performed satisfactorily. Careful records of break-downs, repair bills, and user preference would eventually provide objective evidence of quality.

However, the buyer can still make errors with such records. Manufacturers sometimes change specifications and qualities, and a manufacturer whose products have a good history may currently be producing a product inferior to those of his competitors. For this reason, many purchasing departments try to keep abreast of quality changes by asking users of equipment to report regularly on the quality of all newly purchased items.

Whenever possible, the buyer should be given the widest possible choice of competing brands that are equivalent in quality. Most companies test every major brand. Chrysler Corporation's quality standards for electric typewriters are a good example. All major brands-International Business Machines, Remington Rand, Royal-McBee, Underwood, and Smith-Corona are approved. Individual characteristics of each brand are analyzed in Chrysler's specifications. The specification then provides that "selection of the models shall be determined by the requirements of the work to be performed." It further provides that "all factors being equal, the selection of the manufacturer, based upon competition, shall remain with Central Purchasing."

Restrictive Specifications

To prevent misunderstandings, specifications should be as clear and explicit as possible. They should be written so as to encourage a maximum number of suppliers to bid. Preclusive specifications that restrict the number of bidders to a few are a problem in almost every company, They allow for a minimum of competition, and buyers find it impossible to do a first-rate job.

Materials personnel can never relent in their efforts to prevent specifications from becoming restrictive, Working against them are almost all of their regular suppliers and many specifiers and users of material in their own company. Every supplier dreams of customer specifications tailored to his products or processes. No longer would he have to fight for business against a number of competitors. Instad, he would automatically get an order whenever a need arose.

Brand Name. Supplier sales efforts are directed at both materials personnel and the engineers who specify the material. Salesmen try to convince engineers in particular that their product and processes are uniquely superior. In some cases, they may succeed in convincing engineers that theirs is the only product that will do the job. When this is the case, the engineer feels obliged to specify the supplier's product in his design or requisition. He may simply include the supplier's brand name in his specification, or he may describe the product with performance or technical specifications that can be met only by one supplier's brand.

User brand preference is a particularly acute problem in non-profit organizations. The purchasing manager's argument that profits will be higher if lower cost brands are purchased simply does not carry any weight in an organization where profit is not an objective. It is no accident that companies that specialize in supplying the non-profit sectors of the economy, such as educational and hospital supply firms, enjoy rates of return on capital greatly in excess of those earned by companies whose products are subject to intense price competition.

The buyer can sometimes sidestep the brand-name problem by persuading the user to add the phrase "or equal" to his specifications. This permits the buyer to purchase equivalent, competing brands from a number of suppliers. For example, a specification for electric typewriters might read "International Business Machines or equal." The buyer then would be perfectly free to buy from Remington Rand, Underwood, Royal-McBee, or Smith-Corona if he chose to do so, because they are standard, accepted competing brands.

There are more subtle ways in which to make specifications preclusive than convincing engineers that a certain brand is superior, A supplier can achieve the same objective by persuading engineers to incorporate specifications that are unique to his products or processes. Such specifications need not be completely preclusive; all they need do is give the supplier a slight advantage that permits him to underbid competitors without hardship. This is one of the major reasons that suppliers assiduously cultivate company engineers and other requisitioners of material.

Selling with Service. More sophisticated suppliers do not necessarily spend much time or effort trying to convince engineers of the intrinsic superiority of their product, particularly when they are so similar to those of competitors that such a claim would be an insult to the engineers' intelligence, They have a more positive approach: They assist the engineers in product development. As a result of their help, the specifications either become at least partly preclusive or the supplier gets such a headstart on his competitors that he gains the equivalent of restrictive specifications.

This is the best selling approach, since both seller and buyer may gain from it. The seller gets an edge on his competitors and so does not have to compete quite so vigorously on price. The buyer gets the benefit of the seller's technical know-how. The only problem, from the buyer's viewpoint, is that the loss of competition resulting from his giving an advantage to one supplier may more than offset the benefits of the supplier's assistance. Buyers try to overcome this drawback by retaining complete control over which suppliers are chosen to give technical assistance and by working to keep the specifications that are developed as non-restrictive as possible.

The least restrictive specifications are those that impartially measure technical characteristics or performance. The system of approving certain brands is inherently more restrictive, since such tests can never be completely objective. No set of specifications is foolproof, however. Each inevitably as by freezes out at least some potential suppliers, but so long not an adequate number remain who are eager to bid, the buyer need not worry too much.

Securing Quotations

When the buyer has reviewed specification to make certain that they are as unrestrictive as possible, he is ready to solicit quotations from potential suppliers. With new items, buyers try to get at least three competitive quotations (provided the item is not proprietary). For major purchases, six to eight quotations are not uncommon, and when the buyer has difficulty in finding a supplier, he may issue as many as 100 quotation requests.

While buyers should not hesitate to permit any qualified supplier to bid, they obviously cannot permit every possible supplier to quote for every projected purchase. They simply do not have the time or the clerical help to prepare that many quotation requests. Many buyers methodically rotate their lists of potential suppliers in requesting quotations. If a supplier is high bidder on several quotations, his name is temporarily dropped from the list. Suppliers who already have a substantial amount of the buying company's business may also be dropped temporarily if the buyer wants to avoid taking too great a percentage of their capacity.

Buyers often are too generous with quotation requests. It is pointless, for example, to go to the trouble of formally requesting a quotation from a supplier who consistently refuses to sell at prices different from those shown in his cataloguing or published price lists. Nor should a buyer ever request a quotation from a supplier with whom he has no intention of doing business. Quotations are expensive to prepare, and it is unethical to ask suppliers to prepare them when they will not get an order regardless of what price they quote. In general, price should be the only unknown about the supplier at the time the quotation is requested. The buyer should already have investigated the supplier's potential quality, delivery, and service capabilities, although sometimes it is not worth-while to make a really intensive investigation until the supplier has submitted a favourable quotation.

Exceptions to Quotations

The quotation request should include complete specifications for the material, the quantities required, and a tentative delivery schedule. In addition, most purchasing departments indicate a deadline for submission of quotations; some, including almost all government buying offices, refuse to consider late bids. Some companies also print their purchase terms and conditions on their quotation requests.

If suppliers return quotations with all the information requested and take no exception to any terms or conditions, the buyer is ready to analyze his quotes and select the supplier. However, this is frequently not the case. More often suppliers propose changes in specifications delivery schedules, and purchase terms, and they also may make errors.

Exceptions to Specifications. On production parts, suppliers frequently take exception to specifications. They usually suggest minor changes that will permit them to make the part more economically. Occasionally, they may even propose a complete redesign. Most companies try to encourage such suggestions, since they frequently reduce the cost of the item. Some companies even go so far as to include a statement in their quotation request that suggestions are welcomed.

Changes in Schedule. If a supplier cannot deliver material when it is needed, he is automatically disqualified. But sometimes suppliers propose delivery changes that are not so clear-cut. The delivery date requested by the buyer may be unrealistic, and the supplier simply must be given more time to fill the order. In this case, the buyer may have to propose a change in schedule to the various managers in his company who are concerned.

Occasionally a supplier may make what amounts to a counterproposal on delivery terms. For example, the buyer may have requested a quotation for 10,000 units of an item with delivery in ten monthly shipments. Suppose a supplier suggests either a single shipment of 10,000 pieces or two shipments of 5,000 pieces each. Obviously that supplier's bid is not comparable to bids that agree to the original plan.

The buyer should request the supplier to requote on the same delivery basis as originally requested. Then he should compare the two bids from the same supplier. If the şupplier offers a lower price for different delivery terms, the buyer should analyze them to see if they are really if advantageous. Suppose the supplier quotes a price of $1.00 per unit if he can ship in a lot of 10,000 pieces and a price of $1.10 if he must schedule his shipments over a period of ten months at the rate of 1,000 units per month, In effect, the supplier is offering to reduce the total cost of the purchase by $1,000 ($,10 × 10,000) if the buyer will accept the entire order in a single shipment. For this saving the buyer must carry for ten months an average $5,00 inventory instead of a $500 inventory. The buyer can readily determine if this is worthwhile by applying the principles discussed in the chapters on inventory management. If the savings execeed the additional carrying cost (less the saving in procurement cost by processing a single shipment instead of ten separate ones) and possible obsolescence, then the offer to purchase the larger quantity is attractive, The buyer should then go back to the other suppliers who quoted and ask them to requotc on the same basis.

Purchase Terms. The buyer should study each supplier's quotation to make certain that all offer comparable terms and conditions, For example, one supplier may quote a firm price, another may insist on some provision for escalation for labour and material costs, and a third may insist on "price in effect at time of delivery," Obviously these quotations are not comparable, even if all three suppliers quote identical prices,

The buyer should try to persuade suppliers to revise their bids and accept the terms and conditions he wants, On pricing terms, for example, most buyers prefer fixed-price contracts for short lead-time items, all though they will accept escalation on long lead-time contracts in order to prevent suppliers from inflating their bids to allow for possible higher costs.

If the bidder flatly refuses to quote within the terms and conditions desired, the buyer has two choices. He may disqualify the bid, or he may accept it while making allowance for the disadvantageous terms. In the latter case, the buyer may put a price tag on the supplier's terms. Suppose, for example, that a supplier's current price is $1 and his terms are "price in effect at time of delivery," The buyer may have to inflate this bid to $1.02 or $1.03 when comparing it to the quotations of suppliers who are willing to guarantee fixed prices.

Errors. The buyer should review each quotation carefully to make certain the supplier has made no mistakes in preparing it. He should make sure that the supplier's quotation covers the exact requirements described in his quotation request. If it does not, he should return it to the supplier and ask him to requote. The buyer should be particularly wary of bids that are unusually high or low, If a dependable low-cost supplier submits a bid that is substantially higher than those of his competitors, the buyer should return it and have the supplier check it for errors, The buyer should be equally cautious about exceptionally low bids. Only the most inexperienced and naive buyers will quietly accept a bid of 10 cents for an item that is worth at least $1. This is not only unethical—it is uneconomic. The supplier eventually will detect the error and will either request a price increase or, if he feels he has been treated unfairly, refuse to do business with the buyer's company.

If a supplier rechecks a bid and insists that no errors have been made, the buyer should still be cautious if he is convinced that the bid is unrealistic. If the bidder is not too familiar with the buyer's requirements, the buyer may simply disqualify the bid. But if the bidder is an experienced, reliable supplier, the buyer may wish to review the bid in detail with him to make certain there are no errors. He also may arrange to have the specifications explained to the supplier by product or quality control engineers.

Analysis of Quotations

After exceptions and errors have been taken care of, the buyer is ready to tabulate the quotations on a work sheet for purposes of comparison. If there are no special proposals by suppliers, this .comparison is not difficult to make. For each supplier, the buyer would list:

1. Net unit prices proposed for various purchase quantities.
2. Terms of payment.
3. Setup costs and minimum charges, if any.
4. Cost of any special tools to be purchased by buyer for supplier's use.
5. Unit shipping cost if the item is sold on a basis other than f.o.b. buyer's plant.
6. Other charges, if any.

In some cases, the buyer can select the lowest cost supplier with no more than a glance at his recap sheet. If the low bidder is satisfactory in all other respects, he gets the order. However, many buying decisions, particularly important ones, cannot be made so easily. Quotations must be recalculated to make them comparable, quotations may not be for identical items, or all bids may be too high.

Bids Comparable Economically. Quotations from suppliers frequently cannot be compared until the buyer adjusts them to make them comparable. For example, suppose a buyer gets two bids for a part weighing one pound, having a usage of 10,000 units per year, and requiring an investment in special tools. Shipment is to be made in lots of 1,000 pieces.

Supplier A quotes a unit price of $1 f.o.b. buyer's plant with a $2,500 charge for special tools and a special setup charge of $10 for each 1,000-piece lot. His payment terms are 2/10, net 30. Supplier B quotes a unit price of 95 cents f.o.b. shipping point with a $3,500 tool charge and no setup charges. His payment terms are net 30 days, and the LTL freight rate from his plant to the buyer's plant for 1,000-pound shipments is 70 cents per cwt.

It is not immediately obvious which of the two bids is the lower. The buyer must tabulate them for comparison. He would immediately make the following adjustments in the quotations:

	Supplier A	Supplier B
Unit price quoted	$1.00	$.95
Unit freight cost paid by buyer (1 lb. × $.007/lb.)	—	.007
Unit cost of setup charge for 1,000 piece lots	.01	—
Adjusted unit price	$1.01	$.957
Tool cost	$2,500	$3,500
Payment terms	2/10, net 30	net 30

The table above shows that the adjusted unit price of supplier B is $.053 lower but his tool charge is $1,000 higher. Therefore, B must ship 18,867 pieces ($1,000/.053) before his lower unit price more than offsets his higher tool charge. This would take almost 22 months with a usage of 10,000 pieces per year.

In practice, the buyer would want to be reasonably certain that the part will stay in production for at least two years before he would give the order to supplier B. There are two reasons for the buyer to make the break-even point between A and B more than 22 months' usage:

1. The higher tooling cost for supplier B requires an immediate cash outlay. Cash in hand is always worth more than cash derived from savings made in the future. The cash itself is worth some interest during the period. In addition, if the buyer's calculations are

incorrect and the part becomes obsolete immediately, there is less loss.

2. Supplier A offers a 2 percent discount if bills are paid within 10 days; supplier B does not. If the buyer's accounting department pays bills within ten days as a matter of routine, A's discount is a clear saving of $200 per year and the piece-cost saving by buying from B is reduced from $612 per year to $412 per year. The 2 percent discount is a definite "plus" for A, even if the buyer's accounting department ordinarily takes 30 days to pay bills. The 2 percent discount is earned, in effect, if the bill is paid 20 days earlier; this is equal to an annual interest rate of 36 percent. There are few solvent companies that are so strapped for cash that they can afford to overlook such a profitable short-term investment opportunity. In fact, for most purchases any difference in payment terms between suppliers can be considered a direct difference in price.

If the buyer knows precisely how many pieces he will buy over the life of the tooling, he can compare quotations with precision. If the part in the example were to have a life of precisely two years (or a total usage of 20,000 pieces), then the buyer could make the following comparison between suppliers A and B.

	Supplier A	Supplier B
Total piece cost (20,000 pieces at adjusted prices)	$20,200	$19,140
Tool cost	2,500	3,500
Total cost	$22,700	$22,640
Savings buying from supplier B		$60
Discount earned on payment terms		
Net advantage buying from supplier A	$454	
(including payment terms)	$394	

The bids above are so close that it is a toss-up whether the buyer would give the order to supplier A or B. However, there is no doubt that A offers a slightly better deal when payment terms are considered. The buyer, however, would not necessarily give A the order after making the comparison. He might ask B why he did not offer better payment terms if they were normal in his industry.7 Or he might suggest to B that he review his tooling cost to make certain he had received the lowest possible quotation from the tooling shops he contacted. Many suppliers quote on the basis of rather careless estimates of tool costsmade, in many cases, before they have even obtained quotations from tool shops. Thus, they are sometimes willing to reduce tool quotations after they have studied their needs in greater detail. While it is unethical to disclose competitors' bids, some negotiation of this sort is normal before an order is placed.

Bids far Nonidentical Items. The example above is applicable primarily to production parts made to the buyer's specifications. An entirely different problem is encountered in evaluating supplier-designed items. In such cases, bidders usually are quoting on performance specifications. They may be bidding on a machine tool to do a given job or a component to perform a given function. In each case the supplier is selling both his design efforts and his manufacturing skills. Since each supplier's design is unique, bids are not comparable. Technical evaluation is necessary.

In such cases, engineers carefully review each supplier's proposal. They indicate not only which proposals they prefer but which are acceptable. Suppliers whose bids are not acceptable may be asked by the buyer to requote, especially if their proposed prices are attractive.

The final buying decision is based on both the buyer's evaluation of the economic factors of the bid and the engineer's evaluation of the technical factors. Some companies evaluate bids on a point basis. Engineers assign preference ratings to each bid which reflect their technical evaluation of the supplier's product. They list their preferences in sequence (1, 2, 3, 4) and also indicate separately bids that are unacceptable to them. The buyer lists his preferences in sequence. If a bidder gets a top rating from both the buyer and the engineer, there obviously is no problem. But what of a bidder rated only second or third by an engineer is rated tops by the buyer? In such cases, the buyer and engineer usually try to resolve their differences. In many instances the buyer's preference will prevail if the engineer agrees that the third-best bid is still technically acceptable. In some instances, buyer and engineer may compromise and accept a bid that is second best to both but still fulfills their objectives.

Negotiation of bids. Good buyers do not necessarily accept the low bid even if they are sure it is made by a first-rate supplier and is comparable to competitors' bids. They may even reject all bids if they feel the lowest acceptable quotation is too high.

Buyers do not reject bids arbitrarily, however. They rely as much as possible on objective price data to assist them in negotiation. Even if the buyer is satisfied, there usually still is some need for negotiation. Packaging, freight rates, supplier inventories, split shipments, and so on may be discussed.

❐

9

Price Determination and Negotiations

IMPORTANCE OF PURCHASING IN PRICE MANAGEMENT

The management of purchase prices is a major task given to all purchasing departments in industrial organisation. Traditional purchasing theory has placed equal weighting on the need to obtain the right 'uality, right quantity, right delivery, right place and right price. It would, of course, be incorrect to assert that price should be the dominant factor in the sourcing decision. However price can be seen as a function of the other 'right' characteristics. In other words, the seller will determine a price only when the other factors are known. There are dramatic consequences when inadequate attention is paid to the level of purchase prices. At a minimum, inflated purchase prices can make the end product uncompetitive in its market, with a resulting fall in sales. The implication of purchase prices upon cash flow will not be lost on those who are sensitive to the corporate financial position. In the final analysis the purchasing department is accountable for the organisation's expenditure. There cannot be a more responsible task.

Price can be defined as 'an agreement between seller and buyer concerning what each is to receive, embodied in a formal ratio between quantities of money and quantities of goods or services modified by formal and explicit or informal and implicit understandings'. Such an agreement will be influenced by many factors which explain the subtleties of industrial purchase price management. The nature of the contract; possession and ownership privileges and responsibilities; the form of money to be rendered (including barter arrangements); and the buyer's negotiation ability illustrate the variations inherent in a pricing decision.

Industrial pricing is not a science and cannot be defined in finite terms. There is however a plethora of economic writers who have sought to establish theoretical bases appropriate to various market conditions. The resultant theories seek to explain the pricing mechanism. It is outside the scope of this volume. The reader is directed to Volume 2, *The Economic Aspects of Management*, of this treatise to consider these theories, bearing in mind that in the real world the industrial buyer is usually faced with monopoly or near-monopoly competition. Scherer emphasised one problem facing industrial buyers when he said:

> Collusion to secure monopolistic prices and profits is a venerable, if not venerated institution. It was practised in ancient Babylon, Greece and Rome. Adam Smith remarked sagely that people of the same trade seldom meet together, even for merriment and diversion but the conversation ends in a conspiracy against the public, or in some contrivance to raise prices.

Leighton saw price as the classical economic relationship between supply and demand, but raised the consideration of contests or gaming when he asserted.

Price may be looked at in another way, that is, as the outcome of a power or bargaining relationship. It represents, on the seller's side, an attempt to charge as much as he can get consistent with making the sale; on the buyer's side, it represents an attempt to pay as little as possible and still obtain the product.

Bargaining possibilities are not irrelevant to many pricing decisions when seen from the buyer's viewpoint. The seller's initial offer may be unclear or unacceptable in relation to important contractual features. For example, the proposed price may not take account of desired warranty timing. It is axiomatic that since the buyer is a participant in such negotiations he becomes one of the determinants in the pricing process of industry.

Leighton concluded that little is known about effective price determination. Intuition, guesswork and unsubstantiated assumptions about the behaviour of costs and competitors are alleged to be regular features in the pricing decisions of some organisations. He says that, 'There is remarkably little that is of real practical value to the businessman faced with the problem of price determination. A major gap exists here that remains to be closed.

Some years later, Oxenfeldt, a leading authority on pricing was to refer to the same gap, 'The gap between pricing literature and practice may exist because the authors lack extensive personal experience with the practical problems facing executives in a highly competitive and complex business environment'.

There has been little research into the role of the industrial buyer in the pricing decision. The author undertook an extensive postgraduate study from which much information for this book has been drawn. The examples used are derived from operational situations and are not therefore theoretical in origin.

The background to understanding the role of the industrial buyer in the pricing decision can be found in three specific functions:

(a) establishing the initial price of a purchase;

(b) managing purchase price increase requests;

(c) achieving reductions in the existing purchase prices. Each of these areas is now considered in such a way that the remainder of the book's content will become meaningful.

Establishing the Initial Price of a Purchase

The establishment of the initial price of purchased goods and materials is a critical phase of the purchasing cycle. Provided the buyer can avoid a monopoly source, he has access to the pricing opinions of many potential sellers in the supply market. The precise number will depend on the extent of his search and the seller's responsiveness to the buyer's enquiries.

Buskirk recognised the assertive role for buyers in the pricing process.

The modern industrial marketplace is a professionally-oriented environment with purchasers sophisticated as regards the value and price of goods and services offered. Today, educated and highly trained buyers assisted by the engineering staff, select the best product for the job.

Whilst this ,optimistic note is encouraging there have been many contrary views expressed. Inertial has been identified as a prime element in industrial buying behaviour, and one may there-fore conclude that there is an inadequate attempt by many buyers to define the supply side of the 'supply and demand' equation. Harding concluded that:

1. Inertia is probably the most powerful purchasing influence, the single most important reason for selecting a supplier is that the source has been used before, and
2. The role of middle management is underestimated, particularly in regard to initiation and conclusion of a purchase, while the importance of top management and the purchasing department is correspondingly inflated.

In a detailed study of buyer behaviour in regard to the purchas-ing of sintered components by Winkler has confirmed the inertial approach to source searching.

Inertia is a great weakness of British buying and some suppliers enjoy enormous profit margins because their customers do not want to take the risk of upsetting the settled order of things, or to investigate alternate sources of supply. A study of the steel strip industry revealed that about three quarters of the companies had relied on the same suppliers for ten years, even though there were over 20 companies capable of supplying the goods.

The allegations of inertia will persist as long as the industrial buyer adopts a strategy and uses tactics that do not provide an adequate and continuing overview of the market place.

England and Leenders advance three succinct views on pricing which are relevant to establishing a price:

The determination of price to be paid is one of the major decisions to be made by a purchasing agent. Indeed, the ability to get a good price is sometimes held to be the price test of a good buyer. If by 'good price' is meant greatest value, broadly defined, this may well be true. But if this is interpreted as meaning the very lowest attainable unit price or that price is a residue factor, to be considered only after the underlying elements of technical fitness and quantity have been determined, then the statement is by no means correct.

Resources Management

The task of purchasing management is to ensure that an appropriate level of resources is available to deal with all aspects of the pricing decision. It is clear that the relatively low status of buying in the corporate hierarchy remains a principal weakness in industry. Many organisations have failed to recognise the contribution that can be made by an effective purchasing operation to the achievement of the corporate plan. Purchase prices have a direct relationship to profit. Rs. *n* saved on purchases represents Rs. *n* additional profit, it is so simple!

Understaffing of the purchasing department will inevitably restrict the time available for sourcing studies. It will also prevent detailed efforts to gain an understanding of the supplier's cost structure, competition, future investment plans and market penetration. Almost certainly there will be a failure to penetrate the foreign supply market, which despite its potential hazards, affords an opportunity to control purchase prices. The employment of purchase price analysts remains a relative novelty in the purchasing departments of industry, as indeed does the function of purchase research.

Stigler and Kindahl raise an interesting aspect of resource allocation when they observe that:

A buyer could go out each day and shop for the cheapest seller of copper, but he would be a profligate buyer in his expenditures on search, negotiation, testing of products, and all other costs of creating and maintaining a trading relationship. So he commonly buys on contract, often at a fixed price which is his estimate of the average price over the contract period.

A non-biased observer would believe that Stigler and Kindahl advance excellent justification for a 'profligate' buyer.

In organisational terms, purchase price analysis has become a key purchasing activity in many companies around the world. There are few however who have the capability to analyse all purchase prices. Selective analysis takes place and is usually related to the level of expenditure on individual items. A Pareto analysis is used to identify the top 80 per cent of expenditure. These items are usually designated. 'key' components and are subjected to a rigorous cost scrutiny. In a similar manner any company which receives a significant proportion of total expenditure will be subjected to the same scrutiny.

There remains the opposing view to the claim that purchase price analysis is necessary. Before this is considered it is useful to examine the author's research into this aspect of industrial buyer behaviour. In a study where five hundred industrial buyers were asked of circumstances where they ask for detailed cost break-downs of selling prices, their response is shown in Table 1. The reader should be aware that multiple responses were possible, accounting for N = 1019.

Table 1

Circumstances When Buyers Seek Cost Breakdowns

Circumstances in which Detailed Cost Breakdowns are Sought	*Respondents Indicating Factor*	*Percentage of Total N = 500*
When buying a new item	281	56.2
When buying a modified item	186	37.2
Faced with a request for a price increase	361	72.2

When internal cost pressures force attention on material prices	163	32.6
Other	28	5.6
Total number of responses	1019	

Each of the four major situations shown above represents an opportunity for the buyer to seek cost data. It is clear that the price increase request will stimulate more buyers to seek it than, for instance, when the item is being purchased for the first time. This is a surprising situation when one bears in mind that the learning curve technique is very relevant at the first time purchase, offering the scope for future price negotiations. Note that cost breakdowns at the price increase request stage are of relatively little merit when there is no original data against which to compare it. England comments:

> Regardless of experience, however, some people have an almost uncanny ability to determine a good price. They apparently follow no rule or definite procedure in arriving at these decisions and if called upon to justify their conclusions would have great difficulty in doing so. They have a certain feel of the market which is at once both sensitive and accurate.

The words of England are also pertinent as he seemingly discourages the buyer from enquiring into the seller's costs. He states:

1. In most cases suppliers do not know their costs and it would be useless to Inquire into thom.
2. The interpretation of costs calls for an exercise of judgment and differences of opinion would arise even if all the figures were available.
3. Suppliers would not divulge this information.
4. The seller's costs do not determine his market price.

5. The buyer is not interested in the supplier's costs any way... if the seller's price does not cover costs, either in ignorance or with full recognition of what he is doing, the matter is his problem and not the buyer's.

Developments in the 1970s, in particular the high level of price increases after the 1973 oil crisis, have refuted some of these points. Whilst one accepts that judgment is an element in decision making the observation about 'feel of the market' is spurious logic for academics and no evidence is provided by which the reader may judge its accuracy. One suspects that it may be true for highly organised commodity markets, for example, tin, copper and silver. Such markets offer a responsive information service whose immediacy is unique when compared with the much less organised markets in which the industrial buyer seeks his wares. There are positive reasons to support the view that product complexity, material content complexity and manufacturing methods are fundamental reasons that make a market feel extremely difficult and therefore imprecise. Detailed purchase price analysis has its personal complexity approach and detail, frequently applied after receipt of the seller's quotation. Unless corporate management is prepared to make a commitment to staff the purchasing function at an appropriate level, the inevitable consequence will be wasteful expenditure.

Buyer's Role in Price Management

Divergent opinions may exist, but none deny the buyer's role in price management. This role is now considered in more detail. It may be seen as a purely reactive role in which prices are received from the seller and passively accepted. Conversely, the role may be seen as authoritative wherein the buyer participates in the industrial pricing process and ultimate decision. The tripartite role of the industrial buyer is complete when the regulatory nature of his pricing role is considered.

Ammer considers the regulatory role when he observes that:

> In most cases the supplier does not have the last word on prices. Able buyers can exert tremendous leverage if they

really understand how prices are set and don't hesitate to use their skills. In doing so, they are doing a service not only to their own company but also to the supplier and to the economy as a whole.

This observation is thoroughly constructive and perspicacious. The industrial buyer's investigative role should exert a pressure on sellers to re-check the relationship of costs to prices. For example, a skilled application of purchase price analysis prior to any production start-up may lead the seller to investigate improved productivity and possibly a reduction of the selling price. This aspect of price determination has so far been ignored by economists and business policy authors.

An examination of the collective role of industrial buyers is rarely contemplated. A concerted effort only to award business to low cost producers, forcing high cost producers to re-appraise outdated methods, would indisputably make the international economy healthier and more productive. Above all an effective price challenge prevents complacency in a seller's pricing decision-making process. This consideration raises the importance of taking into account the nature of the purchase. For example, both buyer and seller may be forced into pricing the buyer's 'own' designated item. In this case no previous pricing standard will exist. This situation must be contrasted with the seller's branded item, where totally different pricing criteria may pertain.

Managing Purchase Price Increase Requests

The industrial buyer is being increasingly asked to undertake programmes of cost avoidance. These are conducted in the area of price increase requests made by the seller. There are three main ways in which the buyer can react:

1. He can pay a part of the total increase requested.

2. He can refuse to pay the proposed price increase.

3. He can delay the date of implementation of the percentage price increase agreed.

The method of the inert buyer will be to settle at the full amount without any challenge. If, however, he takes an initiative on items 1 to 3, there are benefits accruing to his company and many reporting systems require regular monitoring of cost avoidance figures. A thorough literature search did not reveal any previous research study on this aspect of the buyer's task. An authoritative and coprehensive study in this vital area is necessary from two points of view. Recent inflation has led to an unprecedented influx of price increase requests, frequently on a three monthly basis. The number of these requests has obvious implications for the method used in handling them, and for the basis of decision judgments of industrial buyers. The second point concerns implications for industrial marketing and the enhancement of knowledge in this field.

Negotiation is a technique that has not been adequately considered in relationship to the management of price increase requests. This is of direct relevance to the regulatory role of buyers in pricing decisions. Risley subscribes to the positive nature of this regulatory role when he says:

> Buyers can and will do everything possible to ameliorate the impact of price increases and to seek price decreases. All this is good. The net result is to help slow inflation and to provide more value, hopefully, the value which serves the customer best.

Development of the perception of a regulatory role for industrial buyers inevitably requires an appraisal of the prime price elemental facets that may be regulated. Profit concepts are one aspect in this regard and Ammer saw a direct correlation between price increases and improvements in profit:

> Naturally when costs and prices go up, profits go up proportionally. Most suppliers follow this convention. Therefore a buyer can assume regardless of what the supplier's cost breakdown shows, that a request for a price increase includes a request for added profit. If competitive conditions warrant it the the buyer should not

> be outraged at such a request. In fact he should not hesitate to use his buying power (if he has enough) to push down the price of an item so far that there is no profit in it for the supplier. However the buyer who feels his supplier 'are entitled to a profit' is naive. It is not the buyer's job to help the supplier to make profits. On the contrary the buyer's.role is to serve as a countervailing force that limits supplier's profits. If the buyer is really effective, he may occasionally eliminate the inefficient and unprofitable suppliers from his ranks.

The management of price increase requests will vary, in detailed approach, from company to company. Meek acceptance represents one extreme, whilst an insistence on the seller substantiating requests with supportive cost data represents the opposite polarity. The view can be advanced that the seller's willingness to provide such substantiation will encourage a meaningful dialogue between the two parties. McGarry put the matter into a context of inherent suspicion by averring:

> ...the parties are at variance not only because of different valuations placed upon the objects of trade but also because, historically, the market place has always been a bloodless battleground where man can match his wits with other men for a material or psychic advantage...the market place has always been the happy hunting groundJor all sorts of shysters, mountebanks and charlatans. Here the predators of every age have looked for their victims among the innocent, the credulous and the gullible.

It is no accident that ancient laws pronounced the maxim caveat emptor.

The warning still applies. The industrial buyer's agreement on trading arrangements, *e.g.*, specifications, delivery and pricing terms, will be formalised by a written contract. Any discussion on pricing should take due account of the pervasive nature and influence of contractual proposals, discussions and agreements.

Many authors have postulated a lack of trust between buyer and seller. One would, in consequence, consider that the pricing process, with its juxtaposing of buyer and seller, would kindle any inherent mistrust. Tucker pointed out that pricing kindle any inherent mistrust. Tucker pointed out that pricing may be perceived as a contest between the individual seller and the individual buyer. This immediately conjurs up an image of a winner and a loser; two ingredients of an unsuccessful negotiation. Tucker continues specifically: 'The buyer is not concerned with the seller's costs nor with his need to make a profit..the market is a potpourri of prices which allows a profit to some sellers and denies profit to others'.

Achieving Reductions in the Existing Purchase Prices

The two prime areas thus far considered represent situations where the buyer is prompted into action by a third party. In the instance of the initial price the actual requirement to buy is the prompter. The industrial buyer, in the case of the new buy, must obtain the materials or components, and must in consequence agree the initial price. The price increase request will emanate from the seller who may therefore be seen as the prompter. There is, however, a further instance in which the industrial buyer is the prompter in the pricing process.

The significant point is the danger of the buyer opting out of this role. Inertia will be truly reflected by an abdication of responsibility for cost reduction in purchased items. Effective cost reduction programmes will require that other functional areas in the buyer's company are involved. For example, a proposed cost reduction may require a change in product design. But the risk of inter-departmental conflict and the implications of product change acceptance in the end-market could well act as a deterrent to such a change.

There are many opportunities for achieving cost savings, as the following checklist shows: changes in specification; substitution of materials and processes; slow moving stock utilisation; negotiation; savings on inter-company purchases; standardisation; volume discounts; rebates; improved transportation and logistics; increased delivery rate prior to price increase; return of obsolete stock for credit; sale of scrap; increased use of long term contracts; reduction in inventory to minimise working capital; enhancement of equipment and tool life; development of new sources to counteract monopoly supply situation; use of corporate agreements; effective use of contract price adjustment formulae; packaging changes; increased quantity offtake for EBQ (Economic Batch Quantity) benefits; systems contracting; value engineering/value analysis programmes.

The Optimum Thinking

At this stage it is necessary to consider the philosophy required to create a purchasing department capable of fulfilling its role in price management. It requires the total support of a corporate management who want an assertive role for buyers. This will require a policy aimed at preventing others in the company, who are lacking in commercial acumen, from interfering in the final decision to buy.

It is also reasonable to expect a purchasing department to the staffed by those who are dedicated to their chosen profession. This demands that they become qualified and continue to up-date themselves on key issues. This will be no mean feat! In the author's view corporate management must take a more deter-mined stance in asking for evaluation of purchasing performance. There remains an unfortunate legacy of some buyers who will not submit to more demanding methods of appraisal. This is quite unacceptable in the field of pricing.

In the larger organisations it is usually necessary to consider reorganisation to meet the demands of effective purchase price management. This may involve corporate negotiations on key items which affect the individual company profit centre concept. In many ways, purchasing theory and organisational approaches are evolving slowly and there remains a considerably gap in the knowledge in these areas.

Finally, in philosophical terms, the purchasing department will never succeed in minimising prices if they work in a vacuum. It will be necessary to harness the skills of internal specialists who can offer advice on the product characteristics. Such advice must be aimed at eradicating unnecessary features. The buyer should then harness the skills of existing and potential sources of supply and maintain a programme of scrutinising purchase prices. This can be done with complete integrity, maintaining supplier loyalty, whilst encouraging potential suppliers to become competitive.

Industrial Buyer Behaviour

The pervasive chacter of the pricing decision makes it necessary to review a wide range of literature upon which industrial buyer behaviour may be modelled. Such a base includes, marketing, finance, economics, purchasing, business policy, and to a lesser extent, production management. This chapter represents the first comprehensive analysis of such literature to appear in book form. It includes references from published books, learned journals, professional magazines and unpublished these emanating from universities.

Individual Characteristics

The Buyer's Expectations will Include:

Product	*Suppliers*
Quality	Known reputation
Quantity	Size and organisational
Technical applications	philosophy
Desired after sales service	Geographical location
Delivery time and reliability	Reciprocity agreements
	Buyer—salesman relationships
Price	Financial stability
Contractual terms and conditions	Responsiveness to abnormal operational requests
Anticipated life of product	Legal and political considerations

The expections will vary in emphasis and consideration according to the following factors:

The buyer's background and technical understanding

The buyer's product knowledge

The buyer's knowledge of alternative sources of supply

The buyer's active search characteristics, stimulus, determinants of range of search beyond national boundaries

The perceived satisfaction with past supplier performance

Generalised self-confidence

Pressure from other organisational members

Accountability for adverse buying outcomes

Purchased items essentiality to the organisation

Purchased items cost implications on finished product sales opportunities

The buyer's perceived role in pricing

The buyer's role within the Decision Making Unit.

The degree of influence that the individual buyer exerts will vary with the organisation's assigned roles. The allegations and observed inertia of buyers raises the question of their perceived role or boundaries of influence. The adage 'Every buyer possesses the right to challenge any specification but not the right to change', signifies one sphere of influence.

It is questionable if many industrial buyers initiate an active programme of effective challenge to specificaitions. There are those who will subordinate themselves without resistance to other members of the organisation. This behavioural style will result in a reactive buying role in contrast to an authoritative or innovatory role. The manner in which the buyer perceives others roles and influence and their consequent acceptance or rejection of his judgement and decisions is also important.

Credibility of the industrial buyer in his internal and external relationships will be achieved in many ways. It is reasonable to believe that achievements stemming from effective decision taking will be pre-eminent. The relationship of the buying department to other functional departments will influence the buyer's expectations and the reward system cannot be ignored. Finally it is necessary to include the individual's characteristics: age, sex, life style, education, family background, cultural, ethnic and geographical origin, value system, social and group affiliation outside his job, personality traits, motivations, ambitions and dependents, and decision-making style.

Interpersonal Relationships

Buying decisions may be made severally, jointly or autonomously, depending upon product and company specific factors. These are shown in Figure 1.

In each instance conflict between those involved in the buying decision is probable and may arise because of different views about products and suppliers. The conflict may be due to criteria used in the evaluation of alternatives or differences in buying goals or determined objectives. The conflict may be latent or patent and may centre on the style of decision-making. The ability of the beyer to resolve the conflict will depend upon his problem solving style, persuasiveness and bargaining skills.

Organisational Variables

Table 2 shows the organisational variables. This final classification includes information inputs to the buying function and their capture. The physical environment will frequently determine the manner in which purchasing decisions are made. The political, economic, legal and cultural pressures and relevance, must also be considered as facets of the industrial buying process.

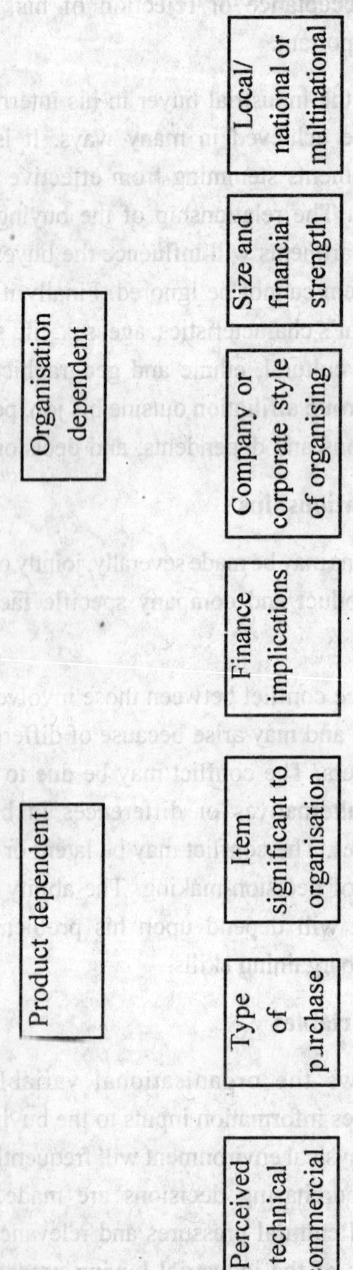

Fig.1. Interpersonal relationship—factors influencing decision.

Table 2

Organisational Variables

Tasks	*Nature of purchase*	*Structure*	*People*
New item Rebuy	General item	Communication system	Users
straight	Pure commodity	Authority system	Buyers
modified	Key item	Status system	Influencers
Buying process	Routine purchase	Reward system	Deciders
Need	Capital item		Gatekeepers
Specification			
Technology			
Search criteria			
Evaluation of offers			
Choice			
Monitor			
Performance			
appraisal			

Expectations

The limited number of research programmes into industrial buyer behaviour indicates that there are many aspects that require more detailed thought. Stogdill defines expectation as readiness for reinforcement being a function of drive, the estimated probability of the occurrence of a possible outcome and the estimated desirability of the outcome. He continues:

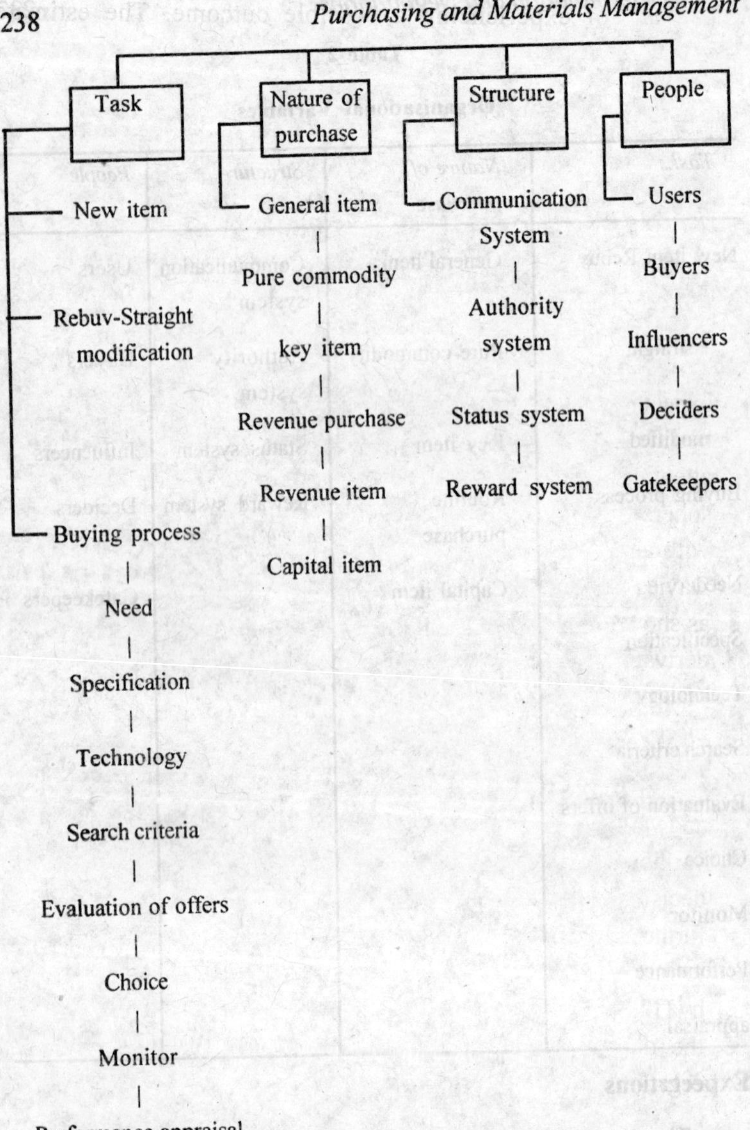

By reinforcement is meant the experiencing of an outcome which tends to meet, fulfil, satisfy or confirm the expectations. By readiness for reinforcement is meant the extent to which an individual is prepared or unprepared to experience or be reconciled or unreconciled to the prospect of experiencing a possible outcome. The estimated probability or occurrence of an out-come refers to an individual's prediction, judgement, or guess, relative to the likelihood that a given event will occur. The estimated desirability of an outcome is an individual's judgement relative to the satisfyingness of need for, demand for, appropriateness of or pleasantness of a possible outcome. Estimates of probability and desirability interact to determine the level of expectation.

A critical study of these views leads to a conclusion that these expectations and their possible satisfying by experience should ideally be integrated with the planning process. There has been increasing attention to the strategic planning necessary in the industrial buying sphere. Ideally, the purchasing strategic plan should be integrated with and be a derivative of the corporate long-term business plan. Davies demonstrated an advanced approach to this aspect of planning as shown in Figure 3, although his schematic presentation is a direct derivative from Humble who presented an overview of the, strategic planning process within which individual decision-making must take place.

Haksansson and Wootz, when considering, the industrial buyer and variables in decision-making, concluded that there are three basic variables. These are concerned with the purchasing situation, the decision-maker, and finally, the decision environment. Prior to a further consideration of Haksansson and Wootz's views it is necessary to introduce the simultaneous nature of decision-making as evinced by Glueck. He identifies four key points; the contents of the decision, the decision process, information necessary for decisions, and organisational design criteria. Their expansive nature is shown below.

Contents of Decision

1. Strategy formulation, design of systems for strategy implementation.

2. Innovation in patterns of products, markets and technology.

3. Economic, socio-political, technological, multinational, multi-industry perspective.

Decision Process

1. Emphasis on anticipation, rational analysis, use of specialists, techniques for coping with novel decision situations.

2. Technology intensive process.

Information for Decisions

1. Formal systems for anticipatory, external environment information.

2. Interactive two way communication channels linking managers and other professionals.

3. Emphasis on continual planning, covering operations, projects, systems resource development.

4. Computer systems emphasising richness, flexibility and accessibility of information.

5. Control, based on cost-benefit forecasts.

Organisational Design Criteria

1. Simultaneous continuous emphasis on efficiency, productivity and innovation.

2. Emphasis in flexible, adaptive response.

3. Emphasis on best design of ad hoc organisation to perform given task.

It now becomes possible to integrate the approach of Glueck with that of Haksansson and Woọtz in order to elementalise the two main variable factors.

Purchasing Situation

Five major variables are relevant:

1. Major changes in the availability of key raw materials, sub-assemblies and other classifications of purchases.

2. Major changes in pricing and contractual conditions affecting major raw materials, etc.

3. Additional entry of potential sources of supply into the global market situation.

4. Exit of existing sources of supply from the supply market.

5. Technological breakdown affecting equipment or system of delivery of products or service offered by the company.

The Individual decision-maker may be characterised according to his personal qualities. These may be instanced by the following: *(a)* leader; *(b)* administrative planner; *(c)* extrapolative planner; *(d)* entrepreneur; *(e)* statesman; *(f)* system architect.

The observed behaviour of industrial buyers suggests that more supplier development programmes are being conducted. These can have direct impact on pricing behaviour and the buyer-seller dyad. It would be possible, for example, to provide the seller with an interest free loan, permitting him to expand his manufac-turing facilities. This could lead to a trad-off on price as a method of loan repayment; a benefit which could continue when loan repayment is complete. In this way both buyer and seller gain advantages.

This logic may be faulted in one major area. It is incorrect to assume that all industrial buying action begins with a purchase requisition. To suggest this is to condemn the function to a reactive ole. There are undoubtedly occasions, depending upon the nature of the purchase mix, when the buyer has an opportunity to take advantage of a market situation. To achieve this it is necessary for the buyer to circumvent the provisioning system and to contract in anticipation of a need. An entrepreneurial environment within business planning is a pre-requisite for this type of operation. This rationale may be pursued to further develop a model of buyer responses.

Stimuli		*Responses*
Marketing actions (a) Product and service variables (b) Price (c) Promotional efforts (d) Distribution mix	THE INDUSTRIAL BUYER	Communication responses (a) Awareness (b) Attitude Purchase responses (a) Product usage (b) Source loyalty

In another model, whose price is listed as a stimulus in respect of industrial buyer the attitude of the buyer is an inclusive factor. The task and non-task theorems of Webster and Wind must be considered in this regard:

1. **Minimum Price Mode.** This has been used in an attempt to explain the behaviour of firms and assumes that the buyer has near perfect information concerning the alternatives in the market,place. This is, however, a major assumption that is unproven. Indeed there is direct evidence and data which contradict such an assumption.

2. **Lowest Total Cost Model.** This is essentially an elaboration of the minimum price model but assumes a goal of profit max-imisation and a very well informed buyer.

3. **Rational Buyer Model.** Buying rationally and patronage of suppliers was first discussed by Copeland in 1924. Research has now advanced far beyond this outline. Rational buying may now be seriously questioned and related to industrial buying methodology.

4. **Materials Management Model.** Materials management has become accepted as an organisational alternative to traditional buying. The search for lowest costs is inherent in this model but is related to a total logistics situation.

5. **Reciprocal Buying Model.** Reciprocity is anathema to many industrial buyers who resent and resist the practice of buying from suppliers on the condition that they purchase the company's products. Some would argue that it is the

seller who would exert pressure on the buyer making a buying' decision.

6. **The Constrained Choice Model.** Most supplier selection decisions involve choosing from a limited set of potential suppliers. The model assumes that inertia is a major determinant of buying behaviour and rightly stresses habital behaviour, the tendency to favour previous sources.

The six models outlined above are task modelling, related to economic emphasis. There are however a wider range of non-task, non-economic factors that must be considered:

1. Self Aggrandisement Model. This emphasises the desire of the buyer to use his position in the organisation as a means to enhance his own income by obtaining favours from potential vendors. Credence must be given to this aspect of buyer modelling. Disturbing events in the United Kingdom in the 1970shave shown that a minority of buyers wire permitting favours to influence their patronage decisions.

2. Ego Enhancement Model. It is logically asserted here that few will take offence at statements or behaviour which recognise their individuality and worth as human beings.

3. Perceived Risk Model. Emphasis is placed upon the buyer's uncertainty as he evaluates alternative courses of action. Various strategies may be adopted to minimise risk. Avoiding a decision and misplaced loyalty are two obvious examples.

4. Dyadic Interaction Model. This emphasises the vital influence of role expectations.

5. Lateral Relationship Model. Consideration of interaction among members of the buying group is rightfully given some prom-inence. On occasions there may be six or more members involved in the decision to buy.

6. Buying Influences Model. This model is directly analogous to the lateral relationship model. The buying influences model concentrates on the influences within the buying department. This is of increasing relevance as the trend towards specialisation within industrial buying takes place. Use of a purchase research specialist will provide outline market and pricing profiles which influence the buyer's decision. Expeditors are having an increasing impact upon supplies rating methodology; continually late deliveries will be a dissuading factor in the decision to rebuy.

Kellogg provided a dramatic extension of the lateral relationship model when he identified the following functional areas within the organisation that could be involved in the industrial buying process:

General Management	Shipping
Finance	Industrial Engineering
Research and Development	Production Control
Engineering	Quality Control
Production	Marketing
Factory Receiving	Sales Management
Stores Control	Purchasing

Other Approaches

Kotler writes as a marketing strategist and offers various interpretative models of the buyer; whilst the emphasis is on consumer behaviour it is equally important to analysis of industrial buyer behaviour. His models are outlined below; although the views expressed are my own.

Marshallian Economic Model

Bentham originally subscribed to the view that man was finely calculating and one who weighed the expected pleasures and pains of every contemplated action. It was however Marshall who consolidated the economic theory and synthesised it into demand-supply analysis, which remains the main source of micro-economic thought. If economic man maximises his utility by carefully calculating the felicitous consequences of every purchase it suggests that industrial buyers have a major task in purchase price management. Simple demand supply theories ignore the detail of how product and brand preferences are formed, thereby omitting a significant factor in the overall situation.

Pavlovian Learning Model

The Russian psychologist Pavlov originated the stimulus response model of human behaviour, based upon the four central concepts, drive, cue, response and reinforcement. This theory is particularly analogous to industrial buying if one considers the effects of advertising on the buying decision.

Freudian Psychoanalytical Model

This model raises the central issue that buyers are probably motivated by symbolic, as well as economic and functional concerns. This view is particularly relevant to the industrial buying process where there is a decision need in terms of specifications. At times the buyer does not have a choice because of the designer's imposition of a predetermined quality specification. The ego aspects of the industrial buyer's decision process cannot be ignored because hopes, dreams and fears may, under some circumstances, stimulate a purchase from a particular seller.

Veblenian Social-Psychological Model

Thorstein Veblen, a distinguished economist who later evolved into a social thinker saw man as a social animal, whose buying decisions were aimed largely at prestige. This can be seen as relevant to industrial buying particularly depending upon the culture, social class and reference groups of the buyer.

Hobbesian Organisational Factors Model

This is specifically a satisfying model where the industrial buyer steers a course between satisfying his own needs and those of his organisation. Rationality of the ultimate decision is now in question.

There are occasions when irrationality would be the concluding opinion, having examined a particular purchase decision. This has applications when price is considered. The lowest offer on price is not certain to be awarded a contract, a decision made on irrational bases. Suspicion that a new source could cause problems is an observed view from industrial buyers.

Influence of the Social Sciences

The social sciences provide a useful basis upon which to enhance the originating influence of Kotler. Four areas ranging from psychology to anthropology can be identified. The considerations in each of the four areas are shown in Table 3.

Table 3

Social Science Influence Model

Psychology	*Social Psychology*	*Sociology*	*Anthropology*
Appeals			
Association			
Attitudes			
Behavirourism		Communication	
Beliefs		Defferentiation	
Cognition	Attitude measurement	Diffusion	
Consciousness	Behaviour	Group deisions	
Dissonance	Interaction	Environment	Attitudes
Emotions	Empathy	Group dynamics	Characteristics
Habit	Interpersonal relations	Impact	Cultural dynamics

Psychology	*Social Psychology*	*Sociology*	*Anthropology*
Identification	Masss psychology	Innovation	Standards
Imagery	Motivations	Opinions	Cultural log
Impulse	Power structure	Propaganda	Satus
Interests	Public opinion	Systms	
Judgements	Situational behaviour	Recognition	
Learning	Role	Recall	
Motivations		Stimuli	
Projection			
Reasoning			
Stimuli			
Sublimation			

The industrial buyer is continually faced with the choice of an appropriate course of action in dealing with a perceived problem. Models of the buyer's behaviour have, correctly, emphasised the organisational influences on the decision-making process. The social science influence model usefully extends the logic to include psychological (and related) factors, which are relevant to the emotive characteristics of pricing management.

Summary of Industrial Buyer Behaviour

The modelling of industrial buyer behaviour has reached a critical stage of development. Recognition has been given to the buyer's role in decision-making, particularly in the context of a broad-based decision-making unit. The macro-modelling has undoubtedly been useful in developing an appreciation of the buyer's corporate role. The outstanding weakness in all the modelling is the lack of conclusive research effort into the micro elements of industrial buyer behaviour. Until these are more fully researched there will be limits on further understanding of both macro and micro situations.

Negotiation Skills

Negotiation is the essential part of positive, authoritative rôle in the industrial pricing process. Many knowledgeable purchasing specialists, involved in price negotiations, lose major opportunities to gain concessions because of their failure to comprehend the finer points of negotiation. An attention on the interpersonal skills required in negotiation is the case topic of the following discussion. Whilst the behavioural specialists have expended considerable effort in researching human interaction, the conflict between buyer and seller remains a misunderstood and misinterpreted phenomenon.

Definitions

Aljian relates negotiation to price when he states that 'The negotiation process provides a legitimate and ethical means for the buyer and seller, through give and take, to eliminate unjustified or unnecessary increments of cost'

The seller will often be reluctant to divulge what is, to him, sensitive commercial data. Nevertheless modern methods of industrial purchase price management, applied over periods of time, involve the use of cost analysis and subsequent application in contractual relationships. As a result the buyer will find himself negotiating for information.

Smith views the concept of decision-making which is at the core of negotiation:

> Negotiation is a system of decision-making characterised by a mixture of common and conflicting interests on the part of the parties involved in making the decisions. The commonality of interests rests in the necessity that both parties must agree to any decision. The conflicting interests are in regard to the disposition of the substantive issues peculiar to the situation. The critical element in negotiation is its mixed motive character. The negotiator is moved to

co-operate, on the one hand, in order to secure some decision. On the other hand, however, he must be competitive in order to ensure the most favourable settlement for himself or those whom he represents. It is this mixture of co-operation and conflict which gives to negotiation its uniqueness as a decision system.

Decision-Making

The concept of negotiation as a decision-making system raises many issues, some of which require a critical self-analysis if the reader is to assess his capabilities in this vital sphere of purchasing. Figure 2 can be used as the basis for a wide ranging inter-pretative study of its relevance to pricing matters. The reader would find it relevant to list details of each item related to events in his own organisation. *Sawyer* and *Guetzkow* developed a negotiation model based upon a decision-making system. This is shown in Figure 2.

There are some key points arising from this model:

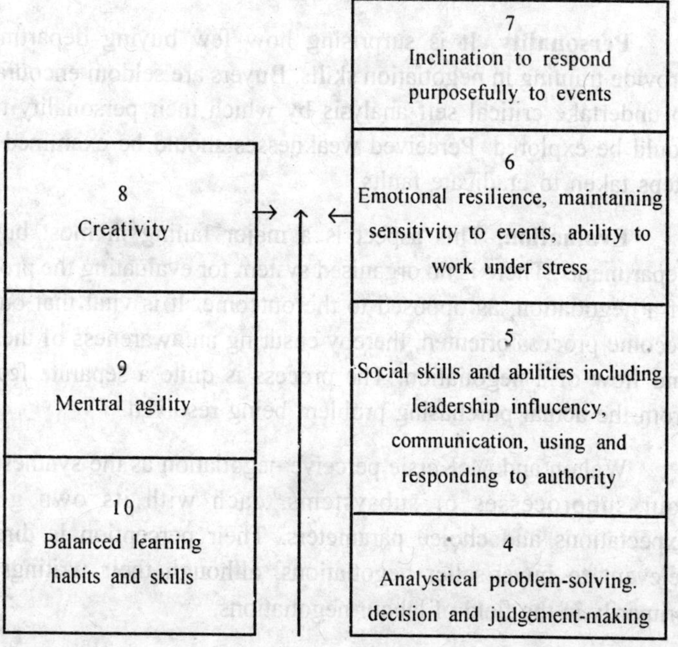

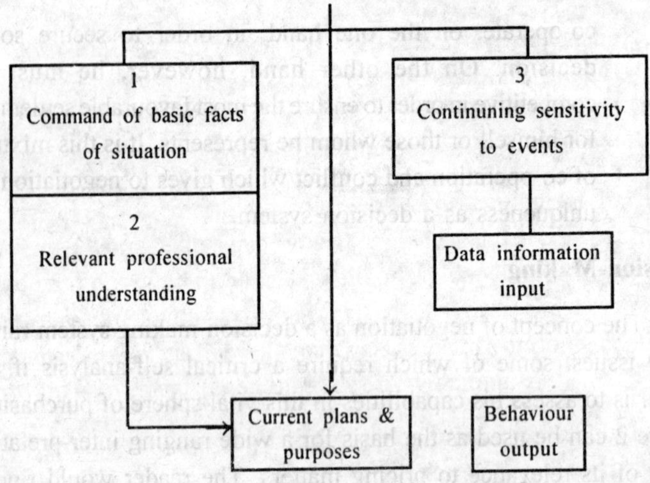

Fig. 2. A model of decision-making (adapted).

Goals. These are essential in a price negotiation and should be based upon high expectation levels. Whenever possible they, should be related to purchase price analysis targets and quotations that reflect a thorough search of the supply market place.

Personality. It is surprising how few buying departments provide training in negotiation skills. Buyers are seldom encouraged to undertake critical self analysis by which their personality traits could be explored. Perceived weaknesses should be examined and steps taken to eradicate faults.

Evaluation. This aspect is a major failing in most buying departments. There is no organised system for evaluating the process of a negotiation, as opposed to the outcome. It is vital that buyers become process oriented, thereby ensuring an awareness of the ebb and flow of a negotiatlon. The process is quite a separate feature from the actual purchasing problem being resolved.

Walton and McKersie perceive negotiation as the synthesis of four subprocesses or subsystems, each with its own goals, expectations and choice parameters. Their perception is directly relevant to buyer/seller negotiations, although their writings are primarily in the field of labour negotiations.

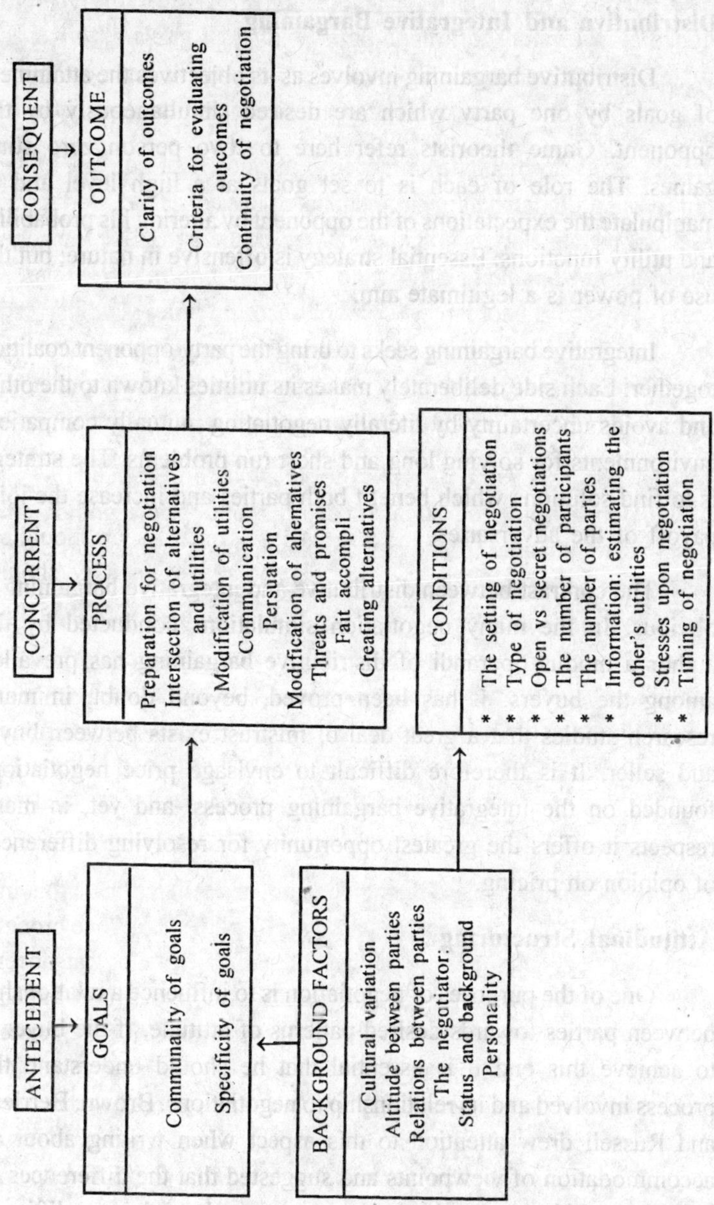

Fig. 3. Sawyer-Guetzkow negotiation model (adapted)

Distributive and Integrative Bargaining

Distributive bargaining involves as its objectives the attainment of goals by one party which are desired simultaneously by the opponent. Game theorists refer here to 'two person zero sum' games. The role of each is to set goals at a high level and to manipulate the expectations of the opponent by altering his probability and utility functions. Essential strategy is offensive in nature; but the use of power is a legitimate aim.

Integrative bargaining seeks to bring the party-opponent coalition together. Each side deliberately makes its utilities known to the other and avoids uncertainty by literally negotiating mutually compatible environments for solving long and short run problems. The strategy is to find solutions which benefit both parties and increase the joint payoff of the adversaries.

The contrast between distributive and integrative bargaining is obvious. In the many negotiation simulations conducted by the author a modus operandi of distributive bargaining has prevailed among the buyers. It has been proved, beyond doubt, in many research studies that a great deal of mistrust exists between buyer and seller. It is therefore difficult to envisage price negotiations founded on the integrative bargaining process, and yet, in many respects it offers the greatest opportunity for resolving differences of opinion on pricing.

Attitudinal Structuring

One of the purposes of negotiation is to influence a relationship between parties towards desired patterns of attitude. If the buyer is to achieve this end it is essential that he should understand the process involved and its relationship to negotiations. Brown, Berriens and Russell drew attention to this aspect when writing about an accommodation of viewpoints and suggested that the differences of opinion could be resolved in various ways, each implying a different approach. Their alternatives are worth serious thought and subsequent application.

An Exercise in Logical Persuasion. This could arise in instances where the buyer has a purchase price analysis that sets a target costing below the seller's offer. It is possible to see the ensuing negotiations as simply a matter of the buyer working through his target costing and logically persuading the seller to reduce his price. This may, of course, be effective. Equally, there are many reasons that may prevent its success. In the first place the seller may not be basing his price on the full cost method of pricing, and therefore logical persuasion is unlikely to convince him to change his approach.

An Application of Power and Coercion. Power is the capability of doing or affecting something. It implies the ability to influence others and must be a possible tactic in negotiations. Only those groups which have power can threaten to use force and the threat itself is power. The industrial buyer has a lot of power; a fact that any seller is conscious of. The buyer can threaten to withdraw contracts, reduce quantities, thereby seriously jeopardising the seller's business in some instances. Power is, however, seldom one sided and the seller can also threaten the buyer's position by rationing supplies or changing the contractual basis. The balance of power will continually change, depending on the market situation, organisational factors and the buyer's knowledge of all the relevant facts.

An Exploration of Mutually Advantageous Concessions. This orientation suggests that the buyer and seller are adopting open tactics whereby each explores areas of conflict, making concessions that will eventually offer advantages to both. It suggests a degree of trust that is not always found in commercial negotiations. The existence of mutual mistrust is often founded on the handling of sensitive commercial and / or technical data. It is natural that sellers are wary of disclosing detailed cost data in case it falls into their competitors' hands. The buyer will probably be reluctant to disclose his company's long-term strategic plans for the same reason. This aspect of buyer-seller relationships requires an understanding founded on total integrity of the buyer.

A Search for Middle Ground Compromise. There have been many negotiations that have concluded with an agreement to settle in the 'middle'. There is a well known expression, 'splitting the difference'. Unless this phenomenon is clearly understood there are major traps for the unsuspecting buyer. An example from price negotiations will serve to illustrate the point. Let us assume that the buyer believes the price should be Rs. 10.00 each. The seller has requested Rs. 15.00 each. The buyer offers to 'split the difference' at Rs. 12.50 each (a common tactic found in simulations), which means he has conceded 50 per cent of his ideal position. It is most unlikely that an experienced sales negotiator will agree to such an offer in the first instance. He will test at a level nearer his ideal position. However, if the buyer then offers to split the resulting difference, the price negotiation is now taking place in the Rs. 13.75 zone. The industrial buyer must consider carefully why the compromise is taking place and who is, in fact, compromising.

❐

10

Legal Aspects of Purchasing

The competent professional buyer does not require the training of a lawyer but should possess an understanding of the basic principles of commercial law. Such understanding should provide recognition of problems and situations which require professional counsel and also the knowledge to avoid legal pitfalls in day to day operations.

Legal Authority of the Purchasing Officer

What is the essence of the purchasing officer's legal status? Briefty put, it may be said that he has authority to attend to the business of purchasing in accordance with the instructions given by his employer. These instructions are usually broad in their character. In general, there should be and. in all progressive organizations there is, a clear understanding as to what the purchasing officer is expected to do. Attention has already been called to the necessity for a clear understanding of his duties simply as a matter of good business policy. The reasons for this clear understanding, cogent as they are from other points of view, are strengthened by virtue of the fact that the law assumes an agreement between the agent and his employer as to the scope of the authority. Presumably, the purchasing officer performs these assigned duties to the full extent of his capacity. In other words, the purchasing officer has a right to expect from his employer a clear understanding as to what his duties and responsibilities are, and he, in term, may be expected to perform these duties to the best of his ability in an honest, careful manner. So long as he does this, his obligations- to his employer, from a legal point of view, are fulfilled. In agreeing to render service to an employer, there is no implied agreement that he shall commit no errors. "For negligence, bad faith, or dishonesty, he is liable to his employer; but, if he is guilty of none of these, the employer must submit to such incidental losses as may occur in the course of the employment." Such losses are incidental to all vocations. Although, by special stipulation, the agent may assume responsibility to his principal for this type of risk, including, indeed, even honest mistakes in the extension of credit, such arrangements are rare. Nevertheless, when a man accepts an appointment to serve as an agent for the principal, there does exist the implication that he possesses the necessary skill to carry on the work that he undertakes. In some cases, a very high degree of skill is demanded, and when a man accepts an appointment under such circumstances he implies that he has the necessary skill. There are, of course, many possible modifications of this general statement. The purchasing officer becomes liable to his employer when he damages the latter through active fault or through negligence, particularly if this negligence arises in connection with the duties imposed upon him. In this connection it may be noted that many difficulties arise in an attempt to define what negligence is, although, in general, it may be said to constitute an "omission of due care under given circumstances."

Since the purchasing officer is acting as an agent for the company which he represents, it follows that he is in a position to bind the company within limits. Actually, of course, the power of an agent to bind his principal may greatly exceed his right to do so. His right is confined by the limits assigned to him, in other words, in accordance with his actual authorization; his power to bind the principal, however, is defined by the apparent scope of his authority, which in the case of most purchasing officers, is rather broad. Furthermore, if he is to avoid personal liability, it must be made clear to the person with whom the is dealing that he is acting as an agent. In fact, the law requires that he go further if he is not to be held personally liable; not only must he indicate the fact that he is acting as an agent but also the person with whom he is dealing must agree to hold the principal responsible, even though the latter is at the moment unknown.

The actual authority delegated to an agent is not limited to those acts which, by words, he is expressly and directly authorized to perform. Every actual authorization, whether general or special, includes by implication all such authority as is necessary, usual, and proper to carry through to completion the main authority conferred. The extent of the agent's implied authority must be determined from the nature of the business to be transacted. These powers will be broad in the case of one acting as a general agent or manager. It is the duty of the third person dealing with the agent to ascertain the scope of the agent's authority. Statements of the agent as to the extent of his powers cannot be relied on by the third party. Any limitation on the agent's power which is known to the third person is binding on the third person.

Personal Liability of the Purchasing Officer

It would appear that there are certain conditions under which the purchasing officer may be held personally liable when signing contracts. *(1)* when he makes a false statement concerning his authority with intent to deceive or, in other phraseology, when his misrepresentation has the natural and probable consequence of misleading; *(2)* when he performs without authority a damaging act, even though believing he has such authority; *(3)* when he performs an act which is itself illegal, even on authority from his employer; *(4)* when he willfully performs an act which results in damage to anyone; *(5)* when he performs damaging acts outside the scope of his authority, even though the act is performed with the intention of rendering his employer a valuable service. In each of these cases the vendor ordinarily has no recourse to the company employing the agent, since there existed no valid contract between the seller and the purchasing firm; and since such a contract does not exist, the only recourse which the vendor commonly has is to the agent personally. However, should the question arise as to who may be sued on contracts made within the apparent scope of the agent's authority but beyond his actual scope, because of the fact that there were limitations on the latter unknown to the seller, it may still follow that the principal can be held. Under these circumstances, the agent has probably put himself in the wrong and is, of course, answerable to his principal. He may also be answerable to the seller with whom he has dealt, on the ground of deceit, on the charge that he is the real contracting party, or for breach of the warranty that he was authorized to make the precise contract he undertook to make for the principal.

Moreover, suits have been brought by sellers against purchasing managers when it was discovered that the latter's principal was for some reason unable to pay the account. For example, such conditions have arisen *(1)* when the employer became insolvent or bankrupt; *(2)* when the employer endeavored to avoid his legal obligations to accept and pay for merchandise purchased by the purchasing manager; or *(3)* when the employer became involved in litigation with the seller, whose lawyers decided that the contract price could be readily collected personally from the purchasing manager.

The Purchase Order Contract

There are many federal, state, and local statutes which relate to purchasing, but the Uniform Commercial Code covers most of the transactions involving purchase and sale of goods and services. The UCC resulted from the joint efforts of the American Law Institute and the Conference of Commissioners on Uniform State Laws. Since the first publication of the Code in 1952, with subsequent revisions and refinements in 1958 and 1962, all of the states have enacted the code into law, except for the state of Louisiana.

Anyone that has had any exposure to commercial law knows that a valid contract is based on four factors:

1. Competent parties—either principals or qualified agents.
2. Legal subject matter or purpose.
3. There must be an offer and an acceptance.
4. There must be a consideration.

The purchase order is generally regarded as containing the buyer's offer and becomes a legal contract when accepted by the vendor: Many purchasing managers have designed the purchase order form with a copy that includes provision for acknowledgement or acceptance. There has never been universal agreement on how detailed the terms and conditions which are printed on the purchase order should be. Some companies use forms that use the reverse side to spell out all the complete terms and conditions which apply to any transaction. Some companies may include a separate printed sheet detailing terms and conditions applying to the order. Some companies provide only for the very basic items necessary for a valid offer and depend on the provisions of the UCC for proper legal coverage. The purchasing officer should depend on the professional legal counsel responsible for handling legal matters for the company in determining the policy to be followed.

An "offer" can be equally valid if made by a vendor, either in writing or verbally. Such an offer becomes a legal contract when accepted by the buyer.

Regardless of whether an offer is made by the buyer or the vendor it can be modified or revoked before it is accepted. However, an offer in writing that includes an assurance that the price would remain firm for a specified period may not be revoked prior to the expiration of the period.

Acceptance of Orders

Since the purchase order form or the sales contract is intended to include all the essential conditions surrounding the transaction, it is customary to include in the agreement a statement such as, "Acceptance of this order implies the acceptance of conditions contained thereon." The purpose of such a provision is, of course, to make all the conditions legally binding upon the seller and to avoid cases in which the seller advances the defense that he was not aware of certain conditions. Statements similar to that indicated are found in practically all purchase agreements, to give warning that there are conditions attached, either on the front or on the reverse side of the contract.

It is important to observe, however, that ordinarily only those terms and conditions which appear above the signature of the purchasing officer may be considered a part of the contract. To append at the foot of the purchase order and below the signature of the contracting parties an additional condition or to append below the signature a statement to the effect that the conditions cited on the reverse side are to be considered as incorporated in the contract is likely to have no binding effect, and such conditions may not be considered by the courts as part of the agreement.

Having placed an order with a vendor, the purchasing officer wishes to assure himself that the order has been accepted. To obtain such assurance, it is customary for him to insist upon a definite acknowledgment, usually in written form. It is not uncommon to incorporate as a part of the contract a clause requiring that the acceptance be made in a particular manner, in which case a form is enclosed with the order and the purchase order contains a clause which stipulates: "This order must be acknowledged on the enclosed form."

The question sometimes arises as to when an offer either of sale or of purchase has been accepted. As a matter of law, the person making an offer may demand, as one of the conditions, that acceptance be indicated in whatever manner he may specifically designate. Ordinarily, however, when an offer is made, the offerer either expressly or impliedly requires the offeree to send his answer by post or telegraph; and when the answer is duly posted or telegraphed, the acceptance is communicated, the contract being complete from the moment the letter is mailed or the telegram is sent.

Sometimes the vendor may use an acknowledgement form of its own design which upon detailed examination may conflict with some of the conditions stated in the purchase order. Often in such situations, a careful detailed examination is not made in comparing all conditions stated in the offer with all conditions stated in the acceptance. If litigation subsequently occurs between buyer and seller the UCC may resolve the question through the provisions of (UCC 2-207) (C) which states:

Conduct by both parties which recognize the existence of a contract is sufficient to establish a contract for sale although the writings of the parties do not otherwise establish a contract. In such case the terms of the particular contract consist of those terms on which the writings of the parties agree, together with any supplementary terms incorporated under any other provisions.....[of this statute].

Under the terms of this provision, the conflicting conditions of both offer and acceptance are disallowed and the applicable provisions of the UCC apply.

Purchases Made Orally

Most professional buyers have occasion to place orders over the telephone or orally in person. Such oral orders are enforceable contracts without written notation if the materials or equipment are suitable for use only by the purchaser. However, the UCC specifies that:

1. Normally there must be some written notation if the value of the order is $500.00 or more.
2. If the seller supplies a memorandum which is not in accordance with the buyer's understanding of his oral order, he must give a notice of objection to the supplier within ten days if he wishes to preserve his legal rights.

Authority of Vendor's Representatives

Another obviously important consideration relates to the authority of the salesman representing a company with which the purchasing officer is transacting business. Subject to the many exceptions arising out of varying circumstances, it may be said that the courts have consistently held that although an employer is bound by all the acts of his agent while acting within the scope of the employment, yet a salesman's ordinary authority is simply to solicit orders and to send them to his employer for ratification and acceptance. It therefore behooves the purchasing officer to know definitely whether the salesman with whom he is doing business has or docs not have the authority to conclude a contract without referring it to the company which he represents. Although a vendor does not authorize his salesmen to enter into binding contracts and although the company may do nothing to lead others to believe that its representative has such power, yet if the salesman does enter into a contract with a buyer, the contract is likely to be held valid unless the seller within a reasonable time notifies the buyer that the salesman has exceeded his authority. In other words, a contract results because the conduct of the employer is interpreted as acceptance. Should any doubt arise in the mind of the purchasing officer, he should be assured that the individual signing the contract for the vendor company is authorized to do so, regardless of whether the person making such claim be the salesman or someone else.

In passing, it may be well to indicate that false statements on the part of the seller or his representative regarding the character of the merchandise being purchased cause the contract to become voidable at the option of the other party.

It is true that this "undoubted right" to rely upon vendors' statements is at best a highly qualified right, the value of which depends upon the circumstances surrounding the transaction. It is of value insofar as the misstatement can be relied upon as a breach of warranty, a condition broken, or a fraud, and, in any event, has no good effect on the purchaser's title. However, it may be said that, aside from any legal question which is involved under ordinary circumstances, the seller is likely to be sufficiently jealous of his reputation and goodwill to make substantial concessions, even though he feels that technically he is right.

One important right which the buyer has is that of inspecting the goods before he accepts them. The purpose of this rule, of course, is to give the buyer an opportunity to determine whether or not the goods tendered comply with the contract description. It is well established that a buyer who inspects goods before entering into a contract of sale is put on his guard and is expected by law to use his own judgment with respect to quality, quantity, and other characteristics of the merchandise. The court is prone, however, to recognize circumstances which may affect the purchaser's ability to judge the accuracy of the vendor's statements. Thus, it has been held:

In order to vitiate a contract of sale on the ground of fraudulent representations, such representations must relate to an existing fact, material to the contract, and upon which the other party has a right to rely and did rely to his injury. If the means of information as to the matters alleged to be misrepresented are equally accessible to both parties, they will be presumed to havc informed themselves, and if they have not done so they must abide by the consequences of their own carelessness.

From this statement, it would seem to follow that where a purchaser accepts merchandise after his own inspection, either as to quality or quantity, he would ordinarily be debarred from raising an issue with respect to these points. Also, as has been pointed out elsewhere, a vendor cannot be held responsible for the failure of equipment to perform the work which the buyer expected of it, if the latter orders merely upon material specifications and without indicating to the seller the purpose to which the equipment or goods are to be put.

The courts have generally held that if a purchaser is not sufficiently experienced to be able to judge adequately the goods which he inspects, or if he relies upon a fraudulent statement made by a seller and purchases in consequence of that fraudulent statement, he may then rescind the contract or hold the vendor liable for damages.

Cancellation of Orders and Breach of Contract

Once a contract is made, it is expected that both parties will adhere to the agreement. Occasionally one or the other seeks to cancel the contract after it has been made. Ordinarily this is a more serious problem for the seller than it is for the buyer, although occasionally a seller may wish to avoid complying with the terms of an agreement, in which event he may merely refuse to manufacture the goods or he may delay the delivery beyond the period stipulated in the agreement. The rights of a purchaser under these circumstances depend upon the conditions surrounding the transaction. Speaking broadly, it may be said that the seller is likely to be able, without liability, to delay delivering purchased goods when the buyer orders a change in the original agreement which may have the result of delaying the seller in making delivery; if, after delayed shipment, the purchaser agrees to accept delivery; and also under certain other conditions.

It is clear that if the seller fails to make delivery by the agreed time, the purchaser may without obligation refuse to accept delivery at a later date. However, the attempt to secure what the buyer might consider reasonable damages resulting from a breached sales contract is likely to be full of difficulty, owing to the fact that the courts experience a good deal of trouble in laying down rules for the guidance of the jury in estimating the amount of damages justly allowed a buyer who sustains financial losses resulting from a seller's failure to fulfill a contract of sale. If there be a general rule, it may be said that the damages allowable to a purchaser if a seller fails to deliver goods according to contract are measured by the difference between the original contract price and th market value of the merchandise at the time when and at the place where the goods should have been delivered. The amount of damages which the buyer can collect for breaches of warranty on the part of the seller therefore will be tremendous.

The seller, in his turn, is sometimes confronted by an attempted cancellation on the part of the buyer. It is not unusual, therefore, to find in the sales contract the following clause: "This contract is not subject to cancellation." As a matter of fact, the inclusion of such a clause has little practical effect, unless, indeed, it is intended merely to indicate to the purchaser that if he does attempt to cancel, he may expect a suit for breach of contract. From a legal point of view, the seller is in no better position that he would have been had this clause been omitted. Moreover, even if an order for merchandise contains a clause by the terms of which the purchaser is notified that the seller will not accept cancellation, the purchaser is legally privileged to cancel the order at any time before the seller legally accepts the order by acknowledgment or by any other act.

However, in a very strong seller's market, where the breach of contract by the seller is related to failure to deliver on a promised date or even to abide by the price agreed upon, the alternatives open to the buyer are almost nil. The latter still wants the goods, and he may be unable to acquire them from any other supplier any sooner or at any better price. Much the same restriction, in fact, exists even where the contract provides for the option of cancellation by the buyer. The purchaser wants goods, not damages or the right to cancel. Since his chances of getting them as promptly from any other supplier are slight, he is likely to do the best he can with the original vendor, provided, of course, that bad faith as to either price or delivery is not involved.

Warranties

Over time the rules governing warranty negotiations between the buyer and seller have advanced from "caveat emptor" (let the buyer beware) to the legal provisions of the DCC which recognizes three types of warranties:

a. Express warranty.

b. Implied warranty of merchantability.

c. Implied fitness for a particular purpose.

Essentially, express warranties include promises, specifications, samples, and descriptions pertaining to the goods which are the subject of the negotiation.

Implied warranty of merchantability has to do with the merchantable quality of goods, and the DCC statutes applying have developed out of mercantile practices.

Accepted trade standards of quality, fitness for the intended uses, and conformance to promises or specified fact made on the container or label are all required as measurement of marketable quality.

Implied warranty of fitness for a purpose usually results from a buyer's request for material or equipment to meet a particular need or accomplish a specific purpose. If the buyer provides detailed specification for the item requested, the seller is relieved of any warranty of fitness for a purpose. There would be a warranty on the part of the seller that his product would meet the buyer's detailed specifications.

Acceptance and Rejection of Goods

The acceptance of goods is an assent by the buyer to become the owner of the goods tendered by the seller. No unusual formalities are necessary to indicate that the buyer has accepted the goods. Any words or acts which will indicate the buyer's intention to become the owner of the goods are sufficient. If the buyer keeps the goods and exercises rights of ownership over them, he will be held to have accepted them, even though he may have expressly stated that he has rejected them. If the goods tendered do not comply with the sales contract, the buyer is under no duty to accept them; but if the buyer does accept the goods, he does not thereby waive his right to damages for the seller's breach of contract. If the buyer does accept goods which do not comply with the sales contract, he must notify the seller of the breach within a reasonable time after the buyer knows or ought to know of such breach.

The question as to whether or not to reject goods delivered under a particular order may arise from various causes and may be dealt with in a variety of ways. For instance, the goods may not have been delivered, on time; may have been delivered in the wrong amount; may not have been in proper condition; or may actually fail to meet the specifications. The problem for the purchasing officer is what to do under such circumstances. The important thing to keep in mind is that it may be safely presumed that the purchaser wants the goods. A suit at law, therefore, is. ,not desirable, even though the buyer is granted anyone of the commonly recognized judicial remedies for breach of contract, such as money damages, restitution, or insistence upon performance, because, aside from the fact that it is goods the buyer wants, legal action is uncertain and the outcome costly; it may be long drawn out and may cause the loss of a friendly supplier. The procurement officer therefore usually seeks other means of adjustment. Several courses are clearly open to him. The first question, of course, is one as to the seriousness of the breach. If not too serious, a simple warning to the vendor not to repeat this failure may be quite adequate. If somewhat more stringent action is called for and if the goods received are usable for some purpose, even though not quite up to specifications, a price adjustment can frequently be worked out to the mutual satisfaction of the buyer and the seller. Sometimes the goods, though not usable in the form received, may be reprocessed or otherwise made usable by the vendor, or perchance by the purchaser at the vendor's expense. If the goods happen to be component parts, they may be replaced by the supplier. If some sort of equipment is involved, or even processed material that is incapable of being efficiently used in its present form, the vendor may correct the defects at the user's plant. Or, as a last resort, the goods may be rejected and shipped back to the supplier, usually at the vendor's expense.

Protection Against Price Fluctuations

Cancellations can, of course, be the direct result of action by the buyer. They arise in two ways:

The first of these methods of cancellation—or attempted cancellation—is rarely to be commended. It comes about because the buyer, if compelled to live up to his agreement, would lose money. Conditions in his plant may have altered, or sales may have fallen off. Therefore, he no longer wants the goods he contracted for. The market price may have dropped, and he finds that he could now buy the goods for less than he agreed to pay. Faced with these conditions, he seeks some form of relief. He becomes extremely watchful of deliveries; and he rejects goods which arrive even a day late, although he would ordinarily have accepted them without question. Inspection is tightened up, and the slightest failure to meet any detail in the specifications is seized upon as an excuse for rejection. Such methods are not to be commended and are never followed by a good procurement officer.

The second form of cancellation may arise in a perfectly legal and ethical manner as far as the price aspects are concerned, through evoking a clause—occasionally inserted in purchase contracts—which seeks to guarantee against price decline. Particularly in periods of declining prices and in purchasing goods subject to price fluctuations, it is in the interests of the buyer to be protected against what might be considered unreasonable prices. Occasionally, too, a long-term contract is drawn up which leaves the ascertainment of the exact price open until some deliveries are called for under it. To meet these conditions, various clauses are incorporated in purchase contracts. Thus:

You warrant that the prices named herein are as low as any net prices now given by you to any customer for like materials, and you agree that if at any time during the life of this order you quote or sell at lower net prices similar materials under similar conditions such lower net prices shall from time to time be substituted for the prices named herein.

These stipulations against price decline are not confined to purchase agreements, and under some circumstances the buyer may receive price reductions upon the seller's initiative. An example of this type of clause is the following:

Should the purchaser at the time of any delivery, on account of this contract, be offered a lower price on goods of equal quality and in like quantity by a reputable manufacturer, he will furnish the seller satisfactory proof of same in which event the seller will either supply such shipment at the lower price or permit the buyer to purchase such quantity elsewhere and the quantity so purchased elsewhere will be deducted from the total quantity of this contract. Should the seller reduce his prices during the terms of this contract. the buyer shall receive the benefit of such lower prices.

Legally such clauses are ordinarily enforceable and frequently work to the buyer's advantage. A tually, the administrative problems involved in seeing to it that these clauses are lived up to and enforced are substantial. The moral effect doubtlessly is greater than the legal.

Standardization of Contract Forms

To avoid many of the pitfalls which the purchasing officer may unwittingly encounter, as well as to create a contract which satisfies the mutual demands of both vendor and purchaser most adequately, efforts have frequently been made to bring about some standardization among the contracts which are in use. Arguments in favour of such a standard con-tract scarcely need any elaboration. However, in spite of the advantages, it is doubtful whether standard contracts would solve the real problem. Whether this statement be true or not, the very general feeling among men engaged in purchasing is that such contracts are neither feasible nor desirable. The fact that this group of men is opposed to a suggested change is not to be considered lightly; and although it need not be a deciding factor, in this case there is good reason to believe that a standardized form is not practical. The most that could be expected, under any circumstances, would be the development of a standard contract which would relate to the purchase and sale of specific types of materials or equipment as between two similar companies.

In practice, purchase agreements differ to such an extent, not only between one industry and another but within the same type of industry, that almost no generalizations can be drawn. It is highly desirable that a company should give the closest attention to the type of agreement which it uses. It is also desirable that a company should make a thorough study of the types of agreements used by other organizations confronted by essentially the same problems. It is possible that a good deal of simplification could be effected without undue restriction of the rights of the buyer.

Title to Purchased Goods

The professional buyer should have a clear understanding of when the title of goods passes from the seller to the buyer. Normally, there will be an agreement on the f.o.b. (free on board) point, and the buyer receives title at that point. Moreover, the UCC code in section 2-401 states that "title of goods cannot pass under a contract for sale prior to their identfication for the contract." On capital goods it is particularly important for tax and depreciation reasons to establish title before the tax year end.

In some instances the buyer is given possession of the goods prior to the passing of a legal title. This is known as a "conditional sales contract," and the full title passes to the buyer when full payment is made. This procedure permits a buyer to obtain needed material without payment until a future time.

❐

11

Materials Scheduling

Manufacture involves the processing or fashioning of materials in order to produce an article. The processes to be performed must, in most cases, be carried out in a particular sequence or pattern. If, for example, a product contains a number of parts which have to be assembled together, no product can be completed until a set of parts is available. Ideally, the manufacture of the parts themselves must be started at points in time which allow their completion on the same date. If the times for manufacture differ then the determination of the individual manufacturing start dates involves working back from the planned start date for assembly. This is illustrated diagrammatically in Fig. 1. The diagram shows that component B must go into

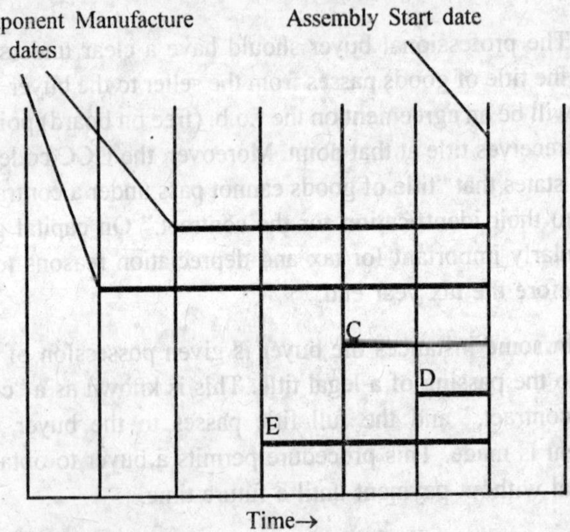

Fig. 1: Determination of component manufacture start dates

manufacture first, followed by A,E, and so on. The length of the horizontal lines is proportional to the time required for manufacture, drawn against a common scale of days, hours, weeks, etc., as required.

Each batch of components may involve several operations, and these will generally have to be arranged for consecutive performance. If sub-assembly is to take place before final assembly, it will sometimes involve similar consecutive operations. In other cases it may be possible to have work performed on several different kinds of sub-assembly consecutively.

Output Based Scheduling

If the machines involved in a manufacturing process have a known output per hour in terms of numbers of parts or metres of material it may prove more convenient to prepare schedules based on quantity rather than time. However, this type or scheduling is fundamentally the same as that already described since output is basically always related to time even if it is sometimes desicrable to express it in other terms for particular purposes.

Manufacturing for Stock

Once the designs of a product which it is intended should become a standard line have been finalised it is possible to prepare a master schedule along the lines already indicated. This implies that the design has been proved and that a pilot batch has passed through the manufacturing process. Special tools and tooling will have been put into use and modifications made, where necessary, to manufacturing methods, sequences and, very probably, times.

Up to this point the master schedule will have been tentative and subject to modification in the light of experience gained with the pilot batch or batches. Strictly speaking, however; it is only possible to say that the schedule is firm at this point in a relative sense. All designs are subject to modifications of one kind or another throughout their useful life. Sometimes the modifications are so far-reaching that it is reasonable to regard the design as a new model. From the point of view of those in the production control department who draw up the schedule each modification, however small, necessitates a critical re-assessment of the previous schedule and in most cases the issue of a new schedule taking the modifications into account. Up-dating of this kind is very important since the efficacy of the planning processes which are required when the production is actually authorised is very largely dependent upon the accuracy of the master schedule used as a basis.

Some companies are concerned only with the production of standard lines of product, and these are made either on a flow line basis or in batches which can be fitted into available capacity in an orderly sequence. In the case of flow line production the processes, once started, follow a well understood sequence and control by reference to the master schedules is relatively easy. This is because capacity demands have been analysed with care and plant and equipment provided to meet the demands. Upward variations in demand are met by the installation of new plant and equipment or by the sub-contracting of some of the additional work. In the case of sub-contract work the delivery dates required of sub-contractors can be derived from a study of the master schedules.

Much the same considerations apply to the batch production. of standard lines. If demand rises it is sometimes possible to meet the contingency by decreasing the interval between the initial loading dates of batches, but this may, of course, have an adverse effect upon the rate of production of batches of other lines. There is obviously less free capacity between loadings in which to accommodate these other lines. Again, therefore; the solution may lie in the expansion of capacity or in sub-contracting.

Another factor to be taken into account in regard to the master schedule is that of method change. As experience of a method of production is gained it is inevitable that better methods will be devised. These may arise from shop floor suggestions, and the supervisor has a big part to play here, or they may be put forward by the work study officers. Whether the changes arise from these or any other sources they will if the proposals aie adopted, almost certainly result in time saving. If that is the case the master schedules must be altered accordingly. Such time saving will often mevement additional equipment or sub-contracting to meet increased demand is not required. This is an aspect of increased productivity which should be the concern of all who have to do with the actual manufacturing processes on the workshop floor just as much as it is the concern of those involved in higher level production management, design, process planning or work study.

Manufacturing to Special Order

The implication here is that an order of precisely this kind has not previously been undertaken, although the class of work will almost certainly be familiar. Equally, although an exactly similar job may be undertaken in the future, there is no certitude that that will be so.

In view of these implications there is often a temptation to dispense with a master schedule and proceed directly to machine loading. Such a practice has considerable drawbacks and is not to be recommended. If it is accepted that the loading of workshops is of such paramount importance that the process should be planned, then it is essential that the whole of the work passing through should do so on a planned basis and not just that which is likely to be continuous or respective. Loading work on to producing units is a highly complex problem, and this applies to all types of work. Therefore, before detailed capacity planning, or loading, can be undertaken it is necessary that broad base or outline plans should first be prepared.

It can be argued, with some force, that scheduling is even more important with non-repeating orders than with continuous flow work. This is because in the nature of things the job which is in continuous production will eventually be sorted out into some semblance of order by mere repetition and the correction of errors. Again it is sometimes argued that non-repeating orders are in production for relatively short periods and the preliminary scheduling work is too lime consuming to be worthwhile.

These arguments are failacious. If relatively short runs of more or less unplanned work are inserted into an otherwise well planned programme the latter will soon suffer. The short-run work, being only partially planned, will almost certainly either over-run the time. allocated for the longer run jobs, or will finish earlier than anticipated and cause idle time or readjustment of the long-run plans.

The difficulties of providing proper schedules for all work passing through the factory are recognised, and the reluctance of management to allocate time for short-run scheduling well understood. Basically, however, the problem is one of policy. If short-run special orders are to be accepted as a policy, then they must receive similar planning treatment to that provided for long-term jobs. If that approach is unacceptable then the sales policy should be that short-term orders are unacceptable. Where the latter policy is adopted there are frequently arguments along the lines that either accepting short-term work attracts customers with long-term work to place, or that short-term work can often be very profitable. There is an element of truth in both these views, but it is far less than the supporters of such arguinents would have us believe.

That short-run orders can appear to be very profitable is true. The occasions where they really are so profitable are, however, infrequent. Merely because the income handsomely exceeds expenditure on labour, material and overheads it is often assumed that a good profit has been made. This is because the losses causes by the disruption of other work cannot easily be calculated. In most cases no such attempt is made. Not only that, but the disproportionate amount of time spent by supervisors and managers in solving the problems of the new job mean that other work suffers. The real drawback to short-run work is that it provides exactly the same problems as does long-run work in the initial stages, but there is no long-run to follow upon which the extra expenditure can be recovered. Thus policy should so far bs possible be directed to accepting either long-run or short-run work. Sometimes a mixture must be accepted, but in anyone of these three cases scheduling is essential.

Scheduling and Sales

Master schedules, or subsidiary schedules derived from them, may be built up from data on the basic operations to be performed, as hown in Fig. 2, or they may start from the broader base of the work to be performed within different workshops or even different factories. Whatever the breakdown might be they all at providing the groundwork for later more detailed planning and permit a properly disciplined approach to questions concerning the giving of reliable delivery dates. If an inquiry is received requesting a delivery date for a given quantity of products the appropriate master schedule can be compared with the charts showing the current and forthcoming load on the factory. The comparison will immediately reveal if the demand can be met and if not what alterations to existing plans would be necessary for it to be met. If alterations are not contemplated then the comparison will enable the best possible delivery date to be determined under the circumstances.

Clearly, when the inquiry is for a quantity of a standard product the necessary schedules for comparison will already be in existance and the process of deciding a realistic delivery date will not be unduly difficult. However, when the factory undertakes special work it is not possible to make the comparison in the manner described without first preparing at least an outline schedule. Because this adds to the cost involved in preparing the estimate for quotation purposes it is often dispensed with. In consequence the delivery promise given is often very little more than an informed guess. In fairness, it should also be pointed out that when a company undertakes special work it is usually in the position, at any particular point in time, of not knowing which or how many of its outstanding quotations are going to become orders. Therefore, offering firm delivery dates can be something of a gamble. If three quotations, A, Band C, are outstanding and only A becomes an order, then the delivery promise will probably be met. If, however, all three develop into orders then one, or possibly more, will over-run the premises given. Despite the validity of this argument there can really be no question that delivery promises derived from even an outline schedule will at thc very least be more realistic than are those which are not, A further point is that although schedules do take time to produce the information required for their compilation is required for the preparation of thc estimate in very many cases. All that is then required is to translate it into the form needed for the schedule.

Enough has already been said about the importance of keeping delivery promises for it to be unnecessary to repeat it at this point. What must, hower, be emphasised is that it is not possible for production control to give reliable promises to sales without some form of schedule for guidance.

Working in the fashion described has also a further advantage from the viewpoint of production control. Immediately an order is received a preliminary schedule; prepared when the estimate was drawn up, can be withdrawn from file, re-examined, and modified in the light of any new relevant information, and entered on to the master schedule. Somtimes this wiil reveal that orders received in the intervening period have absorbed capacity which was not allocated when the original quotation was sent to the customer. If that is the case, production control can immediately advise sales and provide them with a new date; this will mean that sales will have to obtain customer approval of the revision, and sometimes that will be an unwelcome process, either to sales or the customer .or both. Even so, it is better to advise the customer of the true position within a few days of receiving the order. than to hope for the best and then be obliged to advise him of the revision when his expected delivery date is approaching. Provided the company has built its reputation upon keeping dates or alternatively of giving revised dates in good time, then only limited harm will be done. Obviously the ideal position is to keep to the date given in the quotation, but that is not always possible for the reasons given earlier. The company does not know which quotations will produce orders and which will not.

SCHEDULING AND PURCHASING

Reference was made in Chapter Two to some of the problems encountered by the purchasing department when it is endeavouring to play its parts in ensuring a smooth flow of materials to meet the needs of the factory.

One of the most important aspects of effective purchase control is tbe question of time. Time is consumed in finding and selecting sources of supply, placing and chasing orders, and in checking incoming goods. Careful preliminary scheduling provides are purchasing department with a reasonably accurate picture of what are likely to be the future production demands with a maximum margin of warning.

When preliminary schedules for quotation purposes are prepared it is possible in many instances for the purchasing department to carry out a check, if only in broad terms, of what materials are likely to be needed, how much and when. Where the sales department is able, as it often is, to give an opinion about the likelihood of obtaining the order, the purchasing department can, if it so decides, make a few preliminary investigations. These could be internal in the case of material normally held in stock. For example, it may be that certain material will be needed in three months' time if the order is received. Will stock then be adequate to meet demand and, if not, when must orders be placed to ensure delivery in time?

If the materials which might be required are not normally held in stock, the difficulties of obtaining them might be checked. If they are difficult a little deeper investigation might be required. Some at least of this work might well have been done already at the estimating stage and often further pursuit of information would not be justified. The point to be made is that the preliminary schedule provides the buyer with maximum forewarning of a possible order. Reference to sales will frequently provide some indication of the chances of the quotation being accepted and purchasing can then prepare for the work up to a certain point.

Obviously there will generally be only a few occasions when the purchasing department will actually buy material for an order not yet received. On those occasions when that risk is taken the schedule and a knowledge of the delivery date given to the customer will enable the purchasing department to advise the supplier of the dates by which material is required.

When orders are received and the tentative schedules become a part of the master schedule and are thus written into the plan for future production, they provide the purchasing department with invaluable guidance.

Clearly the schedule alone will not necessarily give the buyer all the information he needs. Practices differ from firm to firm. Some schedules, backed by a master material schedule, will give a great deal of detail and the buyer will require no further information before proceeding to order. In other cases the schedule may give only a broad outline of the stages of production. Where this is so the purchasing department will either require a detailed schedule and material list or a dated material list giving the dates by which material will be needed.

SCHEDULING AND FINANCE

In a properly managed concern it will not be the practice to accept orders or to plan production beyond the capacity of the capital available to finance the project. In the initial stages, however, consideration of the sums of money involved may well be restricted to lump sums only loosely related to time. The schedule, either tentative before receipt of the order, or firm afterwards, will show in more precise terms the points in time when production will for example, build up, peak and then decline. Hence the points will be revealed when' the investment will be high and when returns from the customer may be expected. Such information is of great value to those in the company who are concerned with the problems of each flow.

SCHEDULING AND INSPECTION

Quality and reliability of the product are key factors in successful marketing. In order that the work of the inspection department may be effective it is necessary that it should be planned and integrated with the production processes.

Successful planning in this field, as in others, is firmly based upon an adequate supply of information well in advance of the point where action will be required: From the viewpoint of the inspection department the principal source of information about the anticipated forward load is provided by the production control department. Immediately an order is received it is then possible for the latter to issue master or updated schedules giving the dates proposed for the starting and finishing of the various stages of the work to be done. With this information the inspection department can begin any preliminary planning required in order to ensure that inspection facilities in term of manpower and equipment can be available when and where required.

❐

12

Purchasing Capital Equipment

We have been concerned thus far primarily with the procurement of materials, component parts, and supplies. We turn now to the purchase of major equipment.

In most companies it is clear-cut that decisions involving the purchase of major equipment are closely controlled at the top executive level. It is by no means so clear-cut that most companies have a well-thought-out equipment policy which goes beyond a consideration of comparative annual operating costs and wear write-offs. Many interrelated problems should be considered if a sound equipment policy is to be formulated. Some of these problems are stated briefly as follows:

1. Will the new equipment make the best use of available capital funds?
2. Will a desired return on invested capital be received if the new equipment is purchased?
3. Is the equipment flexible in that it has alternate uses?
4. Are technical advances being made which make it likely that more advantageous equipment will be available at an early date?
5. Will the necessary volume be maintained to realize fully the operating cost advantages of the new equipment?
6. What is the effect of taxes?

7. Will the company's competitive position be affected if the new equipment is not purchased?

These problems raise questions which often are not answered easily and, in fact, may raise doubts about the feasibility of having a stated equipment policy rather than considering each new equipment purchase separately.

Definition of Major Equipment

Throughout this discussion, the term "equipment" will be applied broadly to those items the cost of which is more properly chargeable to a capital account than to expense. They are essential "durable" or "capital" goods, as contrasted either with supplies or with those raw materials or fabricated parts which are purchased for direct incorporation into the product that the company is manufacturing for sale. We' shall exclude, however, building and similar construction, which, although both "durable" and "capital," falls for quite obvious reasons into a class by itself. We shall include all classes of power machinery (such as electrical generators, boilers, and internal combustion and steam engines), construction machinery (such as concrete mixers, dredges, steam shovels, and derricks) transportation equipment (such as trucks and elevators), and industrial machinery, both general (such as machine tools, blowers, and pumps) and special (such as looms, various types of shoe repair machinery, and airplane engines). Any complete list of such equipment will be extremely long and varied; this fact must constantly be borne in mind since, although the questions relating to any particular piece of equipment will be common to all types of capital goods, the degree to which any broad conclusion will apply must vary with each individual case.

A useful classification of equipment is the division into multipurpose and single purpose. Multipurpose equipment may have a variety of uses, may be used in several or many industries, tends to have longer technological life, and may have considerable salvage value. Fork lift trucks, certain classes of computers, and standard lathes are typical examples.

Single purpose equipment is designed to do one or several operations well, normally, substantially better than a multipurpose piece of equipment could. On the other hand, its specificity limits its potential use, and its usefulness is closely tied to the need for the operations it performs. Such special equipment is normally limited to one industry and may even be limited to one customer. The purchaser's specifications are important, requiring extensive consultation between the technical personnel of both buyer and supplier. The salvage value of special equipment may be low, and chances are that the need for the tasks disappears before the equipment is physically worn out. Minor or accessory equipment is normally used in an auxiliary capacity and tends to be of much lower dollar value. Its cost may not even be capitalized, and much of it tends to be standardized. Small pumps and motors are typical examples.

The special problems involved in the purchase of equipment, as contrasted with raw materials and supplies, grow out of the character of the product and the purpose for which it is bought. Equipment represents "capital goods:' It does not itself enter into the product being manufactured, as does the raw material. The engineer who recommends the acquisition of a piece of equipment may do so for a variety of reasons. The engineer may believe that manufacturing efficiency will can be improved because of greater speed of output or less variation in the product or greater ease and simplicity of operation, lower maintenance cost, greater versatility of use, lower labour cost, greater dependability, lower pgwer cost, longer life resulting from less depreciation and/or obsolescence. The above reasons tend to be for the sake of efficiency or economy. Other reasons for having equipment may be that they are a necessity by law or a form of insurance. For example, safety equipment as specified by OSHA, such as roll-proof cabs on skidders, and firefighting equipment, may do little to increase operating efficiency. Anti pollution equipment may well decrease operating efficiency and increase costs but is an environmental necessity. Emergency stand-by equipment such as an emergency power plant, an idle lathe in a veneer plant, and an extra crusher at a mine are only purchased to protect against the eventuality that the prime equipment or source may fail. An item of equipment seldom stands by itself—it is operated in conjunction with people and other machines as part of a system; hence, layout must be considered as well as the people and other types of equipment already in use. It is probable that the engineer's conclusions are based on a systems approach.

In the first instance, decisions as to either the replacement of equipment or the purchase of new, untried equipment are normally engineering decisions, based on the ascertainment of a need that usually originates. in the engineering or production department, not in the procurement department. They are, moreover, based presumably on a careful analysis of past costs and in most cases on estimates of future ones.

Special Problems of Equipment Buying

Major equipment procurement raises special problems. Some of the more important of these follow.

1. The buying of equipment usually requires that substantial amounts of money be expended fer a single purchase. Sometimes the sum is so large as even to call for a special form of financing, such as a bond issue or payment on the installment plan. Occasionally, leasing may be resorted to, one reason among several being the inability of the would be user to raise the necessary funds for outright purchase. It is true, of course, that some equipment items are comparatively inexpensive and that the financing of such purchases requires only very incidental outlays, as compared with the necessary expenditure for raw materials or fuel. Even in such instances, however, the necessary funds are tied up for much longer periods of time, and the capital turnover is considerably slower in the case of equipment purchase.

2. Because of its comparatively long life and the investment involved, equipment items, particularly those of a major character, are likely to be bought less frequently than other types of industrial purchases.

3. The final cost of equipment is more difficult to determine with exactness than, for example, the final cost of raw materials. The latter figure can be ascertained with reasonable definiteness. The initial cost of equipment, however, is but part of the total cost, which involves a whole series of estimates, such as the effects of idle time, of obsolescence, of maintenance and repair, of displaced labour, and even of direct operation factors. Some of these items may never be known exactly, even after experience with the particular piece of equipment in question. Moreover, many of the costs, such as insurance, interest, and obsolescence, continue even when the equipment is not in actual use. The income to be derived is also problematical, and, thus, even when it is possible to compute approximate costs, it is often difficult to determine how soon they will be met. These comments are particularly applicable to so-called non-productive equipment, such as cranes and hoists.

4. Equipment purchases are often less affected by current price trends than, for instance, are raw materials. The demand for industrial equipment more than the demand for any other type of industrial goods is a derived demand. Pricewise, the best time at which to buy is, therefore, particularly hard to determine. "Only when the need and the justification of the equipment has been established is there a possibility that its actual purchase may be delayed or hastened by price considerations." Since equipment is not commonly bought until needed, it is seldom bought during periods of business recession, although prices for equipment normally are low at such times and many good arguments can be advanced for buying then. Aside from absence of immediate need, manufacturers in periods of slack business tend to watch their assets carefully. Also, it is true that labor may be cheaper during recessions, and there is less incentive to substitute machinery for labour. The reverse conditions prevail in times of prosperity. The purchase of equipment following the close of World War II and the inflationary period of the late 1960s and early 1970s are excellent examples.

5. The purchase of equipment frequently involves problems concerning the wisest method of disposition of the displaced item, a

consideration which almost never arises in connection with materials or supplies.

6. A decision to purchase equipment, especially major items, is therefore likely to require a careful consideration of many factors involving broad management policy. The decision, once made, may well commit the company in a rather definite fashion to a series of other decisions of a comparatively permanent nature, such as the type of product to be manufactured, the method of its production, and the cost of operation. Put in other words, it is much easier "to get in and out" of a situation involving the purchase of raw materials than one involving the purchase of major equipment. Furthermore, the company's labour policies may be affected. Questions of financial policy, such as bond issues and alternative uses for available funds, may be involved. In short, equipment questions are likely to be procurement decisions of prime importance to management.

We turn now to a brief consideration of some of the specific problems involved in equipment procurement decisions. There are many of them, inevitably, but for purposes of our present discussion, we shall consider only the following:

1. The general principles which should control the selection of equipment.
2. The cost factors immediately applicable.
3. The problem of engineering service.
4. The timing of the purchase.
5. The selection of the source.
6. Some legal questions.
7. The financing of the purchase.
8. The disposition of obsolete or replaced equipment.
9. The purchase of used equipment.
10. Leasing.

General Principles which should Control the Selection of Equipment

The selection of major equipment is clearly based upon due consideration of a wide range of factors, so coordinated that the net result is efficient manufacture of the desired product at the lowest net cost per unit. To achieve this, it is necessary to analyze not only the price of the particular equipment in question but also such elements as plant layout, kind of power used, types of machines used for other operations, and the like. In short, the proposed installation must be looked upon as an integral part of an established production process; and its coordination with the existing plant facilities must be obtained, even though extensive changes may be required to effect economical production.

Decisions as to equipment purchases involve in part engineering and production considerations and in part factors largely outside the scope of these functions. From the former standpoint, there are six commonly recognized reasons for purchase: economy in operation, increased productivity, better quality, dependability in use, savings in time or labour costs, and durability. To these safety, pollution, and emergency protection should be added.

Beyond these engineering questions are those which only the marketing department, purchasing department, financial department, or general management itself can answer. Are style changes or other modifications in the present product essential or even desirable? Is the market static, contracting, or expanding? Does the company have the funds with which to buy the machine which theoretically is most desirable, or is it necessary, for financial reasons, to be satisfied with something that is perhaps less efficient but of a lower initial cost? What should be done in a case in which the particular equipment most desirable from an engineering standpoint is obtainable only from a manufacturer who is not thoroughly trustworthy or perhaps is on the verge of bankruptcy? Such questions are quite as important in the final decision as are the more purety engineering ones, and they are not questions which the engineer is qualified to answer. This merely emphasizes once more the many-sided nature of the problem and the many types of judgment required in reaching a sound solution of it.

Importance of Cost Factors

Once the need for new equipment has been determined, one of the first questions to be considered is that of the cost. To arrive at the right answer to cost is likely to be difficult, calling for a careful balancing of several factors. For example, among the facts called for are the following: Is the equipment intended for replacement only or to provide additional capacity? What is the installed cost of the equipment? Will its installation create problems of plant layout? What will be the maintenance and repair cost? Are accessories required, and, if so, what will their cost be? What will be the operating cost, including power and labour? What is the number of machine-hours the equipment will be used? Can the user make the machine in his own plant, or must it be bought outside? At what rate is the machine to be depreciated? What financing costs are involved? If, as is usually the case, the equipment is for production, what is the present cost of producing the product for which it is intended as compared with obtaining the item from an outside supplier and as compared with the cost of producing the unit with the new equipment?

Since the middle 1950s, there has been a substantial growth in the use of quantitative methods in the analysis of capital investment and capital equipment purchases. Research in mathematics and the increasing availability of computers have provided tools for a depth of economic analysis not feasible in the past. The increased sophistication of business managers in using such concepts as "discounted cash How," "return on investment," and "present value" in making capital equipment and investment decisions has probably resulted in greater understanding and improved decisions."

Life Cycle Costing

The Department of Defense has strongly encouraged the use of Life Cycle Costing (LCC) as a decision approach to capital investments. The philosophy behind LCC is relatively simple. The total cost of a piece of equipment goes well beyond the purchase price or even its installed east. What is really of interest is the total cost of performing the intended function over the life time of the task or the piece of equipment. Thus, an initial low purchase price may mask a higher operating cost, perhaps occasioned by higher maintenance and downtime costs, more skilled labor, greater material waste, more energy use, or higher waste processing changes. Since the low bid would favour a low initial machine cost an unfair advantage may accrue to the supplier with possibly the highest life cycle cost equipment.

The Logistics Management Institute defines LCC as "the total cost of a system during its operational life:" It is the inclusion of every conceivable cost pertaining to the decision that makes the concept easier to grasp theoretically than practice in real life. Since many of the costs are future ones possibly even 10 to 15 years hence of a highly uncertain nature, criticisms of the exactness of LCC are well founded. Fortunately, computer programmes are available varying from simple accounting programmes, which compute eight of the LCC from projected life cycles, to Monte Carlo simulation of the equipment from conception to disposal. The computer allows for testing of sensitivity, and inputs can be readily changed when necessary. The normal emphasis, particularly in governmental acquisition, on the low bid fines, therefore, a serious and preferable alternative in LCC. The experience with LCC has shown in a surprising number of instances that the initial purchase price of equipment may be a relatively low percentage of LCC. For example, computers, if purchased, seldom run over 50 percent, and most industrial equipment falls into the 20-percent—60-percent range.

There are eight steps in LCC formulation. In practice, one may combine some of the following eight steps:

1. Establish the operating profile.

2. Establish the utilization factors.

3. Identify all cost elements.

4. Determine the critical cost parameters.
5. Calculate all costs at current prices.
6. Escalate current labour and material costs.
7. Discount all costs to base period.
8. Sum up all discounted and undiscounted costs.

Problem of Engineering Service

Most sellers of major equipment maintain an intimate and continuing interest in their equipment after it is sold and installed. Two major questions are involved in providing engineering service: why the service is given and accepted, and what the cost of such service is.

Technical sales service is provided by a vendor to a potential Or actual purchaser of equipment, to determine the designs and specifications of the equipment believed best suited to the particular requirements of the buyer and also to ensure that, once bought, the equipment functions properly. It is nearly always related to the "individualized buying problem of particular users:" Some sellers feel that the equipment they sell is so complicated or requires such fine adjustment that none but their own experts can either install the machines or service them after installation. The vendor may feel further that the buyer's operatives need to be specially trained, perhaps for weeks or months, before they can be trusted to handle the equipment themselves. Occasionally, equipment is sold which carries with it a production guarantee, an additional reason for supervising both the installation and the operation of the equipment. Even after this initial period, the seller may provide for regular inspection to ensure the proper operation of the machine.

In many instances, services of these various types are thoroughly warranted; and it is to the best interests of buyer and seller alike that they be offered by the vendor and utilized by the purchaser. Smaller companies may well be most in need of such assistance because they are unable to employ their own consulting engineers. Furthermore, regardless of the size of the company making the purchase, the greater the amount either of pres ale or postsale service rendered by the seller, the greater the responsibility of the latter for proper and satisfactory performance.

There is, however, another side to this question of sales service. For one thing, the prospective buyer may ask for and receive a great deal of presale service and advice without real intention of buying or knowing full well that the firm providing the service will under no circumstances receive an order. Not only is such a procedure unethical, but the buyer who pursues it will sooner or later find the organization's reputation for fair dealing has seriously suffered.

Yet abuses are by no means confined to the buyers. It is well known that salesmen often solicit requests for export consulting service from buyers without any real inquiry as to whether or not a sale is likely to materialize. Furthermore, the theory that such services are mutually advantageous is not always substantiated by the facts. The seller's claims as to the necessity of vendor-supervised installation and instruction are not always warranted.

The problem of engineering service is really twofold, both phases, however, involving cost. The first phase relates to the method followed by the seller in charging for presale service. Such service is clearly a matter of sales promotion, and, when no subsequent sale results or when the profit on the sale is insufficient to cover fully the cost of the service, some other means of caring for it must be found. If the total costs of all such service are borne only by the firms which actually do buy, the price paid will appear unduly high; yet this method may prove the only feasible way of handling the charge. The problem is complicated further when a firm produces, two lines of product, one requiring service and the other not. If presale service cost is charged into general sales promotion overhead, clearly the one product is likely to be overpriced and the other underpriced; this situation places the seller in an awkward competitive position. One suggestion that has been made for meeting this problem is that a specific charge, either a flat fee or one computed on the basis of actual cost, be made for presale engineering service, the recipient of the service paying this charge irrespective of whether or not a purchase is made subsequently.

The second phase of the probl,em relates, to posts ale engineering service. The prime abuse of postsale services arises from those firms which insist upon furnishing it and upon charging for it, whether or not the buyer feels a need for it. Such charges naturally become a part of the price paid for the equipment, irrespective of whether they are included in a single quotation or are billed to the purchaser separately. When the service is really needed, no objection to such charges can be raised by the buyer, provided, of course, that they are fair. The purchaser must see to it, however, that the service actually is necessary and that the charges are legitimate and reasonable. Such considerations are matters of price negotiation and should be settled before the purchase contract is signed.

Timing of the Purchase

The determination of the proper time at which to make a purchase of equipment is significant although its importance varies both with the amount of money involved and with the character of the item. One requiring a large expenditure naturally receives more attention than one necessitating only a small sum; the purchase of a piece of "productive" equipment such as a turret lathe is likely to be more carefully considered than the purchase of a "non-productive" item such as a desk, although both are, properly speaking, "equipment."

Productive equipment, particularly of an expensive nature, is usually bought on a basis of known requirements. The equipment is bought only when, after an analysis of all cost and other factors, it appears probable that the purchase will "pay for itself" within a definite period of time. The exact length of this period naturally varies widely both with company policy and with the item in question. It may range from six months to several years or more. Obviously, in spite of all the formulas, this evidence is often somewhat difficult to produce, since it calls for judgment as to future sales and prices as well as cost figures.

For one thing, the need for expansion is normally felt during prosper ous periods. Demand may be artificial, in the sense that it is caused by cantracting ahead ar by purchasing in advance of immediate requirements ar through fear of inability to abtain supplies when needed, and is greatest at such it time. Pressure from the sales force through complaints that orders are not filled promptly, from the production department, which is campelled to work overtime, and from stackholders, who demand that the company get its share of the business all these lead to the expansion. During periods of recession, this need is not apparent. Furthermore, the funds available during the prosperous periods are not available in a period of recession, even if the managers were willing to' invest in equipment at such a time. True, during prosperous times a concern might set aside money to be used for plant improvements or expansion in a time of recession. Actually, this is seldom done partly because it is difficult to invest money in such a way that the company will receive a satisfactory profit and still be able to liquidate the investment without being forced to take an inordinate loss. Expansion thus occurs during times that are already prosperous and thus still further pramotes overcapacity and overproduction, even though from some points of view the reasons do not appear entirely logical.

Selection of the Source

Selection of the proper source requires careful consideration in any purchase of majar equipment. In the purchase of raw materials and supplies, quick delivery and the availability of a continuous supply are impartant reasons for choosing a particular supplier. These characteristics are not so important in equipment purchases. The reliability of the seller and a reasonable price are, of course, important, regardless of what is being bought. But, as contrasted with raw materials, what may be called "cooperation" in selecting the right type of equipment, proper installation, comman interests in efficient operation-in short, a long-continuing interest in the product after it is sold—becomes very important so, too, does the availability of repair parts and of repair services throughaot the entire life of the machine. Satisfactory past relationships with the equipment supplier weigh heavily in the placing of future orders.

During the 1960s and early 1970s there was a substantial increase in foreign-made capital equipment sold in Narth America. Whether this was caused primarily by availability, price, technology, or other reasons is not entirely clear. The difficulties of obtaining service from non-domestic manufacturers may be considerable even for such simple reasons as poor translations of service manuals.

Normally, the interest of operatians, engineering, or technical personnel in capital equipment is such that their source preference is a normal rather than unusual problem with which the purchaser must cope.

Manufacture of a needed item may at times be quite possible, particularly of comparatively simple standardized equipment, such as a coal crusher. Furthermore, it may be the mast economical method of procedure, even thaugh a payment for the use of same patented feature is involved. The basic questions involved in "make or buy" have been covered in another chapter and need not be reviewed here, even thaugh the manufacture of a piece of equipment does call for some modificatian in the application of the generalizations there laid down.

Some Legal Questions

Attention should also be directed to the legal questions that arise in connection with equipment buying, although no attempt will be made to discuss them here. The danger of liability for patent infringement constitutes onc such problem. The extent of liability for accidents to employees is another. Again, the equipment sales contracts and purchase agreements are often long and involved, offering many opportunities for legal controversies. Various forms of insurance coverage are used and are often subject to varying interpretations. Any purchased machine must comply fully with the safety regulations of the state in which it is to be operated, and these safety regulations vary greatly in the different states.

As of recently the Federal Government OSHA requirements have to be followed. The question of consequential damages is a particularly touchy one. Should the seller of a key piece of equipment be responsible for the loss af sales and contribution when the machine fails because of a design or fabrication error? Such losses may be huge for the buyer. In one company gross revenue of $1 million per day was last for six manths because of the failure of a new piece of equipment casting $800,000 These and many ather situations exist which call for careful scrutiny and interpretation by qualified legal caunsel. The impartance of this phase of equipment buying should not be averlooked.

Financing of the Purchase

Before any commitment to buy a major item is authorized, careful thought must be given not only to the desirability of the purchase but also to the means by which payment is to be provided. Regardless of what else may be said for the equipment, unless it can be paid for, obviously no action can be taken.

When the financial budget is set up, it is customary to make provisian for two types of capital expenditure. The first type covers probable expenditures which, although praperly chargeable to some capital account, are stiII too small to be brought directly to the attention of the finance committee or controller. Customarily, some limit is fixed, as, far example, $500 ar $1,000.

The second type includes expenditures for larger amounts. These are also provided for in the budget, because large sums are involved and because the practice may induce those responsible for such purchases to plan their equipment needs well in advance. The inclusion in the budget, however, constitutes neither an authorization to spend that amount of money nor an approval of any specific equipment acquisition. This authorization must be obtained subsequently from the appropriate executives concerned, and their specific approval is given only after they have examined carefully a preliminary, although detailed, analysis of the project. To secure such authorization, a formal appropriation request is called for, giving a detailed description of what is to be bought, estimates of the costs involved, the savings likely to result, the causes which have created the need, the effect of the purchase upon the organization as a whole, and whatever other information those initiating the request feel is pertinent or the financial authorities may request. In the light of these facts, together with the data regarding other financial requirements of the company and its financial position, a decision is made as to the wisdom of authorizing the particular expenditure under consideration.

In years past, no major capital expenditure was possible unless the company either had the necessary funds on hand or could secure them through what may be termed the "orthodox channels." More recently, however, the sellers of equipment have made possible purchase on a deferred payment plan, and today there are very few types of standardized machinery that cannot be secured on this basis. The wisdom of buying equipment on such a plan is, of course, a matter which each individual company must decide for itself and then only with reference to the particular purchase in question. Two general comments only will be made at this point.

In the first place, it in undoubtedly true that such financial arrangements have made it possible for some manufacturers to secure needed equipment more promptly than they otherwise could. Improvements in both design and type are continually being made in almost all kinds of machinery and other equipment. If a manufacturer is to continue to compete effectively, one means of keeping costs down is to reduce, as far as possible, the disadvantages of operating with obsolete equipment. But, although fully cognizant of the need for new machinery, a manufacturer may not be able to raise enough cash to pay for the purchase. Deferred payment plans or leasing may make it possible to meet this problem.

In the second place, before placing an order on a deferred payment basis, the purchaser must be doubly sure that the purchase is really wise. Installment selling is essentially a device by which sellers develop a market much more intensively than they could otherwise often, it should be added, to the disadvantage of buyer and seller alike. From the buyer's angle, the anticipated savings may never develop, or at least are materially less hoped for. Again, the buyer may be tempted not only to replace existing equipment but, either through additional machines or through the acquisition of equipment of greater capacity, to overexpand. The financing charge may be excessive and, in any event, must always be considered in arriving at the total cost. Finally, the dang that the new equipment may become obsolete before it is paid for will be greater in the case of installment purchases, because of the longer time over which payment is made. From the seller's standpoint, we need only point out that if such sales are made unwisely, it is quite possible that the market may be overdeveloped, with all the attendant problems.

An interesting variation of the deferred payment plan has developed in recent years, particularly in some industries, based on the theory that the payments to the seller are dependent upon and proportional to the anticipated savings.

Leasing, a popular method of financing equipment, is described at the end of this chapter.

Disposition of Obsolete or Replaced Equipment

This problem takes various forms—all resolving themselves into a decision as to the most economical and profitable method of disposition. One procedure is to trade in the old machine on the new, the vendor making an allowance and assuming the burden of disposing of it as best he can. A second procedure is to sell the old equipment to a used equipment dealer directly. A third method is to find a direct buyer. A fourth method is to sell the old machine as scrap. A fifth method is to destroy the machine to assure no one else will have access to it.

The responsibility for disposing of the displaced machines commonly rests on the purchaser. This responsibility is clear when dealing directly with prospective users or with used equipment dealers. Trade-in allowances raise a somewhat different problem in that all such allowances are likely to be price concessions on the new equipment instead of being based solely upon the actual market value of the machine traded in. The responsibility for excessive allowances of this nature rests essentially on the seller and not on the buyer. The latter may go too far in getting price concessions. The chief abuse of the trade-in practice has been committed not by buyers but by sellers.

The purchase of used equipment rather than new often raises some interesting issues. In general, the same rules of evaluation apply as in the case of new equipment. One important difference, however, may be that, ordinarily, manufacturers' services and guarantees do not apply to such purchases. The value of these intangibles is difficult to determine. Many buyers would say that they are more important with used equipment than with new and that their value may be greater than any differential in price. The matter, however, is one of individual judgment as applied to each particular purchase.

Procurement of Major Equipment—used and Leased

In our discussion of equipment purchases thus far, it has been largely assumed that the buyer was acquiring new equipment. An alternative to such a procedure is the purchase of used equipment.

Why used Equipment Comes on the Market

Used equipment comes onto the market through a variety of reasons. One obvious result of the modernization of a plant is the disposition of the displaced equipment. It can, of course, as a last resort, be demolished and sold as scrap. It may be possible, however, to utilize at least some of the machinery in some other department or plant of the company. But if this is not feasible, then the equipment may be sold at a price yielding a return well above the scrap values In addition to this somewhat general reason, there are other explanations as to the appearance of used equipment on the market. Some of these may be listed as follows:

1. Loss of contracts.

2. Change in process or in line of manufacturing.

3. Obsolescence in a specific use.
4. Insufficient productivity to meet the needs of the original owner.
5. Trade-in on a new machine.
6. Inadequacy to meet new requirements.
7. Discontinuance of entire manufacturing operations because of bankruptcy, insolvency, death of owner, etc.

Sales Contract Terms

Having used equipment either to sell or to buy, a manufacturer has at least two problems. The first relates to the terms of contract. Here there are three choices: *(1)* The equipment may be disposed of "as is" and perhaps "where is." A sales "as is" means that the contract carries essentially "no warranty, guarantee, or representation of any kind, expressed or implied, as to the condition of the item offered for saie." "Where is," of course, is self-explanatory. *(2)* The equipment may be sold with certain specific guarantees, preferably expressed in writing. This practice is found more generally among used equipment dealers, though they sometimes may offer equipment "as is;" (3) Finally, the equipment may be sold "guaranteed and rebuilt." The desirable interpretation placed on this is that the equipment has been rebuilt or is in condition equivalent to that of a rebuilt machine and is invoiced as such; that it has been tested; and that it carries a binding guarantee of satisfactory performance for not less than 30 days from the date of shipment.

Organization of used Equipment Market

The next query relates to the channels through which the equipment is bought and sold. Here, too, there are various alternatives. Briefly, they are:

1. Trade-in as partial payment on new equipment.
2. Direct sale to a user.

3. Sale through a broker or liquidating agent.
4. Sale at auction.
5. Sale to a dealer in used equipment.

Trade-in as Partial Payment on New Equipment. Generally speaking, manufacturers of equipment are unwilling to accept used equipment as part payment on new. Under certain circumstances, however, in the interest of customer goodwill, they may be willing to assist a prospective buyer of new equipment to locate a buyer for the used. This is most likely to be the case *(1)* when the item to be sold is non-competitive with anything manufactured by the seller or *(2)* when the buyer is a regular customer of the particular equipment manufacturer. When the seller is unable to make delivery of a new item in time to meet the buyer's requirements, he may even go so far as hot only to suggest a market for the equipment to be replaced but to indicate where it may be possible to locate a piece of used equipment of the type sought.

It must be recognized, however, that, except in the obvious case of direct sale to user, the utilization of one of these channels does hot necessarily preclude the use of another. Thus, a used machine may be sold by the owner to a dealer, who in turn sells to another user. Or a liquidating agent may sell either to a dealer or to a us.er and may do so either directly or through an auction. Although direct purchase from the seller is an important method of acquisition, in the brief description which follows, major attention will be devoted to the dealel, probably the most important single agency in the market.

Direct Sale to User. Direct sale through the company's own organization is often a profitable method of disposal. Through advertising in trade journals or some other media, the attention of potential buyers may be attracted to the offer, and negotiation initiated either by mail or by direct visitation. Used equipment is frequently disposed of in this manner. Since this procedure eliminates the use of an intermediary, it suggests a saving of the latter's profit.

Finding a buyer, moreover, often does not appear to be a serious problem, particularly since the potential buyers are likely to be somewhat limited in number and the seller ordinarily has a sales organization already set up. However, experience has shown that in many cases the "saving of the middleman's profit" is illusory and that direct sale actually is time-consuming, troublesome, and ineffective so far as securing as high a return as can be secured through other methods is concerned. This is particularly true when, for instance, an entire plant is being closed down and the equipment sold.

Sale Through Broker. Brokers, in theory at least, do not take title to the equipment in which they are interested but seek only to bring buyers and sellers together. In fact, however, they may act in the capacity both of brokers and of dealers, though obviously not for the same equipment. Used equipment brokers are more important in some industries than in others. Comparatively few of them, for instance, specialize in general machine tools, largely because of the multiplicity of regular dealers. Brokers frequently employ personal selling and advertising to liquidate equipment and commonly realize a commission of 10 to 15 percent on the gross sale.

Sale at Auction. Auction firms vary in type and character. Some are highly reputable. Others are not always so regarded. One type of auction firm is the trader who buys stock and auctions it off. This type of firm frequently has representatives both at its own sale and at other auctions to encourage bidding and to acquire good machines that, for one reason or another, do not bring high prices on the day of the initial auction. While the auction commission is less than that for a broker, the price realized on the merchandise frequently is lower, inasmuch as it is impossible to bring together in a local region as many interested buyers as can be reached through direct-mail advertising. On the other hand, by the use of the auction method, it is possible at times to realize higher prices because it gives play to the emotional factors involved when bidders openly compete against one another.

From the standpoint of the buyer, both equipment and material can often be obtained economically through an auction sale. However, to buy well calls for a rare degree of ability on the part of the bidder, since it requires an intimate knowledge of one's requirements, judgment as to the economic worth of the items, an understanding with management in advance as to the amount of funds available, and skill in the difficult art of bidding.

Sale to Dealers. There are many types of dealers who buy and sell used machinery tools and other used equipment. Certain dealers act as brokers in handling some sales, while at other times they purchase outright. Another class of dealers stock new as well as used machines, but many-perhaps most-dealers specialize only in used equipment. In addition, many dealers rebuild equipment. The largest dealers of this type maintain plants which manufacture parts for used machinery, and they also employ an engineering staff to design improvements for the rebuilt machines. They then offer the machines "rebuilt," including guarantees which often are more comprehensive than those given by new machinery manufacturers. A large number of dealers stock used machinery in warehouses and sell to manufacturers and other dealers. Still a different type is the merchant who buys machinery by placing a deposit against it and then sells it before moving it from the premises were it was purchased, thus eliminatin the necessity of warehousing.

Plants about to be closed down or liquidated following bankruptcy are sometimes bought by another type of large buyer, a speculator who attempts to keep a liquidated plant in operation for a time. Often these plants are operated only long enough to process the material on hand.

A used equipment dealer may acquire used equipment from several sources. Many large manufacturing firms ask a dealer to inspect a plant that is being closed down and to make an offer for the machinery which it contains. While some of these firms have previous buying or selling relations with the dealer, others are influenced by the dealer's advertising or by customers' recommendations. In prepared trade journal advertising and on sales brochures, a dealer may indicate a willingness to buy any quantity of good used machinery and offer to send a representative to inspect such equipment. The dealer may also invite firms that are contemplating the purchase or sale of surplus equipment to write for sales bulletins, which outline the services which the dealer offers.

Some large used equipment companies do not undertake to repair and rebuild the equipment they purchase, but instead they have the machines overhauled and repaired by various organizations that specialize in specific types of machines. They believe that no one dealer can adequately rebuild the machines which these larger companies handle. Such concerns, moreover, do not acquire the real estate when they purchase entire plants but concentrate only on the machinery and equip-ment contained therein. It is obviously difficult to keep track of the fluctuating real estate values in the many different cities in which some companies operate, and they consequently prefer to stick to the line in which they specialize.

While many purchasing officers say they are opposed to purchasing used equipment, virtually all do buy it in larger or smaller quantities. The policy varies widely from company to company. Some apparently buy it only under unusual circumstances, while others buy used equipment in preference to new whenever a satisfactory purchase can be made.

Reasons for Buying used Equipment

Some of the reasons for the purchase of used equipment follow:

1. When price is important either because the differential between new and used is vital or the buyer's'funds are low.
2. For use in a pilot or experimental plant.
3. For use with a special or temporary order over which the entire cost will he amortized.
4. Where the machine will be idle a substantial amount of time.

5. For use of apprentices.
6. For maintenance departments (not production).
7. For better delivery when time is essential.
8. When a used machine can be easily modernized for relatively little or is already the latest model.
9. When labour costs are unduly high.

Leasing Equipment

It was pointed out earlier that purchasing used equipment was one of two alternatives to purchasing new equipment, a second being leasing equipment. Some attention needs to be directed to this possibility. Since the end of World War II, there has been a substantial increase in the number and diversity of manufacturers of capital equipment who lease as well as sell their equipment. Those who advocate leasing point out that the concept of leasing involves payments for the use of the assets rather than payment for the privilege of owning the asset.

Short-term rentals are a special form of lease with which everyone is familiar. Short-term rentals make a lot of sense when limited use of the equipment is foreseen and the capital and/or maintenance cost of the equipment is significant. Often an operator can be obtained along with the piece of equipment rented. The construction industry is a good example where extensive use is made of short-term rentals.

Most lease contracts can be drawn to include an "option to buy" the equipment involved after some stated period. It is important for anyone considering the lease of capital equipment to be sure that the latest Internal Revenue regulations are understood. On October 15, 1955, the Internal Revenue Service announced its position on ascertaining the tax status of leases as follows:

In the absence of compelling factors of contrary implication the parties will be considered as having intended a purchase and sale rather than a rental, if one or more of the following conditions are covered in the agreement:

1. Portions of periodic payments are specifically applicable to an equity to be acquired by the lessees.
2. The lessees will acquire title upon payment of a stated amount of rentals.
3. The agreed rental payments exceed the current fair-rented values.
4. The total amount which the lessee is required to pay for a relatively short period constitutes an inordinately large proportion of the total sum required to be paid to secure transfer of title.
5. The property may be acquired under a purchase option which is nominal in relation to the valur of the property at the time when the option may be exercised, as determined at the'time of entering into the original agreement, or which is a relatively small amount when compared with the total payments which are required to be made.
6. Some portion of periodic payments is specifically designated as interest or is otherwise recognizable as the equivalent of interest.

Unless the lease rental payments are allowed to be treated as an expense item for income tax purposes, some of the possible advantages of the equipment lease plan may not be realized.

In the past, some large manufacturers of machines and equipment employing advanced technology have preferred to follow a policy of leasing rather than selling their equipment. Government antitrust actions have aimed at giving the user the right to determine whether he wished to lease or purchase. The leasing may be done by the manufacturers of the equipment, by distributors, or by companies organized for the specific purpose of leasing equipment. At times, as in the construction industry, an owner of equipment who has no immediate use for his equipment may lease or rent it to other concerns that may have temporary immediate need for it.

Types of Leases

There are two main types of lease, the financial and the operational. The financial lease is primarily financial in nature and may be of the full payout or partial payout variety. In the full payout form the lessee pays the full purchase price of the equipment plus interest and, if applicable, maintenance, service, record keeping, and insurance charges on a regular payment plan. In the partial payout plan there is a residual value to the equipment at the end of the lease term and the lessee pays for the difference between original cost and residual value plus interest and charges.

The financial lease cost is made up of the lessor's fee, the interest rate and the depreciation rate of the equipment. The lessor's fee depends on the services offered and may be as low as .25 percent of the gross for straight financing without other services. The interest will depend both on the cost of money to the lessor and the credit rating of the lessee. The depreciation normally varies with the type of equipment and its usc. For example, trucks are usually depreciated over a five-year period.

The operational lease is in its basic form non-cancellable, has a fixed term which is substantially less than the life of the equipment and a fixed financial commitment which is substantially less than the purchase price of the equipment. Service is the key factor in the operational lease with the lessor assuming full responsibility for maintenance, obsolescence, insurance, taxes, purchase, and resale of the equipment, etc. The charges for these services must be evaluated by the lessee against other alternatives which may be open.

Categories of Leasing Companies

According to J. P. Matthews careful analysis of how the lessor will profit from the leasing arrangement is vital in obtaining a satisfactory price. Since most leasing companies have standard procedures for calculating leases but are seldom willing to disclose these or the vital figures behind them, it behooves the buyer to search carefully before signing. Since lessors are more likely to disclose competitors' procedures and figures than their own, the search need not be seen as an impossible task. Matthews identifies four major different structures of leasing relationships, each with its special implications.

Figure 1

FOUR LEASING STRUCTURAL RELATIONSHIPS

THE FULL SERVICE LESSOR THE FINANCE LEASE COMPANY

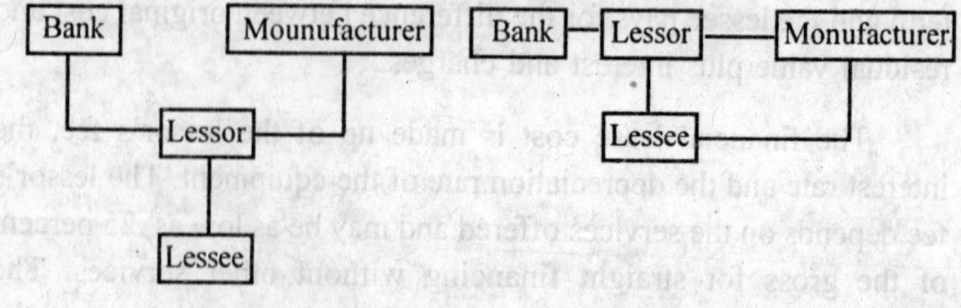

THE CAPTIVE LEASING COMPANY BANK PARTICIPATION

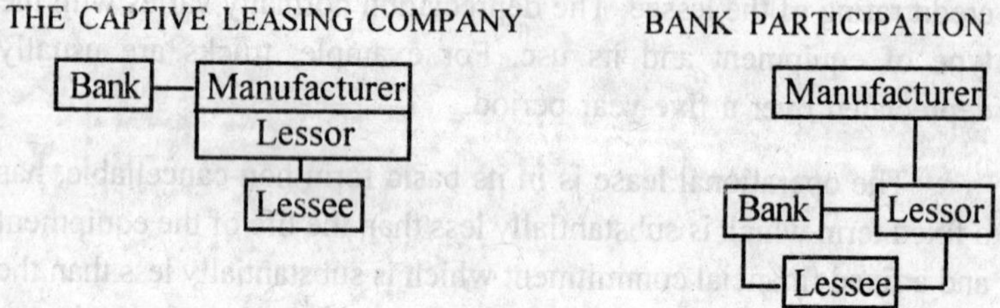

1. The full Service Lessor. Full service lessors are most common in the automotive, office equipment, and industrial equipment fields. The lessor performs all services, purchases the equipment to the buyer's specifications, and has its own source of financing. This type of lessor generally obtains discounts or rebates from the equipment manufacturers which are not disclosed to the lessee. Profits are also obtained on the maintenance and service charges which are included in the lease rate. Care should be taken on long-term leases which contain an escalation provision to allow such escalation only on that portion of the lease on which costs might rise.

2. The Finance Leaae Company. This type of lessor does not purchase or maintain the equipment, so that the lessee deals directly with the equipment manufacturer. The lessor frequently has access to funds at close to prime rate and is able to make its profit by lending above this. Occasionally, if a relatively short lease is involved, the lessor may wish to profit from the resale value of the equipment and may offer unusually low lending rates. A profitable lessor may benefit from the investment tax credits and depreciation which to a less profitable lessee may be meaningless. When a lessee has already reached the limits on its investment tax credits because of large capital expenditures but the lessor is not yet at the limit, leasing may similarly benefit both.

3. Captive Leasing. The prime purpose of captive leasing is to encourage the sale and use of the parent's equipment. The reasons why the original manufacturer of equipment may choose to lease rather than to sell are several.

1. To secure either wider distribution or a higher margin.
2. To reduce the credit risk.
3. To sell a full line or to increase the volume of sales of supplies.
4. To control the secondhand market.
5. To stabilize the company's growth through securing distribution in times of recession when sales, especially of new as contrasted with used equipment, are difficult to make.

The lease agreement has also been of value to some manufacturers in protecting their patent position.

These advantages, of course, usually apply only in part and to some what special situations. All of them are somewhat debatable. But where they do apply, the company making use of the leasing device, while at the same time well aware of its dangers, is often in a strong position.

Obviously, a transfer price for the equipment holds between the parent and the lessor. Sometimes a lessor will quote a 2 percent sales tax figure on the rental value when in reality the lessor may only be charged with a use tax which applies to only 50 percent of the rental value. A lessee might expect to gain at least a 1 percent benefit from negotiation here.

4. Bank Participation. There are advantages to bank participation in cases where the lessee has a good credit rating. The bank may be willing to finance part of the lease at rates slightly over prime, because it is a low-risk and low-nuisance lease. The lessor looks after the purchasing, servicing, and disposal of the equipment, relieving the bank of tasks it normally has little expertise in.

Advantages and Disadvantages

We are here more concerned, however, with the user of the equipment, particularly the company with option to lease or buy. Without undertaking to elaborate upon them, for they are self-evident, the advantages of leasing may be listed as follows:

1. Burden of investment shifted to supplier.
2. Small initial outlay (may actually cost less).
3. Availability of expert service.
4. Risk of obsolescence reduced.
5. Adaptability to special jobs and seasonal business.
6. Test period provided before purchase.
7. Lease rentals are expenses for income tax purposes.

On the other hand, there are certain equally clear disadvantages:

1. Final cost likely to be high.
2. Surveillance by lessor entailed.
3. Less freedom of control and use.

Many leases are definitely one-sided in their terms, placing virtully all the risks on the lessee. These terms, therefore, need to be watched with the utmost care. For instance, what are the arrangements for replacing equipment when obsolete or no longer serviceable? Is the lessee in fact free to buy supplies anywhere, such as paper for copying machines? Are the actual charges what they appear to be? Are there onerous limitations on either the maximum or the minimum output or other such operational factors as the number of hours per day or number of shifts the equipment may be used or on using attachments? What limitations, if any, are there to the uses to which the equipment may be put?

Evaluation of Advantages and Disadvantages

To evaluate these advantages and disadvantages is no easy task. Take, for example, the matter of cost. A buyer might be tempted to assume that if the purchase price equaled approximately five times the annual rental charged, this would be an excessive price for leasing. Yet, before coming to this conclusion, the buyer must remember that the annual rental in dollars includes more than merely recovering the cost of the equipment, since the lease rate presumably includes allowances for such charges as service and maintenance, insurance, and interest. Moreover, should the buyer purchase the equipment not only these charges would be assumed but the very intangible risks of depreciation and obsolescence.

Or take the moot question as to the freedom of a lessor to buy supplies from someone other than the owner of the leased equipment:

In some cases manufacturers of both supplies and basic equipment have used their equipment installations as a method of promoting the sale of supplies by leasing the equipment at very low annual rates in order to secure the lessee's orders for supplies. From the user's standpoint this may have an important impact on purchasing. Selection of supplies may be based more upon the evaluation of the basic equipment installation than on the price and quality of supplies from competing sources.

Users must recognize that their choice of equipment introduces certain pressures for purchasing supplies and auxiliary equipment from the equipment manufacturer. A lease may serve to accentuate such pressures.....The effective performance of the machine, as well as its cost of maintenance and repair, may be materially affected by the type of supplies used. Obviously, the vendor's reputatio is threatened if his equipment does not live up to performance claims. Consequently it may be argued that if his own supplies are used, the equipment will operate at maximum efficiency......But under the lease, the argument will be more forceful, since the lessor can show that he has a direct interest in the particular equipment installation.

A lessor assumes a great interest and responsibility for the servicing of leased equipment. Since ownership remains with the lessor under the lease, he must take precautions against damage to his equipment resulting from improper use by the lessee. If an improper supply item is used, it may increase the amount and cost of servicing required. If the rental is based upon units of output, the use of inferior supply items can reduce the lessor's revenue from the lease. In either case, the lessor can argue that he has a direct interest in the type of supplies purchased by the user....

Even if it is assumed that there is no contractual agreement concerning the purchase of supplies, and that the lessor does not actively push the argument that his own supplies are essential for the maximum performance of the equipment, this purchasing consideration still exists. The user should anticipate that there will be an inclination to assume that supplies provided by the company who makes the equipment will be superior for use with that particular type of equipment.....

Quite aside from any weighing of the specific advantages and disadvantages and beyond the actual terms of the lease, any prospective lessee of equipment needs to exercise the utmost care in passing judgment on the lessor. Is the lessor:

1. Reasonable and fair in dealings with customers?

2. Devoting as much attention and money to research as alleged?

3. Strong financially?

4. Fully protected by patents?

5. If a sole source, prone to be arbitrary in the periodic adjustment of rental and other fees?

What effect would a fire in the lessor's plant have on the repair and servicing requirements of the user?

There is neither formula nor theory which can provide the right answer to all these questions. The solution to each particular problem can be found only in the sound judgment of the procurement personnel within the buyer's organization.

❐

13

Material Logistics—Material Handling & Warehousing

The role of the stores has at long last been recognized as a management function, and it takes its rightful place alongside purchasing, stock control, production planning and control, and materials control.

Stores has much to offer to the viability of the organization it serves if it is managed by well-trained, experienced and responsible management who make integrity the hallmark of everything they do. One of the roles in which the stores must operate is as the 'bank' inside the company, for it is in the stores that huge sums of money-in-kind have to be taken care of, looked after and controlled. This money-in-kind has to be controlled and accounted for, and only issued on presentation of a properly authorized document, in the same way that money from a bank is only issued on the presentation of a properly authorized cheque. All the same rules by which a bank secures the money it holds should be practised by the stores to protect the large sums of money-in-kind that it contains. The staff in a bank are trained personnel, many of whom hold a qualification in banking while others are still being taught. They are people of high integrity and know they are in the bank to give a service to customers. They are affable, but strictly cautious. They refuse to hand out any money without correct authority: No one is even allowed behind the counter of a bank unless they are employed in the bank. All these same rules and personal behaviour pattern should be exercised by and in the stores if we want to have an efficient and effective function contributing to the overall viability of the company.

Another role the stores function has to perform is the responsibility for seeing that the company's outgoing cash for materials, supplies and services, which today exceeds 55 per cent of the total outgoing cash of the company, is at all times fully safeguarded, by making absolutely certain that we get value for money for everything we accept into stock. Also, claims for goods damaged in transit or short-delivered must be dealt with in the proper manner and on time, working very closely with the finance department to make sure we do not pay anything to anyone for materials, supplies and services until stores have authorized payment through the issue of a goods receipt note.

Another role to be discharged by stores is to make certain the whole operation works like a transit camp, through which many thousands of items will pass on their way into use, at which tinte they viill start to earn money for the company. Storehouses should never be built to be filled with stock, but only as places through which items will pause for the shortest possible time on their journey to an end use. The shorter the time they are allowed to pause, the greater the savings will be in stocking costs and the smaller will be the strain on company cashflow. The slogan for the stores must always be 'Keep it on the move,' because while we keep stocks on the move we create a healthy position for business. Another role of the stores is accountability. The stores must be accountable in two directions if it is to be effective. It has to be accountable for every item it contains, right from the time of receipt up to the time of issue. Stock-taking exercises tell us how well or how badly we are performing in this arca of accountability and, when the results are not as good as they should be, it is up to the stores to see the matter is put right in the shortest possible time.

This service level can be measured, and stores must regularly monitor it so that again we can remedy any faults and shortcomings that this may reveal. If we can remember in the stores function that 'The best today is good buy tomorrow it will be better, we shall never falter in our pursuit of giving the company the very highest standard possible, so that we can always compel senior management to need us in their corporate thinking and planning.

Before we look into details, how the stores function a brief discussion on planning the stores will not be out of order.

Stores Planning

A store which has been properly designed or planned can be operated efficiently and makes economic use of space and equipment. Planning involves a number of compromises. Space can be saved at the expense of time. TIme can be saved by using more space. Manpower usage can be balanced against labour-saving machinery; in contries where land is cheap, wages are low and people are looking for work, the automatic warehouses used in high-wage economies do not make economic sense.

Location of the store should be planned so that goods coming in from suppliers and goo s going out to customers can be moved in and out freely. Inside the store, the internal layout and the equipment and operating procedures should facilitate off-loading, checking and putting away of goods coming in, and picking, issuing and despatch of goods going out.

The store should have adequate heating lighting and ventilation, the floor should be dust-free and strong enough to support racks and fork-lift trucks. Security is important. It is a legal requirement that the health and safety at work of employees is fully provided for.

A typical central store serving several locations is an industrial building which allows four or five pallets to be stacked on top of each other, with some clear space above the stack for safety. (This corresponds to 5 to 6.5 metres, or 16 to 22 feet). Vehicle access needs to be convenient, with enough room for delivery vehicles to park, unload and turn. Loading bays should be about a metre above road level, and under cover.

Much information needs to be collected and evaluated for the design of a new store; stock range, transaction volume, space requirements, and the extent to which mechanical handling is to be used. Four questions need to be answered:

(1) What things will be received, and in what quantities? Production inputs depend on what is to be produced. Each product would need to be broken up into lists of parts and materials needed to make it, multiplied by projected production rates, in turn depending on sales estimates. Maintenance requirements depend on the plant to be installed, plant utilization—single shift working or round the-clock operation and the importance of avoiding breakdowns.

(2) Which of these items will be stocked? Some requirements may be large enough and regular enough for arrangements to be made for suppliers to deliver direct into the production process, no stock, or just a buffer stock being held. At the other extreme, some requirements will be too occasional to be carried in stock and will be bought as needed. Between these extremes lies the broad range of stockable items.

(3) How much room will these stocks take? This depends on stock levels multiplied by space requirements per item, and is also affected by holding and handling arrangements.

(4) What are the average stocks, and the maximum stocks, to be carried of each item? Volume of usage, supply conditions, stock control policies, and cost factors affect this.

The next step therefore would be to plan the racks, pallets, tote-boxes, etc. in which the stock will be held, and the use of fork trucks, overhead cranes, conveyors, etc., for handling the stock.

Finally, the layout of goods receiving sections, issue areas, storekeeper's offices, inspection, and other auxiliary service areas need to be planned, and the gangway system laid out.

In practice, something like this has to be done when a new warehouse or a new factory is purpose-built for new products or processes. But when the new stores or factory is intended to replace or expand existing ones, stores design often starts with the shortcomings of the present arrangements, and aims at better ways to solve known problems.

Unit Loads and Containers

When goods are handled in large quantities, there are advantages in standardizing unit loads. The idea is to make a more convenient unit for handling and storage purposes by loading a certain number of goods into a container and keeping them in it as long as possible. Th number of goods which make up a unit load depends on: the size of the item, the size of the container, storage, transport and handling methods, convenient delivery quantities for the supplier, convenient issue quantities for the user. Ideally goods are made up in unit loads at the point of origin and these are not broken into until the point of use, remaining in the standard lot through all intermediate transports, storages and moves.

Containers used with unit loads include: pallets, stillages, tote-boxes, freight containers. No-container unit loads are also made up by shrink-wrapping or strapping together such rigid items as bricks or cartons.

Freight containers are now widely used. Special container ships to take them, specially equipped docking areas to load and unload the ships, rail terminals and container trains, road terminals and fleets of special road vehicles for container transport have all appeared on an increasing scale. Freight containers facilitate transport rather than storage, but they have obviously influenced materials handling in the places which send or receive them.

Pallets and Stillages

Both pallets and stillages are types of load board, defined as a portable platform, with or without superstructure, for the assembly of a quantity of goods to form a unit load for handling and storage by mechanical appliances. Load boards include flat pallets, box pallets, post pallets and stillages.'

The meaning of the word stillage varies from one industry to another. A common type of stillage is a wooden platform mounted on wooden or metal skids which raise it 15 cm (6 in.) or so off the ground. This is used in conjunction with a stillage truck, often a simple angle iron fram on wheels with a tow handle. The operator pushes this frame under the stillage and pumps it from its low position to its high position, by a foot-operated hydraulic cylinder or a mechanical link with the towbar. The high position lifts the whole assembly off the ground on to the truck wheels, where it can be towed about. Semi-live stillages are also common, these are fitted with wheels at one end and the towing arrangement has only a single pair to take the front end load.

Any kind of frame for holding things can be called a stillage, and many types are made, with special attachments to hold bottles, carpet rolls, oil drums, etc.

Pallets are defined as 'a load board with two decks separated by bearers or a single deck supported by bearers, constructed with a view to transport and stacking, and with the overall height reduced to a minimum compatible for handling by fork lift trucks and pallet trucks'. Terms used in connection with pallets include the following:

(1) **Two-way Entry.** The bearers allow the forks to enter from two opposite entry sides.

(2) **Four-way Entry.** Forks can be inserted from all four sides; on two sides known as 'restricted-entry sides' the truck's load wheels have to pass over the bottom slats of the pallet.

(3) **Deck.** Top or bottom flat surface.

(4) **Bearers.** Blocks or longer pieces which separate upper and lower decks or support the upper deck if there is no lower deck.

(5) **Stringer.** Flat horizontal member connecting the bearers and supporting the deck.

(6) **Wings.** Parts of the deck which project beyond the bearers.

Types of pallet include:

(1) **Flat Pallet.** Usually made of wood or plastic; can be single decked, if the goods will not be stacked, or are strong enough to support stacking for example, wooden crated or if the pallets are going to be held in pallet racks; can be double-decked, reversible, etc.

(2) **Post Pallets.** These have comer posts so that they can be stacked on top of each other, the posts taking the weight rather than the contents. Pallet converters can be used to turn flat pallets into the equivalent of post pallets. The posts are usually made of metal and fitted with special feet which help in locating one pallet on top of another; sometimes lifting eyes or trunnions are also fitted.

(3) **Box Pallet.** These have at least three mental or timber sides, and are used to hold items which do not stack easily and would probably fallout without the sides; the sides can be solid, slatted or mesh; one or more can be removable to make it easier to put goods in and get them out; all the sides can be collapsible so that the pallet takes up less room when returned or stored empty.

(4) **Expendable Pallets.** One answer to the problem of getting your pallets back from the customer when you send palletized unit loads to him, is to use non-returnable or expendable pallets. These have to be strong enough to stand the various moves and handlings they encounter en route, and are still in a state of active development. Another answer is the pallet pool: a group of organizations use a common pool of pallets on hire or loan arrangements of some kind. A national pallet pool for the United Kingdom has been discussed, but firms are not willing to meet the cost and inconvenience of scrapping the 1200 pallet sizes they are currently using in favour of the two or three sizes

a pallet pool would use. The two preferred sizes are 12cm × l00cm (48in. × 40in,) and l00cm × 75cm (40in. × 30in.).

Pallets can be stacked on top of each other, or where this would overload them or damage the goods, in pallet racks.

Storage Racks

An extensive range of standard or semi-standard racks is available from manufacturers, as well as variops kinds of slotted angle which can be cut and fitted together to make purpose-designed shelving. The main alternatives are:

(1) **No Racks.** Floor storage is used for very heavy goods.

(2) **Fixed and Adjustable Racks.** A popular choice is the double-sided rack 2.2m (7ft 3in.) high, 2.7m (9ft) wide, and 0.9m (3ft) deep, allowing 45cm (18in.) deep shelves each side. Shelves are 0.9m (3ft) wide, the racks being made in 0.9m (3ft) bays bolted together. Distance between shelves can be adjusted to suit the size of the goods, and special drawers, dividers and cupboards are readily available. The overall height is fixed by the maximum reach of the average man standing on the ground. Heights greater than this can be reached by ladders, or by climbing up specially reinforced rack fronts, but a better way is to split high racks into levels with walk-ways or mezzanine floors at 2.0m (7ft) intervals, with at least two stairways and a gravity chute.

(3) **Sliding Racks.** Popular for items required infrequently. Small installations are moved by hand, larger blocks of shelves can be powered. Mobile racking saves space for storage, at the expense of time in getting goods out and putting them away.

(4) **Live Racks.** A system useful when items are issued continuously in large quantities, providing automatic stock

rotation. In one type, goods are accommodated on lengths of roller conveyor sloping towards the picking end.

(5) **Pallet Racks.** Fixed or adjustable racks designed to hold pallets.

Gangways between racks should be sited in line with windows to exploit natural light. Artificial light is best provided by lamps mounted above the ways, and also above receiving, checking, and issue points. Columns and stanchions should be in the rack area, not blocking gang-ways. Care should be taken that cables, pipes and sprinklers remain accessible.

The ways between racks and bins are usually divided into main roads and side streets. Main roads should be wide enough to take trucks and move the bulkiest goods: 105m (5ft) is the minimum practicable width; 1.8m (6ft) wide is a popular spacing for these main gangways. Side streets should be short to reduce walking, at right angles to main roads, and at least 0.7m (2½ft); a width of 0.9m (3ft) is easier to work.

When several trucks are in use it is a good idea to make as many gangways as possible one-way streets. The width of one-way gangways should then be 0.6m (2ft) wider than the widest truck. Two-way gangways should be 0.9m (3ft) wider than two vehicles side by side. Provision should be made for trucks to turn round.

Clear spaces must be provided for receiving, unloading, unpacking, checking and inspecting incoming goods; for keeping returnable packages; and for assembling and making issues.

Stores Location and Centralized Storage

Physical storage facilities are part of the organization's manufacturing strategy, in the case of production stocks, and part of its marketing strategy, in the case of stocks held for customers. They are links in the supply chain.

The basic principle is to store things where least work will be involved where handling, rehandling and internal transport will be minimized and journey distances for the stores customers shortest. In a factory producing a single product or a group of similar products for instance, raw material might be stored near the first operation machines, work-in-progress between first and subsequent operations, finished product near the shipping and despatch area, and small tools and works supplies near the middle of the factory area. In a factory producing different products for example, a textile factory producing jute yarn, woollen yarn, woven carpets, and operating a dyehouse—each department would store its own raw materials and central storage would be confined to common-user items such as maintenance and operating supplies.

That is one way to do it. There are others. Some very large on a world organizations operating on a world scale, for instance armies and air forces, make extensive use of centralized storage. Local authorities and government departments have to consider the extent to which storage should be centralized. Even at the level of a factory it is common to find a single central store which receives all incoming goods, and makes issues either direct to users, or else in bulk lots to sub-stores like a wholesaler supplying retailers. Setting up a central stores of this kind adds another tier to the organization structure and another set of handling's and transports to the operations sheet, which must increase costs.

If common-user items are few and the combined demand for them small, centralization will not pay in the absence of special considerations for instance maximum security for certain high priced and readily saleable goods, or the need for special testgear and trained inspectors for certain deliveries.

But if there are enough common-user items, centralizing stocks of them can save money through lower stocks, lower prices, and perhaps other reductions in overhead. How can central storage reduce stocks? If four departments have independently stocked between three and 12 months' supply of an item they all use, obviously stocks come down if better stock control enables a central stores to supply them all with two months' stock. Departmental stores are usually small and their stock control may be amateurish.

Less obviously, if four departments have independently kept three months' supply, and the item is switched to a central stores which still keeps three months' supply, there can still be a reduction in the quantity held. This is because the aggregated demand is stabler and hence more predictable than the four individual demands. The space saving may be greater than the direct stock feduction; bulk stocks take less room.

A switch to central storage should also mean fewer, larger orders—with possibilities of negotiating lower prices. Other considerations include:

1. increased opportunities for standardization, leading to fewer stock items;
2. overstocking and redundancy is usually easier to see and stop;
3. greater security against pilferage and theft may be possible;
4. administrative costs should be reduced, with fewer orders and fewer deliveries;
5. there may be a net saving space and personnel;
6. materials which can best be bought forward in bulk on long delivery may be best handled centrally. This need not mean central storage, but sometimes it is a help.

Considerations which may weigh in the other scale include:

1. extra transport cost;
2. possibly worse communications with users;
3. possible transport delays;
4. unless there is excellent service and strict control, sub-stores will build up private buffer stocks and total stocks will increase, while the expected saving in space and personnel may fail to materialize;

5. unless operating routines and paperwork are well designed, administrative costs may actually be increased.

Materials Handling

Maximum use if space with minimum waste of times is the aim in planning storage and handling facilities. It is easy to save space by keeping goods in high-bay racks or in mobile racks which have to be moved to gain access. Whether it is more important to save space, or to save time, depends mainly on the throughput. For low transaction rates, over-the-counter service by hand is suitable. For high transaction rates, mechanization and automation can pay. In some applications goods are off loaded straight into conveyor systems which feed production, the stores being represented by loops and sidings in the system.

Four main types of materials handling are:

1. By Hand. Widely used; goods are picked manually with the aid of steps, trolleys and ladders, and are carried to the issue point, with the aid of trolleys, sack trucks, etc.

2. Overhead Cranes and Hoists. Overhead travelling cranes have complete access to the area covered by their long and cross travel, without needing gangways except for storeman access.

3. Fork Trucks. These are available in considerable variety, both electric-powered and diesel-powered, as well as unpowered. They are primarily used for moving goods on pallets. Stacker trucks are mainly used for lifting or stacking pallets. Counter-balanced fork-lift trucks are perhaps the gencral purpose device for moving as well as stacking pallets, but there are several variations which operate in much narrower aisles than the counter-balanced type: for instance the reach truck, whose forks reach forward within the truck's wheel-base; the rotating-fork reach truck, which can work both sides of an aisle without the truck itself having to turn, and the stacker cranes, used in high-bay storage installations with narrow aisles.

4. Conveyors. These include:

(a) unpowered roller conveyors;

(b) powered roller conveyors;

(c) powered belt conveyors;

(d) chain-driven overhead conveyors, which move goods in carriers suspended from trolleys linked by a chain running on an overhead track or rail;

(e) underfloor dragline conveyors, in which trucks or trol leys are drawn round the floor by a chain in a channel in the floor. These are used in warehouses, where goods have to be picked from a number of different bays, the' trucks being routed automatically to spurs in the bays required. Other materials-handling equipment is also used in stores, for instance dock levellers, mobile cranes, stillage trucks.

The objective is to arrange for material to be shifted over the shortest route in the safest manner, by the quickest means, in the largest convenient unit loads, and to cut out needless movement of men and materials.

Firms without a materials-handling engineer can obtain expert free advice from manufactures of materials-handling equipment (who would not however be human if they did not have an unconscious bias in favour of mechanical handling), or can call in their own work study and industrial engineering department, since materials-handling engineers are simply method studiers with trade knowledge. Some simple rules which may be worth keeping in mind are these:

1. Least handled is best handled. Every time parts and materials are handled, costs increase; and handling commonly accounts for 15%, occasionally as much as 85% of final cost. So eliminate unnecessary handling, and simplify necessary handling as much as you can.
2. Try not to handle things twice. Some rehandling cannot be avoided if goods are to be stored at all, of course.

3. Try to cut out bending and stretching, stooping, putting down and picking up. If incoming goods have to be held between unpacking and inspection, can they be held on bench-high roller conveyors? Getting things out of racks is usually easier than getting them off the floor. Floor storage usually requires goods to be stacked and lifted by hand.

4. Use gravity instead of muscle or motor where possible to move things. In a two-level stores, a gravity chute will bring things down quicker and more safely than a man.

5. Avoid manhandling where possible; handle mechanically where justifiable on a cost basis. Mechanical handling devices include cranes, hoists, conveyor fork-lift trucks and their attachments, jack trucks and stillage trucks, pallets and soon.

6. Try to handle in unit loads. Load standardization can save a lot of time in receiving, storing, checking and issuing goods. For goods of suitable size bought in an adequate volume, the ideal is for the supplier to deliver palletized unit loads, which are not broken into until the actual production operation.

The changeover from manhandling to mechanical handling, apart from its cost advantages in an economy where men are not treated as beasts of burden, is part of the movement towards humanizing work, finding human uses for human beings.

Mechanical handliug in the stores improves the storeman's lot, by taking some of the donkey-work out of his job. It should reduce labour costs. Whether or not it will reduce overall costs depends on a comparison of the wages saved, and perhaps other savings in time and space, with the depreciation and operating costs of the machinery.

Material handling represents 35% to 401% of all production costs-in some basic industries, as much as 75% or even more. It is one of the few areas where costs can still be substantially reduced as shown by the fact that handling costs vary widely among plants with the same general volume of output, even in the same industry. The plant hampered by the limitations of old buildings, the plant that "just grew," the plant where materoal handling is regarded as not specially related to basic manufacturing, all these can often be helped to lower handling costs. However, lack of proper planning of buildings has in many cases made the task, if not impossible, at least impractical from an investment stand-point. Only when management becomes sufficiently alerted to this problem to pinpoint actual material handling costs and analyze the effect of efficient handling on other functions can their true significance in overall cost control be appreciated.

Where only warehousing operations are concerned, handling problems are usually more readily identifiable. It is in the complexity of manufacturing or processing areas that the handling factor often becomes obscured and must be isolated by careful operation analysis.

In the face of the increasing pressure on costs, the ultimate solution is of course the complete new facility. This calls for a true integrated handling system, based on the concept of a complete producing unit, planned with an eye on the full effect of each single function on all other functions. Production processes may even be modified to tie them in better with material handling. Actually, this kind of thinking goes even beyond the bounds of a plant facility. The scientific material handling system starts with the packaging of raw materials at the supplier's plant and ends only when the product reaches the customer's receiving dock.

The activities which comprise the total material handling system are many. The following list is generally accepted:

1. Packaging at vendor's plant.
2. Transportation from vendor.
3. Unloading.
4. Receiving.
5. Stores (indoors and out).

6. Issuing to production.
7. In-Process handling.
8. Intradepartmental handling.
9. Interdepartmental handling.
10. In-process storage
11. Workplace handling.
12. Intraplant handling.
13. Packaging (protective).
14. Finished goods warehousing.
15. Handling related to auxiliary functions.
16. Packaging (consumer).
17. Loading.
18. Record keeping.
19. Shipping.
20. Transportation.

Each of these areas may be studied and improved separately. Package design, for example, can have as much influence on handling methods as can more obvious factors such as floor capacities and the like. A significant increase in effective floor space can often be attained by slightly altering the dimensions or type of a shipping container. Such an approach requires an examination of raw material sources and the effect of their packaging and Shipping methods on costs. At the other end, the handling costs of market distribution facilities must be considered.

"Processing on the Move"

The integrated material handling systems concept seeks to eliminate material handling as such. The key word is "flow;" that is, processing on the move, with coordinated flow lines extending from the raw material source, through receiving, processing, warehousing, and shipping, and ultimately to primary distribution centers.

Recent years have produced a number of outstanding examples of the effectiveness of this approach. Some are large-scale operations. But even in medium-size plants, the processing-on-the move approach has been used with highly effective results.

The trend toward integrated handling systems is by no means confined to completely new plants. The approach has been used to modernize existing plants, at least to the extent permitted by building limitations. The highly competitive brewing industry, for examples, has taken some noteworthy steps in this direction. In the most modem brewing operations, empty cans come from the supplier's plant in large, specially designed bulk bins from which they are fed by gravity directly to the filling lines. Intermediate handling has been eliminated, but this saving was made possible only by coordinating the shipping methods of the can supplier with the best system for the user.

Because an integrated handling system means lower costs, it has an important place in the planning of any new production facility. This calls for a free interchange of ideas. The architect, the industrial and process engineers, and the product designers, all must participate.

Terms like "integrated handling" and "systems concept" often conjure up a visIon of highly specialized automatic equipment. This is a misconceptlon. To be sure, strides have been made in the design of highly specialized handling equipment. But a wide variety of near-standard equipment can be fitted to a specific situation with the use of various accessories. In fact, about 400 different kinds, types, and varieties of material handling equipment are presently available. They are classified by the International Material Management Society and the American Society of Mechanical Engineers into nine major classifications as follows:

Either mobile or fixed

1.000 conveyors

2.000 cranes

3.000 positioning equipment

Mobile

4.000 industrial vehicles

5.000 motor vehicles

6.000 railroad cars

7.000 marine vehicles

8.000 air transports

Fixed

9.000 containers and supports

There may be as many as 1,000 pieces of equipment or devices in some of these classifications. The following paragraphs describe a representative few of the devices commercially available.

Monorail systems are a highly efficient means of handling loads on an intermitent basis the advantages are no rigid floor requirements, better use of overhead space, and little or no need for aisle space. However, routes and areas served must be more or less fixed, arid auxiliary mobile equipment may be needed to supplement the system.

Conveyors are one of the mainstays for handling material in various forms, and some innovations in the conveyor field have still further increased their versatility. In the so-called "power and free" overhead conveyor system, loads are actually suspended from the "free" overhead conveyor line and are moved along by spring-loaded pusher bars connected to a parallel overhead power chain. Use of the spring-loaded pushers permits banking or backing up of loads when desired, thus providing storage for anticipated peak requirement at the production unit, and the flexibility of varying load speeds.

In the field of roller and belt conveyors, automatic control, combined with standard conveyor equipment, has produced mass-handling of high capacity with the advantages of en route storage, stop-offs for processing, and automatic package sorting.

Other interesting types of conveyor equipment have been developed in recent years. Thus a flexible steel belt conveyor can be made to go around turns in snakelike fashion, eliminating the roller curves required with a conventional belt conveyor; and the oscillating trough conveyor carries bulk materials along in a uniform, continuous forward movement (even upgrade) by vibration.

Conveyors are also being used as moving assembly benches which make for better control of workers' output and simplify inventory control because materials can move more directly.

Forklift trucks have been greatly improved in versatility and maneuverability, with direct bearing on effective use of floor space. Not so long ago, a ten-foot-wide aisle was the narrowest in which a conventional 4,000-pound forklift truck could turn 90 degrees, pick up a load, and return to its original position. Innovations have reduced required aisle widths considerably in the last few years. The trend now is to look upon the basic fork truck as a power source for various attachments or devices that can be changed quickly to meet varying needs.

Out of doors, forklift trucks are becoming bigger and more stable. The trend is toward greater maneuverability, and at the same time, better balance, plus (as an outgrowth of OSHA), all-weather driver protection and a full complement of safety features in relation to both the driver and the load.

The driverless tractor and train is a development that is commercially applicable. Such a system can be used to dispatch individual loaded cars to remote points, where they are dropped and empties are picked up all without the need for a driver-operator. Guidance and motive power for the tractor come either from a single wire hung overhead or running in an inconspicuous groove in the floor, or from a line painted on the floor that reflects light rays to light-sensitive devices within the tractor which keep it "on the beam" as it moves along its path. Overall control of the system is handled from a central programming panel where routings, stop-overs, and pickups may be preselected in a few seconds.

The unit load concept is becoming standard practice. The idea is not new, but as the full potential of integrated handling has become apparent, it has taken on new meaning. Materials and products are being moved in unit loads, not only in the plant and warehouse, but over highways and railroads and by air. Unit load is based, to a great extent, on modules (sizes in multiples) which coordinate carriers, pallets, package shapes and sizes, etc., so that they square off and fit with minimum wasted space and dunnage.

The idea of a container of full trailer-truck size, sepatate from the rolling stock, opens up tremendous possibilities not only for lowering loading and unloading costs, but for reducing breakage and spoilage. Full trailer-size, the cargo unit can be loaded and blocked for shipment at the output end of the production line, with a free choice of transportation media. The "packaged" cargo unit may be conveyed by railroad car to a seaboard ship for over-water shipment. Each transfer between media is performed at a fraction of the cost of manual handling. Other outstanding advantages offered by these sealed cargo units are protection against pilferage ann elimination of special export packing.

Modern pallet handling equipment has helped greatly to sell the "unit load" idea. Plant-wide pallet systems now include automatic stackers (palletizers), unstackers for depalletizing incoming loads, pallet conveyors, and automatic fast-acting floor-to-floor pallet elevators. The automatic pallet loaders available today can take many different packages from production lines, sort and stack them in any desired sequence, and forward the loaded pallet by conveyor to warehouse or shipping dock—all without manual effort. Systems like this can save as much as 90% oithe cost of manual stacking.

Here again, the integrated handling system concept comes in. When all loading and unloading were done manually, the type of truck or railroad car was of minor consequence. The only requirement was manual labour and plenty of it. For pallet handling, however, highway truck bodies must be suitable for handling pallet loads.

Pallet manufacturers are trying to develop standard pallet sizes, but the multiplicity of package sizes makes this difficult. Meanwhile, the concept of unit loading without pallets is growing. This can be accomplished by using a fork truck clamping arrangement for gripping and moving the assembled stack as a unit.

Automatic Warehouses

It is always interesting when considering the current state of the art in anything, to look at the leading edge, which in storage is the automatic warehouse. This is a warehouse in which a substantial part of the receipt, storage and despatch functions are performed without manual handling of the goods. They are expensive installations, which pay only when a very high throughput of goods can be achieved not less than 4530 kg (10,000 lb) per hour according to one estimate.

The history of the first of the automatic warehouses is instructive. This was designed by Donald Gumpertz for Brunswick Drug Co of Los Angeles and went into operation in 1957. The client supplied some 2000 retail outlets with a range of 1800 drugstore items, and increasing delays in filling orders from the central warehouse prompted the client to commission the design and installation of a high speed automatic warehouse. The design solution was suitable for base stores handling upwards of a thousand issues a day. Each stock item was held in a steeply canted shelf or chute, loaded manually at the top by storemen, and unloaded automatically at the bottom by a solenoid-operated gate with remote control. Goods were discharged on to a system of conveyor belts leading to packing and despatch bays.

Customers orders were fed into data processing equipment which sorted the orders, printed advice notes and shortage notifications, updated stock records and operated the gates at the appropriate locations. When the gates opened goods were discharged by gravity feed on to branchline conveyors, which fed mainline conveyors. Goods furthest from the output end were picked, first, so that the hole order for a given customer would arrive together at the packing and despatch bay, at rates of up to ten items a second.

The installation is reported to have worked well-only ten minutes lost through equipment malfunction in the first 18 months. But if its technical functioning was admirable, its economic viability became increasingly dubious. Los Angeles residents were moving further and further away from the city centre. So were the retail outlets which served them. Traffic congestion got steadily worse. Holdups in supplying goods to retailers were the result not of processing delays in the central warehouse, but of transit delays in moving goods from the central warehouse. The solution was to open warehoused in the outskirts of town. This reduced throughput in the costly high-volume automatic store until it became a white elephant and was shut down.

Work Study in the Stores

The objects of work study have been defined as getting the most effective use of existing or proposed plant; the most effective use of human effort; and a reasonable workload for the people employed. These objects are as important in the stores as in any other part of the organisation.

Work study has two aspects: work measurement, and method study. Work measurement consists in measuring and timing work with the object of setting standards of performance which a person trained for and used to the job can keep up day after day. These standards can be used for planning work, defining the size of the labour force, devising financial incentives and payment-by-result systems, and job costing. Work measurement begins by actually observing.and recording what people do. Any storeman who knows his job could probably write down a list of the operations it entails; but actual observation is required to make the right allowance for delays, interruptions, waiting time, and frequency of various operations. A closely allied topic is job evaluation, or assessing the value of different jobs in relation to each other.

Method study also begins by observing how things are done, but with the object of devising better ways of doing them. Jobs which have for a long time been done in one way often turn out on examination to be capable of being, done in a different way which is quicker and less tiring. After all it is obvious that the layout of many stores, factories, offices and indeed towns, just developed piecemeal, bits and pieces being added here and there wherever they could be fitted in. These haphazard arrangements have their own charm but things could be ordered better if thought were given to the functional aspects. Much work, especially work which is taught on a craft apprentice system, is equally piecemeal and haphazard in its organization. Method study entails a systematic consideration of process, procedure, equipment, layout, and anything else relevant, in order to make the work less tiring, more effective, efficient, and economical.

The work studier's main tools are analysis, ingenuity, and observation, together with a mind trained and skilled in work study. Nevertheless some tools or aids have been developed which all can use. String diagrams to check travel distances, flow charts to devise optimum routes, scale plans and models aid in designing both stores layouts and materials handling.

Planning Aids

The simplest planning aid is to make a map of the stores; the usual scale is 6.5 mm (1/4 in.) to 30 cm (1 ft). Walls, windows, doors, roads, railway sidings, lavatories, pillars and other obstructions should all be marked. Trucks, trolleys and equipment, racks, bins and fixtures are drawn to scale on thin card and cut out. The effect of various layouts can be tried out by moving the cardboard cutouts about on the base plan. When a good layout has been found the cutouts can be stuck down with transparent adhesive tape. A more permanent planning board can be made by using balsa wood, which is easy to cut, for the movable parts. Magnets set into the cutouts enable them to be moved about the metal-based board without falling off. This shows how much room for manoeuver there is and whether alleys are wide enough to take trucks. By pushing truck cutouts along alleys you can tell when spacing between racks has to be increased and where trucks can go.

Some pins and a piece of string enable the same map to be used to check walking distances required for various jobs. The average storeman spends at least a third of his time walking from point to point either to get goods out or to put them away, so it is important to design stores layout and locate stock items in a way that will reduce this walking distance to a minimum.

One washing machine manufacturer used a string diagram to redesign their stores in this fashion. A scale map of the stores was made and pins were stuck in points corresponding with issue counters and storage locations. By running a string round the pins corresponding to the points a storeman has to visit, the distance he covers in doing his work can be measured. It turned out that to collect parts for the main assembly of the washing machine a storeman had to walk about 6.km (3.8 miles).

The string diagram also shows how alternative arrangements affect travel distances. By better stores layout and improved parts location, this company's work studiers were able to reduce this long walk by one third. In the course of the investigation they also saved a fifth of the space required for storage.

Flowcharts, diagrams showing where items go and what happens to them, are useful in plotting better layouts and improving work routines or forms routing. Scale models are useful in following three dimensional material flows through multistorey build-ings, in devising applications for roller conveyors and gravity chutes, and in showing overhead obstructions and planning high stacks. Perspex, being transparent and easy to work, is a suitable material for walls and floors in the model, while racks, machines, raised loading bays and so on can be modeled in softwood. Making the model could be an interesting project for a management student or apprentice; or it could be made by the firm's joiners or pattern shop, or let' out to a specialist firm of architectural modellers. The standard scale is again 1/4 in. to the foot.

Table 1

A Code for Special Hazards to which Stock may be Subject

Code Letter	*Keyword*	
A	Attractive	Attractive to thieves—portable, high-value, saleable
B	Breakable	Easily broken-handle with care-for example, glass
C	Corrosive	Acids, other chemicals, which may corrode containers, etc.
D	Dry	Must be kept away from moisture
E	Explosive	Certain Chemicals
F	Fire hazard	Highly inflammable items-petrol, oil, paint
H	Heat-sensitive	Deteriorate above certain temperatures
L	Light-sensitive	Fade or deteriorate in strong light
M	Magnetic	Should not be kept in strong magnetic fields
W	Warpable	Bend or break if not supported properly
O	Other	Subject to special hazards not listed above

Certain stock items require special treatment. Rubber must be kept dark and within certain temperature limits, paper must be kept dry and clean, timber so that it will season and will not rot, inflammable and explosive goods out of harm's way. It is sometimes advisable to code stock items that call for special treatment', and Table 1 may be useful in this connection. Security must always be borne in mind when designing stores. According to J. Edgar Hoover, 25% of factory employees were dishonest and 25% were honest. He did not know about the other half. Even if 75% of employees can be trusted, we would not wish to put temptation in the way of honest folk.

Obviously thieves do not want to steal everything in the stores. Portability, desirability, cost and marketability are the key factors. Strict security regulations which would be appropriate for diamonds would not be suitable for 2 tonne lathe bed castings, for example.

It is standard practice to keep stock behind a perimeter fence or wall, with thiefproof windows and locked doors. Nobody is allowed into the stores unless they have business there which cannot be done over the counter. Goods receiving bays are walled off from actual storage.

Let us now step inside and look at the stores operation in action. We shall start here all the action starts: ,that is, in the receipts section of the stores. This is the most vulnerable section and needs a great deal of planning and attention.

The Receipts Section

This very important section of the stores is without doubt the most vulnerable, for a number of reasons:

1. It is the place where the whole operation begins. If we get it wrong here, then by the time the goods arrive in the binning area it will be more wrong, and by the time we get to the issuing side it will be chaos.

2. We need to exercise more discipline in this area than any other, because it is where the company's outgoing cash is either protected or wasted.

3. There are legal connotations associated with this function, which means that the personnel employed in this section must be trained to understand the implications of what they are doing.

Likc all othcr scctions of the stores, the receipts section has to operate under authority. With this in mind, we must remember that the stores has no authority to receive anything at all into the stores from outside suppliers unless they possess a stores copy of the company's official order to cover the receipt. The copy order is the only official document that gives our suppliers the authority to deliver anything to the stores, and without that document in the stores we have no authority to accept anything.

This places the responsibility of purchasing to ensure that copies of all orders placed by them today are delivered to the stores, by hand if necessary, by 9 a.m. to tomorrow morning without fail.

The copy orders are to be filed away not in the stores office or the stock control office but in the receipts section of the stores, and filed in such a manner that they can be retrieved easily and quickly so that as each delivery is made to us, and before we start to off-load or receive it, we will check to see that we have a copy order to cover the item(s). If we have we will accept it; if we have not, we will contact purchasing and find out more about the delivery wanting to be made.

Having received the item(s) because we have a copy order to cover them, we then proceed to accept them. Every company and carrier delivering to the stores will need a receipt signature from an authorized person in the receipts section. These authorized personnel must be trained to sign for receipts and always to put after their signature the word 'Unex,' which means 'We are signing for what is delivered, but at the time of receipt we have not inspected or examined the goods'.

To sign for everything 'Unex'must be a rigid discipline, to be exercised in every storehouse. We must never just give a signature. This has to be done to protect the company's interests so that, if, when we do examine and later inspect the goods, we should find any damage or short delivery, we shall have a clear and legitimate claim to have the matter dealt with by the supplier, and to protect the company's outgoing, hard-earned cash.

Having examined the receipt carefully for quantity and satisfied ourselves that they are all as per the description stated on the copy order, we must now proceed to have them carefully inspected before they are placed into stock to be used.

Everything, no matter what it is, that arrives in the stores must be inspected, and we must check for quantity and description from the stores' copy of the official order, and not from a supplier's delivery note or packing slip. This is another rigid discipline that must be followed in the receipts section of the stores. The supplier's advice note and packing slip are not official documents as far as stores are concerned. They are supplementary documents that can be attached to the official document the copy order.

Inspection

When receipts are taken into the stores we must ensure that we have a very clear company policy to cover the inspection process.

It is not necessary to have everything received inspected by a skilled technical inspector. Therefore we must grade our stocks into four categories for inspection, and as receipts are taken in, so the correct grade of inspection will be carried out on them.

The grades of inspection are classified into A, B, C and D categories the decision into which category each item of stock falls is made by the company's chief inspector or chief quality assurance engineer. Behind the B category of inspection a number will be shown; this can be any number between 5 and 95, for reasons we shall explain.

The four categories of inspection will adequately cover any type of receipt which any stores is likely to receive in its lifetime:

Category A	Visual inspection
Category B	Batch inspection
Category C	100 per cent inspection
Category D	Laboratory test inspection

Visual Inspection

When we grade our stockholdings in this way for the purposes of inspection, we shall discover that approximately 50 per cent of all receipts coming through the stores annually fall into category A. These are items which only need to be visually inspected by an experienced responsible person(s) in the receipts section of the stores; depending upon the results of this visual inspection, the receipt will either be accepted or rejected.

Batch Inspection

A much smaller number of items fall into category B, which is batch test inspection. If it was a B 10 inspection it would signify to the receipts section of stores that 10 per cent of the quantity received would be selected at random and passed to the technical inspector for inspection. If the 10 per cent passes inspection and is accepted, then the whole consignment would be accepted on the strength of the 10 per cent test. This is why it is known as batch inspection.

Full Inspection

An even smaller number of items will be found in category C, which involves 100 per cent inspection. These are items which are so critical in their end use that every single one received has to be inspected by a technical inspector. Any rejections will be immediately dealt with by stock control and purchasing, for free replacement or otherwise.

Laboratory Tests Inspection

The smallest group of all is in category D. From items in this group a sample will be taken, which will be sent to a laboratory for testing. If the tests prove acceptable, a laboratory report will be issued to stores, who will file it very carefully, and the whole consignment will be accepted on the evidence of the test made. Conversely, the whole consignment would be rejected if the sample did not pass the test in the laboratory.

It will be seen then, that a policy of inspection is vital in any company. A master stock list or stores vocabulary should be presented to the chief inspector or chief quality assurance engineer, who should be asked to mark against each item the grading symbol of inspection he requires to be carried out upon receipt. When this is done, this symbol-A, B, C or D will be recorded on the stock record; whether this is manual or on a computer does not matter. In future, every time any item is replenished the correct symbol ill automatically be passed to purchasing who will type the symbol on the purchase order, a copy of which will go to stores. When the item(s) are received, stores will know right away what kind of inspection has to be carried out and they will see that this is done without fail.

When the inspection process has been completed, stores will raise a goods. received note, which will show quantity advised, quantity received, and quantity accepted after inspection, as well as other important information. It is against 'Quantity accepted after inspection' that our invoices will be paid. All invoices received in the company must remain in the accounts department. They must never be sent to stores for signature. This is totally wrong from a security point of view. The invoice must be paid on the evidence of the goods received note, a copy of which must go to the accounts department. All goods received notes should be pie-numbered by the printer and a careful record kept of whom they are issued to and where. This is necessary again for internal security purposes and enables auditors to make checks on their validity. Having received the results of inspections of goods coming into the receipts section of the stores, the items will be passed into the binning area for stocking and ultimate issue.

With the advent of the use of computers in stores, and providing we have a terminal situated in the receipts section, it is now possible to put all receipts into the computer within an hour of receiving them and before the receipts have passed through inspection. This enables the expeditors, purchasing, and production planning and control to know that the items have arrived. Expediting will cease and production planning can prepare to proceed with their plans.

A special digit, placed at the end of the code number, part number or description of the item received, will indicate to all concerned that the item has been received but will not be available for issue until it has been accepted by inspection. When inspection is completed, and if the item is accepted, stores will eliminate the special digit in the computer and people will know it is now available.

If only part of the quantity delivered is accepted by inspection, then stores will cancel the first entry into the computer and replace it with the accepted quantity only, showing no special digit. In other words, the quantity accepted by inspection is all that is available for issue. In these circumstances, stores will advise purchasing, production planning and control, and stock control about the rejected items so that immediate remedial action can be taken.

In the event that the whole consignment is rejected by inspection, stores will simply cancel the item from the computer altogether and immediately advise all three departments named above, because the need for remedial action now becomes urgent.

One of the major disciplines in the receipts section of stores that must be continuously in operation is that of making absolutely certain that the receipts section of the stores is physically cleared every day.

Nothing received today must be left unattended until tomorrow. If we embark on this sloppy method of operation, it can only lead to chaos and disaster as far as a successful and effective stores operation is concerned.

Obsolescence

Every store suffers from obsolescence. Retailers hold sales to clear their shelves of material which has not sold. Factory stores must also clear out obsolete and surplus and excess stock regularly, because it takes up space, makes some demands on stores labour and record-keeping, and contributes nothing to operations.

How does this dead stock cease to be live? Progress, fashion, Improvements in available materials may be the reason. Alterations to designs or to manufacturing policy or in sales are the most usual reasons; these all change or abolish requirements for certain items. As requirements alter, so must stocks; new stocks must be bought in, old unwanted stocks disposed of. There is always the temptation to hang on to goods because they are sure to come in useful one day. So they may; but meanwhile they are wasting a valuable asset—space—and they are not likely to be improving in stock.

Purchasing should insist on being informed by the department which institutes a change affecting requirements, at as early a date as possible, so that goods do not go on being bought after they have ceased to be required. Purchasing people themselves should keep reminding other departments of the importance of this.

But it is not enough to try to keep up with changes as they happen; some will slip through undetected and others will happen gradually. Systematic checks should be made on stock periodically, to identify the items for which stock levels have got out of step with demand. This is often done in conjunction with periodic stocktaking.

A three-way check after each 6 monthly stocktaking can be made. First, the two previous inventory sheets are compared with the one just completed, ,and a list extracted of items whose stock-level was similar on all three occasions. Second, the chief store-keeper makes an independent list of items which to his knowledge have not moved for months, or are moving but not fast enough to clear existing stocks inside a year. Third, the stock record section prepares a similar list from records by comparing stock balances with consumption. The lists are then compared and reconciled to give a final list of surplus.

Then steps are taken first of all to see that no more is bought of any of these items. (This sounds obvious and it is; but it can still happen that a stock clerk ignorant of the true position will requisition more of an item which is already overstocked simply because the balance is below a maximum stock figure or near an ordering level which is no longer appropriate.) Second, an effort is made to use up the excess material. Perhaps the design department can suggest a way to use some of it. The sales department may also be consulted; it may be possible to dispose of excess stock occasioned by discontinued or modified products by making a few more of the old products, perhaps for sale at special prices. Third, if all else fails, the rest of the dead stock is sold or scrapped and cleared out of the stores.

Variety Reduction In Stock Purchasing

Most industrial stores stock a great variety of things; 10,000 items is quite common in small or medium-size engineering stores.

In many cases this variety is greater than it need be; items are duplicated or triplicated under slightly different names, or the range of sizes is uneconomically large. A determined attempt at variety reduction can then be well worth while.

Variety is not of course in itself good or bad, and the mere fact that variety exists is no reason to try to reduce it. As consumers we all want a choice. One of the early steps in variety reduction, Henry Ford's famous dictum that his customers could have their Model T and colour they wanted so long as they wanted black, was a long step in the wrong direction. As now practised, variety reduction may actually increase the useful variety of end-products; it is the useless variants it aims to eliminate, ana it ought also to reduce cost to the consumer. Steps in the right direction are simplification, specialization, and standardization.

Specialization is restricting the range of products coming from a particular group of productive resources, as when a plant special-izes in screws and studding and refuses to branch out into turned products generally. Simplification is achieved by reducing the types and sizes made, although the word obviously has wider meanings some of which are relevant even in this connexion. Standardization is the process of agreeing and adopting precise detailed specification or descriptions, whether of procedures, products or components. The dimensions, composition, quality, performance, method of manufacture or method of test may all be standardized.

Variety reduction has several advantages. With a smaller range of stock items, the demand for each item tends to increase and also to become more predictable. For instance, demand for items which are components in several end-products may well be easier to forecast than demand for anyone of the end-products; consolidating the requirement tends to smooth out the fluctuations. Having fewer items in the stock range is likely to lead to lower totaJ stocks even if total demand is not reduced. Making fewer and bigger purchases provides opportunities to obtain lower prices.

Categorization of Stock

Stocks held in the stores are, to the layman, just stocks, but to the experienced stores personnel they fall into many categories and groups. Stores have to be constantly aware of which category or group items fall into, depending on what treatment we are giving the stocks and for what purpose, because how we carry out this treatment affects other departments as well as the company.

We have already seen, for instance, that for the purpose of stock-checking we have to grade the stock into three categories. A, B and C. In other circumstances we would have to segregate the stocks we control into:

* Capital stocks.
* Revenue stocks.
* Consumable stocks.
* Quarantine stocks.
* Issue stock.
* Customer stock.
* Personal issue stock.

Although overall these are all stocks housed by the stores, each group requires its own treatment, and stores personnel must know which stock falls into which category or group. Each group has to be accounted for in different ways. In some cases the recording of the groups also differs.

We have to know that capital stocks can become revenue stocks—even the same item of stock-and conversely revenue stocks can become capital stocks. It all depends on the treatment they are given. Although certain stocks are called free issue stock we know that nothing is free, and so the treatment of these items has to be understood.

Over and above all this there are 'assets withdrawn from use', which are held temporarily in stores not as stock items but as items which can be used again when the occasion arises. These are items which were capitalized when they were first put to use-that is why they are called assets but that original use has now ceased, so we keep them safely in the stores-sometimes at an agreed value depending on how much they have been depreciated in value while they were in use. Sometimes they are kept in stores at 'no value'. If a project or demand arises for these assets, we deploy them again, and it saves the company having to find new cash to finance them. Such assets withdrawn from use have to be carefully recorded and allocated to possible uses; when issued again they have to receive special attention as regards accounting.

Storage

A storehouse that is not fully utilized is wasting the capital expended upon it; but one holding too much is wasteful of time and labour. Quick response is essential in economic warehousing operations, since time is money and each day of delay involves holding a further day's worth of stock.

If stores are packed too tightly on the ground, access becomes impossible, and the same applies if they are stacked too high. Concentration rises at the expense of access and vice versa.

We are aiming at the maintenance of continuous work flows through the warehouse, so that they can operate without hindrance caused by the closing of gangways or the blocking of accesses. The nature of the flows themselves must be examined. First, identify the main areas of work:

1. Goods inwards; receipts; inspection and storage.
2. Picking; goods outwards; packing and despatch.
3. Stock-taking.
4. Stock maintenance; turnover of stock; rebinning; protection; etc.

Each of these tasks has its own work flow, either beginning or ending with the location in which the stocks are held. Here it is necessary to consider which items are fast moving and which slow moving; whether they are lightweight, heavy, awkwardly shaped, or difficult to handle; what type of container is needed; and What type of storage facility has to be provided.

Storage Methods

These are many different kinds of storage methods in use today, some of which are associated with particular methods of material handling. The tasks of storage and handling should therefore be considered together. Some different types of storage are:

1. Binning.
2. Racking and shelving.
3. Flat pallets and stillages.
4. Post and box pallets.
5. Block stacking.
6. Floor storage for very heavy items.
7. Containers.

The essential thing in storage is that an item can be found when it is wanted. Thus a store demands tidiness, method, and discipline. It will be easier for everyone concerned if each item has a stock number, and that each location in the store has a location code.

Bins

Binning is used primarily for the 'picking' face in a warehouse. The difference between binning and shelving is that bins have vertical regular divisions, or, alternatively, drawers for keeping smaller items. Items are often stored within a bin in the packing boxes as sent by the supplier, after they have been checked and counted by incoming inspection, or in 'tote pens' or containers.

Racking

Racking can be used as the picking face for items that are too big or heavy for bin accommodation, or for reserve stocks for replenishment. It is advisable to keep these two classes separate.

Racking can be built from prefabricated section, has adjustable height shelving, and is often built to accommodate complete pallet loads.

Pallets

Pallets are specially designed platforms for the stacking of goods with a view to the whole load being removed to wherever it is required by a fork-lift truck. There are a wide variety of pallets of different sizes and made from different materials from steel or wood to disposable fibre. Pallets may be flat, have posts to which cages can be fitted to hold loose items, have boxes wi lids, or just be batons screwed to the underside of large crates.

Block Stacking

This is often the way of stacking box or cage pallets, where one pallet is stored on top of another, it can also describe the storage of boxes on top of one another. However, one has to be sure that crushing does not result if the boxes are cardboard. Cardboard boxes are often blocked on flat stillages.

Floor Storage

Awkward or heavy items are normally stored on the floor, always making sure that the floor will support the weight to be placed upon it.

Sheet metals, metal bars and steel sections are usually floor-stored on racks or heavy pallets. It is important that these kinds of item be accessible and tidy, so as not to block the movement of other stores items. Special lifting devices, jibs and cranes may be needed for handling.

Hazardous Materials

There are often national regulation for the storage of potentially dangerous materials, where the following hazards may be present:

1. Fire risk.
2. Poisons.
3. Toxic fumes.
4. Explosions.

For instance, paint stores are usually separate fire-resistant buildings, and especially dangerous materials are locked and secured.

Special consideration apply in different conditions, such as in tropical storehouses where hot, humid conditions are present-free air flow around stored items may be necessary. Arrangements for protecting the stores and for the rapid collection and disposal of water are necessary and adequate safeguards against insects, bacteria, viruses and other organisms may also be required.

Containers

The traditional methods of moving retail goods are rapidly being replaced by the introduction of containers, which dramatically reduce the number of times goods have to be handled. With the design of large handling devices it is now quite feasible to load containers at plant and unload them again at the destination, completely untouched by human hand.

The container concept calls for a standard design so that the containers can fit special trailers on lorries, or railway truck bases. There are now special container sizes for container air freight. The dimensions adopted by the International Standards Organization (ISO) are length 9.125m, width 2.438 m, height 2.438m; modules can be made to fit these overall dimensions.

Materials Handling Equipment

The main types of handling equipment, linked to the type of storage used, are:

1. Manual platform or stillage truck.
2. Power-driven platform or stillage truck.
3. Hand-operated crane.
4. Fork-lift trucks.
5. Hand-operated stacker.
6. Gravity conveyors (wheel or roller type).
7. Lifts, chutes, hoists, cranes.
8. Vocuum and pressure systems.
9. Powered conveyors (belt or monorail).
10. Lorry equipment (tail lifts, lorry crane, etc.).

The cost and amount of handling involved in moving items from one stage to another are often underestimated as are the economies which can be made by properly designed storage and handling methods. Considerations of safety, cleanliness and stock deterioration are also important.

Warehousing

Much care needs to be taken over the design of the operating system within the warehouse. It is vitally important to consider each of the different activities that take place. Typically, these are:

1. Unloading and receiving goods.
2. Putting away in the bulk store area.
3. Transfer from bulk storage to order picking section.
4. Order picking.
5. Checking.
6. Packing.
7. Assembly of orders.
8. Despatch.

All these activities have to be planned and coordinated into a single system. Within this system there may be a need for several different methods; different products with different characteristics may call for different treatment. It is necessary, therefore, to classify products handled and stored by type, quantity, and number of lines, so that appropriate methods can be designed and implemented.

The prime objective of the system must be to minimize handling and distance travelled. This calls for careful design of the layout, not only to use the system selected but also to optimize the use of the buildings available. Once again, maximum flexibility must be built in at all times; and this also applies to the warehouse staff. Wherever possible they should be trained in the appropriate skills so that they are able to undertake the whole range of activities within the warehouse. The problems facing warehouse management include the peaks and troughs of the different activities, even within the span of a single day, and the mark of the success ful manager is the ability to transfer his staff to meet these peaks and troughs.

The flow concept, which has found such favour in the production field, is not really applicable in a warehousing environment, for there is no need to take everything the length of the ware house. It follows from this that the despatch area should be adjacent or close to the goods reception area so that the fast-moving Items come straight in and out of the warehouse; almost without getting into the system itself at all.

It is not possible in this section to consider all the different activities within the warehouse, or even to describe the different types of equipment that are available, so let us look at one or two examples of systems that have been introduced in different situations.

Raw Materials-Metal Bars and Coils

First, let us take an example from the engineering industry and consider a company using as raw material both metal bars and metal coils. Now, pigeon-hole racking is a most effective way of storing small quantities of a large number of differing grades of bar. A point to watch here is that the bars are delivered in stipulated lengths. In the company we have in mind, the stipulation was that bars should be between 8 it and 11 ft long. And, indeed, they were stored in racking which was designed to house bars of these limits. Visual inspection soon indicated that something was seriously wrong, and we found bars up to a length of 19 ft in the system. You can imagine what effect this had on the working area of the store.

However, as the quantities increase, then pigeon-hole racking and the manual system it embraces becomes less satisfactory and the use of stackable storage cradles with an overhead hoist becomes quite attractive. This method is satisfactory if the number of qualities or grades is limited, otherwise a large amount of double-handling is going to be incurred. If this is the case, then we have to look for alternative methods, such as powered mobile firtree racking served by a four-way reach truck. This enables us to get maximum accessibility with minimum storage space.

Now, when storing metal coils, none of the methods just described seems to be appropriate. A different solution has to be sought, and one that comes to mind is double deep racking equipped with cradles in which the coils can rest, served by a fork-lift truck fitted with a probe and pantographic reach mechanism. This example illustrates some of the alternatives available to a company, just for its raw materials stores.

Finished Parts

Let us now look, in a second engineering company, at the finished parts store, which contains small engineering parts. Here there is a very successful system based upon a series of captive stacker cranes. As the cranes move along the aisles under manual control, the operators place the items they have picked onto small conveyors running along the racking at mid-level and these, in turn, transport the picked items to the order packers. The storage area is set out with alternative picking and replenishment aisles; each racking is two deep with live storage rollers transferring parts from the replenishment to the picking face.

Palletized Cartons

For the third example we go to the food industry, where the traditional warehouse system is based on pallet racking with order picking taking place at the first two levels. Overhead is the bulk storage area which is organized on a semi-random location system. Back-up pallets are placed as near to the picking station as possible. Order picking stations are in fixed locations and the picking lists are made up in order of warehouse sequence. Computers can be of considerable help in this area, sorting orders into the correct sequence of items. Manual systems, on the other hand, are based on a pre-listed order form (PLOF) which is also made out in warehouse order.

Automation can take a lot of hard work out of the warehouse operation. It is most often found in the bulk storage areas where computers, possibly with manual intervention through consoles, put away and retrieve palleted goods. The stacking of these pallets is quite critical to the success of the system and all pallet loads have to be checked to see that they do not exceed dimensional tolerances. The repacking of pallets can be a costly business.

So which system ought we to choose? Naturally, a system which reduces overall the total work load of the operation and which gives us the best utilization of storage capacity. We are most unlikely to come upon this solution by mere chance, and it calls for an objective assessment of all the different activities within the warehouse and of the product lines and throughput which have to be accommodated by the system.

Choice of Storage System

Which storage scheme will give us the most efficient system? Before we can decide this we have to balance the need for accessibility against that of storage space utilization. It will help if, for a moment; we think in terms of square footage of floor space rather than in terms of cubic capacity. The most effective system from a storage capacity point of view is, without a shadow of doubt, a block stacking system which may be five, ten or even more, pallets deep.

The problem comes, of course, when you have to retrieve the pallet that is at the back of the row. Then you are faced with a fairly formidable doublehandling operation. Still, the fact remains that the most simple method of storage is block stacking, either placing pallet upon pallet or, if stability or protection is required for the load, using cage pallets in place of the conventional wooden pallet.

If we wish to improve accessibility we can only do so at the expense of storage space and by the installation of racking. Once we start considering the installation of racking we have to deter-mine what aisle widths we wish to use and this will be linked directly to the type of lifting truck or stacker crane we wish to employ. The problem with that proven old work-horse, the counterbalance fork-lift truck, is that it requires an aisle width of approximately 11 ft in which to operate, and therefore it is not very satisfactory for use within the racking system of the warehouse.

It was with this purpose in mind that the 'reach truck' was designed, in which the forks can move within the framework of the truck. The aisle widths required by reach trucks vary, but if we take 7 ft 6 in as being typical we shall not be too far out. However, even with a reach truck, we shall be lucky if we are able to utilize more than about 50 per cent of the floor space.

Two different developments have taken place to improve this figure. The first is the so-called 'double deep reach truck', which has a pantographic action that effectively doubles the depth of the racking. The second is the development of narrow aisle trucks, such as the turret truck and the side loading truck, which can operate in aisles as narrow as 4 ft 4 in. wide.

Further developments have narrowed the aisle width even further, and stacker cranes and rack stackers can operate in widths as low as 3 ft. We must be careful, however, not to leap to too rapid a conclusion, because as the aisle required by the truck becomes narrower and narrower, the dimensions of the pallet itself begin to assume importance; if we are using a standard ISO pallet, for example, the minimum width without any allowance for working tolerances must be 3 ft 8 in, irrespective of the type of truck used.

A fairly recent development, which tackles the problem of utilization from a different angle, is that of 'powered mobile racking', where the racks themselves are moved, so that a single aisle can service a great number of lengths of racking. The figures below give some indication of the percentage space utilization one can expect to achieve with the different types of equipment, using an ISO pallet:

Counter balance fork-lift	44%
Research truck	53%
Narrow aisle turret truck	63%
Stacker crane	66%
Pantograph	69%
Power racking	89%

These figures are based on typical installations, but they do serve to illustrate how, by changing our equipment, we can improve the use of our storage capacity yet still retain accessibility.

In selecting a system we have to consider the storage task, the space available, and the costs of the alternatives. As our system becomes more sophisticated and our storage utilization increases, the cost starts to climb, as you might expect. As a general rule the simplest system will be the most satisfactory, providing it meets the two requirements of storage capacity and accessibility. Where space is at a premium, more sophisticated systems are likely to provide the required solution.

One important aspect of efficient storage is whether we choose a random or fixed stock location system for bulk stock. The advantage of a random system is that all space is available to all products, but to be successful it requires a foolproof control system, otherwise the identification and rotation of stock can become a nightmare. Simple systems of recording the location of each pallet as it enters the warehouse should in theory work without a hitch, but in practice human error intervenes to bedevil the system. It only requires one pallet to be placed in the wrong location for the system to start to fall apart.

Fixed stock locations are not so sensitive to human error because these can be picked up and visually identified quite quickly. On the other hand, they are inflexible and unable to cope with fluctuations in stockholding of different items. With a fixed location system, one either has to accept a relatively. lower utilization figure or seek some other alternative. An attractive alternative is what we will call, for want of a better expression, a semi-random stock location system. In such a system, families of products will be restricted to certain areas of the racking and within these sections the storage will be quite random. this allows, within product groups, for fluctuations in the storage requirements of individual items yet permits fairly easy stock identification.

The bulk stock can be held either ill its own section of the warehouse or, as we have already seen, above the picking stations. In some systems it can be found in both. Again, careful consideration has to be given to which is the most efficient and satisfactory way of handling and storing the stock. In one warehouse, the bulk stock was held on one side of the section and was transferred by fork-lift trucks to a block of live racking some seven pallets deep, where picking took place at the remote face.

The Centre of Movement

The task of distribution is deceptively simple. It is to move goods from the production line or area of primary production to the customer in an acceptable time, and to do so economically. The first part is simple, enough, and we often tend to think of the whole operation as errand running. But this is far from the case, since in most distribution problems there is quite literally an infinite number of solutions. Optimum or near-optimum solutions are difficult to find and often involve much more than errand running!

What are the options?

1. How many warehouses should there be?

2. Where should they be located?

3. What capacity should they hold?

4. What administrative arrangement are necessary?

5. What area are we expected to serve?

6. What is the delivery specification our customers are likely to want?

7. Shall we use road, rail, air or water for our main transportation?

8. What packaging is necessary?

9. How do we programme the delivery schedule?

10. Can we collect different orders together to minimize transport runs?

The total number of warehouses could be calculated from a consideration of two main factors-but others must be taken into account as well.

Transportation Costs. These vary with mileage; the greater the number of warehouses, the smaller will be the total mileage. Transportation costs usually reduce with greater numbers of warehouses.

Warehousing Costs. These costs will increase in proportion to the number of warehouses built; the larger the number of ware houses, the greater the warehousing costs.

❐

14

Traffic and Transportation

TRAFFIC FUNCTION

Traffic management is a big job in most industries. In the typical manufacturing company, transportation services are the third greatest expenditure; only purchased materials and labour are more important. Producers of bulky, low-cost materials may spend as much as one-fourth of their sales dollar on transportation, and even those who produce items of very high value may directly or indirectly payout 5 or 10 percent of their sales dollar for transportation services.

Most larger companies have a separate traffic or physical distribution department. The traffic manager is a major executive; in some cases he reports directly to the president of the company. Even when he does not, he may be only one echelon lower in the organization, reporting to the materials manager, purchasing manager, or marketing manager. Growing recognition of the importance of the physical distribution function is not only upgrading traffic but bringing it closer to related materials activities.

Most organizations, however, rely on common carriers for most or all of their transportation needs. In the economic sense the common carrier is like any other supplier the company might have. The carrier performs a service and gets paid for it. The main difference is that common carriers whose vehicles cross state lines ard very tightly regulated by a federal government agency, the Interstate Commerce Commission, as well as by various state agencies.

Were it not for the unique character of its regulation, transportation services would probably be just another purchasing function in most organizations. However, complex regulations make transportation purchasing sufficiently different from conventional purchasing activities so that in larger companies it is usually not carried on in the purchasing department but in a separate traffic department.

Basic Responsibilities

The traffic department is responsible for problems related to the purchase of transportation services, including the selection of mode of transport and of carrier, negotiation of rates, tracing and expediting of shipments, filing and negotiation of claims for lost or damaged shipments, and audit of freight bills. In addition, as the company's experts on transportation, traffic personnel are involved in many special studies designed to minimize transportation costs or to advise management about the effect that various decisions (such as plant location or product distribution) would have on transportation cost.

Traffic is intimately involved in materials management and physical distribution even in companies where there are no organizational ties linking traffic with other materials management activities. The choice of a carrier automatically influences inventory levels. Fast, highly reliable modes of transportation permit less inventory than is required for slower, more erratic modes. The traffic function is also intimately related to problems of warehouse and plant location. In simple cases, the location must be easily accessible to low-cost transportation; in more complex cases, inventory investment, transportation cost, and other variables combine to determine optimum location.

The typical traffic department also has a number of miscellaneous functions, including the handling of all passenger reservations for employees traveling on company business and the moving of household effects the employees transferred from one company plant to another. Sometimes the traffic manager also is responsible for the operation of all company-owned vehicles; even if he is not, he should always be consulted prior to their purchase.

Traffic also is concerned with packaging material. The heavier the package, the higher the freight costs to ship the product. On the other hand, lightweight packaging is more liable to damage in shipment. For this reason, many tariffs are based on shipments being made in certain types of packaging.

Traffic usually is concerned with both inbound and outbound shipments of materials and finished products. Many traffic departments become intimately involved with charter carriers or company-owned trucks.

Normally, however, most of their dealings are with various common carriers, including railroads, trucks, pipelines, and water carriers.

Picking the Carrier

Railroads are by far the most important common carriers in terms of tonnage handled (about half the total). Trucks are second in tonnage but lead in dollar volume. Pipelines handle almost as much tonnage as trucks but get only a small fraction of their revenue. The reason for the discrepancies between shares of tonnage and revenue of the various carriers is obvious: the rate per ton-mile for all commodities is not the same. A trucker who hauls a ton of household goods for one mile may get 100 times as much as a pipeline gets for moving a ton of crude oil the same distance.

A company should buy transportation services just as it buys any other commodity on the bases of quality, price, and service. It should try to direct its business to carriers that provide prompt delivery with a minimum of lost or damaged shipments, cooperate readily in tracing and rerouting shipments, make a minimum of errors in invoicing, and so on. These are sound criteria for selecting among like types of carrier, which charge identical rates when they are subject to regulation.

The transportation buyer must also select among various types of transportation service. His two basic criteria should be price and service. Carriers that give fast service charge relatively higher tariffs and those charging the lowest rate usually provide the slowest service. Shipment over water is the cheapest and usually the slowest way to ship any commodity—particularly in specialized bulk carriers that transport on coal, grain, and like commodities. Pipeline is the lowest-cost overland mode of shipment—so cheap that even coal is pulverized and mixed into slurry so it can be pumped through special pipelines. Most matenals cannot be transported in ships or pipelines, however, and shippers must choose among a variety of higher cost, but usually faster, carriers.

Rail Freight. Although the relative importance of railroads has declined substantially since World War II, they still are the most important carriers. Rail freight rates in carload lots are always lower than air freight, parcel post, or rates charged by freight forwarders. For many commodities they are cheaper than truck rates, and sometimes. they are competitive with barge and ship rates. They rarely are cheaper than pipeline rates.

With the exception of materials that can be pumped through a pipe-line for most commodities rail shipment—particularly in trainload quantities with oversized box cars—is the cheapest possible mode of overland shipment. Shippers of manufactured goods rarely are able to generate enough traffic to move their goods in trainload quantities; their lowest-cost mode of shipment is often in full carload lots for shipments between points equipped with railroad sidings. When a company does not have a siding, it must transfer its shipment from the railroad boxcar to a truck. This creates extra transport and handling expenses which usually make it more economic to ship 100 percent by truck or may even force a company to relocate near a siding if its costs are to remain competitive.

Truck Freight. Almost every factory is equipped with a dock to receive truck shipments; in fact, truck lines are the most important common carrier for many types of manufactured goods. Truck rates often are as low as those charged by railroads for finished manufactured products, and service usually is faster. Trucks are especially competitive on shorter hauls. They may offer overnight service between cities that are only a few hundred miles apart. Both interstate truck and rail rates are regulated by the Interstate Commerce Commission, which tries to set rates that permit fair competition between the two carriers. Trucks have substantially increased their share of traffic at the expense of the railroads since the 1950s, but recently the railroads have been holding their own despite fierce competition from competing carriers.

Shipment by Air. Air cargo shipments have increased at a fantastic rate as technology has worked to reduce real costs. Since the end of world War II physical volume of air freight has increased at least 50 times, although total tonnage is still a small fraction of that carried by rail and truck. The only factor that has tempered growth is the fact that air tariffs are still two to ten times higher than those charged by railroads and truck lines.

If rates are so high, how have air shipments managed to gross so fast? Obviously because for some shipments, speed is the only important factor and the shipment must be made in the fastest possible manner, almost regardless of the cost. There are at least two other reasons for the rapid growth of air shipments. First, air tariffs are not as high as by appear. In most cases, it is possible to use much lighter containers when shipping by air, and sometimes no packaging at all is needed. Thus the total weight paid for when shipping by air is often less than it would be if shipment were made by surface transportation. This reduces the premium paid for air shipment. For certain extremely fragile shipments that would require especially heavy packaging if shipped by surface freight, it may actually be cheaper to ship by air. Air shipments also perI!lit buyers to carry lower inventories. If they can get overnight shipment, they need not carry an item in inventory. For this reason, air shipment is quite commonly used for repair parts for machinery.

The cheapest type of air shipment is air freight. The shipper delivers the goods to his local airport and they are handled by a regularly scheduled passenger airline or air cargo carrier. For a substantial premium (usually about 200 to 300 percent), the shipper can get faster more complete service with air express or by using an air freight for warder. The tariff for such shipments includes pickup and delivery by truck and routing over the best available commercial air routes.

The. U.S. Postal Service provides the forwarding service if the shipper uses air parcel post. This is economic on very light shipments but, for larger shipment, the shipper should (and sometimes must) use private forwarders or the airlines themselves,

Barge and Pipeline. Shippers of bulky, relatively inexpensive raw materials try to ship by water or pipeline whenever possible in order to keep transportation costs at a minimum. In fact, chemical, aluminum, steel and power plants often are intentionally located at deep-water ports or on inland waterways in order to reduce the cost of inbound raw materials. Water shipment is slow, but the rates always are low. Also, when railroads or trucks are faced with competition from water carriers, they are more prone to offer rate reductions.

Only fluids can be shipped through pipelines, and pipeline shipment often is more expensive than water shipment. However, the pipeline is the most economic vehicle for shipping natural gas, oil products and anything else that can be made into a fluid to inland points.

Piggyback and Fishyback. Sometimes the most efficient way to ship is by using two carriers—truck trailer and either railroad or ship. "Piggy-back" shipments are made by loading truck trailers aboard railroad flatcars for shipments between cities. The trailer is delivered from the shipper's plant to the flatcar by truck, which also moves it to the customer's plant. "Fishyback" shipments are made by loading the truck trailers on a barge or ship. After the water shipment, the trailers can be towed by truck to their final destination.

Piggyback and fishyback shipments combine many of the advantages of shipping by rail, barge, or ship with those of shipping by truck, including the following:

1. Reduced Handling Expense. Material need be handled only when it is loaded into the truck trailer and when it is unloaded at the final destination.

2. Lower Rates. Shipment between points not on rail sidings often is cheaper by piggyback than by motor freight, since the long intercity haul can be made by rail. With fishyback, it is possible to eliminate extra handling and packaging for export by loading the truck trailer directly onto the ship.

3. Faster Service. Since they minimize handling and enable shipments to be routed by the best service available, piggyback and fishyback usually permit quicker deliveries than the conventional approaches to surface transportation.

Piggyback and fishyback are by far the fastest growing modes of shipment and, in recent years, their expansion has been limited largely by carriers' ability to buy and finance additional equipment.

Routing, Delays, and Damages

Once the carrier is selected, the traffic manager's job would seem to be complete but it rarely is. The carrier does not necessarily carry out its part of the bargain. Trucking companies do not always have trucks immediately available and, if they are busy, do not maintain their promised schedules. With railroads, the problem may start when boxcars are requested. Plenty of them are usually available in periods of depressed business, but during boom periods there is often a shortage. The shipper frequently has no recourse but to wait his turn, although he can ask the Interstate Commerce Commission for help. The ICC has the power to allocate cars to various railroads (and even can, for example, order a railroad to supply some of its cars to a competing road that is hard pressed). But, of course, the ICC cannot create cars out of thin air so shipments are delayed during periods of car shortage.

Routing. The traffic manager's problems do not end when his shipment is loaded on the railroad boxcar or truck. If he is on the job, he will direct the originating carrier to use a particular routing.

Railroad and truck lines crisscross the United States in a huge grid. There are almost always two possibilities on an interstate shipment, and there may be dozens. For example, one of several possible routings between Portland, Maine, and Greensboro, North Carolina, would be the Boston and Maine Rail road to Hartford, Connecticut; the New York, New Haven and Hartford Railroad to New York City; the Penn Central Rail road to Washington, D.C.; and the Southern Railroad to Greensboro.

If you are a shipper in Portland, Mair.e, all you need do in theory is to tell your friendly Roston & Maine freight agent that you want a car to go to Greensboro, North Carolina, and he will pick the routing for you. But the best routing from the point of view of the originating carrier is not necessarily the best one for you as the shipper. Left to his own devices, the originating carrier may carry you as far as possible on his own lines. This may not be the fastest routing, but it gives the originating carrier maximum revenue. Then the originating carrier may turn the car over to another railroad with whom it has friendly relations either common financial control or reciprocal agreements on freight. This again is not always the quickest route. Occasionally. it is not even the cheapest way although, in general, tariffs between two points are identical regardless of the routing.

Thus, companies with professional traffic managers always give their carriers precise routing for each shipment. In most cases, responsibility rests with the firm that is purchasing the material rather than the supplier. The routing becomes a standard part of the purchase order, and the supplier's traffic department follows its customer's instructions.

Tracing. The supplier's traffic department may trace shipments for its customers. Typically, the buyer follows up with the supplier's sales department to determine why a particular shipment has not yet been received. The sales department may then discover that the item has been shipped. It might give the appropriate bill of lading or way bill number to the buyer so his own traffic department could trace the shipment, or it might do the tracing for the customer.

In big companies, dozens of traffic clerks spend almost all of their working lives on the telephone tracing shipments. The procedure is fairly simple. Given the waybill or bill of lading number (*i.e.*, the shipper's receipt for the shipment), the carrier's clerk can determine, precisely what boxcar or truck the shipment is on. The clerk then traces the car or truck and reports back to the shipper when it is due at its destination.

Big shippers often find it convenient to reroute full truck or carloads. For example, at any given time an auto producer might have hundreds of boxcars en route from its major manufacturing plants in Michigan to assembly plants scattered throughout the country. If shortages develop at a particular assembly plant, a boxcar can be rerouted in transit to that plant. This practice cuts lead time substantially and permits the firm to get along with a lower inventory investment.

Damage Claims. Even if cars are not rerouted, goods are shuffied back and forth a great deal while they are in transit. Not surprisingly, there is a good deal of damage. Common carriers are forced to pay out more than $200 million per year in damage claims to shippers. Even if the shipper is reimbursed in full, damaged shipments cause production delays, and the processing of claims is a huge burden on the typical firm's traffic department.

Not all claims are the carrier's fault. In fact, the carriers maintain that most claims occur as a result of inadequate packaging. One problem is that frugal shippers keep using the same cartons over and over again. Carriers maintain that most corrugated cartons are designed for one-shot use and should then be discarded.

The exact cause of damage is not clear-cut in many cases. The shipment would certainly not have been damaged if it had been handled with sufficient care. But it might also be true that there need not have been any damage had the merchandise been packed more carefully in costlier containers. Traffic departments spend a great deal of time investigating damaged shipments and making claims against carriers. They also work with their own company's packaging engineers and others on ways to reduce damages. Shippers are becoming increasingly conscious of the simple truth that they are losers on damaged shipments even if they are reimbursed in full by carriers.

The procedure for claiming damages is fairly straightforward. He also gives him his bill of lading, the paid freight bill, and a copy of the supplier's invoice or other evidence that establishes the value of the damaged merchandise. The claimant may include photographs of the damage both to help verify his claim and to serve as a basis for the development of ways to prevent future damage. Naturally, carriers must include an allowance for damage claims in their tariffs, and it is to everyone's interest to help minimize such claims.

Tariffs of Common Carriers

Like other prices, the tariffs charged by common carriers are influenced by supply, demand, and cost of production. They also are influenced by peculiar variables of their own. Unlike most other sellers of goods and services, common carriers are not free to set their own rates, nor can they operate wherever and whenever they please. Each carrier must have a franchise to operate at all, and, as a condition of the franchise, almost every phase of the carrier's business is subject to regulation. In fact, carriers are not even free to cease operations without getting approval from one or more regulatory agencies.

The Interstate Commerce Commission is the most important regulatory agency for interstate railroads, motor carriers, and barge line operators. The Federal Power Commission regulates pipelines. Intrastate shipments are regulated by various states agencies.

Economics of Rate Structures

Regulatory agencies try to set rates that are fair to shippers and at the same time permit carriers to earn an adequate return on their investment. This is not an easy job. It is almost impossible to determine the cost of handling a particular type of shipment. In addition, regulatory agencies are subject to considerable non-economic pressures.

Cost Determination. Each carrier ships thousands of different items between thousands of different terminals. A big railroad, for example, is available to carry any type of shipment from any terminal on its own or another railroad's line to any other station. It would be a difficult enough job to determine the cost of an individual shipment if all costs were direct. Unfortunately, most costs do not vary directly either with the type of shipment or with the distance it is carried. They are fixed, or non-variable.

For example, railroads must spend prodigious sums on maintenance of their roadbed. Most such expenditures are necessary regardless of whether the road handles one train a minute or one train a year. How then does one calculate the wear and tear on the road from an LCL shipment of shirts from the factory in Troy, New York, to a department store in Memphis, Tennessee? The shipment may move over several railroads, and chances are that several alternate routes are available. The expenses of each road involved will be almost exactly the same whether or not the shirts are shipped.

It is impossible for a carrier to determine the real cost of any single shipment or even any group of shipments. About the best it can does determine the average cost per ton-mile for all shipments by dividing total costs shipped by total ton-miles. It also can calculate the average cost per shipment by dividing total costs by total number of shipments. Special studies also can yield valuable information concerning the relave costs of handling various types of shipment. But when it comes to determining what the costs and rates should be for transporting a particular commodity such as shirts from one point to another, arbitrary asumptions must be made.

Almost any rate can be justified, depending on the assumptions that are made. Competition can sometimes be used as a basis for rate setting but competing modes of transport often find themselves in the same boat. None of them can assign costs so well that rates make much sense. Competition does work in some respects, however. Carriers "discover" that costs are lower when competing modes of transport are available. Costs often are high and service is poor on routes where a carrier enjoys a monopoly.

Pressures on Rates. Tariffs are influenced by both political and economic forces. Since a company in a given community can compete more effectively if it has favourable freight rates, regulatory bodies often are pressed by local communities and industries to set low rates. In fact, much of the original pressure for regulation of carriers came from farmers and small businessmen who believed that the railroads were getting too big a share of their output by charging high tariffs to ship their goods to market.

Even today, rates are almost always lower when carriers have competition. For example, on coast-to-coast shipments, railroads are conscious of competition from ships using the Panama Canal. This some times makes the coast-to-coast rate lower than rates charged for shipping identical commodities to inland points. Competition from barge traffic on the Mississippi and Ohio rivers keeps rail rates low in those areas. Railroads in the Great Lakes area have been forced to reduce some rates because of competition from ships using the St. Lawrence Seaway.

Even if a carrier has little effective competition, it cannot afford to charge too high a tariff. If it does, the traffic may simply disappear. A rock quarry, for example, will go out of business if it cannot negotiate a competitive freight rate. The major cost of the rock delivered to the user is freight. The lower the freight rate, the greater the distance from the quarry that the rock can be shipped and still remain competitive with rock from other quarries.

In some cases, the traffic is created only if the rate is sufficiently attractive to make it possible for the shipper to earn a profit. For example, the Kaiser Steel Corporation began shipping sheet-steel coils across the country from its plant in Fontana, California, to Hennepin, Illinois, in 1972 only because it was able to negotiate a special 50-car-unit train load rate of $19 per ton. This rate, which is divided among the carriers the Southern Pacific, Rock Island, and Milwaukee railroads is less that half that of the single-car rate. Without it Kaiser Steel could not possibly hope to compete with steel firms in the Midwest for business in the part of the country.

What Traffic Will Bear. In general, most tariffs are based on "whatever the traffic will bear." If the product has an extremely high value perpound, freight cost is relatively unimportant to the shipper. For example a freight cost of $5 would have an almost insignificant effect on the cost of a very fine chair designed to sell for $400, but it would be quite significant for a chair intended to sell for $40. Whenever possible, carriers try to distinguish between inexpensive and expensive products in order to charge what the traffic will bear. Usually only part of the premium paid to ship the higher cost commodity is justified by the greater cost of damage claims and other costs that characterize the more expensive item.

To add to the confusion, the rate is not necessarily identical in both directions. For example, the lowest rate at which one could ship a truckload of "printed matter" from Boston to Philadelphia is 87 cents per cwt. But one could ship a truckload of the same printed matter from Philadelphia to Boston for only 72 cents per cwt. The rates should be identical. Why do they differ by more than 20 percent? The most likely explanation is that shippers of printed matter from Philadelphia to Boston were more successful in negotiating with carriers and arguing the validity of a lower rate before the Interstate Commerce Commission than shippers in the opposite direction were. Or possibly there is more southbound traffic, so that trucks sometimes must travel partly loaded or empty northward from Philadelphia to Boston. The northbound traffic will not take as high a tariff as the southbound traffic, so the carriers established a differential designed to encourage more northbound shipments.

Similarly, it has traditionally been cheaper to ship something from Europe or Japan to the United States than vice versa. For example, iron or steel pipe costs $38.25 per ton to ship from New York to Germany but only $20.75 to ship from Germany to New York. Similarly, it costs $0.00664 per ton-mile to ship automobiles from New York to Rio de Janeiro but only $0.00222 to ship from London to Rio. American manufacturers have complained bitterly that this discrimination in ocean freight rates puts them at a competitive disadvantage with foreign manufacturers. The conference of shipping lines that sets the rates justifies them on the basis that cargo space that is outbound from the United States is relatively more scarce than inbound space. This, of course, is a roundabout way of saying that rates are set for what the traffic will bear.

The density of the product also is important in determining tariffs. A carload of lightweight, bulky material costs almost as much to transport as a carload of very heavy materials. The carrier naturally must charge a higher rate per hundredweight for the low-density material in order to recoup his costs. For example, the National Motor Freight Classification' indicates the following rates per hundredweight on LTL (less than truckload) shipments from Washington, D.C., to Atlanta Georgia:

Density (per cu. ft.)	Rate (per cwt.)
Less than 6 pounds	$7.31
6-12 pounds	3.79
More than 12 pounds	3.26

Class and Commodity Rates

So complex are rate structures that it is even possible to pay two different rates for identical shipments with identical origins and destinations. For example, the tariff for shipping a carload of steel from Baltimore to San Francisco can be either $3.98 per cwt. or $2.43 per cwt. The higher is the "class" rate, the lower is the "commodity" rate.

Carriers have class rates for almost everything. As the term implies, the rates are created by dividing goods into classes (or classifications) and setting rates for each class. An occasional shipper of a commodity will check first to see if there is a commodity rate for the shipment he wishes to make. If there is not, he will always find a class rate.

A frequent shipper of a commodity between two points is foolish to pay a class rate. When no commodity rate is available, he negotiates one with the carrier. The proposed rate is reviewed by the ICC and hearings are held. At these hearings, the shipper's competitors may object if they feel the proposed rate is too low and gives him an "unfair" competitive advantage. Competing carriers also may protest if they feel the rate is too low, and will cause them to lose traffic. The final commodity rate' usually represents a compromise among the conflicting interests of the shipper, his carrier (or carriers), competitors of the shipper, and competing carriers. However, in every case the commodity rate is lower than the class rate, so it is well worth a big shipper's trouble to obtain commodity rates for all key commodities he handles.

Cost-reduction Opportunities

Because rate structures are so complex, there are many opportunities for traffic experts to make tremendous savings in buying transportation. They often can save their companies millions of dollars by finding "loop' holes" that permit shipments to be made at lower tariffs and also by spotting errors that carriers make in computing charges. For example North American Aviation Division of North American Rockwell Corp. was able to reduce its $2,929,400 annual freight bill by $597,344 in a traffic cost-reduction programme. More than $180,000 of the savings came from overpayments detected in audits of freight bills that had already been paid. The balance came from more economical shipping methods.

More than $143,000 was saved by making increased use of pool carshipments. Savings of more than $230,000 came from consolidation of service from air cargo carriers, use of company-owned trucks returning empty from deliveries, special fixtures in freight cars, and so on.

Auditing Freight Bills

Of the savings made by the North American Aviation traffic department, the most surprising may well be the huge sum recouped by auditing freight bills to detect overcharges. It might appear that North Amercian had been extremely inefficient to accept such overcharges in the first place or that its carriers were either inefficient or dishonest. Neither is true.

Every well-managed company audits its freight bills and makes enormous savings as a result. The rate structure is so complex that errors are inevitable. Moreover, when two different rates apply to the same commodity (and there is always the problem of classifying the shipment), who is to blame the carrier if it charges the higher of the two rates? Many such mistakes are the shipper's fault. The carrier's rate clerk never sees the shipment and must rely on the shipper's description of the material. If the description is incomplete, he naturally applies the higher rate. The lower the class number, the lower the rate. In other words, a Class 77½ rating carries a lower tariff than a Class 100 rating. Class ratings vary substantially with the completeness of the shipping order description. For example:

If you ship:	*And describe them as:*	*They will be rated:*	*They should be rated:*
Cotton work shirts	Cotton shirts	Class 100	Class 77½
Crude sulfate of soda	Chemicals	Class 100	Class 50
Wooden forks or spoons	Woodenware	Class 100	Class 50
Portable phonographs	Phonographs	Class 125	Class 110
Solid toy blocks	Toy blocks	Class 85	Class 70
Cotter pins, iron or steel	Hardware	Class 70	Class 50

Even after freight bills have been audited once, it is still possible for a skilled auditor to detect errors. For this reason, almost every big corporation sends bills that its own auditors have checked to an independent auditing firm for a second review. Such firms find it profitable to check clients bills for a commission of 30 to 60 percent on the errors they detect. They will also provide complete traffic management service for smaller companies.

Not every freight bill is incorrect, of course. In fact, more than 99 percent usually are not challenged. Monsanto Chemical's experience is not untypical. It limits its audit to invoices that exceed $100; at that must check about 600 of them a day. About 20 of these are "pickups" that is, bills picked up for further investigation because of Some dicrepancy. On about half of the pickups there is a discrepancy between the rate charged by the carrier and the rate Monsanto feels should be paid. The balance of the pickups result from errors in computation. Monsanto's experience in auditing freight invoices is typical of most large companies with first-rate traffic departments.

Charter Truck

Switching from common carriers to private chartered truck has been a surefire cost-reduction technique for many traffic departments. For example, Montgomery Ward cut its transportation costs by $2,500,000 a year with a company-operated fleet of 280 trucks. Big savings result mainly because charter rates are not regulated. A company can carry the "cream" of its traffic in its own trucks and ship the balance by common carrier. It saves enormous amounts in this way because common carriers charge rates much higher than their true cost for some shipments in order to offset losses on other shipments. For example, almost all common carriers lose money on LTL and LCL shipments, whereas carload and truckload rates for most finished manufactured goods are extremely profitable, especially when shipment is between two points on the carrier's main line.

Interstate Commerce Commission regulations may prohibit common carriers from cutting rates in order to hang on to business they might lose to captive carriers. Only common carriers of agricultural products are exempt from ICC regulation. In some cases, manufacturers make use of farm trucks to haul merchandise one way and the trucks presumably haul produce the rest of the time. Care must be taken to avoid violation of ICC regulations, however. And, in recent years, the ICC has tried to crack down on what are really unlicensed common carriers.

It is perfectly legal for a company to use a chartered truck to deliver goods and then return empty to the plant, and many companies believe that this seemingly uneconomical mode of transport is much cheaper than common carrier. Naturally, traffic managers try to route their trucks so that they expend a maximum amount of time traveling with payloads. One way to do this is to use the trucks to pick up materials from suppliers after they have made deliveries to customers in the same area. One New York-based manufacturer of steel laboratory furniture uses a charter truck to make weekly deliveries to customers in the Milwaukee and Chicago area. The truck returns with steel purchased from Chicago mills. In this particular case, the company's choice of steel suppliers is influenced by the fact that many of its customers are in the Chicago area. Were the company to buy its steel from mills nearer New York—in Bethlehem, Pennsylvania, or Sparrows Point, Maryland, for example—it would have to ship by common carrier, since it does not have many customers in these areas.

Individual firms can also cooperate with one another in order to make more efficient use of charter trucks. For example, a manufacturer in New York might have heavy outbound traffic to Chicago, while a Chicago manufacturer might have heavy shipping to New York. If the two can cooperate in some fashion, they can get more efficient utilization of their charter trucks. They have to be careful to avoid acting as a common carrier, but in many cases such cooperation is possible and does not violate ICC regulations.

Many companies claim they would prefer charter trucks even if they made no direct cost saving with them. With their own trucks they are able to work on tighter schedules and enjoy lower cost packaging and materials handling. The trucks may even be used as a promotion device with the firm's brand name prominently displayed on them.

Tighter Scheduling. When a shipper controls his own fleet, he can more easily regulate relative priorities of various shipments. Sometimes he also can offer prompter service to customers or reduce his in-transit inventories. For example, the Admiral Corporation reduced its average time to ship TV sets from several plants near

Chicago to its New York distributor from 50 to 30 hours when it started using chartered trucks.

Packaging and Materials Handling. It often is practical to equip chartered or company trucks with special racks or other materials-handling devices to cut packaging and materials-handling costs. Comparable savings often can be made by leasing specially equipped railroad cars from common carriers. Even when special racks will not eliminate pack aging, it still is possible to cut packaging costs by using company trucks.

Since carriers are responsible for damage to goods in transit, they naturally insist that shipments be securely packaged. In some cases, it is possible to ship in lighter, cheaper containers with little increase in damage. For example, the Douglas Furniture Company cut packaging costs $25,000 per year because it was able to use 150-pound test cartons in its own trucks instead of the 200-pound test cartons required by common carriers. In addition, it cut its damage losses 80 percent because merchandise was handled more gently in company-operated trucks.

Good will and Convenience. A company-owned truck with the company name and trademark emblazoned on its side is a rolling advertisement. In addition, customers are more likely to be impressed when delivery is made by company truck instead of by common carrier. There is good reason for this. A company often can give better service with its own truck's, and it is almost always more convenient to dispatch a company-owned vehicle than to call on a common carrier.

Despite their advantages, however, there is no doubt that charter trucks would not be used so widely today were it not for the rate structure and antiquated regulations governing common carriers. Few manufacturers or distributors can operate truck lines as efficiently as common carriers, and most would not want to do so were it not so advantageous.

Other Cost-reduction Techniques

Sometimes a company can get common carriers to reduce rates simply by threatening to charter its own trucks. The process is an involved one, because the carrier cannot cut rates unless it has approval to do so from the ICC or some other regulatory body. The carrier's competitors will often resist its request for rate reduction. Competitors of the shipper benefiting from the reduction also may protest:

Classification Change, An easier route to rate reduction sometimes lies in creating a brand-new rate classification for the item. The shipper must convince the carrier and the regulatory body that his product is unique and should get a lower rate because it either costs less to ship or is worth less than other products in the same rate class. For example, the National Motor Freight Classification shows the following classifications for a simple item like a garment hanger:

Hangers, garment, aluminum, aluminum alloy, magnesium metal, or magnesium metal alloy, NOI, in boxes,	Class 100
Hangers, garment, plastic, or plastic and metal combined, in boxes	Class 100
Hangers, garment, NOI, in barrels, boxes, or crates	Class 100
Hangers, skirt or trouser, cast aluminum, in boxes	Class 85
Hangers, garment, wire, or wire and paper combined, in barrels, boxes, or crates	Class 70
Hangers, garment, wood, or wood and wire combined, in barrels, boxes, orcrates	Class 70
Hangers, garment, pulpboard, printed or not printed, in barrels, boxes, or crates	Class 55

The lower the class number, the lower the tariff that will apply. Thus the cheapest hanger to ship is one that is "garment, pulpboard, printed or not printed, in barrels, boxes, or crates." The most expensive is the first one listed. If a company should develop a new type of garment hanger-one of molded Fiberglas, for example—how does it determine what rate class should apply? Of course, it always can ship the prodlict as "hangers," but then the carrier would apply the highest tariff. Or it could describe the item in terms of the rate class that best fitted it. Fiberglas hangers presumably would be considered "hangers, garment, plastic, or plastic and metal combined in boxes." In this case they would be shipped as Class 100.

If there were any legitimate basis for doing so, the traffic manager would try to get the Fiberglas hangers assigned to a lower class than the plastic hangers. He might claim, for example, that Fiberglas hangers had a higher density, were of lower value, or less subject to damage than ordinary plastic hangers, and therefore they were entitled to a lower rate class. In this particular case, he probably would not be successful since Fiberglas would probably be considered a superior form of plastic.

Needless to say, shipper should be extremely careful in describing shipments. To earn a lower rate, the shipment not only must fit the specifications of that rate but must be described as such.

Reducing Demurrage Charges. Railroads allow 24 to 48 hours to unload a boxcar. If the car is held beyond this free time, they make a penalty charge called "demurrage." This charge has been increased several times in recent years because railroads complained that approved demurrage rates did not permit an adequate return on their investment in boxcars. However, the charge has apparently not increased enough to make it profitable for railroads to invest in boxcars, and idle cars remain a problem for the railroads. From the shipper's point of view, the boxcar is a reasonably cheap storage area even if demurrage charges must be paid. However, shippers naturally try to keep demurrage charges low, and the traffic department makes periodic studies to analyze charges and recommend changes in procedure that will reduce them.

In many cases, materials managers can reduce demurrage charges substantially by carefully scheduling shipments so that unloading facilitites are never overtaxed. Periodic studies show whether or not cars are being handled in the most economical fashion. They must take account not only of demurrage charges but also of unloading and storage costs. Sometimes it pays to incur extra demurrage charges; for example, it may be cheaper to pay demurrage than to have an unloading crew work overtime at premium rates. Also, many companies prefer to pay demurrage during peak production periods rather than to invest in the additional storage space that would be required to eliminate it. Partly as a result of this practice, the average boxcar moves loaded in trains only about 23 days per year and moves empty for 14 days. The rest of time the car sits idle on various sidings.

Specific Projects

Every traffic department always has at least one or two special cost reduction studies underway, Particularly promising for cost reduction are changes in packaging specifications, various pool car arrangements, and various facilities studies.

Packaging. Although it may not be directly responsible for package design, the traffic department should be concerned with packaging specifications. It can analyze damage claims, and, if there is almost no damage because of poor packaging, perhaps a less expensive package can be used. If damage claims are high, more costly packaging might be Worthwhile. Needless to say, traffic men prefer to select the lightest possible package. A shipper must pay freight not only for the product but also for the package that holds it. In some cases, costs can be reduced by selecting a container that weighs less even though it may cost slightly more.

Pool Cars. Shippers try to avoid paying high LCL and LTL rates whenever possible. One way to do this is to pool a number of small shipments headed in the same direction. For example, many Eastern manufacturers load orders for a number of West Coast customers in a single car. Thus a manufacturer may load orders for distributors located in a number of California cities in a boxcar with a San Francisco destination. When the car arrives, the orders are separated and carried by company-owned truck or by some other conveyance to their separate destinations.

Pool cars also can be used for purchased materials. In this case the company pools all shipments from suppliers in a given area. For example, an auto company with a Los Angeles assembly plant might arrange for pool cars to leave at regular intervals from all cities in \ which it has a number of parts suppliers. Suppliers then deliver to the loading point, where a carloading firm pools their shipments. Such arrangements may save hundreds of thousands of dollars. Needless to say, purchasing and traffic must work together closely when there are pool car arrangements. In many cases, choice of a supplier will be influenced by his proximity to a pool car loading point.

Facilities Studies. Traffic considerations also are important in determining the location of any new facilities. Using linear programming and other operations research techniques, the physical distribution or traffic manager can determine the relative transportation costs to and from various proposed locations. Frequently there are substantial differences.

❐

15

Disposal of Scrap and Obsolete Materials

Managers have long been concerned about the effective and efficient handling of the salvage of surplus, obsolete, and waste and scrap materials generated within the firm. In recent years, salvage problems have become more complex, as well as more important, as companies have become larger, more diversified in product lines, and more decentralized' in management. More recently, a new dimension has been added to the overall salvage problem, the need to develop and use new methods to avoid the generation of solid waste products and better means of salvaging and disposing of other wastes which are discharged into the air and waterways, causing pollution.

While it is the purpose of this chapter to analyze and discuss the purchasing department's role in disposition of surplus and waste, the alert purchasing executive must also keep abreast of the new technology concerned with avoiding and eliminating causes of wastes which result in pollution.

The salvage of all types of materials in U.S. industry is big business. It is estimated that sales of scrap and waste materials of all types are in excess of $6 billion per year. Not only does the sale of scrap and waste result in additional income for the seller, it also prevents pollution and serves to conserve raw material resources and energy. For example, every ton of iron and steel scrap recycled saves 1½% tons of iron ore, 1½ ton of coke and ½ ton of limestone.

Sources of Waste and Surplus

No matter how well a company may be managed, some excess, waste, scrap, and obsolete material is bound to develop.

Every organization tries, of course, to keep such material at a minimum. But, try as they may, this can never be wholly successful. The existence of this class 794 of material is the result of a wide variety of causes, among which may be mentioned overoptimism in the sales forecast; changes in design and specifications; errors in estimating mill usage; inevitable losses in processing; careless use of material by factory personnel; overbuying resulting from attempts to avoid the threat of rising prices or to secure quantity discounts on large purchases.

We are not now concerned with the methods by which excess, waste scrap, and obsolete material may be kept at a minimum, for these have already been discussed in connection with proper inventory and stores control, standardization, quality determination, and forward buying. The immediate problem has to do with the disposition of these materials when they do appear. In attacking it, we first need to distinguish among the four categories in question.

Excess of Surplus Material

Excess (or surplus) material is that stock which is in excess of a reasonable requirement of the plant. It arises because of errors in the amount bought or because anticipated production did not materialize. There are various ways in which such material may be handled. In some cases it may be desirable merely to store it until required, particularly if the material is of a nonperishable character, if storage costs are not excessive, and if there is a reasonable expectation that the material will be required in the future. Occasionally it may be substituted for more active material. Or, if the company operates a number of plants, it may be possible to transfer the excess to another plant. There are times, however, when these conditions do not exist and when fairly prompt sale is desirable. The chances for change in the style or design may be so great as to diminish considerably the probability that this particular material may be required. Or, it may be perishable. Factory requirements may be such as to postpone the demand for large amounts of this material so far into the future that the most economical method is to dispose of it and repurchase at a later date.

Many companies set some rough rule of thumb by which to determine when a stock item is to be classed as "surplus." Thus, according to one manufacturing organization:

Generally speaking, the question of excess material should be decided on a six-month basis. Customarily, the excess would be that amount of material on hand which represents more than a six-months' supply. There are exceptions, however. Some material deteriorates so rapidly that any quantity on hand greater than two or three months' supply be treated as excess material. In other cases, where it takes six months or longer to procure new material, more lengthy supply periods are frequently essential.

This rule suggests that all materials should be grouped into rough classifications, and normal requirement and supply periods established for each. Mere classification in itself is not sufficient. As with all classes of material considered in this chapter, systematic, physical stock-taking, continuous review of inventory records, and occasional "cleanup campaigns" are also necessary.

Another source of excess material usually appears upon the completion of a construction project. The company just referred to covers this situation as follows: "All new material for a specific property on order and not used on the project in question constitutes an inventory and must be treated as such. As soon as the work is completed, all new, unused material should be transferred immediately to the custody of the stores department. The original cost of the material should be charged to "Reclamation Stores" which is an unclassified segment of the Stores Account and credited to the property order or authorization.' Provision is also made for the proper accounting of used material created or resulting from demolition work carried on in conjunction with construction projects.

In the case of one large manufacturing company, if the sales department has definitely obligated the company to make a certain quantity of an item, or has set up a sales budget for that quantity subsequently accepted by the management, and later finds itself unable to dispose of its quota, the losses sustained on the excess material are charged to that particular item or sales classification. The same practice is followed if the sales department, by virtue of recommending a change in design, creates an excess of material. This company feels that the loss should not be absorbed generally or distributed over other departments.

Obsolete Material

Once material has been declared obsolete, it is wise to dispose of it for the best price that can be obtained. Obsolete material differs from excess stock in that whereas the latter presumably could be consumed at some future date, the former is unlikely ever to be used inside the organization which purchased it. Material becomes obsolete as a result of a change in the production process or when some better mate-rial is substituted for that originally used.

Although material may be obsolete to one user, this need not mean it is obsolete for others. An airline may decide to discontinue using a certain type of airplane. This action makes not only the plane, but also the repair and maintenance parts inventory, obsolete. Both may have substantial value to other airlines or users of planes.

What are "scrap" and "waste"? Scrap and waste material differ from excess or obsolete stock since they cannot properly be classified as new or unused. The former terms are sometimes used indiscriminately, and from the standpoint of their disposition no harm results by so doing. However, the causes which produce them and their effect on costs are very different. "Scrap" is a term which may be applied to material or equipment which is no longer serviceable and has 'been discarded. It includes such items as worn machinery, old tools, and the like. In such cases, scrap arises because the company is replacing old machines with others which are more modern and more productive. A concern buying new machines, tools, and other equipment normally maintains a depreciation charge intended to cover the original cost of such items, so that the value of a machine has been written off by the time it is finally discarded. Such a depreciation charge normally covers an obsolescence factor as well as ordinary wear and tear. Actually, however, a discarded or scrapped machine may still have a value for some other manufacturer in the same type of business or in some other industry. It consequently may be disposed of at a price which will show a profit in many instances. This replacement of old or obsolete machines by others capable of larger production at the same or lower cost provides a profit-making opportunity not to be overlooked.

Another form of scrap is represented by the many by-products of the production process, such as fly from cotton spinning, warp ends from weaving, and metal scrap from boring and planing machines. Start-up adjustment scrap is frequently significant, and, in industries like paper making, paper converting, printing, polyethylene pellet manufacture and many others, it is one major reason for a significant price increase for small custom orders. The faster and the more automated the equipment, the higher the start-up scrap will be as a percentage of the total material used in small orders. Commonly, items' of this class, which are quite unavoidable, are considered a form of scrap; such material may frequently be salvaged and handled in one of several ways, to which reference will be made later. In the metal industries, the importance of scrap in this form has a definite bearing on costs and prices. For instance, a selection from forgings, stampings, or castings may depend upon the waste weight. The waste weight to be removed in finishing plus labour costs of removing it may make a higher priced article the better value. In turning brass parts, the cost of the material (brass rod) may be greater than the price of the finished parts, because the recovered brass scrap is such an important element in the cost. Indeed, so valuable is scrap as an element in cost that it is not unusual for the purchase contract on nonferrous metals to include a price at which the scrap will be purchased by the supplier.

Waste has been defined as material or supplies the original forms of which have been changed during the production process and which "through carelessness, faulty production methods, poor handling, or other causes have been spoiled, broken or otherwise rendered unfit for further use, so far as concerns the particular manufacturing process." This definition is not entirely adequate.

There is a form of wastp not due to obsolescence and yet not a result of carelessness or poor handling. Waste, for example, may be brought about by the fact that the material is not up to specifications, because of faulty machinery or breakdowns or because of chemical action not foreseen.

Theoretically, waste should not exist. Actually, 'however, there probably will never be a time when some waste will not exist in every plant. This statement does not mean that every effort should not be made to reduce the waste factor to the lowest possible point. Its reduction can be brought about in a great many ways, such as the installation of new processes, by improved production layout, and by employee motivational programmes.

Some differences of opinion may exist between accountants and engineers as to the exact definitions of scrap, excess, and waste. From the standpoint of the purchasing manager who has to dispose of the material, these differences are secondary. The commercial term "scrap" is for all practical purposes all-inclusive and as such can be used in a general discussion of the problem.

Value of Reclaimed Scrap. In one respect, it is surprising that more attention has not been given by more companies to the whole problem of scrap. The reasons are probably several. One of the most important is that scrap is suggestive of something which has no value and which the junkman can take away-in other words, something which a company is willing to sell if it can get anything for it, but which, if not, it is willing even to pay somebody to haul away. Another reason, is that many concerns are not large enough to maintain scrap and salvage departments, since the amounts of scrap they have do not appear great enough to warrant particular attention. Yet scrap may well be a source of potential profit.

An illustration may be in point. A man purchased old burlap and other items from the salvage department of a large organization. He then called on the sales department of the same company and disposed of the material at a substantial profit. He made $20,000 in these transactions merely because the salvage and the sales departments of the same company were not cooperating.

At times of raw material shortages scrap is likely to have very high prices. The example of copper scrap at $1.30 per pound compared to the government controlled price of 60 has already been mentioned. The director of purchases of a large equipment manufacturer said in early 1974 that he had about 40 tons of a special bronze alloy scrap in the yard, and he received telephone calls from potential buyers from all over North America.

England found in 1973 and 1974 that its domestically controlled price of waste rags of about $60 per ton was well below that of the European market, resulting in an exodus of this material for which a special domestic collection programme had been set up to encourage local manufacture of toilet, tissue. The result was a shortage of raw materials for the English mills, and a tissue shortage forcing imports of an item that could well have been manufactured locally.

The disposition of all kinds of scrap materials should always be so handled as to reduce the net loss to the lowest possible figure or if possible achieve the highest potential gain. The first thought, therefore, should be to balance against each other the net returns obtained from each one of several methods of disposition. Thus, excess material can frequently be transferred from one plant of a company to another of the same company. Such a procedure involves little outlay except for packing, handling, and shipping. At other times, by re-processing or re-conditioning, the material can be salvaged for use within the plant. Such cases clearly involve a somewhat larger outlay, and there may be some question as to whether, once the material has been so treated, its value, either for the purpose originally intended or for some substitute use, is great enough to warrant the expense. Since the decision whether to undertake the reclamation of any particular lot of material is essentially one of production costs and of the resultant quality, it should be and commonly is made by the production or engineering departments instead of by the scrap department. The most the purchasing manager can do is to suggest that this treatment be considered before the material is disposed of in other ways. In some companies there is created, within the manufacturing department, a separate salvage or "utilization" division to pass upon such questions as possible reclamation. Indeed, the place of the "salvage engineer" is well established among many larger firms.

Marketing of Scrap. If the material is such that profitable reclamation is not possible, other opportunities present themselves. It may be sold to a local scrap dealer. It may be sold, either directly or through a broker, to some large consumer, as a great deal of steel scrap is sold. It may be sold back to the original supplier, who may resell it "as is" or who may be in a more strategic position for its reclamation than the seller.

The Elimination of Waste Committee of the American Society of Mechanical Engineers some years ago developed a Dictionary of Waste Elimination in which it points out four important alternative methods for disposing of scrap:

(1) Can the material be used, either "as is," or with economical modification, for any purpose other than that for which it was purchased? *e.g.*, substitution for similar grades and near-by sizes, and shearing or stripping sheet metals to obtain narrower widths. *(2)* Can it be returned to the Manufacturer or Supplier from whom it was purchased, either for cash or for credit on other purchases? *(3)* Can any other manufacturer use the material either "as is," or with economical modifications? It should be noted that sales can often be made direct to other users, and there are surplus materials dealers in most cities who either purchase such material outright or dispose of it on a commission basis. *(4)* Can the material be reclaimed or modified for use by welding? Welding has become a very important factor in disposing of materials to advantage. Defective and spoiled castings and fabricated metal parts can be reclaimed at little expense, short ends of bar stock, pipe, etc., can be welded into working lengths and worn or broken jigs, fixtures, and machine parts can be built up or patched. Furthermore, castings and fabricated metal parts can be reduced in size by either the are or acetylene cutting process.

If all of these fail, the material will have to be salvaged.....A major point to keep in mind is the fact that metals for salvage should be broken, sheared, or torched to small charging size, because they then command a much better price than can be obtained for large materials. Also before proceeding with the dismantling of finished apparatus and assembled parts, it should be determined that the salvage value will exceed the cost of labour and overhead—otherwise, the material should be disposed of as mixed scrap.

Different kinds and grades of material.....should be kept separate and clean at the source because it is expensive to separate them when mixed.....

Standardization with consequent reduction of grades, sizes, shapes, etc., will accomplish more in the way of waste prevention than any other single thing.

When scrap is sold, careful attention should be given to the selection of a buyer and to the procedure for handling the sale. The yellow pages of the telephone directory provide lists of dealers who buy scrap and waste products. The *Waste Trade Journal* which is published weekly provides price information for most waste and scrap products for the major markets in the United States. The Waste Trade Directory published annually provides comprehensive coverage of all segments of the market.

Procedure for Disposing of Scrap

The procedure for handling the disposal of waste and scrap is important. One writer has said:

In connection with the selling and delivery of the material, a system should be set up which will be consistently followed and will afford the company protection against all possible loss through slipshod methods, dishonest employees and irregular practice on the part of the purchaser of by-products. All sales should be approved by a department head and cash sales should be handled through the cashier and never by the individual whose duty it is to negotiate the sale. All delivery of by-products sold should be effected through the issuing of an order form and sufficient number of copies made to provide a complete record for all departments involved in the transaction. The shipping department should determine the weight, count, etc., and this figure should go to the billing department without going through the hands of those who negotiate the sale.

Any department responsible for the performance of this function should maintain a list of reputable dealers in the particular line of scrap and waste to be disposed of and should periodically review this list. At frequent intervals the proper plant official should be instructed to clean up the stock and report on the weights and quantities of the different items or classes of items which he has for disposal.

A common procedure is to send out invitations to four or five dealers to call and inspect the lots at the factory and quote their prices f.o.b. factory yard. Such transactions are usually subject to the accepted bidders' check of weights and quantities and are paid for in cash before removal. Not infrequently, acceptable and dependable purchasers with whom satisfactory connections have already been established are relied upon as desirable purchasers, and no bids are called for from others. In some cases, it has been found desirable for the purchasing department, in order to maintain a record of such sales, to issue a formal purchase order on the production department giving the particulars, such as the dealer's name and address, the weights, prices, shipping instructions, and terms, and requesting that department to issue a regular sales order on the factory for delivery as arranged.

After the purchasing department has been notified that the buyer has accepted and paid for the shipment, a copy of the order on the production department is marked with the date and amount of payment, stamped "COMPLETED," and filed away in a special folder. For future reference, these sales of scrap and waste are recorded on a special card or sheet designe for that purpose.

❐

16

Inventory Control

The inventory management can be interpreted as the avoidance of over-investment or under-investment in inventories, as an essential step in improving overall operational efficiency. Determination of the right level of investment in inventories; consistent with production/ operation schedules and prompt services, is the crux of inventory management.

Inventory control is that function of materials management which attempts to maintain stocks at their predetermined levels. It is exercised by planning required stock levels at regular intervals, by counting and validing the stock at the same intervals and by comparing the two sets of figures to feedback warning of variances. It has the following main purposes:

(i) To determine maximum, minimum and reorder stock levels.

(ii) To ensure that least possible working capital is blocked without allowing stocks to rise so high or fall below the predetermined minimum levels. A balance of stocks must be maintained.

(iii) To guard against theft, depreciation and obsolescence.

(iv) To dispose of scrap and unserviceable items economically.

(v) To carry out physical verification and reconciliation between the actual stocks to accounting records.

Determining and maintaining stock levels, inventory classification, inventory costs, economic order quantity and inventory control methods are being discussed here, which literally constitute the scope of this chapter. However, obsolescence and scrap, their disposal, physical verification, storage, stores accounting, etc., will be discussed in the next chapter.

Inventory Classification

Inventories may be classified under the following categories:

ABC Analysis

This inventory classification model is an adaptation of Vilfredo Pareto's Law of 80-20 distribution of wealth and income. This is the most important and widely used technique of classifying inventories. This is based on the principle of 'Vital Few-Trivial Many'. A higher degree of attention is focussed on the vital few, which offset the results significantly.

ABC classification, or the alphabetical approach, or always better control system is based on the annual consumption value. It has been found that about 10% of the number of items contribute to about 70% of the consumption value known as 'A' category. The middle 20% in number accounts for about 20% in value, and is known as the 'B' category. The remaining 70% in number accounts for about 10% of annual consumption value, and is the 'C' category. However, the exact cut-off points for A, B, C will vary from organisation to organisation.

The distribution of inventory in a normal organisation may be of the following pattern:

(a) 5-10% of the top number of items account for about 70% of the total investment in inventories. These are 'A' items and require rigorous control.

(b) 15-20% of the total number of inventory items account for about 20% of total investment in inventories. These are called 'B' items and require a moderate degree of control.

(c) The remaining 70-80% items account for 10% of the total investnent. These are 'C' items and require less degree of control.

Since P&MM wing of PDD does not follow any scientific inventory classification model, the researcher has on his own done classification on ABC basis, taking into consideration consumption value of selected 112 items of the Central Stores Division, Jammu. This has been depicted in Table 1 and also in Figure 1.

Table 1

Distribution of Inventories according to Size of Consumption Value in Electric Central Stores Division, Jammu

Category	*% of Inventory*		*% of Consumption Value*		*Degree of Control*
	General	*Cumulative*	*General*	*Cumulative*	
A	13	13	68	68	Rigorous
B	16	29	23	91	Moderate
C	71	100	9	100	Less

Source: Tabulated Data.

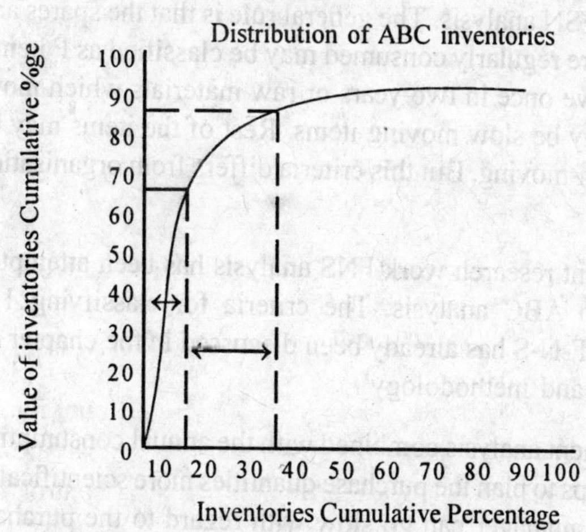

Fig. 1.

The Bombay Electric Supply and Transport (BEST) has been following the undermentioned inventory classificationl:

Items	*Annual Consumption Per Item*
A	Rs. 15,000 Above
B	Rs. 500-15,000
C	Below Rs. 500

It maintains nearly 350 'A' items and 520 'B' items and remaining 'C' items. Model of inventory classification of BEST in unsuitable for the PDD, keeping in view the nature and value of its items.

ABC Inventory classification of regular centrally purchased items has been recommended by Tata Consultancy to the Himachal Pradesh State Electricity Board (HPSEB). The work of ABC inventory classification is presently in progress in HPSEB.

FNS Analysis

One of the important ways of finding the usage of materials is according to their movement. For this purpose we have fast moving, normal moving and slow moving items or FNS analysis. Some managers classify their stock items as fast moving, slow moving and non-moving *i.e.*, FSN analysis. The general rule is that the spares and materials which are regularly consumed may be classified as F items. Spares which move once in two years or raw materials which move once in a year may be slow moving items. Rest of the items may be categorised as non-moving. But this criteria differs from organisation to organisation.

In the present research work FNS analysis has been attempted to, in addition to ABC analysis. The criteria for classifying 112 selected items as F-N-S has already been discussed in the chapter on 'research design and methodology'.

The movement analysis combined with the annual consumption value analysis helps to plan the purchase quantities more scientifically. For example, the manager can go slow with regard to the purchase of items falling under C&S category. But has to be very vigilant and has to expedite the purchase process of A&F items. Exceptionally high degree of control has to be exercised on A&F category items.

This is essential because overs tocking of this category of items not only entails greater investment, but carrying and other associated costs increase *pari passu*. Further, out of stock position jeopardises the operational flow, vis-a-vis efficiency.

The commonality of FNS and ABC analysis of 112 selected items of the Electric Central Stores Division, Jammu may be worked out as under:

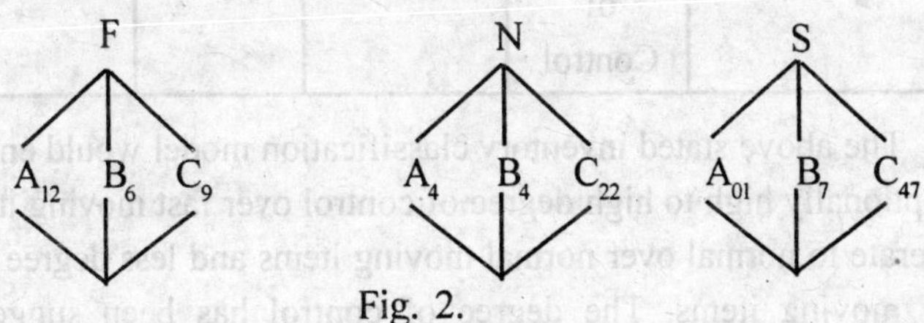

Fig. 2.

Table 2

Inventory Movement Analysis of Items of ECSD, Jammu

Inventory Value	*Fast*	*Normal*	*Slow*	*Total*
A Top 13% number 68% consumption value	FA-12	NA-04	SA-0l	17
B Medium 16% 23% consumption value	FB-6	NB-4	SB-7	17
C Remaining 71 % number 9% consumption value	FC-9	NC-22	SC-47	78

Inventory Value	*Fast*	*Normal*	*Slow*	*Total*
Degree of control	Exceptionally High and High Degree of Control	Moderate and Normal Control	Less Control	112

The above stated inventory classification model would ensure, exceptionally high to high degree of control over fast moving items, moderate to normal over normal moving items and less degree over slow moving items. The degree of control has been suggested vertically in Table 2.

VED Analysis

Under the classification 'V' stands for vital, 'E' for essential and 'D' for desirable. The absence of V category of inventory items whose absence will completely paralyse the work. They may not be very costly items but very indispensable for the operation of the organisation. For example, insulators are not very costly but essential for maintenance of electric lines. E items are those whose absence will temporarily stop the work or affect efficiency adversely. In electricity boards/ departments, electric meters are the best example of E items. D items are those whose absence will not result any stoppage of work but their availability may improve efficiency of the organisation. For instance, use of high rating conductor than that is normally being used in our country for transmitting power may reduce transmission losses of power significantly. This has been successively experimented in the USA and Russia.

This utility analysis brings out the criticality factor in inventory. Obviously, it would be preferable to hold higher stock levels of vital items, lower stock levels of essential items and the lowest levels of desirable items.

It has been found that BEST is using both ABC and VED analysis simultaneously for effective control of inventories. For transport organisations this model may be the better model for controlling inventories. But in case of electricity organisations ABC and FNS analysis is the best model as it takes care of vital and essential elements of inventories also in addition to their movement analysis and consumption value.

SDE Analysis

SDE items are those items which are scarce, difficult to obtain and easy to obtain. Scarce items are normally imported items. Obviously, it would be desirable to hold higher stock of scarce items and would need rigorous and constant control over them. Presently electricity organisations including J&K State PDD are mostly using indigenous items. Everything is being manufactured in India including the turbines.

Difficult items are those which though available involve lot of problem in their obtainment. For the POD 'D' items may be the non-local items. Items which are not available in J &K State may be termed as non-local and available within the State as local. 'E' items for the POD may be local items. Stock levels for 'D' items should be slightly higher than the 'E' items.

XYZ Analysis

As ABC analysis is based on annual consumption value, XYZ is based on the year end stores inventory value. X items are the top 10% items, accounting for about 70% of stock value, Y the middle 20% accounting for middle 20% of stock value and Z the remaining items.

XYZ analysis of inventory classification of POD inventories has not been attempted in the present study on account of two reasons. First, stocks in the central stores are managed quite unscientifically. Many fast moving items may either be out of stock or under stock and many slow moving and non-moving items may be overstocked. Second, disposal of surplus and unserviceable items has not been carried out since long.

Keeping the above factors in view XYZ analysis of the Central Stores Division items has not been attempted as his may give misleading picture.

GOLF, SOS & RAM

Some of the organisations make use of technique like GOLF, SOS or RAM in addition to some major technique of inventory analysis.

GOLF : Government controlled, ordinarily available, locally available and foreign supplies.

SOS : Seasonal and off-seasonal.

RAM : Reliability, availability and maintainability.

Presently, the PDD does not purchase Government controlled and foreign items.

INVENTORY COSTS

The following classes of costs are involved in inventory decisions:

Ordering Cost

These costs are those which are associated with making purchase requisitions. In this process two types of costs are involved: *(I)* the fixed cost, and *(II)* the variable cost. It may be pointed out that with every increase in the number of requisitions the ordering costs continue to rise because of variable costs involved. The fixed costs remain constant up to the optimal limit. If the number of orders surpasses that particular limit, even the fixed cost may also increase.

$$\text{Ordering cost} = \frac{T_{CO}}{A \times N}$$

T_{CO} = Total cost of ordering.

A = Average number of items purchased.

N – Total number of orders placed.

It may be pointed out that ordering costs incase of P&MM wing during the year 1992-93 were Rs. 22. But if three items, *viz.*, insulators, cement and nuts-bolts are not considered ordering cost would be Rs. 189. However, for subsequent analysis average of the two would be considered *i.e.*, Rs. 105. This means that ordering cost has mainly been influenced by these three items dominating in number. On the whole this indicates that there is much to be done in this direction.

Inventory Carrying Costs

These costs include all expenses incurred by an organisation because of the volume of inventory carried. The following elements are usually included in inventory carrying cost:

(a) Obsolescence

(b) Cost of foregoing some other investment opportunity

(c) Deterioration

(d) Storage and handling charages

(e) Taxes

(f) Insurance

(g) Transportation

(h) Pilferage and losses, etc.

In general inventory carrying costs range between 25% to 30% as reported by the Bureau of Public Enterprises of the Central Government. In case of Central Stores Division, Jammu of PDD, inventory carrying costs have been calculated around 26%. Keeping in view the stock holding position of Rs. 486.20 lakhs at the end of 1992-93 financial year; a reduction of just 1% in carrying costs would mean saving of Rs. 4.861akhs in a year. It appears that concerned executives do not realise that money saved through better management of inventories releases additional capital for being used elsewhere.

Out of Stock Costs

In case of the POD out of stock is mainly responsible for two things: *(i)* delay in project completion, and *(ii)* power failure. Due to out of stock problem project completion gets delayed and as a result completion costs escalate. Power failure which causes sufferings to the public is such a social loss which is difficult to calculate. However, loss due to escalation in compeletion costs of projects and industrial production loss can be calculated, which is enormous. It has been observed that cost of out of stock in the PDD is very high due to poor inventory management. In case of 12 A&F items out of selected 112 items in 1992-93 in a range of 12 months period 7 items were out of stock ranging between 1 to 3 times.

Economic Order Quantity (EOQ)

One of the oldest (1915) methods of scientific inventory control, the 'economic order quantity' has endured because of its ability to balance 'some major costs and to be very flexible and adaptable for many situations. The basic model of EOQ is generally referred to as Wilson Formulation. The EOQ is of great importance for those organisations which purchase/manufacture goods in bulk, not only because of its wide use, but also because of its relative simple analysis which brings out the nature of the faced trade-offs that must be used in any inventory system. The materials manager is faced with a peculiar situation; the cost of acquisition increases, as smaller quantities are procured each time, but the decrease in inventories also decreases the inventory carrying charges. Thus, the manager has to balance the two opposing costs, in order to strike the optimum level of inventories, which may minimise the total cost in an organisation.

Economic order quantity is that size of order which minimises total annual costs of carrying inventory and cost of ordering. When the carrying and ordering costs have been properly balanced, the total cost is minimised and the lot size so determined will be the EOQ.

The EOQ concept applies under the following conditions:

(i) The item is replenished in lots or batches either by purchasing or manufacturing.

(ii) Sales or usage rates are uniform and as such annual demand can be predicted with reasonable accuracy.

(iii) This technique is useful for less value but more number items. For all 'A' category items this technique may be unsuitable.

The purchase executives of PDD should make use of this technique to determine economic lot sizes of items like Insulators, Steel Tubular Poles, PCC Poles, Nuts and Bolts, Cement, Steel, etc.

Derivation of EOQ (Mathematical Approach)

In order to derive the EOQ model, following notations may be used:

Q = Economic order quantity

C = Cost of one unit of item

I = Inventory carrying costs

S = Ordering cost per order

R = Total annual usage/demand

Total inventory carrying costs over a period are equal to:

$$\left| \text{Average inventory quantity during the period} \right| \times \left| \text{Cost of one unit} \right| \times \left| \text{Inventory carrying cost in percentage} \right|$$

$$= \frac{Q}{2} CI$$

The total ordering costs may be given by:

Numbers of orders per period × Odering cost per order $= \dfrac{R}{Q} S$

Thus, we have

$$\frac{Q}{2}CI = \frac{R}{Q}S$$

i.e., $$QCI = \frac{2RS}{Q}$$

or $$Q^2 = \frac{2RS}{CI}$$

or $$Q = \sqrt{\frac{2RS}{CI}}$$

Calculs Approach:

Using the earlier notation, the total cost (TC) is given by:

$$TC = \frac{Q}{2}CI + \frac{R}{Q}S$$

Inventory Control 115 Differentiating the above expression with respect to Q, we get:

$$\frac{d(TC)}{DQ} = \frac{CI}{2} - \frac{RS}{Q^2}$$

The first derivative is set equal to zero in order to find the optimal value of Q.

i.e., $$\frac{CI}{2} - \frac{RS}{Q^2} = 0$$

$$Q^2 = \frac{2RS}{CI}$$

$$Q = \sqrt{\frac{2RS}{CI}}$$

In order to find out whether total costs are at a minimum or maximum with respect to the economic order quantity, the use of second derivative may be made.

CONTROL METHODS

Inventory control as already stated is a technique by which the quantity of materials is held between the predetermined levels. The following techniques of inventory control are normally used to keep investment in inventories at the lowest possible level and operational efficiency at the maximum:

1. Perpetual or Fixed Quantity System
2. Periodic Review System
3. Optional Replenishment System
4. Two Bin System
5. Materials Requirement Planning System.

Perpetual Inventory System

Before discussing the perpetual inventory system, it is pertinent to discuss some of the vital components of the system, such as safety margin, reorder point, etc. Safety stock is the extra inventory held as a buffer or protection against the possibility of stock out. In other words, it is the minimum level of inventory which an organisation would like to keep to avoid any exigency relating to stoppage of work. The reorder point is defined as a point in time at which a purchase order should be placed to replenish the inventory stock. Thus, three variables, usage, lead time and buffer stock are an integral part of the reorder point. The reorder point may be calculated as under:

$$R.O.P. = U \times t + SS$$

U = Average monthly or daily usage

t = Lead time in months or days

SS = Safety or buffer stock

or

Reporder point = Buffer + Safety + Reserve

or

Reorder point = Demand during lead time + Reserve Stock

As stated above the reorder point comprises of three components: *(i)* buffer stock-average demand during average lead time, *(ii)* safety stock-average demand during delivery delay, and *(iii)* reserve stock-variation in demand during average lead time. The maximum limit of order is equal to the safety margin plus standard order quantity. The standard order quantity may be the EOQ or modification of it to suit the need.

Under the perpetual inventory system, the reorder quantity is fixed but the frequency of ordering varies depending uypon the fluctuations in usage. Whenever the inventory reaches a minimum level, known as the reorder point, an Grder for a fixed quantity (EOQ) is placed.

The perpetual inventory system is also known by other names such as fixed order quantity system or Q-system. Figure 3 illustrates the way in which the perpetual inventory system operates. Small circles in the said Figure are the reorder point *i.e.*, whenever the inventory is depleted to such point, an order for fixed quantity is triggered off. This control system is suitable for A category, V category, S category, H category and F category of items barring few exceptions.

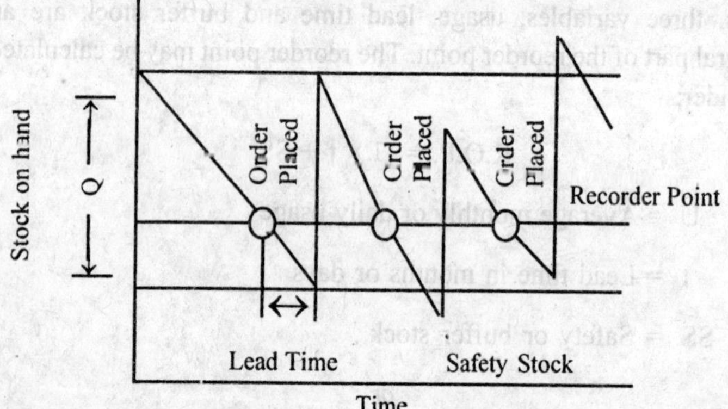

Fig. 3. Perpectual Inventory System

Periodic Review of P System

Another major inventory control tool is the periodic review technique, frequently called the fixed-cycle technique. In this, inventory records are reviewed periodically and replenishment orders are placed for each itern at each review. The review period may be a week, month, quarter, etc., whichever is best for the situation. At each review period, an order is placed for an amount equal to the difference between a fixed replenishment level and the actual inventory level. Thus, the order quantity is variable in size, whereas period between placement of orders is fixed. For example, the order quantity would be larger than usual when the demand has been greater than the expectation, and it is smaller than usual when the demand has been less than the expectation. However, the review period is fixed in this inventory system.

The review period can be fixed by dividing EOQ by the annual consumption. The replenishment level (S) may be calculated as under:

S = u (t + ro) + SS

u = Average monthly or daily usage

t = Lead time in days or months

to = Review period

SS = Safety stock

Maximum stock level (M) is defined as :

$$M = B + D (t + to)$$

or

$$M = B + Dt\ to$$

With the uniform depletion of inventory during the review period, the average level (S) of inventory in this model is:

S = B + ½Dt to

B = Maximum desired stock

D = Average demand

This technique may be contrasted with the conventional order point where the inventory records are reviewed each time an entry is made and a replenishment order is placed when the balance on hand reaches a predetermined order point. In the order point technique, the order quantity is fixed and is usually the EOQ.

Under this system, enough stock is ordered to bring the total on hand or on order up to a predetermined target level. This system is some sort of a replica of what is known as 'imprest system of cash control' is financial accounting. The periodic review technique is useful under the following conditions:

(i) When there are many small issues of items from inventory, so that posting records for each issue is impracticable.

(ii) Ordering costs are relatively small.

(iii) It is desirable to order many items at one time to make up a production schedule.

(iv) Determining levels for fast moving spare parts.

The above points have also been supported by George W. Ploss1. In general this system is considered suitable for high value and fast depreciable items, because it allows for a close control. Figure 5 illustrates the operation of periodic inventory system.

The periodic review system requires more inventory on hand, for a given frequency of shortages, as compared to the perpetual inventory system. On the other hand, since the perpetual inventory system requires perpetual auditing of the system, the cost of operating the system is normally higher. However, because of the computer facilities, cost advantage of periodic review system is withering away and many companies are resorting to perpetual inventory system.

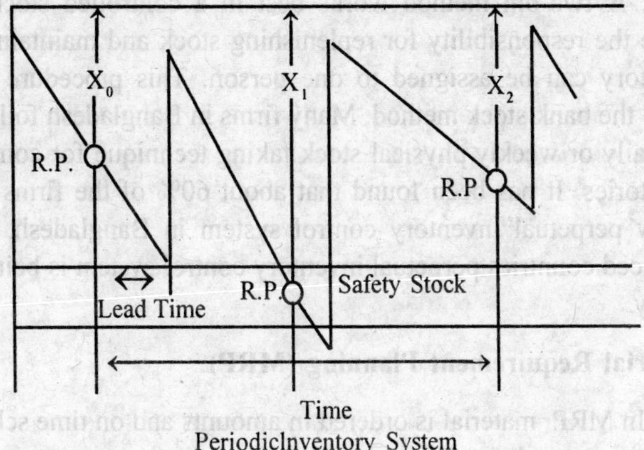

PeriodicInventory System

Fig. 4. Order quantity X_1 = S - inventory level of review period

This system is combination of periodic and perpetual inventory systems. Optional replenishment system is useful in situations where the cost of reviewing the inventory is high or the cost of ordering is very significant. Under this system if perpetual records cannot be maintained; due to high costs, then use of periodic review can be made. This system is more advantageous in case of bulk items, where physical assessment of stock is costly and could be inaccurate. Under this system an order should be placed for Q (quantity).

Where $So + qo < s$ $\qquad Q = S - So - Qo$

So = Stock on hand

Qo = Outstanding quantity against previous orders

s = Reorder point

S = Replenishment level

Two Bin Method

In this system an amount of stock equivalent to the order point is physically segregated either into a second bin or container. When all the open stock has been used up, the second bin or reserve container is opened and material control is notified to order more stock. This is a practical method for keeping control of low value items. A two-bin method works best in a controlled stock room where the responsibility for replenishing stock and maintaining the inventory can be assigned to one person. This procedure is also called the bank stock method. Many firms in Bangladesh follow this and daily or weekly physical stock taking technique for controlling inventories. It has been found that about 60% of the firms do not follow perpetual inventory control system in Bangladesh. But in advanced countries perpetual inventory control system is being used widely.

Material Requirement Planning (MRP)

In MRP, material is ordered in amounts and on time schedules to meet a preplanned programme of production or construction. Under this technique detailed requirement schedules are prepared in respect of the project or annual normal consumption to maintain the system in case of electricity organisations. MRP schedules contain the following elements:

(i) Projected annual demand/usage.

(ii) Month-wise usage.

(iii) How much of each of these items are already in hand?

(iv) How much are already ordered in addition and when will they arrive?

(v) Maximum level of each item.

(vi) Reorder point of each item.

(vii) Order placement at the appropriate time.

(viii) Ensure minimum carrying and ordering costs and also the minimum investment in inventories without risking stock outs.

It is worthnoting here that stock levels and reorder points under this system are determined on the basis of inspection and estimate of experienced executives.

❐

17

Material Distribution Control

A very important part of any manufacturing system is the need to plan and control the movement and storage of all materials and processed goods. This is relevant not just for the in-plant activities of a company but also for the associated tasks of delivery and distribution of its goods to its customers, whether they are local or based overseas. As far as internal movement and storage are concerned, recent research studies have shown that, typically, materials in a factory are being worked upon for only 30 per cent of the manufacturing cycle time; for the bulk of the time-*i.e.*, 70 per cent they are waiting in a queue for a machine or a process to become available, or they are being temporarily stored before the start of the next stage of manufacture. In this context, the need for designing the appropriate systems for handling and moving these materials, as well as storing them as and when required, is clear.

This first section in the chapter puts forward the concept of an 'integrated' physical distribution management system and recommends a particular form of it. The important role of the 'Freight Forwarder' in moving goods internationally is discussed in Volume 8, Marketing Management. The issucs involved in organizing thc routine and scheduling of vehicles for the distribution of finished goods, the role of computers, and several measures of performance for physical distribution management, including financial, operational, and customer service levels, are described in this chapter and recommended.

Physical distribution management is that part of management concerned with the design, administration, and operation of systems to control the movement and storage of raw materials and processed goods.

It should therefore be concerned with:

* Warehouse systems.
* Freight transportation.
* Materials handling.
* Inventory control.
* Depot site location.
* Protective packaging.
* Information and data processing systems.
* Order processing.

Or concerned at least as far as these factors have a bearing upon the physical distribution operation.

Some companies have incorporated the production control function within the scope of distribution. There is a distinct inter-face between production flow and distribution, and at some time the costs associated with set-up time, processing, and delivery have to be assessed together and controlled. Whether this should be the responsibility of distribution depends upon the extent to which the production schedule can be distribution orientated. In some companies this can be achieved completely, with salutary effect on distribution costs.

Advantages of Establishing Materials Distribution As a Separate Function

In some companies, the responsibilities falling within the full concept of physical distribution management are split between different management function. This makes it difficult to make an overall assessment of the distribution operation, to measure its true performance and to ensure that the separate parts fit neatly into an efficient whole. There is a real danger that parts of the distribution operation will become the poor relation of some other function and lose the sharpness of their edge. Split responsibility, like a canker, may eat out the heart of an efficient operation.

In other companies, physical distribution is solely the responsibility of one other function. True, this allows for unified control and the development of a coordinated system and as such it passes muster. The danger lies in distribution drifting into a role subservient to more powerful interests and in its being starved of the resources and development which it needs.

There is no generally acceptable solution suitable for adoption by all companies large and small. In the smaller company, the scope of physical distribution may not be sufficient to merit the establishment of a separate distribution function. In the larger company, special factors may demand the curtailment of the responsibilities of PDM.

Nevertheless, the case for an integrated physical distribution system is a strong one; it leads to a balanced distribution system in which all activities are soundly interlocked. It encourages the development of a coordinated system in which each constituent part is built for the benefit of the total system and is not the result of piecemeal action taken by one department or another.

The advantages of setting up a separate distribution function are:

1. Single responsibility for all distribution activities leads to better coordination and use of resources.
2. Distribution is rapidly becoming more complex and professional; it can no longer be treated as a secondary interest of a busy manager. A well balanced, efficient operation calls for the application of a wide range of distribution skills which can normally only be found in an individual dedicated to the distribution task.
3. A true measure of operational performance embracing the use of all distribution resources can only be attained when all distribution activities fall under the control of a single individual.

4. The need for a strict control of distribution costs and capital expenditure; the goal is to minimize total company distribution costs within the defined level of service and to make the right capital investments. This goal is difficult to attain where responsibilities are split and each manager is striving to reduce his own individual costs, or where distribution is subservient to some other activity.

5. It facilitates the formulation of an overall company distribution policy and long-term distribution plan.

This is not to say that there is a blueprint which can be applied to every company. Each situation has to be assessed to see how far the PDM concept is applicable, what advantages its adoption will bring, and where the boundaries around the different activities should be drawn.

Potential Benefits of Coordination of Group Distribution Operations

Where a group of companies operates a series of distribution operations, consideration should always be given to the coordination of these operations. Among the potential benefits may be numbered:

1. Shared resources.
2. Purchasing power.
3. Standardization.
4. Design of unified systems.
5. Technical advice.
6. Development of company-wide distribution concepts.

To take an example in the field of transport scheduling, the combination of deliveries of different classes of goods leads to:

1. Increased flexibility.
2. Composite loads-fewer, larger drops per load.

3. Coincidence of calls-fewer calls.

4. Mixed loads-fewer refusals.

Company Attitudes to Distribution

A survey gave an interesting insight into company attitudes to the allocation of responsibility for the different activities.

In terms of percentage of companies participating, distribution held the responsibility as follows:

Transportation	100%
Warehousing	88%
Stock control	54%
Materials handling	54%
Data processing	54%
Depot site selection	46%
Protective packaging	42%
Production control	6%

Sources of Conflict

The conflict which so often exists between the different functions of a company is highlighted in the field of level of service. It is for this reason that decisions affecting level of service have to be taken at the highest level. The interests and reactions of the different functions can often be at odds, as each endeavours to be as efficient as it can.

A sense of conflict is to be found at the interfaces between the responsibilities of the different functions, and where a decision taken by one will influence the performance of another.

The interfaces of PDM with the finance, production and marketing functions of a company are numerous; some of those met most frequently are given below:

Finance and Administration

* Capital tied up in stocks.
* Capital investment.
* Costs of operation.
* Control systems.

Production

* Production control.
* Siting of stocks.
* Materials handling methods.
* Delivery of raw materials.
* Warehouse design.
* Protective packaging.
* Unit pack size.
* Loading methods.
* Collection of empties.

Marketing

* Delivery frequencies.
* Lead times.
* Scheduling disciplines.
* Promotions.
* Minimum order size.
* Urgent deliveries.
* Stock levels.

COSTS RELATING TO THE CONFLICT AT THE INTERFACES

Transport

(a) Marketing: frequency of delivery, customer delays, drop size, promotional activity, changes in customer size, seasonality factors, expediting policy, fixed-day or fixed-interval delivery.

(b) Purchasing: backloads.

(c) Production: batches released in geographical groupings to follow orders.

(d) Administration: the release of orders.

Warehousing

(a) Marketing: number and size of orders, promotional activity, seasonality factors.

(b) Production/marketing/finance: stocks held.

Inventory

(a) Marketing: of service product range.

(b) Marketing/production: buffer stocks.

(c) Finance/marketing: policy stocks.

Situations which can Give Rise to Interdepartmental Conflicts

	Situations	*Advantages*	*Disadvantages*
1.	Bulk purchases of Material	(Purchasing): large discounts	(Finance): Working capital tied up (Disribution): Warehousing costs increased
2.	Long Production runs	(Production): low costs	(Finance): working capital tried up (Marketing): narrow

Situations	Advantages	Disadvantages
		product range (Distribution): warehousing costs increased
3. Broad product range	(Marketing): more sales through wider customer appeal	(Purchasing): discounts small on low-volume pruchases (Production): short high-cost runs (Finance): finished goods stocks high (Distribution): higher costs through more administration and warehousing space
4. Tighter credit control	(Finance): greater use of working capital	(Marketing): possible loss of sales
5. Shorter delivery lead times	(Marketing): increased sales as a result of better service	(Finance): higher operating costs (Distribution): systems costs increased in order to meet service requirements
6. Unit loads	(Production): lower operating costs (Distribution): systems costs can be lowered by eliminating uneconomic calls	(Finance): loss of sale to small customers

The Role of the Freight Forwarder

Forwarding can be defined as: 'Help forward: send on to further destinations.' We feel that forwarding needs to be defined more clearly in the context of the company's interest in the activity.

The movement of goods in international transit is a chain of various stages/movements by differing carriers/modes of transport.

We consider the role of a freight forwarder to be 'assisting the efficient flow of goods down the international transport chain.' The traditional position of a forwarder was to act as a buffer between the manufacturer/exporter and the sea carrier. The manufacturer's primary interest was in production and selling of goods, and the sea carrier's in transporting cargo by sea. The forwarder filled a gap between the manufacturer and the sea carrier by looking after the manufacturer's interests, in booking space with the carrier, calling forward goods down to the dock, ensuring safe loading, arranging Customs clearance and producing the documentation to and from the sea carrier. The sea operator usually paid the forwarder commission (mostly 5 per cent of sea-freight) for this service.

Depending on the terms of shipment, a forwarder could be responsible for import work. This consisted of notifying the receiver of the arrival of goods. arranging Customs clearance, presenting original bills of lading to certify ownership and obtaining a release/ out-of-charge note to enable the receiver to pick up his goods.

The forwarder was therefore the representative or agent of the exporter/shipper or importer/receiver,and thus was often referred to as a 'Forwarding Agent Income was mainly obtained for documentation and Customs work. He was referred to as 'Mr 5 per cent' in the international transport industry and his primary work was in handling documentation.

This type of activity still exists today with some companies specializing in this area. Shipments to the under-developed parts of the world, and the majority of airfreight, is handled by companies purely handling functions F to I for a percentage commission, or K to P for a scale of charges. Although this work is declining in the international market for movements by sea, it is widely used by Continental exporters/importers where the role of the forwarder is more clearly defined and accepted as a necessity to international transportation.

The introduction of containerization presented the forwarder with a dramatic change in his trading environment, to which he needed to respond to ensure continuation of his activity. Goods were being packed in a container at an exporter's own factory and transported all the way to an overseas receiver's depot. Although the modes of transport for carrying the container changed, the goods themselves were always in a common unit owned by the sea carrier.

The sea carriers had invested vast amounts of capital in building up a sophisticated through transport system between exporter and importer. To ensure traffic flows, many ship operators saw the role of forwarder as unnecessary.

The concept of an 'integrated carrier,' who provided the client with his equipment, haulage, vessel, and forwarding expertise as a package deal, has become an established sector of the international transport scene.

A large proportion the traffic carried by the deep-sea container consortia moves on a door-to-door integrated basis. Examples of deep-sea import traffics are:

1. S. Daniels traffic from Australia *via* OCL.
2. Green Giant on CP Ships.

Integrated services are primarily concerned with full container loads (FCL). The forwarders' response was to offer their clients similar door-to-door quotations and handle the less-than-container load (LCL) traffic. The forwarders bought shipping space with other (non-conference) carriers to the extent that the major consortia had to abandon the concept of having a totally integrated service carrying all traffic and had to accept the need for forwarders. Deep-sea forwarders, offering door-to-door rates, either subcontract the movement to the sea carrier, or operate a non-vessel operating common carrier (NVOCC) system to effect the overseas movement.

The NVOCC system is basically the bulk buying of slot space on a container vessel and filling it with traffic where he can recover more from the client (wholesale buying/retail selling). Several forwarders may co-operate to offer such a service to increase their bargaining position to obtain lower rates from the sea carrier.

Particular concentration has been made by forwarders on LCL traffic because the sea carrier is not geared up to cover this market, preferring to let forwarders consolidate LCL traffic into line-owned equipment to present the sea carrier with an FCL load for shipment. A comparison would be the company's consolidated retail distribution service as opposed to the manufacturer attempting to deliver small lots with his own transport. The forwarders' consolidation service is referred to as 'groupage'.

The short-sea services developed at the same time as containerization, but the 12-metre tilt trailer was used as the base unit of the service, rather than the container. The concept of roll-on, roll-off (RO-RO) is that the sea route is a link between two road systems. Since Britain is an island, this has had particular importance; 75 per cent of unitized cargo between the United Kingdom and Europe is carried by RO RO, mainly using 12-metre trailers.

The forwarders who specialized in trailer movements become known as 'trailer operators' offering door-to-door services on either a regular or spot basis. The majority of trailer movements are 'unaccompanied', ih that the traction unit is not carried on the sea leg, as opposed to 'self-drives,' where the driver and his unit cover the total door-to-door transit.

There are trailer operators who are totally integrated; as well as owning the trailers and vehicles, they own the ships providing the connection between the two road systems. This is a specialized type of freight forwarding, operated by such companies as Ferrymasters and Norfolk Line.

The more numerous type of trailer operator is the freight for warder who, in addition to any other forwarding activity, has a fleet of trailers and/or traction units operating services to and from Europe using the various ferry companies for the sea leg of the transit.

The European scene contains group age operators using containers, or more often trailers, running a liner-type operation, point-to-point transit on a reguiar basis.

Small loads are consolidated at strategically located depots and carried to a similar depot overseas for deconsolidation. Transport to and from the depots is often undertaken by, the exporter/importer.

The container plays a minor role in inter-European movements, in comparison to the carriage of heavy goods or valuables subject to theft.

Most short-sea container movements are carried on an integrated basis, where the carrier acts as forwarder, such as Bell Line and Geest. It can be seen that an exporter has a wide choice of options open to him to convey his goods to an overseas importer. (see below), which may or may not involve the use of a forwarder. There are a few companies that are sufficiently large, or have large export volumes, to enable them to operate their own forwarding departments or companies. This possibility is only available to a select few of Britain's largest industrial groups.

Table 1

Exporter Option on Export System

Service	*Type of movement*	*System*
Deep sea	Conventional	Use traditional forwarder who obtains 5 per cent commission from shipowner.
	FCL	Use shipping line door-to-door service-no forwarder. Use forwarder who subcontracts to shipping line for movement. Use forwarder operating NVOCC service.
	LCL	Use shipping line LCL service Use forwarder with groupage service.

Service	*Type of movement*	*System*
Short sea	FCL	Use shipping line door-to-door servic no forwarder
		Use forwarder operating NVOCC service
	F trailer L	Use integrated trailer operator
		Use forwarder trailer service
	LCL	
	L trailer L	Use forwarder with groupage service.

In order to obtain traffic, a forwarder needs to provide a service-orientated package which meets the client's requirements on cost, service and reliability. Competition from shipping lines and integrated carriers demands that a forwarder must offer a competitive package to retain his position as the exporters'/importers/agent.

Terms of Shipment Routeing Control

Manufacturers sell their export products with a clear indication of the terms of shipment. Most sales are made on the basis of the four most common terms:

1. **Ex -works.** The importer is responsible for all costs beyond the exporter's works/warehouse.

2. **FOB (Free on Board).** The exporter is responsible for all charges up to loading on the ship/aircraft. The importer covers all costs beyond this point to final delivery.

3. **CIF (Carriage Insurance Freight).** The exporter is responsible for all charges up to end of point of discharge in overseas port/airport. The importer covers all costs beyond this point to final delivery.

4. **Free Delivered.** The exporter is responsible for all costs up to final point of delivery at the importer's warehouse (except overseas Customs clearance, which is usually paid by the importer).

The traditional terms of shipment used were FOB and CIF. British exporters have always tended to sell on a FOB UK port basis, leaving the importer to pay the sea freight and delivery charges. Overseas exporters sending goods to the United Kingdom usually specified CIF terms so that the UK importer only paid for the delivery costs in the United Kingdom.

The introduction of container and RO-RO operations have had a significant effect in variations in use of terms of shipment. The introduction of a simple door-to-door cost, in place of the complex rates levied for each link of the transport chain, enables both importers and exporters to cost the movement of their goods more easily. Exporting could now be costed as easily as a domestic sale involving a single cost for a haulage movement.

Greater use is made of Ex-works and Free Delivered terms, especially in the trade between the United Kingdom and Europe. UK exporters started to realize the benefits of control up to the point of sale in making them more competitive, and importers are willing to consider taking delivery of goods at source.

The terms of shipment are important to the forwarder because they signify who has overall routeing control and where his role begins and ends. A rough guide is that whoever (exporter/importer) is responsible for the payment of sea freight effectively routes the traffic: Ex-works—importer controls whole movement; FOB—exporter pays charges to port but importer dictates route; CIF—exporter dictated route, importer pays charges ex-port; Free Delivered—exporter controls whole movement.

There is a negligible income opportunity for a forwarder from an exporter who sells Ex-works, or an importer who buys Free Delivered (except to advise his overseas agent to obtain the routeing of the traffic on a joint service).

Significantly reduced potential is available to a forwarder from an exporter selling FOB or an importer buying CIF. The prime target for forwarders and integrated carriers is the exporter selling Free

Delivered and the importer buying Ex-works, because the total door-to-door price is higher and therefore profit potential is greatest.

The predominance of UK exporters still using FOB UK port and importers buying CIF UK port effectively means that much of Britain's overseas trade is controlled by principals overseas. This tends to reduce the market for the UK forwarder, and increases the importance of having a good overseas agent obtaining routeing orders to feed traffic into a joint operating system.

As a service industry, the forwarder has to respond, rather than dictate, in satisfying his clients' needs. He is therefore unlikely to be able to alter the types of terms used by his clients.

The potential of changes in the use of terms of shipment is greater on export traffic than imports. The gradual moves by exporters towards control up to the point of overseas sales opens up new markets for the forwarder as routeing control is exercised by the exporter.

The predominance of CIF and Free Delivered terms on imports is unlikely to change in the short term, which will clearly restrict their value to a forwarder.

Vehicle Routing and Scheduling

There are three fundamental types of vehicle task:

1. Trunking.

2. Short distance shuttle.

3. Multi-drop radial delivery.

Each exhibits its own characteristics and requires its own system.

Trunking

This normally involves long journey distances and often comprises a unit load, used for delivery direct to customer, or to carry stock to an intermecliate depot for onward distribution to the customer. In this latter role, it is complementary to the radial delivery operation. Journeys can include staging posts where drivers exchange vehicles or loads, enabling the drivers to return to base each night. The economics of trunking can be considerably improved by the carrying of a back load. This may be obtainable through a clearing house, or be achieved by collecting a load of raw materials from a supplier. The ideal back load is a full load which can be collected when an empty vehicle is in the area. Care should be taken that the costs associated with the collection of a back load do not outweigh the cost advantages of running home loaded.

Short Distance Shuttle

Vehicles based upon a central depot make a number of relatively short trips a day with a unit load. Examples of this type of task are:

(a) Inter-factory delivery.

(b) Collection from the docks.

(c) Supply of distribution depots close to base.

This task may provide a considerable scheduling problem. Individual journeys have to be allocated to a driver so that, in total, his trips comprise a full day's work. Pitfalls to be avoided include time wasted waiting for the next load, and queuing and delays at the delivery depot. A fast delivery service can be achieved where an articulated vehicle is able to drop its loaded trailer and pick up an empty one in exchange.

Radial Delivery

Usually, this is the final stage in the distribution chain—the delivery from distribution depot to final customer. The task is characterized by multi-drops and a high driver involvement in unloading. It presents a routeing rather than a scheduling problem. Methods of approach to the problem depend upon whether routes are variable or fixed. In the former case, a system has to be designed which will produce fresh routes for each day of operation.

In all three types of task, vehicle routes and loads should be selected to utilize transport resources most efficiently. In building up the transport plan, the driver should be regarded as the prime resource and his utilization should be maximized as far as possible. His time in a sense, is unique, whereas the capacity of a vehicle can be used more than once during a working shift. This is not to say that one neglects vehicle capacity utilization-to no so may lead to an excessive fleet but that this should be used as a secondary control.

The maxim of good transport planning is: First fill the driver's day, then ensure that vehicle capacity is sufficiently well utilized to carry the load.

Operating Standards

In order to put transpart planning an a sound objective footing, it is necessary to develop a framewark of operating standards for all tasks undertaken by the driver. These tasks are likely to include:

1. Depot work at the start .of the day.
2. Driving through different environments.
3. Calling at the customer.
4. Unloading at the customer.
5. Depot work at the end of the day.

During a recent survey of 118 companies, in connection with driver payment and productivity schemes, we found that the tasks of drivers, in terms of number of companies participating, included:

Checking vehicle	115
Unloading, or assisting to unload	115
Collecting documentation	110
Refuelling	106
Washing vehicle	94

Collecting empties or returns	87
Assisting in vehicle unloading	77
Shunting in yard	77
Checking contents of load	75
Roping and sheeting load	54
Wheel changing on road	42

This list indicates the variety of tasks which may make up his daily work load. Whether a skilled driver should undertake some of these tasks is open to question. There is no simple answer; in practice it will depend upon whether other employees are available to undertake the task, and how well specific tasks fit into the pattern of the driver's work-load. An allowance has to be made in the transport plan for all activities undertaken by the driver.

Operating standards should be derived for all driver tasks and these should be expressed in the form of standard times based upon 100 performances on the British Standard Scale. Contingency allowances should be built into the standard values wherever possible. Contingencies, from the point of view of standard deviation, can be broken into two types:

1. Those which are anticipated and should therefore be built into standards; these are generally of frequent occurrence and relatively short duration.
2. Those which are unexpected, occur infrequently, and are usually of fairly lengthy duration (*e.g.*, a blocked motorway, a major mechanical failure of the vehicle); allowantes cannot be sensibly built into the standards, and some other form of compensating mechanism has to be devised.

Delivery Systems

There are two fundamental delivery systems: nominated day delivery (NOD); and fixed interval.

An NDD system gives:

1. Regular, reliable service.

2. Reduced distribution costs.

3. Greater degree of control.

4. Fewer delays or refusals.

It is the more disciplined of the two systems, and implies a deadline for the customer to place his order, and for the sales representative to call. It enables the transport planner to draw up a semi-permanent schedule, and allows him to optimize the use of his resources more easily. It is, however, more difficult to operate for the smaller operator, who lacks the flexibility to meet the constraints placed upon him by customers.

A fixed interval system is appropriate when:

1. Quick service is essential.

2. Demand is random.

If the interval is realistic, fixed interval systems give some flexibility of routes and allow good utilization of resources. They call for dexterity on the part of the scheduler.

Vehicle Routeing

The first step in all vehicle routeing methods is to separate the fixed work-load (depot work, calling at customer, and unloading times), from the variable work-load (driving time), 'Variable' and 'fixed' are defined in the sense that they change/do not change with the route that is taken.

There are three basic methods:

1. **Pin and String Method.** This is used for fixed routes. The name illustrates well the approach to solving the problem, but in practice the need for a series of speed standards makes its physical application difficult.

2. **Gated Grid Method.** This involves the design of a route-planning network and is well suited for use with the random daily load where vehicles are required to make a number of drops. By clustering demand points together, a standard allowance can be made for driving work within a cluster. The variable element of the driver's task is thus 'reduced' and the route planner can concentrate on controlling the arterial mileage travelled when building up the route.
3. **Computer Methods.** These can be used for both types of routeing problem, or to check out vehicle schedules.

Pin and String Method

This method is applicable for the permanent or semi-permanent route. Each customer is represented on the map by a pin. The driving element of the task, *i.e.*, the variable cost, is separated from all other elements and its value is represented by the length of a piece of string. Work associated with each call is marked on the appropriate pin head, and the pattern of drops on each journey determines the driving time that is available, and hence the length of the string. Routes are traced out on the map until the length of string is completely taken up. Repeated simulations will indicate the best pattern of routes and the number of vehicles required.

Gated Grid Method

This route planning system is designed to deal with the random daily load, where vehicles are required to make a number of drops en route. Its objective is to optimize the utilization of driver and vehicle resources. The system revolves around the route planning network which has first to be drawn up.

There are three fundamental steps in the building of the network:

1. Selection of Clusters. The demand points are marshalled into clusters, and the number of clusters controlled, to keep the network to a manageable size. (Our experience indicates that a total of about one hundred clusters is ideal.) The size and configuration of the clusters is determined by geographic constraints, *e.g.*, rivers and road patterns, and the need to apply a common inter-drop driving standard within a cluster.

2. Determination of Connecting Links. Each cluster is examined, and all direct connecting links with other clusters are identified. These direct links represent all routes that may be used operationally, and form the basic logic of the network.

3. Building the Network. Each cluster is represented by a cell in the network and the cells are so assembled that the connecting links can be described simply and logically. This calls for a certain dexterity, similar to that required in drawing up a critical path network when all the events and activities have been determined.

Each cell is given a title, for means of ready identification and this conveniently can be the name of the chief town within the cluster demands.

Use of Computers

Computer programmes commonly work on a basis of minimizing mileage. A number of different forms of input are used:

1. Coordinates of each customer as given, for example, by the Ordnance Survey grid, are fed mto the computer, which then calculates the distance of every possible connecting link. Physical barriers can give a very false picture of actual route distances and provision has to he made in the programme for this type of constraint.

2. Actual distances between pairs of points are fed into the computer. This method, though more accurate, is extremely laborious as all possible routes have to be measured.

3. A series of nodal points are defined and distances measured between all points in the series. Coordinates of each customer are fed in. This method, which is a compromise between the first two, overcomes the physical barrier problem of

the first method, and reduces the manual task of the second.

Computer routeing programmes have progressed a long way since the first commercial programmes were released in 1963 and the following list, which is not exhaustive, indicates some of the facilities which are commonly available:

1. Variable vehicle speeds.
2. Routeing limitations-time, mileage, number of calls.
3. Vehicle capacity, ability to handle a mixed fleet.
4. Time restrictions on delivery.
5. Geographical factors.

The advantages and disadvantages of computer routeing are shown in Table 2.

The success of a computer routeing system will depend to a large extent upon the environment in which it is to work. To impose it upon an essentially manual system may well invite disaster, but, as part of an integrated computerized system, considerable benefits may be obtained.

Computer routeing programmes have been used quite successfully to check out schedules at six-monthly or yearly intervals.. The route pattern of the first run can be of considerable value to the scheduler, and subsequent runs serve to monitor the 'state of health' of the schedule.

Table 2

Computer Routeing

Advantages	*Disadvantages*
Computer plans entirely logically	Routes often bear little relationships to the manual or visual solution

Advantages	*Disadvantages*
Speed of operation, allowing a greater number of factors to be considered	Minimizes mileage, which may not be the prime criterion
Freedom from calculation errors	Produces unacceptable routes which may be hard to justify with the driver
Extensive search leads to a superior route plan	

Vehicle Scheduling

Scheduling is the allocation of journeys to drivers. In practice, it is often difficult to find a 'good fit' of journeys which gives each driver a full day's work. Other constraints that may have to be reckoned with are:

1. Availability of loads when required.
2. Return of empties, *e.g.*, at milk processing plants.
3. Inability of a customer to unload more than one vehicle at a time.
4. Queuing.
5. Back loads.

The scheduler not only has to send out the vehicle at the correct time but also schedule it back into the depot when it is needed. The vehicle fleet can often be regarded as an extension of the production line and must work in phase with it.

In drawing up the schedule, the sequence of steps is as follows:

1. Determine total work load and number of drivers required.
2. Allocate loads to each driver.
3. Draw up schedule, observing all production and delivery constraints.

Role of Computers

With the development of the minicomputer and microcomputer, computer facilities have become very much more accessible to distribution management. Software programmes have now been developed specifically for use in the distribution field, and a number of software houses have developed modular systems which can be purchased singly and added to as and when the need arises. Typical modules are as follows:

1. Order processing.
2. Stock control.
3. Vehicle routeing and scheduling.
4. Vehicle maintenance.
5. Operational performance.
6. Sales ledger.
7. Purchase ledger.

Terminals can be located at distant sites, so that it is not necessary to provide a computer (however small) at each location. Computers can be split into three categories:

1. Mainframes. General-purpose machines used for high-speed batch processing and for multi-user interactive applications. Typically, they will be used for overnight batch processing of customer orders and the updating of stock files.

2. Minicomputers. High-speed interactive processing for multiple users. Essentially based upon 'on line' operating. Typically used for vehicle routeing and schedullig systems, and for warehouse stock location and rotation systems.

3. Microcomputers. Small machines, normally only supporting a single user and with limited storage capacity. Operationally they are slower than the larger machines and only one application can be run eft anyone time. Typically used for 'standalone' local applications in vehicle workshops, ware-houses or distribution administrative functions, *e.g.*, tachograph analysis.

Technical advances are blurring the demarcation lines between the three categories and, for example, it is now possible to have multi-user micro systems.

Computers are extremely good at searching, selecting, and listing and as such they can relieve management of a considerable clerical burden.

They can play a number of basic roles in support of physical distribution management:

1. **Information Processing.** The collection, storage, transfer and representation of data. Data can be collected at one source (*e.g.*, sales office), transformed (*e.g.*, the accumulation of orders) and transferred to another location (*e.g.*, a ware-house).

2. **Data Preparation.** Data is processed and produced in a different form. For example, sales orders may be processed to represent them in the form of metric tonnes or cubic metres, as these are more meaningful in distribution terms.

3. **Data Evaluation.** Data is evaluated against a series of decision rules and mathematical relationships which have been previously determined. Simulations may be run on these programmes to determine the best solutions under varying circumstances for example, where to site a distribution depot given various production locations and sales fore casts;

4. **Assistance in Direct Decision-making.** The programme can recommend decisions based on the evaluation of data against specific rules. For example, in a stock location and rotation programme, the computer will allocate a particular pallet to a specific station, *i.e.*, it will have optimized the solution of a pallet position from all those that are available.

Computers also play a central role in automated warehouse systems. Signals generated by computer programmes control the movement of equipment and the placing and selection of ware-house goods. In many cases there is no manual intervention at all.

Typical control applications are:

1. Acceptance or rejection of incoming goods.
2. Driving of automated carrier systems.
3. Pallet storage and retrieval systems.
4. Automated picking systems.
5. Diversion of orders to packing stations.
6. High-speed parcel sorting systems.
7. Issue of orders to fork-lift drivers and other operatives.
8. Automatic transfer of stock to picking stations.
9. Container park control.
10. Direction of incoming vehicles to unloading/loading docks.

A recent study has identified 20 different potential computer applications in the distribution field:

Strategic Decisions	*Operating Decisions*
Depot size and location	Stock location and rotation systems
	Customs administration
Tactical decisions	Retail replenishment
Transport planning	Vehicle workshop activities
Ware-house planning	Training
Logistics planning	Transport mode selection
Distribution costing	Vehicle maintenance and management

Strategic Decisions	*Operating Decisions*
Performance monitoring	Tachograph analysis, ware-house maintenance and management
Operating decisions	
Vehicle routeing and scheduling	Pallet control Shipping control Sales opportunities Security system

Measuring Distribution Performance at All Levels

At departmental level there are basically three different methods of measuring performance:

1. In financial terms.
2. In operational terms.
3. How well we are meeting the levels of service laid down.

At company level the chief parameters are:

1. Cost.
2. Level of service.

Taking the distribution chain as a whole, these parameters change slightly and might best be combined and defined as the value added for the required level of service. Distribution is a service industry and adds no intrinsic value to the goods it handles, except in the abstract sense of delivering these goods undamaged to the right place at the right time. For a given level of service, therefore, a high performance along the distribution chain is one that succeeds in minimizing the value added as a result of distribution activities.

❑

18

Storage of Materials

Proper storage facilities and systematic arrangement of stores precede proper functioning of any well organised store. In a systematic arrangement, coding the materials for easy identification and giving it a location address containing rack or bin number for quick location assumes importance. A well organised arrangement not only facilitates its issue for use but also facilitates speedy varification which is very essential for its periodic assessment. It also is the surest means of finding the condition of stores, the difference, if any, between the actual stock and the book balance, overstocking and understocking of materials and the quantity of scrap and unserviceable items which can be done away with to make room for useful items.

With the help of three main factors storage efficiency of the Central Stores Division may be evaluated:

(i) Storage facilities.

(ii) Safety and security.

(iii) The losses suffered on account of wastage/obsolescence or economies realised through proper stores planning and control.

Storage Facilities

Efficiency of storage system depends on the storage facilities and trained and committed personnels. Recently some sheds have been constructed by the Department to facilitate storage of inventories but they do not cater to the needs.

It has been observed by the researcher that storage facilities in the Central Stores Division are improper, inadequate and quite primitive,

Many items which should be stored in sheds remain in the open yards and keep on gathering rust. Some of the items even in the sheds are stored at improper places, which has increased number of inserviceable items and also the loss of the organisation. In one of the cases due to improper storing of cement which got set, the Government had to suffer a loss of Rs. 30 lakhs. This has been corroborated by the Audit Inspection Report of 1991-92. There are many such instances, where due to wrong storage or inadequate storage facilities the Government had to suffer huge losses.

General aspects of storage cover a wide range of activities. However, some of the specific aspects of storage may be as under:

(i) Storage should facilitate easy handling, *i.e.*, counting, checking and issue apart from security and safety of materials as well as men.

(ii) The controller of stores should continuously monitor/ review storage capacity needed and this depend on the forecasted levels of materials to be purchased and held. There should be maximum economy exercised in relation to the volume of space.

(iii) Every material requires a specific method of storing to obtain the maximum efficiency with respect to ease of handling and prevention of deterioration. Suitability of storage equipment is, therefore, a major factor to be decided.

(iv) Bins must be of right size. Otherwise, untidy stacking will result.

(v) Apart from wastage, spoilage of materials may also occur due to improper storage. Dampness is another major problem in stores because it leads to corrosion of metals, solidifices powder, fades colour, etc., prevention of dampness is a vital factor especially in the storage of sensitive materials like electrical or electronic equipment.

(vi) Another aspect of storage is prevention of losses due to evaporation, pilferage, theft, etc. It should be out-of-bound for outsiders and unauthorised officials also, unless special permission has been sought.

Safety and Security

The term safety envisages the safety of materials in stores, including materials handling equipment, and the safety of the personnel working in stores. One of the important responsibilities of the stores officer is to prevent accident from taking place in stores. These days science of ergonomics is gaining importance as the complexities of store-keeping have increased.

Freedom of access by outsiders into the stores involves security risks. Sometimes transport drivers or workers may come to deliver goods or take goods. It has been seen that in the ECSD they invariably come under the supervision of a member of the staff. Even loaded materials is checked against challan at the exit gate. During closed hours a watchman remains inside the stores premises. It has been noted by the researcher that stores premises remain unclean and untidy. Neat and orderly premises are not only a morale booster but are an important element in accident prevention.

It is usually said that theft is a latent instinct, activated when the environment is congenial to its manifestation. Precaution against theft involves the creation of an environment which is not congenial for these instincts to be manifested. Despite all the precautions of security arrangement a theft of steel worth Rs. 1.59 lakhs took place in the stores premises sometime back. Keeping in view the nature of the item and security arrangement connivance of staff members can not be ruled out in this theft case. Such events may again happen if erring officials are not punished for lapses and, moreover, adequate publicity should be given to any punishment awarded to employees for pilferages.

One of the major hazards in stores relates to fire. It is necessary to take every possible precaution against fire and ensure that all fire regulations are strictly observed by all the staff. The Factories Act,

1948 makes various provision for fire precautions. Number of measures have been suggested by the experts to prevent theft or fraud.

The following specific measures may be taken against malpractices by stores staff :

(i) All incoming materials must be first received in the receiving section. These should not directly go to the stores. The receiving section and the stores, therefore, act as a double check on each other. If necessary, an independent inspector may be attached to the receiving section to certify the quantity received.

(ii) Materials coming in by trucks, particularly expensive raw materials, should be weighed for both gross and tare weight, preferably on weighing scales within the stores premises.

(iii) The registration numbers of the incoming and outgoing vehicles must be recorded at the gate. A copy of the record should go to accounts section so as to tally with the vehicle numbers mentioned on Goods Inward Notes and thus ensure that delivery purported to have been effected by lorries have been really received:

(iv) A separate set of records should be maintained by accounts section. Records of accounts section and stores should tally periodically.

(v) The audit party from the Accountant General's office should also carry out independent physical verification. In routine the 'Inventory Control Section' is supposed to carry out physical verification. These reports should be compared at the end. This may reduce chances of bias and negligence on the part of any inspection team. Moreover, surprise-random checks should be done by the Chief Engineer and Superintending Engineer, Procurement and Materials Management Organisation. If discrepancies are found explanations should be sought of erring officials and exemplary punishment should be awarded to them. This will be threat to many.

Losses on Account of Wastage/Obsolescence

At the end of 1993-94 value of dead and slow-moving items in the ESCD (Jammu) was Rs. 335.67 lakhs. This was around 28.42% of the total purchases made in 1993-94. In addition to this blockade of capital/loss, thefts, shortages in stores and setting of cement call for urgent attention of the Department.

All this may be attributed to the following factors:

(i) Inadequate storage facilities.

(ii) Unscientific materials purchase planning and control.

(iii) Improper materials layout and handling.

PHYSICAL VERIFICATION OF MATERIALS

Presently stock verification or stock-taking is done once a year by a team of engineers constituted by the Chief Engineer, P&MM. This team is headed by an XEN or AEE. Under the present system of verification book balances are compared with ground balances and shortages, if any, are reported and recovered from the concerned stores officer. Physical verification once a year for such a huge store does not serve its purpose. It has been learnt that sometimes verification is not carried out at all, and whenever done, it is carried out to adjust book balances to physical balances. This is not a well defined and carefully planned programme of physical verification. Whenever verification is carried out, the disorganised arrangement of stores makes it difficult and reduces the speed of operation.

For a huge store like that of the size of the POD, it is essential to take stock on perpetual basis without creating peaks in work load. A monthly stock taking schedule fixing the length of the cycle according to the importance of items could be introduced. 'A&F' items could be covered once every quarter; 'B&N' items every half year; and 'C&S' items once a year. As already stated Inventory Control Section should work round the year to carry out physical verifications, etc. It is also important that in addition to checking the quantities, the stock-takers verify the apparent quality of the stores to ensure that scrap, damaged or otherwise sub-standard material is quickly identified. It is equally important that all shortages and excesses are listed and all material differences are investigated. Differences, if any, may be reported to the concerned officer so that accountability for the lapses could be established. The scope of physical verification activity should also include identification of unserviceable/non-moving items, so that their quick disposal could be arranged.

An effective stock verification system is necessary to ensure that stocks shown in the books are accurate and reflect the actual physical position. The reconciliation of stock quantities should be carried out to match:

(i) the physical quantities with those in the bin cards; and

(ii) the bin card quantities with the stock ledger.

Three separate levels for this verification activity may be proposed:

(i) Verification by Inventory Control Division.

(ii) Random Verification by Auditors.

(iii) Random Check by the CE or SE.

Verification by Inventory Control Division

A schedule of verification should be drawn to provide coverage for all the items during a financial year. This activity should be quite independent of the verification conducted by the independent bodylike auditors etc. Any discrepancy observed should be investigated and adjustments for any wrong/non-posting of receipts/issues or arithmatical errors should be brought to the notice of the concerned official for correction on the bin cards and stock ledger. Discrepancies due to other reasons should be reported to the concerned top executive(s). However, discrepancies within the tolerable limit can be written-off with the consent of the CE or SE concerned. Apart from this all items should be physif:ally as well as value-wise verified. An exercise should also be carried out to identify unserviceable and non-moving items.

Random Verification by Auditors

Stock verifiers should be personnels of an independent external office, such as Regional A countant General's Office, etc. Association of an external office is necessary to establish the credibility of the verification exercise. The existing verification system by auditors confined to the financial matters is inadequate. Verification of physical stock should be done for randomly selected items in each stores sub vision. Items covered should include major part of the stores value. The physical verification report should be submitted to the CE, P&MM as a secret document.

Random Check by CE or SE

The CE or SE concerned should conduct surprise verification of selected items to enhance propriety of the system. They can make it a part of administrative inspection.

Management of S0S Materials (Surplus, Obsolete and Scrap)

Management of SOS materials has assumed tremendous importance in materials activities, in view of the "financial sringencies. Various estimates of money locked up in the obsolete items are available in the Indian scenario. The first estimate was provided by the then Finance Minister Mr. C. Subramaniam, who mentioned on December 10, 1974 (The Hindu, December 11,1974) thatthe amount of money blocked in obsolete and surplus material was estimated around Rs. 2500 crores in India; presently with further industrialisation and inflation, this figure today is expected to be over Rs. 10,000 crores. Keeping this in view identification and disposal of such items is necessary from both materials and financial view point.

In the Central Stores of PDD, at the end of financial year 1993-94 the amount locked-up in slow-moving and non-moving items was around Rs. 254.43 and Rs. 81.241akhs respectively. So much high blockade of Government money speaks height of ineffective purchasing and storage system. The abovementioned slow-moving items are likely to become redundant shortly.

The money locked up in scraps at the Central Stores Division and workshop could not be evaluated for technical reasons. The management of surplus, unserviceable and scrap items has not been given the attention that it deserves in the PDD. Though it is not an important item of day-to-day activities, a little attention given to it at regular intervals by institutionalising the mechanism of periodical declaration of surplus and obsolete equipment and their disposal at regular-intervals not only would augment working capital/resources but it would also clear space and release pressure on inventories, apart from preventing their deterioration in quality and value due to efflux of time and exposure to risky elements. The type of materials or equipment that become obsolete are as varied as their operations.

The Central Stores Division and workshop report unserviceable and surplus items including the scraps to the concerned Chief Engineer. The concerned Chief Engineer has to decide if such materials can be put to alternative use. If not, the Chief Engineer decides the future course of action including their disposal either because they are not required or are unserviceable. Last time such items and scraps were disposed of by the P&MM wing in 1988-89. Since then disposal of scrap and dead items has not taken place. Obsolete and surplus goods should be disposed of as soon as practicable, provided adequate steps are taken to ensure that such an action will not result in unethical premature disposals, which could in turn result in stockout of the same item. It may be pointed out that delays in disposing of redundant stocks not only increase the inventory carrying costs, but creates the risk of deterioration and loss of sale value of the stocks. It sounds, ironical that due to faulty planning, an item which is bought for usage becomes non moving and unserviceable and has to be disposed of. The disposal can be effected through the following ways:

(i) Inviting offers from time to time from possible scrap dealers.

(ii) Annual contract system.

(iii) Public auction.

(iv) *Ab initio* negotiation.

Power Development Department either invites offers from registered dealers or adopts public auction system. As stated above such items are sold either through auction or inviting tenders but the sale is effected on 'as is where is' basis. Though this protects PDD legally (audit objection), it gives an impression to the prospective buyer that they are in a bad condition. Moreover, once the materials are survey reported as unserviceable, the Government departments do not spend any money thereon except on watch and ward. This gradually reduces their sale value—a little cleaning up to make it more presentable is not done. This may fetch better slaves value to the PDD.

In respect of Madhya Pradesh State Electricity Board (MPEB) and Himachal Pradesh Electrictty Board (HPSEB), once the obsolete and unserviceable materials have been survey reported to the CE, he grants appropriate permission to the custodians and others for their disposal. The survey reporting system in MPSEB is very sound from theoretical point of view as the officer who is empowered to dispose of the materials is expected to give his considered views in regard to why these items have become unserviceable or surplus? A lot of information as to the quality, quantity, the date of their purchase, their value, the reasons for their becoming obsolete, surplus or unserviceable, their present value, etc., are all to be given. This prevents the hasty disposal of useful items. But the record keeping in all State Electricity Boards including the PDD of J &K is perceptibly poor or officials are reluctant to give information. This is quite fallacious that either larger quantity than required have been bought or materials of sub-standard have been accepted, or the equipment is not functioning or serving the purpose for which it has been bought for whatever reason. In almost all the Boards except MPSEB and HPSEB large quantities of materials were awaiting disposal, deteriorating further in quality due to negligence in their preservation or lack of adequate care. Despite many difficulty MPSEB has been able to dispose of large quantities of obsolete, surplus and unserviceable materials and scraps through vigorous and sustained action. Large quantities of scrap and surplus and unserviceable materials were lying with Andhra Pradesh, Uttar Pradesh and Tamil Nadu Electricity Boards.

Management of SOS may be discussed under the following four heads:

(i) Surplus and obsolete materials.

(ii) disposal of scrap and unserviceable items.

(iii) Reclamation and recycling.

(iv) Wastage reduction.

Surplus and Obsolete Materials

Faulty forecasts and planning, incorrect purchasing practices, buying in bulk, faulty storekeeping methods, inadequate stores preservation, inefficient material handling, poor manufacturing methods, improper codification, etc., are other causes leading to obsolescence. The problem of obsolescence is more acute and deserves attention in the capital intensive industries, like power, processing and transport sectors. Strategies for identification, minimization and disposal of obsolete items need a good computerized information system for generating periodic reports for action.

The researcher has observed that in PDD, materials have become surplus or obsolete more because of the purchase of larger quantities than required than technological changes. MPSEB has an effective High Power Committee consisting of Head of Departments which examines monthly the computerised statement of non-moving and slow-moving items. With a view to finding alternative use for surplus and obsolete items, fix reserved prices for those which are to be sold and review action on earlier decisions. They have been able to find alternative use practically for all their surplus and obsolete items, with slight alterations and modifications. The redeployment of surplus materials to places where they are required is systematically done in the MPSEB. In the MPSEB, when an equipment is declared surplus, its spares are also put up for sale along with it. No such practice is in vogue in the PDD of J&K.

The PDD may follow the example of MPSEB by a constituting a committee to review quarterly or half-yearly as the case may be, non-moving and slow-moving items, unserviceable items and scrap in such a way that complete action on all of them in a year can be taken according tome plan. In place of the committee this function can be performed by the 'Inventory Control Division' also (creation of which has been suggested elsewhere in this thesis). The committee can function only when reliablelists of non-moving and slow-moving items are available and is assisted by a small cell created for the purpose.

The following measures are necessary for the avoidance of surplus, obsolete and unserviceable materials:

(i) Materials of the correct specifications may alone be bought and their proper packaging by suppliers stipulated;

(ii) quality control and inspection must ensure acceptance of materials of required quality;

(iii) maintenance of accurate records and keeping them up to date;

(iv) efficient handling and storage thereof;

(v) alternative use for them may be explored; and

(vi) there should be an efficient system of recovery, recycling and reuse.

Disposal of Unserviceable and Scrap Items

In this regard the tender is called by the CE or SE Procurement and Materials Management, PDD and final disposal is done by the

XEN Central Stores. If the disposal is to be done through public auction, the CE, P&MM wing authorises the XEN Stores incharge to conduct all the proceedings. But since long this exercise has not been carried out in any of the wings of PDD. In MPEB the controller of stores personally conducts the auctions with the active help of zonal CEs. There are sufficient evidences that disposal of surplus, obsolete unserviceable items and scrap has not been given the attention it deserves in almost all the State Electricity Boards including the PD D of J &K—MPSEB to some extent is an exception.

Table 1

Book Value of Scrap and Unserviceable Items of Central Stores Division & M&RE Wing, Jammu 1994-95

S.No.	*Particulars*	*Number*	*Amount (Rupees in Lakhs)*
1.	Non-moving Items	37 Nos.	81.24
2.	Copper Wire Scrap	94.73 Mts.	84.60
3.	Aluminium Scrap	9481.57 Kg.	1.90
4.	Items likely to become redundant		254.43
	Total		422.17

Source: Compiled from Central Stores Division, Jammu of P&MM Wing (POD).

The copper wire scrap lying in the stores of various divisions of The Electric Maintenance and Rural Electrification (M&RE) wing of PDD was assessed in 1985 at 80 Mts. which further increased to 94.73 Mts. in 1994 having a book value of Rs. 84.60 lakhs. But, its disposal had not been arranged till th end of 1994-95. Non-disposal of copper scrap over such a long period of time is fraught with the chances of losses due to pilferage, etc., besides occupying space and entailing avoidable expenditure on its which and ward. 37 dead items having book value of Rs. 81.24 lakhs purchased between 1983 and

1990 against different purchase orders had not been lifted by the user divisions resulting their damage/breakage or expiry of life and consequential loss to the Government. These stores were awaiting disposal till the end of 1994-95. These items with further passage of time may result in further loss to the Government. Sometime back aluminium scrap of Rs. 1.90 lakhs value became irrecoverable on account of non-provision of clause for recovery of scrap value in respect of supply of aluminium rods for conversion into AAC/ ACSR conductors to J&K Small Scale Industries Development Corporation (SIDCO). There is a need to incorporate all the necessary conditions in the order of whatever type.

Slow-moving items purchased between 1983 nd 1993 having a book value of Rs. 254.43 lakhs have resulted in blockade of Government money over a considerable period. With further passage of time, these items are likely to become redundant

The following suggestions may be made for selling these items:

(i) The items should be sorted out in tenus of quality so that items of uniform quality are put in each lot. The materials which can be put to use readily should be separately sorted out and auctioned for fetching better prices.

(ii) If the materials put to auction are cleaned, dusted and made a little more presentable with negligable expense, they may fetch a higher price.

(iii) Sale of these items at regular intervals or on fixed days, as in Karnataka Electricity Board, could attract more scrap dealers.

(iv) Rate contracts for items which arise regularly like drums (which are reconditioned and used by oil companies) fetch good prices without having deteriorated in quality in storage.

(v) Since scraps and other materials are 'bought' and not 'sold', which means that scrap dealers buy scrap only when there is demand for it. It would be better if the functionaries who deal with the sale of scrap, study the market and put them up for auction when it is likely to fetch good prices.

The scrap should be reduced to the minimum. In an industry in Pune it was reduced from 36% to 6%10 through better management. Efforts should be made to find end use of the scrap. These investigations will prove financially beneficial. It has a value, as such, should be accounted for properly and someone should be made responsible for it.

Reclamation and Recycling

Since PDD is material-intensive and capital-intensive, it would be desirable to recycle or recondition as much material as possible. This is particularly so when most of our natural resources are getting depleted due to large scale consumption thereof and in view of financial stringencies. Most of the Electricity Boards do the reclamation of transformer oil but this process is more effectively done in M.P. where they have a full-fledged reclamation plant, the product of which conforms to the specifications of fresh transformer oil. Some of the Electricity Boards, like A.P. and U.P. do mostly filteration of transformer oil. PDD officials have not paid any heed towards reclamation of transformer oil. The Department should take effective steps to collect the reclaimable oil. The same can be either sold, if reclamation facilities are not available within, or it can be got reclaimed from the private firms. The Electricity Boards can also reclaim used engine oil as is being done in M.P. by collecting it in the stores whenever fresh oil is issued and a proper account of it is kept. As some of the Boards have a large fleet of vehicles, the reclamation of oil could be attempted, if economical. If it is not, it could be sold to p.c.c. pole factories, etc., which can us it as lubricant. This reclamation theory of engine oil may not be of much relevance/ importance to the PDD, for two reasons. Firstly, the Department has not a very large fleet of motor vehicles. Second, the department has not its own vehicle workshop. The recycling business of engine oil may be totally uneconomical for this Department. However, used engine oil can be collected and sold as lubricant.

Wastage Reduction

PDD uses a large number of materials, particularly cables, wires, conductors, insulators, poles, steel rods, etc. An amount of consciousness to reduce wastage should be developed and propogated so that the wastage reduction in materials is possiblle. Wastage can be reduced by ensuring that small lengths of conductors and cables are not left out. Steel rails and poles can be welded together where economical to form full lengths, reroiling scraps where economical, etc.

While it is not possible to quantify the extent of saving in respect of the above items, it is pretty certain that all these could be effected without much expense or additiohal staff, besides ensuring a small inflow of working capital, clearance of space in store yards and prevention of their deterioration in storage.

A multi-pronged effort in this direction would be necessary. The staff should be motivated to avoid scraps and wastage from arising, to arrange for its efficient collection, where practicable and economical, to arrange for its recycling and reuse and where this is not possible to arrange for its profitable disposal. Various techniques of waste reduction, like recycling, salvaging, standardisation, methods study, quality control, zero defects, etc., enable to create a consciousness amongst all persons, to effective waste control programme.

METHODS OF INVENTORY VALUATION

The process of valuation of the material range from the conservative practice, such as market price or cost of procurement, whichever is less on one hand, to modem developments such as replacement cost and standard cost on the other. Each method has its own advantages and disadvantages. For income-tax purposes, only one of the following methods, *i.e.*, the FIFO system or standard price or actual price or market value, whichever is lower, is accepted. However, for internal control purposes the organisations can choose any of the following methods.

First-in and First-out (FIFO)

Under this system materials are issued in strict chronological order, *i.e.*, whatever is received first is issued first. This method ensures that the materials are issued at actual cost and the stocks are valued as per the latest price paid. The operation of this system is simple, so long as fluctuation in price is not much. In an inflation in-built economy, where the material costs are increasing, the production costs lag the actual prices, thus indicating higher profits. But the advantage is that the value of materials in stock does not vary significantly from the market price. One of the main disadvantages of this method is that this may create a highly unsettled state of affairs because of too many variations in the prices of products sold by the manufacturer within the same month.

Last-in and First-out (LIFO)

Under this method the materials which come in last are issued first at the market rate, *i.e.*, the cost of the last lot of inventory will enter the cost of production. But stocks are valued at older prices. In times of falling prices, the LIFO method is disadvantageous as this may create an erroneous state of affairs as the cost worked out may be less than the price paid for materials. Therefore, this method also suffers from the defect as it fails to accommodate price variation.

Average Cost

Under this method of valuation issues are valued on the basis of arithmetic average of the cost of different lots of inventories purchased during a particular period (month, quarter, etc.). It will at least remove the problem of price variation on the onc hand and perhaps the problem of inconsistent inventory valuation on the other. This way problem of too many prices being quoted by the manufacturer during the same period will be solved. In spite of these facts, the problem of price variation cannot be completely set aside.

Weighted Average Cost

The weighted average takes into account the price and quantity of the materials in store. It gives a reasonably accurate picture of the situation, with the issues charged to production and values of closing stock resembling the market conditions. Under the periodic weighted average system issues are priced at the end of the period and the price is a weighted average price of all the purchases during the period. It may be pointed out that the weighted average cannot be calculated until the end of the review period. Moving average method computes an average unit cost after each purchase or addition to purchase. It is well suited to the perpetual inventory system and for computerized inventory operations.

The standard cost after considering the market conditions, usage rate, storage conditions, handling facilities, obsolescence of items, depreciating nature of the item, and past experience and the future variations in the prices of that item of inventory. Finally, to the forecasted price standard administration and sales and distribution overheads to find out the total cost of inventory. The standard cost may be ascertained at least in relation to a year's time. This may take care of all possible fluctuations. In case of wide variations between the standard cost and the actual cost, the standard may be revised to make it relevant to practical situation.

The weighted average cost and standard cost methods are widely used by the manufacturing concerns for valuation of inventories. These techniques are regarded as scientific techniques of inventory valuation. The standard cost method was hitherto used by a manufacturing concerns but now Government departments have also realised its importance, where materials are purchased by a centralised body and issued to the user divisions at no-profit no-loss basis. After studying pros and cons of all inventory valuation methods, it has been found that Standard Costing Method can be of great help to the Government departments to make objective and meaningful valuation of inventories.

In the POD, the issues are made from one Government department to the other, where cost determination has no relevance, as has in case of manufacturing concerns. The actual price plus handling charges (ranging up to 3%) becomes issue price of an item.

It may be added that the Stores Division should evaluate the old materials at the end of every financial year on the basis of price of the latest lot received plus handling charges or actual cost plus bank rate of interest say 16% + 3% handling charges. But the latter part appears to be more practicable for electrical items. This should be compounded for the subsequent years. This may put some pressure on the user divisions to lift expeditiously the requisitioned materials. This would be a sort of inbuilt system to put pressure on both users as well as stores management. The users would be pressurised to life the requisitioned materials and stores management to dispose of unserviceable items and not to buy excess materials. Moreover, the extent of loss towhich the Government is put to on account of wrong planning, excess purchasing and over stocking can be determined effectively. In order to work out avoidable loss or avoidable investment, value of safety margin should be subtracted. On account of over-purchasing/over-stocking, blockade/loss of investment in case of only A&F items within the surveyed population has been worked for the year 1991-92 as under:

Value of Surplus Purchasing:

Issue price of A&F items (including 3% handling charages)	= Rs.2,11,83,702
Add: 16% opportunity cost (bank rate of interest)	= Rs.29,21,890
Total	Rs.2,41,05.592*

*This amount excludes value of inventories which existed prior to 1992-93 and were part of stock in the said year.

This exercise may be termed as Standard Costing.

The Government could have spent this blocked investment somewhere else for some development purpose. That way this was a social loss also in which the society had been exposed to in a already financially crippled state. It is difficult to calculate social loss accurately. Thus, over-purchasing has a serious repercussion from economic, financial and materials management point of view.

AN EVALUATION

Management of stores and SOS has become increasingly important in view of volume of inventories to be handled and technological changes.

The inspection activity at suppliers' factory appears to be an avoidable activity. It has been observed that this activity has dubious character of gratification, which has been deliberately kept in the operational hierarchy. Inventories received at the Central Stores Division are subject to thorough check-up as regard to the physical damages. In view of the researcher the scope of this inspection activity should be broadened to cover technical specifications also. Further, th re should be clause in the purchase order for strict adherence to quality specifications, otherwise, manufacturers would be supplying at their own risk and responsibility. Moreover, manufacturers should be asked to follow Indian Standard specifications in general and Planning and Design wing specifications in specified cases. This way without compromising with the sanctity of the purchase system, savings would accrue both in time and money terms. The establishment expenses would be reduced by 2% and external lead time on an average by about 25% in case of non-local orders. However, this sort of inspection activity should not be generalised.

The existing issue procedure in the PDD is 'sales oriented' as it takes care of sale of materials from the Central Stores Division to the user divisions. But from materials management point of view and to have proper track of materials, the system should provide for correct recording of all issues from each user division and return of materials 'unused' or 'surplus' to the Central Stores Division or at least a record of that should be sent to the Central Stores. In addition, there should be procedure for stock transfer from one user division to the other or for that matter from any store to any other store. For this purpose, a Stock Transfer Note (STN) should be used. Moreover, for effective accounting of stores, codification system is must. This system can work very effectively with the support of a computerised system that can keep record of individual stock items in any store and provide guidelines for transfer of items to where they are needed. For proper recording of issues of any item from any store a personal computer installed at the Divisional Stores should be used. The issue records can be transferred in a magnetic media (floppy disk) periodically to the Central Stores Division for management decisions. To avoid wastages, the surplus materials should be returned to stores, using a 'Material Return Note' (MRN). In order to have such functioning of the storage system of PDD — two things are important:

(i) Management Information System (MIS): materials should be effective enough, especially computer based.

(ii) A little more centralisation of purchase function irrespective of item ratings.

Keeping in view the procedural formalities inherited in the Government departments and stretched operational field of the Department under study, it may take sometime to implement the above stated materials recording and transfer system. Therefore, till the above stated system is introduced, as a gap filling measure, *i.e.*, short-term measure the Department may continue with the existing system of materials issue with the following modifications/ improvements:

(i) There should be provisions for effective inter-branch transfer of materials from those divisions where they are surplus to those where they are needed especially at the time when such items are out of stock in the Central Stores Division.

(ii) Scrap and surplus/ obsolete materials should be returned to the Central Stores Division for disposal, etc., after passing accounting entry of internal adjustment. It would be economically feasible for the Central Stores to dispose of unserviceable and scrap items.

(iii) The construction materials/equipment after the completion of the project should be either returned to the concerned store or shifted to some other project cite where they are needed. This has been done in a limited way.

(iv) The user divisions should be impressed upon to project their demand quite judiciously so that over purchasing or under purchasing could be minimised. It has been observed that projected demand lacked scientific base and judgmental vision.

(v) No division/circle should be allowed to get more quantity than requisitioned, unless a special case has been made out. At the same time, there should be inbuilt system that the user divisions lift the requisitioned quantity within the stipulated time.

Physical stock verification should be a continuous process and must not be limited to annual checks only. The existing physical verification system is an inadequate system and is a procedural formality. In order to ensure proper accountability and reporting of deficiencies / discrepancies, three separate levels for this verification activity have been proposed.

In addition to revealing discrepancies in physical ground balances and stores records, verification activity should also seek to identify disposable inventory. Under the present system of verification, 'identification of disposable materials' is not within the purview of the verification committee. Such activity should be carried out by the stock verifiers, especially by the Inventory Control Division and reported to the CE or SE concerned for further necessary action. Usually large organisations set-up a high power committee consisting of representatives of different departments to decide on disposable action. On the similar pattern the CE, P&MM wing should constitute a committee comprising of; he himself as the Conventor and Director Industries, FA/DFA, SE/XEN StDres, XEN Workshop and representatives of user divisions as members. Disposable action may be undertaken by entering into annual contract with intending purchasers, or by periodically inviting offers, or by public auction. Any cost-effective method under Government norms may be opted. However, dealing with scrap buyers who gang themselves into cartels should be avoided.

Periodical analysis of waste and scrap, with reasons thereof, help to reduce the incidence of waste. The huge amount blocked in slow-moving items which was around Rs. 3 crores would be a wastage as these items were purchased prior to 1993 and are likely to become redundant. The % age of such wastage would continue to increase if suggested steps will not be taken. Problem of obsolescence can be reduced by introducing formal documentation, known as 'effective point advice' (EPA). It helps in tapering off the old model stocks and in better coordination for profitable introduction of changes with minimum side effects. In general various techniques of waste reduction like recycling, salvaging, value engineering, standardisation, work study, zero defects, etc., create a consciousness amongst all persons, to effective wastage control programme.

A combination of first-in and first-serve (FIFS) and standard cost method may turn out to be effective for inventories from issue and valuation point of view respectively.

❐

19

Management Information System: Materials

Management systems are in fact as old as the writings in the world. The oldest evidence of writing by man discovered so far consists of clay tablets excavated at Sumer in Mesopotamia and dated approximately 3000 B. C. They contain records from an inventory system of receipts and issues made to individuals from a temple grain store. When Babylonia, merchants were keeping records on clay tablets, at about the same time, the ancient Egyptians made a great improvement in record keeping when they developed Papyrus (the fore-runner of paper) and a sharp pointed pen called a 'calmus'. Today, businessmen and all others keep records and process data, but the technology by which data is processed has had a quantum leap forward especially in the last 15 to 20 years. Around 15th century Luca Pacioli developed the double entry book-keeping system, the forerunner of our modern financial accounting system. In the twentieth century computers revolutionised the whole information system. The world has gone through the agricultural revolution, industrial revolution and we are in the midst of the so-called 'Information Revolution'.

In fact, many historians believe that writing arose in response to the need for such management information. For example, W.H. McNeill, Chairman of the Department of History at the University of Chicago, says "At first, Sumerian priests used writing mainly to record deposits and withdrawals from temple store houses. A persistent problem here was how to find ways to record, the names of the men who engaged in these transactions. Eventually the effort to record individual men's names in recognizable form induced the priests to resort to equivalences between syllables in men's names and the sound of some easily pictured word. Then by developing enough standard syllable pictures the scribes would easily learn to record all the sounds of ordinary speech."

He goes on to add:

"It seems probable that all known forms of writing derive directly or indirectly for the Sumerian Invention."

It would be no exaggeration to say that few areas of management have stirred more acrimonious debate—management information system is one of them. A management information system is an integrated man-machine system that provides informatiort to support the planning and control functions of executives in an organisation.

For the increased importance of management information system, two main reasons may be cited:

(i) Increased complexity of organisations.

(ii) Increased complexity of management.

Increased Complexity of Organisations

Organisations have grown in complexity to levels which are unprecedented and information plays a vital role in holding together and coordinating organisations. Information is the mortar that holds together the edifice of the modern multi-division, multi-location and multi-product organisations. The role of the management information system has become very similar to that of the nervous system in animals.

This complexity can be attributed to four primary causes:

(i) the technological revolution;

(ii) research and development activity;

(iii) product changes; and

(iv) the information system.

Increased Complexity of Management

There have been four developments in the field of mangement that, when integrated with earlier systems, may provide a break through in improving the management process. These four developments are:

(i) information feedback system;

(ii) decision-making;

(iii) operations research or management science techniques that permit an experimental or simmulation approach to complex problems; and

(iv) the advent of electronic computer, which are able to have both access and record information and perform calculations at speed which is almost unbelievable.

MIS: A Conceptual Analysis

Management information system comprises of three words: Management—Information—System.

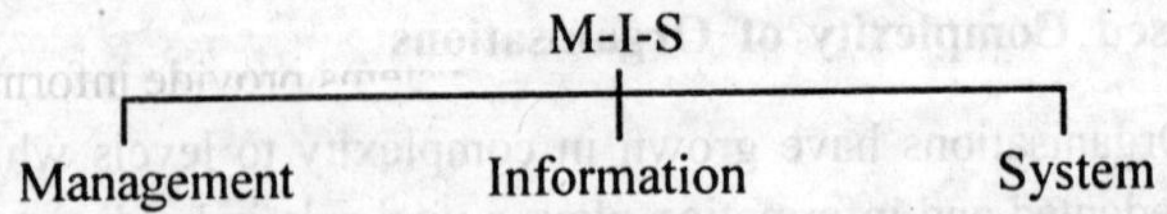

Management has been defined in a variety of ways, but for our purpose it comprises the processes or activities that describe what managers do in the operation of their organisation, *viz.*, plan, organise, initiate and control operations. They plan by setting strategies and goals and selecting the best course of action to achieve the plan. They organise the tasks necessary for operational plan, set these tasks up into homogenous groups and assign authority and responsibility. They control the performance of the work by setting performance standards and avoiding deviations from standards.

Information could be defined as sets of facts, figures, and data that have been retrieved and processed for forecasting or decision-making purpose.

A system is a set of elements forming an activity or a a processing procedure/scheme seeking a common goal or goals by operating on data and/or energy and/or matter in a time reference to yield information and/or energy and/or matter. In other words a system consis of inter-department sub-systems; anything wrong with any of the sub-systems is reflected ultimately in the system whole. The systems concept helps to optimize the output of the organisation by connecting the operating sub-system through the medium of information exchange.

Putting all the three components together, it could be seen that management information systems are sets of related processes, activities, individuals or entities interacting together to provide processed data to the individual managers. The objective of management information system is to provide information for decision making, planning, initiating, organising and controlling the operations of the sub-systems of the firm and to provide a synergistic organisation in the process.

The main ingredients of information system may be highlighted as under:

(i) The management information systems provide information from the data after processing them. The informa-tion systems do not generate data. The data is generated, collected, recorded, stored, processed and retrieved after it has been generated by performance operations in an organisation. The information systems follow the procedures designed for processing this data which has been generated within the organisation.

(ii) The information systems are designed for the job positions rather than for individuals in the organisational hierarchy.

(iii) The information systems are designed for different levels of management—they are supposed to cater to the information needs of decision makers at top, middle and junior levels of management.

(iv) The information systems are designed for supplying information to managers in different functional areas.

(v) The information systems should be integrated by way of data base. The redundancy in storage of data, processing of data and generation of reports is avoided by way of integration of information systems. Single point data entry and updation of master data files should be ensured to minimise chances of discrepancies in the data integrity.

(vi) The information systems are facilitated with electronic equipment such as computers.

(vii) Integrated planned systems are essence of MIS not "Island of mechanization" or data processing systems.

Relevance of MIS to Different Levels of Management

In fact management is a process of achieving an organisation's goals and objectives by judiciously making use of resources of men, materials, machines, money, methods, messages and moments (the last two in context of information being a vital resource to the managers/decision makers). Management may be structured into three hierarchical levels, namely, top level, middle level and bottom level or strategic, tactical and operational levels respectively. Although lines of demarcation are not absolute and clear cut, one can usually distinguish certain layers within the organisation.

Top management establishes policies, plans and objectives of the organisation as well as budget estimates are laid down. These factors are promulgated and passed down to middle management. They are translated into specific revenue, cost and profit goals. These are reviewed, analysed and modified in accordance with the overall plans and policies until agreement is reached. The middle management then issues the specific schedules and measurement yardsticks to the operation management. The operational level has the responsibility of producing goods and services to accomplish the objective, which in turn will enable the organisation achieve its overall plans and objectives.

In context of MIS, management can perhaps be best defined as a process of : *(i)* creation of objectives; *(ii)* judicious allocation of resources; *(iii)* determining operational plans and schedules; *(iv)* keeping control of progress; and *(v)* evaluation through feedback. Each of these areas require certain decisions to be made. Strategic decisions are taken at the top level, tactical decisions at the middle level and operational decisions at the junior level as can be seen from Table 1.

Table 1

Job Contents of Management Levels

Sl. No.	*Character Mangement*	*Top Mangement*	*Middle Mangement*	*Operational*
1.	Focus on Planning	Heavy	Moderate	Minimum
2.	Focus on Control	Moderate	Heavy	Heavy
3.	Time frame	One to five years	Upto one year	Day-to-day
4.	Nature of activity	Relatively unstructured	Moderately structured	Highly structured
5.	Level of complexity	Very complex	Less complex	Straight forward
6.	Result of activity	Plans, policies and strategies	Implementation and schedules	End product

Source: J. Kanters, Management Information Systems, 3rd Edition (Englewood-Cliffs: Prentice Hall International, Inc.)

MIS Development

Systems development is an iterative process and it consists of the following identifiable stages presented in tabular form:

	Stage	*End Result*
1.	Problem Definition	Statement of scope and objectives.
2.	Feasibility Study	Economic/technical/political feasibility. Financial viability and modification of system.

Stage	*End Result*
3. System Analysis	Logical model of the system consisting of details such as data flow diagrams, data dictionary, etc.
4. System Design	Alternative solution along with revised cost-benefit analysis, hardware specifications manpower requirements, plan for implementation, user sign-off, test plans, formal system test procedures, security, audit and operating procedures.
5. Systems Development	Actual programming as per the user sign-off, compilation and testing of the programmes.
6. Systems implementation	Training of the user staff, system documentation and implementation.
7. Post-Implementation Maintenance and Review	Refined and tuned system along with revised documentation and satisfied users.

Richard Nolan in 1979, developed Stage Growth Hypothesis of MIS development. The six different stages presented in the model are: *(i)* initiation, *(ii)* contagion, *(iii)* control, *(iv)* integration, *(v)* data administration, and *(vi)* maturity.

The Research Team of Sloan School of Management, suggested a creative approach termed as 'Critical Success Factor' (CSF) for information requirement analysis, which is an improvement over John F. Rockart's CSF approach.

The CCSFs for any business are the limited number of areas in which results, if satisfactory, will ensure successful performance. These are the areas where things 'must go right' at the right time. The CSFs must receive constant and consistent attention from the management.

MIS in Procurement and Materials Management Organisation

From hierarchical view point management of the Procurement and Materials Management wing of PDD can be divided under the following levels:

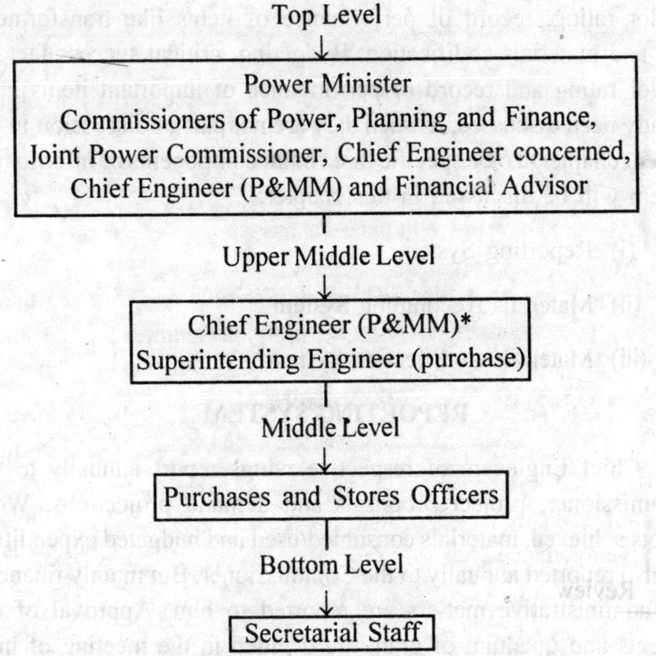

*The Chief Engineer (P&MM) is invariably the member of all purchase committee and is also responsible for purchase and procurement planning, as such his role is strategical as well as tactical.

In the said Department the top level management is concerned with deciding policy matters, as such the main focus is strategic planning aspects. The upper middle level of management concentrates on purchase scheduling and inventory control. The middle level of management helps to perform purchase scheduling and inventory control functions. The bottom level provides secretarial assistance and fulfils official formalities.

In this part of the chapter, the materials information function and its associated activities of the Procurement & Materials

Management organisation have been studied in totality to find out suitability of the existing MIS. Efforts will also be made to identify the materials information requirements at different levels of management. On the whole MIS of the organisation under question has been studied with regard to reporting system, books of account and registers, analysis of critical success factors, purchase budgeting, vendor rating, record of performance of items like transformers, etc., and materials codification. Budgeting, critical success factors, vendor rating and record of performance of important items have already been discussed, as such they are not part of discussion in the present chapter. To be specific three main components of information system will be discussed in this chapter:

(i) Reporting System.

(ii) Materials Accounting System.

(iii) Materials Codification System.

REPORTING SYSTEM

Chief Engineers of respective wings report annually to the Commissioner, project proposals and demand projections. Work targets achieved, materials consumed/used and budgeted expenditure are also reported annually to the Commissioner. But mainly financial and administrative matters are reported to him. Approval of the projects and quantum of grant are decided in the meeting of high power committee. But one of the most important aspects of information system, *i.e.*, monitoring performance of the purchases and stores executives is conspicuous by its absence. What is required is that either the Power Commissioner or Joint Power Commissioner should monitor the performance of the Chief Engineers and other senior functionaries periodically in context of time bound purchasing and other related job schedules. These executives in turn should fix work targets in the light of broader objective with regard to procurement, etc., for the junior executives and appraise their performance accordingly. The performance appraisal should be on the basis of management by objective (MBO) technique. The conventional system of writing , Annual Performance Report' (APR) has no meaning as it is a subjective approach. By objectively evaluating performance of executives, the top mangement would be able to fix the accountability—a concept which is altogether missing in Government organisations. When one knows that his performance would be monitored by somebody he endeavours to perform better. The executives who perform better shculd get preference in the matters of promotion to higher ranks and other incentives.

A monthly 'materials status statement' is sent by the Stores organisation to the Commissioner and Chief Engineer, which is a good practice. But no such annual 'consolidated materials status statement' is prepared by the Stores Organisation, which is must to have instant information about the yearly materials status. Monthly 'materials status statements' in addition to the demand requisitions become base of purchase decisions. But there is no practice of reporting periodically, dead, absolete and scrap items. Moreover, age-wise analysis of slow-moving items is also not done. Physical verification reports are prepared annually by the duly constituted committee, who submits the same to the Chief Engineer (P&MM). He may send a copy of the report to the Commissioners if he so likes. It should be mandatory to send copy of each physical verification report to the administrative head.

Standard forms are not used for sending requisitions, placing orders, writing off materials discrepancies, etc. However, standard forms, are in vogue for bin cards, proforma bills and for recording receipt and issue of materials (price store ledger). Further, there is no system of reporting of stocks in stores of user divisions, inter-division transfer of items, materials at site and scrap lying in different stores. These matters ought to be reported to the Chief Engineer (P&MM) or Central Stores organisation for management decisions.

On the whole it has been observed that job responsibilities of functionaries and information flow do not match properly. Either reports are not provided or provided quite late. As a result, the receiving functionary is unable to take appropriate decision and timely action. This has been found to be one of the main causes of delay in demand requisitions and purchase orders, excess or under purchasing and inaction on disposal of scrap and dead items. Moreover, there are no standards against which the actuals should be monitored for planning and control of inventories.

In order to keep proper track of materials, following 'Forms' may be suggested in addition to those already in use:

(i) Stock Transfer Form

(ii) Materials Return Form

(iii) Materials Requisition Form

(iv) Material Discrepancies write off Form

(v) Purchase Order Form

(vi) Age-wise Analysis of Items Form.

Power Development Department is supposed to review periodically performance of all the four wings. To assist the Department in achieving its objectives, the following structured elements of information (presented in tabular form) may be needed:

S.No.	*Objective*	*Information Need*	*Source of Information*
1.	Expansion & development of infrastructural work	For policy matters	Projection reports of all the wings
2.	Work targets achieved and materials consumed vis-a-vis budgeted expenditure	Review and Control	All the four wings
3.	Inventory Status	Review and Control	Annual materials status statement
4.	Check pilferages	Control and Administrative action	Physical verification report
5.	Performance appraisal	Commendation/ administrative action	Periodic performance report
6.	Timely action	Allocation of funds	Requisitions of all wings

The CE (P&MM) is primarily responsible for purchase of specific items for all the user wings. The information need of the CE may be presented in tabular form:

S.No.	*Objective*	*Information Need*	*Source of Information*
1.	To issue purchase orders	– Projected circle-wise material requirements	– Requisitions of user wings
		– Inventory status of items in circles	– Circle stock status report
		– Tenders that are not finalised within validity periods	– Tenders finalisation report
		– Inventory norms	– Tender documents
		– Spill-over orders and expected receipts	– Purchase orders
2.	Follow-up of purchase orders	– Purchase orders against which total supplies have not been made	– Purchase orders
		– Actual receipt of materials	– Material Receipt Report
		– Quantity rejected or supplied short	– Defective/Short Supplies Report
		– Supplies received against purchase orders	– Net materials Budget Variance Analysis
3.	Monitor vendor relibility	– Quantity rejected or supplied short	– Defective/Short Supplies Report
		– Actual receipt of material	– Material Receipt Report
4.	Monitor stock movements	– Inventory levels in various stores	– Stock Status Report
		– Monthly material receipt	– Material Receipts Report
		– Emeregency purchases	– Field Purchases Report

S.No.	Objective	Information Need	Source of Information
5.	Monitor replacement/rectification of items from suppliers	– Quantity rejected or supplied short	– Defective/Short Supplies Report
6.	Authorise material transfer	– Identification of surplus items	– Age-wise analysis of non-moving items
		– Anticipated shortages	– Material shortages Report
		– Inventory Status	– Stock Status Report
		– Request of transfer of material	– Field

Since the Superintending Engineer assists the Chief Engineer, Procurement and Materials Management; he needs almost the type of structured information as is needed by the CE.

The position of the Chief Controller of Stores may be as under:

S.No.	Objective	Information Need	Source of Information
1.	Receipt of items	– To execute indents	– Bills of suppliers
2.	Issue of items	– To execute indents	– Indent of user division
3.	Aggregation of receipts and consumption	– Inventory control	– GRN and Indents/Bin Card
		– Monitoring Stock Status	– GRN and Indents/Bin Card
4.	Expected arrivals information	– User divisions can be assured of supply after a stipulated period	– Suppliers intimation
5.	Identity scrap and dead items	– Disposal	– Physical verifications Report/Stock Disposal Report
6.	Total requisitions division-wise	– Ensure requisitioned Supply	– Requisition Form

S.No.	*Objective*	*Information Need*	*Source of Information*
7.	Anticipated shortages	– To enable CE to take timely action	– Stock Status Report
8.	Determine stocking policies	– Past consumption trends	– Stock Status Report
		– Future expansion progammes	– Demand projection reports

STORES ACCOUNTING, BOOKS AND REGISTERS

Stores accounting has two aspects, the value of materials stored and the physical quantity of materials stored. In regard to the first, stores accounting is necessary as they represent assets of an organisation and it provides basis for inventory control and costing the manufactured items. As regards the second aspect, it is necessary all the time to ensure that all the materials that have been received have been accounted for.

Stock records are necessary for the following purposes:

(i) They indicate the amount of any material in stock at any time without it being necessary for the item to be counted physically.

(ii) They enable the physical stock and the stock as indicated by stores accounts to be tallied.

(iii) They provide a means of providing how much be ordered to maintain stoccks at the required level.

(iv) They serve the purpose of a price list.

Table 2

Excess Stock Holding by ECSD, Jammu

S.No.	*Year*	*Reserve Stock Limit*	*Stock Position*	*Below the Limit*	*Excess*
1.	1991-92	400.00	439.54	–	39.54
2.	1992-93	400.00	486.20	–	86.20

3.	1993-94	400.00	335.67	64.33	–
4.	1994-95	400.00	887.90	–	487.90

Source: Compiled from the Records of Electric Central Stores Division, Jammu.

Against the sanctioned reserve stock limit of Rs. 400.00 lakhs the value of stocks actually held by the ECSD, Jammu at the end of 1991-92, 1992-93 and 1994-95 far exceeded, as mainfested in Table 2. This was alarmingly high in 1994-95.

There may be two reasons for this:

(i) excess requisitioning by the user divisions vis-a-vis non-lifting of items by them; and

(ii) non-disposal of surplus and unserviceable items.

Sanction to hold stocks in excess of the reserve stock limit had not been obtained from competent authority.

Agreement between quantity and value accounts of the stock had not been carried out since long. Non-recording of value of individual receipts/issues and delayed posting and non- authentication of entries in many cases were also observed by the investigator in the price store ledger. A test check of 112 store items revealed that balances of 10 items shown in the price store ledger differed with the corresponding balances shown in the stores bin cards. This is a serious lapse and ought to be checked by the officer incharge by monitoring the balances periodically.

The details of payment made in advance of receipt of materials is generally kept in a subsidiary register called 'register of advances'. The amounts recorded in this register are subsequently cleared by recording details GRs of the supplies received or reference to cash vouchers or receipts of the amounts refunded by the concerned. At the end of 1993-94 unadjusted advances aggregating to Rs.1162.25 lakhs stood in the 'advances register' maintained by the ECSD, Jammu. The materials against these advances had been received but recording of reference to GRNs of materials against the relevant entries of advance was pending. This indicates lack of control on advance payments and poor information system.

Public works deposit registers were incomplete as full particulars of the deposits had not been recorded and reference to cash vouchers for credits/debits were not quoted Reconciliation of deposits to ascertain reasons for minus balances had not been conducted. Periodical reviews to clear unclaimed deposits due for credit to Government revenue in terms of para 393 of the State Public Works Account code had also not been conducted.

Under rules the recoverable debts not pertaining to the accounts of works and losses, shortages and sales on credit can be debited to 'miscellaneous public works advances' but these items have to be reviewed monthly for expeditious clearance. In the ECSD, Jarnmu the outstanding balances under the aforesaid head amounted to Rs. 39.54 lakhs out of which Rs. 36.62 1akhs were outstanding against firms and other agencies towards the cost of unexecuted supplies, shortages and non-adjustment of accounts of advances, etc. This is unethical on the part of the Department as specific steps should be taken to clear the outstandings.

Rupees 2.92 1akhs were recoverable from various employees of the Department out of which Rs. 53 thousands were outstanding against officials who had since been transferred from the Stores Division. No perceptible action for the recovery of dues had been taken.

The value of supplies received prior to their payment were credited to 'suspense sub-head purchases', which were cleared when the value of the materials had been paid or adjusted. Though the operation of this sub-head was abolished long back, yet a credit balance of Rs. 17.42 1akhs stands in this account.

Presently the following books and registers are being used by the organisation under study:

(i) Cash Book, *(ii)* Deposit Register, *(iii)* PWD Advance, Register, *(iv)* Price Store Ledger, *(v)* Gross Receipt Book,

(vi) Advance Payment Register, *(vii)* Contractor Ledger, *(viii)* Index Register, *(ix)* Establishment Records:

(a) Pay Acquaintance Roll

(b) T.A. Register

(c) Despatch Register

(d) Receipt Register

(e) Telephone Register", etc.

On the whole there has been casual approach towards record keeping, as such information system is ineffective.

CODIFICATION: A CONCEPTUAL ANALYSIS

A good codification structure is essential for a modern materials management system. Action oriented inventory control and purchase management system requires that information needed by the management for any individual item or a group of items be available instantaneously. If considerable time has to be spent in arranging groups of items based on specifications or evaluating the stock of individual or groups of items, the time of action may pass and the inventory may be burdened with items that should not have been purchased or accepted into stock. The present section of the chapter has been designed keeping in view the above factors.

The materials manager is the largest spender of resources, as such, he has to constantly on the look out for cost reduction techniques and prompt availability of materials information. The starting point of any cost reduction technique and quick approach to information is to identify the materials, which in materials management terminology is called 'Codification'. Confusion in locating the materials lying in store leads to avoidable delays, reducing the very concept of a storing system to a farce. The importance of a proper codification structure can be gauged from a classic example of the 'Electric Company' in UK., where a screw with a diameter of 3/8" and length of 6" had as many as 111 names, depending on the type of usage and the department using the screw. A proper codification removed the additional 110 stocking bins with associated entries, inventories obsolescence, clerical efforts, etc.

An item code is a meaningful identification assigned to each item of inventory. This code may be expressed as a pure numeral, alphabetical or alpha numerical. It provides unique identification leading to quick and accurate referencing of items. Coding of items is a primary requisite for streamlining the inventory control system. Codification is the process of representing each item by a number or alphabet, the digits of which indicate the group, the sub-group, the type and the dimension of the item. The number of digits vary from 7 to 13 depending upon the number of items, use of check digit, number of manufacturing sister oganisations, inclusion of vendor, etc.

The structure should be flexible to provide for future additions of items without entailing the risk of duplication or necessitating changes in the existing code. For instance, BHEL, had only eight code when it started, but later on when inter-plant common codes were thought of, it had to re-do the coding and presently a twelve digit common code has..been developed. The code structure should be compact, conside and consistent. The total number of digits should be constant for all items. Each code should represent one item and each item single code.

Objectives of Materials Coding

The specific objectives of materials coding are as under:

(i) Provision of correct specification of the item coded. These specifications refer to detailed description of the item in terms of its physical dimension, chemical analysis, performance characteristics or a combination of these. Such complete specification of items are vital for procurement of items, without the delays involved in seeking clarification of items as well as resolving disputes between the purchaser and the vendor. Further complete specifications enable procurement with adequate competition from reliable sources of supply.

(ii) Introduction of standardization in items of inventory. This refers to standardizing specifications of items with the associated advantages of:

(a) reducing inventories by eliminating varieties of items due to brand names and sizes;

(b) lowering procurement costs through purchase of fewer items in large quantities; and

(c) ensuring uniformity of the materials used by different divisions and thus facilitating movement of such materials amongst divisions in times of emergency.

(iii) Enabling better controls to be exercised on consumption, purchase and storage of inventory items, especially by use of electronic data processing.

(iv) Prompt availability of information with regard to stock positions for management decisions.

CODING SYSTEMS

The following systems of codification are commonly used:

(i) Alphabetical System.

(ii) Numerical System.

(iii) Decimal System.

(iv) Alpha numerical System.

(v) Kodak System.

(vi) Brisch System.

The Kodak and Brisch systems of codification are the modern systems of codification. Hence only two systems have been discussed. Others are more of an academic significance and hence have not been discussed.

Kodak System

Eastman Kodak Company of New York, developed this 10 digit numerical code. The logic of major grouping under this system is based on source of supply. All materials are divided into 100 basic classifications, contributed by procurement—considerations. Each class can be divided up to 100 sub-classes—arranged alphabetically, which represent the third digit. Within this sub-class, kinds of items are arranged alphabetically and significant numbers like 00,10,20,30...90 are assigned to each item, forming the fourth and fifth digit of the numerical code. Thus 10 times as many items of a new kind may be absorbed under this system without any trouble. The sixth and seventh digits of the code signify the types; while eighth and ninth digits are allotted to 'sizes' in the similar manner and the tenth digit is left free to accommodate any minor variation.

If, however, there are more types, sizes or minor variations in any class or sub-class than are normally allowed, the allocation of digits may be changed without disturbing the neighbouring items to which numbers might have already been allotted. Kodak system is thus flexible and elastic and can accommodate ten items as many kinds or ten times as many sizes in a ratio of 10:1 at any point.

Brisch System

The Brisch System, named after a prominent consulting British Engineer in the UK, consists of seven digits and is applied in three phases. The items are grouped into suitable categories, such as main groups, sub-groups, etc. After these preliminary categories, items are grouped within the respective clans, in order to bring similar items together. The Brisch System, though it consists only of seven digits, is quite comprehensive, as the basis is on logical major groupings. If two digits are used for this, then we can have 00 to 99 major categories, within this major category, the splitting is done on the basis of materials, or use, or size. Such a logical bringing together of like items is very useful in standardisation and variety reduction.

This is not necessary that a codification system should be applied exactly in the form developed by the pioneers. These systems can be used with objective modifications to suit to the needs and nature of the organisation.

PROPOSED CODE STRUCTURE

Since the Procurement and Materials Management wing of PDD has not been using codes. in the Central Stores-a comprehensive coding system may be proposed to help the management to streamline the stores management and procurement procedures.

Considering the variety of characteristics that need to be incorporated in the code structure to provide complete specifications of an item, a basic seven digit (including check-digit) numeric code may be proposed. This code structure will provide considerable flexibility in introducing new items without the risk of duplication with the existing code items. This system has been proposed keeping in view tile need of the Department. The Kodak System is the lengthy in operation, but can accommodate more items as compared to the proposed system. But keeping in view the present and future needs of the Department, the proposed system appears to be quite adequate. Therefore, the proposed system is need-based, practicable, comprehensive and result-oriented.

Under the proposed system first, items are identified into major groups and each group is characterised by an alphabet. Sub-groups under each major group are represented by two-digit number. Under each sub-group further classification is done. This classification is assigned a four digit running serial, such as 0001,0002, 0003, etc. In addition, for the purpose of detecting input errors during the operation of a computerised inventory control system, a self-checking digit is applied.

The structure of the code shall be as under:

G		S	G		S	L	N	O		C	D

The code structure comprises of:

G = Group................. alphabetic character

SG = Sub-group................. 2 digits

SLNO = Serial Number............. 4 digits

CD = Check Digit............... digit.

Major Groups and Codes

For five major group codes for instance may be as under:

Code	Group
C	Cables
M	Measuring and Testing Instruments
O	Oil and Lubricants
P	Protective and Control Devices
T	Transformers.

Sub-groups and Codes

Each major class of primary materials can be further divided into convenient sub-groups based on the essential difference in type, shape, usage, design, etc. Each such sub-class is assigned a two digit numeric code which forms the second and third digit of the item code.

Transformers for instance may be grouped as:

(i) Current Transformers;

(ii) Distribution Transformers;

(iii) Power Transformers; and

(iv) Potential Transformers.

These sub-groups of transformers may be assigned the following two digit number:

Code Item	*Sub-Group*
10	Current transformers
15	Distribution Transformers
20	Power Transformers
25	Potential Transformers

Serial Number

Under each sub-group within a particular group of materials and equipment a four digited running serial is given. For this purpose the researcher has taken distribution transformers to substantiate the whole gamut of code structure.

Code	*Item*
150001	630 KVA Distribution Transformers
150002	400 KVA Distribution Transformers
150003	250 KVA Distribution Transformers
150004	100 KVA Distribution Transformers
150005	25 KVA Distribution Transformers

The check digit can be used to check the code of any item to guard against erroneous input under the computerised system of coding. It is worked out as under:

First group code is converted into a numerical code:

A	1
B	2
C	3
D	4
E	5
F	6
G	7
Z	26

Group code $\times 1 = N_1$

$S \times 2 = N_2$

$G \times 3 = N_3$

$$S \times 4 = N_4$$

$$L \times 5 = N_5$$

$$N \times 6 = N_6$$

$$O \times 7 = N_7$$

$$\text{Sum} = N_1 + N_2 \ldots\ldots\ldots\ldots\ldots N_7$$

Check Digit = Σ of N $\div$ 9

= 9 – remainder (Nine minus remainder)

Now the full code for 630 KVA, 400 KVA, 250 KVA, 100 KVA and 25 KVA distribution transformers can be substantiated along with check digit:

T15OO012	630- KV A
T1500024	400 KV A
T1500036	250 KV A
T1500048	100 KV A
T1500051	25 KVA

BENEFITS OF CODIFICATION

The codification structure so proposed by the researcher for the P&MM wing of the PDD, would:

(i) reduce investment lock-up considerably without experiencing stock-outs;

(ii) cut down the lead time both internal and external by making information available promptly;

(iii) ensure proper control over material issues, their return and inter-division transfer;

(iv) facilitate bulk ordering on a staggered delivery basis;

(v) avoid long descriptions with detailed specifications in purchase requisitions or stores indents; and

(vi) ensure easy identification, simplification and standardisation;

(vii) enable elimination of duplication, avoidance of cumber some names, and systematic logical grouping of similar items;

(viii) facilitate computerisation to strengthen MIS of the organisation.

The proposed code structure will help in curbing pilferages and unnecessary lock-up of investment in inventories in addition to providing instant information about the stock positions. Materials codification structure should be developed as a part of integrated information system.

It is imperative for the Procurement and Materials Management wing of PDD to make indepth study of feasibility, system analysis, system design and system development before implementing the proposed materials information system.

EPILOGUE

MIS from materials point of view is an organised network of information flow aimed at supporting materials activities (purchase planning, procurement, inventory control, stores handling, etc.) by furnishing relevant, reliable and timely information.

The CSFs for any business are the limited number of areas in which results, if satisfactory, will ensure successful performance. These are the areas where things 'must go right' atthe right time. The GSFs must receive constant and consistent attention from the management. In the Procurement and Materials Management wing of PDD, the CSFs, which deserve special attention have been identified with the help of network analysis in chapter on "Material Planning and Procurement".

The main observations with regard to the MIS in the Procurement and Materials Management organisation are as under :

(i) Job responsibilities of functionaries and information flow are not properly matched. The information supplied has not been adequate for the functionary concerned to initiate meaningful action.

(ii) There has been no periodic exchange of historical data as well as revised forecasts which are essential to foresee problem areas.

(iii) The existing report formats are not standardised. Moreover, reports are provided quite late. As a consequence, the receiving functionary is unable to take appropriate and timely action. This has been the main cause of delay in demand requisitions and purchase orders, over and under purchasing, and inaction on disposal of scrap and dead items.

(iv) facilitate arrangement of bin cards, stock carads, etc., in a uniform manner;

(v) help in accurate posting of receipt and issue of materials in the appropriate records;

(vi) Aggregation of data elements contained in documents such as indent requisitions, stores ledgers, etc., has not been done properly to have instant information to enable the functionaries to exercise control. Such aggregation at different levels would be useful to provide information on demand and usage trends and to device possible measures of control. Further, there is no well defined information system which can be used for strategic planning, management control and operational control.

(vii) There have been no standards or budgets for materials usage against which actuals can be monitored for better planning and control.

(viii) Since vendor rating is not done by the P&MM organisation, there has been no proper rapport with the reputed suppliers.

(ix) Easy identification of materials and availability of relevant information about them is not possible without proper codification.

It may be pointed out that the existing MIS does not cater to the needs of the functionaries of the organisation under question. There is an urgent need to develop an integrated MIS so that instant information flows among functionaries. In the proposed system efforts have been made to link information flow to specific job responsibilities of purchase and stores executives. Information needs of the Administrative Head have also been kept in mind. It has been stated earlier that reports should be promptly sent to concerned officers so that appropriate action can be taken at the right time. The materials coding system proposed should be made part of the overall information system. In order to strengthen the MIS, reporting system should be periodical, informative and result oriented. Use of standard forms is necessary to ensure accuracy, simplicity and comprehensiveness in the system. Budgeting or MRP should be used both as a planning and control technique. Budgets and schedules are must to monitor actual results against the targets. Preparation of annual 'materials status statement' on the pattern of monthly statement is also necessary to have instant information about the stock positions. Another statement known as 'age-wise analy is of items' should also be prepared to decide usefulness of stocked items. With the help of this, dead and unserviceable items can also be identified and their disposal can be arranged.. Vendor rating is necessary to add reliability in the system and analysis of CSFs is necessary to decide stress areas. Even a slight disconcentration in these areas can delay the execution of projects and cost and time trade offs get disturbed.

❐